THE MELLON CHANSONNIER

Volume 2

COMMENTARY

THE MELLON CHANSONNIER

Volume 2

COMMENTARY

Edited by Leeman L. Perkins and Howard Garey

New Haven and London, Yale University Press

1979

Published with assistance from Paul Mellon
and the Yale University Library

Designed by John O. C. McCrillis
and set in Baskerville type by
Asco Trade Typesetting Limited, Hong Kong.
Printed in the United States of America by
The Murray Printing Company, Westford, Mass.

Published in Great Britain, Europe, Africa, and
Asia (except Japan) by Yale University Press,
Ltd., London. Distributed in Latin America by
Kaiman & Polon, Inc., New York City; in
Australia and New Zealand by Book & Film
Services, Artarmon, N.S.W., Australia; and in
Japan by Harper & Row, Publishers, Tokyo Office.

Library of Congress Cataloging in Publication Data

Mellon chansonnier.
    The Mellon chansonnier.

    Chansons, for 3 or 4 voices; principally French
words.
    Photoreproduction and transcription (on facing
pages) of a 15th-cent. ms. in Yale University
Libraries.
    Include bibliographies.
    Includes indexes.
    CONTENTS: v. 1. The edition.—v. 2.
Commentary.   1. Chansons, Polyphonic.
I. Perkins, Leeman L.   II. Garey, Howard B.
M1495.M513M4   784'.3063   75-43329

ISBN 0-300-02234-4 (vol. 1)
       0-300-02241-7 (vol. 2)
       0-300-01416-3 (set)

To
Paul Mellon

in gratitude for his gift of
The Mellon Chansonnier
and for his support
of this publication

CONTENTS

The Edition

ABBREVIATIONS

Sigla used for the periodicals cited most frequently.

AM	*Annales Musicologiques*
AfMw	*Archiv für Musikwissenschaft*
JAMS	*Journal of the American Musicological Society*
MD	*Musica Disciplina*
MQ	*The Musical Quarterly*
MGG	*Die Musik in Geschichte und Gegenwart*
ZfMw	*Zeitschrift für Musikwissenschaft*

THE MUSIC

Leeman L. Perkins

CHRONOLOGY OF THE REPERTORY

The secular song forms of the fifteenth century have been the object of considerable scholarly and critical attention.[1] Whether considered verse, music, or a combination of the two, much commentary has focused on their limitations, and the aesthetic judgments have been largely unfavorable. Undeniably, the subject matter is largely confined to the highly stylized amorous sentiments of aristocratic courts. In addition the recurrence of certain themes, notably the all-too-cruel suffering of the unrequited lover; the strict adherence to the fixed forms of *ballade, rondeau*, and *virelai*; the conventional turns of phrase; the stereotyped imagery; the excessive reliance on a basic vocabulary generated by the use of rhyming dictionaries; and the acceptance of versification as one of the indispensable skills of the noble and educated classes—all have been derided to some extent by modern critics.[2] Even the music, though less commonplace than the verse and consequently less vulnerable to similar criticism, has not escaped censure for its lack of formal variety and for the strictures imposed on melodic development by the need for clarity and articulation in presenting the poetry as song. In fact the positive qualities of the genre—concision, economy of expression, and structural cohesion—have been construed in an unfavorable light by unwarranted comparisons with essentially different categories of musical composition, the contemporary mass and motet.[3]

1. Of the many studies that could be cited here, restrictions of space will allow the mention of only a few that have been judged particularly informative. The incisive comments of Knud Jeppesen in his introduction to *Der Kopenhagener Chansonnier* continue to be basic for a study of the genre; the collected essays of *Chanson and Madrigal 1480–1530*, edited by James Haar (Cambridge, Mass.: Harvard University Press, 1964), shed light from several vantage points; Howard Brown opens his discussion of "The Transformation of the Chanson at the End of the Fifteenth Century," *Kongressbericht Ljubljana*, with an admirably concise descriptive synthesis; and Gustave Reese provides analyses of the works of the most significant masters in his *Music in the Renaissance*.

2. See, for example, the comments by Jeppesen, ibid., pp. 20 ff., or the more extensive discussion by Marcel Françon in the introduction to *Poèmes de transition*, pp. 27 ff., 91 ff., and passim.

In view of the great quantity of fifteenth-century chansons produced and the relatively modest skills of many of the authors, it should surprise no one that negative judgments concerning their literary value are sometimes warranted. At the same time it should be evident that the most gifted poets, turning the conventions of the period to their advantage, created some exquisite jewels of lyrical verse. And many of these poems were provided with musical settings of comparable value.[4] Their scope and expressive means are intentionally limited. They are musical miniatures, and their charm and artistic effectiveness are necessarily to scale. It is on such matters as the elaboration of detail or the inflection of nuance, in short the subtle manipulation of conventional means and devices, that an aesthetic judgment can be most properly made.

Obviously, any meaningful critical assessments of this nature must be based on historical criteria deriving from an understanding of the social and artistic functions of the created work in its own time and place, of the importance it held for those who produced and perceived it, and of the processes of change and development to which it was subject. The courtly society of the fifteenth century that provided the context for the chanson has been discussed repeatedly in considerable detail and is now understood reasonably well.[5] Less is known about the social uses of music on a practical, day-to-day basis, even for those courts whose musical institutions have been the object of carefully documented studies.[6] And the fine stylistic distinctions that are to be discerned in the development of secular music through the fifteenth century, particularly from midcentury on, have yet to be elucidated as carefully as they must be if serious aesthetic judgments are to be possible. Not that studies of style are wanting for the secular music of

---

3. Such is the case with the doctoral dissertation of Peter Reidemeister, *Die Chanson-Handschrift 78 C 28 des Berliner Kupferstichkabinetts*, pp. 33–67. The arguments presented are apparently intended to establish the aesthetic inferiority of the fifteenth-century chanson within a contemporaneous frame of reference.

4. There are analogous examples from other periods of history, such as Shakespeare's use of the sonnet or Mozart's adherence to the musical forms and conventions of the eighteenth century.

5. See, for example, Otto Cartellieri, *The Court of Burgundy*, or Johan Huizinga, *The Waning of the Middle Ages*.

6. This state of affairs is perhaps most evident with respect to the ducal court of Burgundy. Despite the wealth of detail provided by Jeanne Marix in her archival study of the *Musique et musiciens de la cour de Bourgogne*, there is little to indicate the nature or extent of the routine involvement of the chapel musicians with the preparation and performance of secular music at the court.

the period;[7] but thus far the majority of them have been concerned with generalizations, with questions of synthesis and historical continuity. Before turning to an examination of subtle stylistic detail, it was necessary to establish that for the chanson "there was in fact no fundamental change in its basic premises" from the generation of Binchois and Dufay until the end of the century.[8]

It is clearly not within the scope of the present edition either to make definitive critical judgments or to embark upon the kind of comprehensive stylistic study that might provide a basis for such an assessment. However, because the repertory of the Mellon Chansonnier is both manageable in size and representative in content, it offers an opportunity to examine some of the more notable stylistic refinements that made their appearance in the chansons of the second half of the fifteenth century. In this respect it is of special interest because it consists of two definable layers that derive, with some marginal overlapping, from separate chronological periods.

The bulk of the manuscript (ff. 1v–59r) is comprised of works by the immediate contemporaries of Tinctoris, composers representing the musical culture of his native region.[9] This generalization is valid even for the Italian and Spanish pieces by Vincenet placed at the end of the section (Nos. 43 and 44), for although this composer, like Tinctoris, was in the service of the Neapolitan court, he obviously had been trained in the northern musical tradition. The only identifiable exceptions are the compositions by the English masters Frye and Morton, but even they are not truly alien. Morton's prolonged residence at the Burgundian court, beginning as early as 1457, led to an assimilation of typically Continental compositional procedures. Walter Frye cannot be shown to have been on the Continent, but his setting of *Tout a par moy* (No. 35) is not only written on a French poem cast in the typical rondeau form; it displays as well stylistic

7. In addition to the publications cited in n. 1 there are, for the first half of the century, Heinrich Besseler's *Bourdon und Fauxbourdon*, a valuable and informative piece of work even though some of its basic assumptions have been seriously challenged; Catherine Brooks, "Antoine Busnois, Chanson Composer"; Sylvia Kenney's study *Walter Frye and the Contenance Angloise*; Isabel Pope's discussion of "La musique espagnole à la cour de Naples"; Edward Kottick's comparison of the French and Italian traditions in "The Chansonnier Cordiforme"; and the introduction to the edition of the *Odhecaton* by Helen Hewitt and Isabel Pope, to mention but a few; see also the bibliography below and that given by Geneviève Thibault in her article on the "Chanson."

8. The expression is that of Howard Brown, "The Transformation of the Chanson," p. 83.

9. See above, Tinctoris and the Compilation of the Chansonnier, vol. 1, p. 17.

traits that are distinctly modern compared to those of some of his demonstrably earlier works. A few of the pieces in this initial segment of the chansonnier—works such as Morton's *N'aray je jamais mieulx que j'ay* (No. 24), Binchois's *Comme femme desconfortee* (No. 27), and *Tout a par moy* itself—had apparently already been in circulation for a number of years when the copying was begun. They were undoubtedly included because of their exceptional popularity, particularly in Naples. The earliest of these compositions is probably not to be dated much before the late 1450s, and the most recent were probably written in the early 1470s shortly before the compilation of the chansonnier was begun.

By contrast, the last two gatherings (ff. 61^v–80^r) contain a repertory that is manifestly earlier, with the exception of the devotional motet by Tinctoris on the final opening. Of the twelve works in question, half are also found in the manuscript now in Berlin at the *Kupferstich-kabinett*, 78 C 28.[10] This means that all but two of the pieces common to both sources are located in the closing segment of the Mellon Chansonnier. The Berlin collection was apparently copied prior to 1465 and presented to the Florentine patricians Margherita Castellani and Bernardino Niccolini as a wedding gift.[11] It provides therefore a terminal date for the pieces it contains and suggests as well that the most recent of those imported from England or France (apparently all but one were English or French) were composed a few years before. The earliest, however, may date from ten to twenty years before. Three of the chansons included in the closing segment of the Mellon Chansonnier are also found in manuscripts copied during the first half of the century. A fragment of Frye's *So ys emprentid* (No. 45) is found in the Ashmole manuscript of the Bodleian Library in a layer probably dating from the 1440s; *Or me veult* (No. 49) was copied into the Emmeram Codex of the Bavarian State Library in Munich, 3232a, and into the Strasbourg manuscript 222.C.22; Dufay's *Par le regart* (No. 51) was incorporated into the Porto manuscript 714. In every instance these pieces were written in the black notation of the early fifteenth century in at least one of the sources cited.[12]

That the particular group of pieces under discussion (Nos. 45–56)

10. See the Concordant Sources for Nos. 45, 46, 51, 52, 54, and 56.
11. See the description of the manuscript in The Sources, p. 152.
12. Consult The Sources and the Comments for discussion of the manuscripts and compositions in question.

represents a distinctive repertory is suggested by its separation from the remainder of the collection by two vacant openings—the only such gap in the manuscript—and by the fact that it just fills the final two gatherings, from the ·verso of the first leaf of the section to the recto of the last. It is as if those two quinterns had been copied separately, albeit by the same scribe, from a different set of exemplars and then joined to the six gatherings into which the more contemporary pieces had been similarly written without bridging the small gap between the two segments of the chansonnier.[13]

If this interpretation of the evidence is correct, what was the source from which these works were drawn? Eight of them (Nos. 45–47, 51–54, and 56) were also copied into the Escorial manuscript IV.a.24. This means that all but three of the compositions common to the two chansonniers are located in the final segment of the present manuscript. Significantly, there is good evidence that the Escorial codex, like the Mellon, originated in Naples, apparently in the 1460s.[14] This seems to suggest that these particular pieces, although partially known in Florence as is indicated by the substantial number found in the Berlin manuscript 78 C 28, appear to stem from a repertory of secular works apparently accumulated at the Aragonese court during the reigns of Alfonso il Magnanimo (1416–58) and of his successor Ferrante up to 1465.

Consequently, the final two gatherings may be seen as a reflection of the preeminence claimed by Raffaelo Brandolini for the musical life of the kingdom of Naples while under the aegis of those princes.[15] They apparently contained perennial favorites that continued to be prized there two and three decades after they had first become current. It is not surprising, then, that Tinctoris would have included them in his compilation. Even the substantial representation of English composers of the first half of the century is understandable in view of the praise he gives them in his theoretical writings as leaders in the development of the mellifluous style of his period.[16] Since the original poetry of the English songs (Nos. 45, 47, and 55) is found only in the Mellon

---

13. Cf. the discussion above, Physical Characteristics, vol. 1, pp. 1–2.

14. See below the observations concerning the manuscript in The Sources, p. 157.

15. See above, Conclusion, vol. 1, p. 30.

16. Tinctoris's observations in this regard are to be found in his prologues to the *De arte contrapuncti* and the *Proportionale musices*; see Coussemaker, *Scriptorum* 4: 76–77, 154, and the English translation in Strunk, *Source Readings in Music History*, pp. 195 ff.

Chansonnier and in none of the concordant sources—even those of
Neapolitan provenance such as the Escorial manuscript IV.a.24—it
may even have been the theorist who brought it or had it sent to
Naples from his native region in the northern realms under Burgundian
sway for inclusion in the collection at hand.[17] Furthermore, it is
possible to suppose that a part of this earlier repertory reached Florence
by way of Naples rather than directly from the North. It is of special
interest in this regard that the initial owner of the Berlin manuscript
78 C 28 was the son of Ottobuono Niccolini (b. 1410), who served
Florence as ambassador to the court of Naples at a date as yet un-
specified but presumably well before his death in 1470.[18]

There is, then, a gap of approximately twenty years separating the
two layers of the Mellon repertory. Obviously, this generalization
concerning their chronological relationship cannot be applied indis-
criminately to individual works, but it does provide a frame of reference
for the following discussion of musical style that will perhaps allow a
more precise definition than would otherwise be possible of the trends
and developments in secular music during the third quarter of the
fifteenth century.

FORMAL STRUCTURES

Early in the fourteenth century the cultivation of secular polyphony
came to be restricted almost wholly to the setting of poetry in the
so-called fixed forms: ballade, rondeau, virelai, or their non-French
analogues. This ascendancy was to be maintained until late in the
fifteenth century. During that period each of the verse forms generated
a corresponding musical structure that was invariably followed.[19] It
is not surprising, therefore, that virtually the entire repertory of the

---

17. See above (The Composers) the discussion of anglophile tendencies attributable to Duke
Charles, vol. 1, p. 8.

18. See Peter Reidemeister, *Die Chanson-Handschrift 78 C 28*, pp. 17–18, and Vittorio Spreti,
Enciclopedia Storico nobiliare Italiano 4 (1931):816. Francesco Guicciardini indicates in his *History
of Florence*, pp. 19–20, that Niccolini represented Florence at negotiations that took place in
Naples in 1469 but mentions no earlier mission for him to that city. Lewis Lockwood, who
searched through the inventories of the Florentine archives, found nothing to document Niccolini's activity as ambassador to the kingdom of Naples prior to 1465, nor is he cited by name
in the accounts of the Aragonese court published by Nicola Barone, "Le cedole di Napoli,"
pp. 5 ff. However, mention is made of a Florentine embassy that was present in the city of Naples
in the course of 1465 (ibid., 9:33).

19. See below (*Formes Fixes*) the description of the poetic forms and their relationship to
the corresponding musical structures (pp. 84–97).

Mellon Chansonnier is cast in one or another of the traditional poeticomusical forms then commonly in use.

It seems reasonable to expect that the relative esteem in which the individual genres were held in the early 1470s should be reflected in the proportion of each to the total number of works in the collection. Consequently, when one considers the distribution of the pieces in the manuscript according to category (see table 1), the inclusion of no fewer than five ballades may appear at first blush unusual for the period, for by the mid-1400s that particular form was rarely set in regions of French culture. After having predominated through much of the fourteenth century—most notably in the works of Guillaume de Machaut (c. 1300–77)—the ballade began to decline rapidly in popularity toward the beginning of the fifteenth century. Composers of the generation of Busnois and Ockeghem had abandoned it almost completely,[20] and northern manuscripts roughly contemporary with the Mellon such as the Copenhagen, Dijon, Nivelle de la Chaussée, and Wolfenbüttel chansonniers contain only an occasional example.[21]

This anomaly is more apparent than real, however. On the one hand, four of the ballades included in the present collection are almost certainly of English origin, and the fifth, *Or me veult*, most probably as well.[22] On the other hand, the entire group is located in the earlier of the two layers in the manuscript and includes two of the three pieces having concordances in sources from the first half of the century. These compositions, then, are primarily representative of the musical taste of the British Isles, where the ballade continued to be cultivated well after it began to be neglected on the Continent, and they are also among the oldest of the repertory.

By contrast, the *bergerettes* collectively form one of the most up-to-date groups in the collection. Their generic ancestor, the virelai, was

20. According to Brooks, "Antoine Busnois, Chanson Composer," pp. 114, 125, only one of the 71 chansons that have been attributed to Busnois is a ballade. It is an unusual piece on the Flemish text, *In mijne sin*, transmitted by a single source. Likewise none has survived under Ockeghem's name except the bitextual lament on the death of Binchois, *Mort, tu as navré/Miserere* (a motet-chanson) (see the list of works in the forthcoming edition of *Grove's Dictionary of Music and Musicians*).

21. For example, none of the ballades found in the present collection is included in any of the manuscripts cited, and only one in the Laborde Chansonnier (cf. the description of those codices in The Sources).

22. Regarding the presumed original text of *Gentil madona* (No. 46) and related problems of form and provenance, see above, Italian and Spanish Elements and Versification in the Critical Apparatus for the compositions in question.

TABLE 1. The Compositions of the Chansonnier by Formal Type

Ballades

No. 45 So ys emprentid Walterus Frye
No. 46 Gentile madona [Bedingham]
No. 47 Myn hertis lust [Bedingham]
No. 49 Or me veult bien Esperance mentir
No. 55 "Alas, alas, alas" is my chief song [Frye]

Bergerettes

No. 5 A une damme [Busnois]
No. 12 Je ne puis vivre ainsy [Busnois]
No. 14 Ja que li ne s'i attende [Busnois]
No. 30 Ma bouce rit Okeghem
No. 31 Se je fayz dueil G. le Rouge
No. 36 S'il est ainsi Caron

Canción

No. 44 La pena sin ser sabida Vincenet (à 4)

Rondeaux quatrains

No. 1 Bel Acueil [Busnois]
No. 8 Ung plus que tous Busnoys
No. 10 A qui vens tu tes coquilles Busnoys
No. 22 Se mon service vous plaisoit
No. 25 L'omme banny Barbingant
No. 32 De tous biens plaine Heyne
No. 33 Dona gentile G. Dufay
No. 42 A vous sans aultre [Busnois]
No. 51 Par le regart Dufay
No. 53 Puis que je vis le regart
No. 56 Nos amys, vous vous abusés A. Basin

Rondeau quatrain layé

No. 41 Paracheve ton entreprise [Morton]

Rondeaux cinquains

No. 2 En soustenant vostre querelle [Busnois]
No. 3 Accueilly m'a la belle [Caron]
No. 6 Loing de vo tresdoulce presence
No. 7 Est-il merchy Busnois
No. 9 Ce qu'on fait G. Joye
No. 13 Non pas que je veuille penser [Joye]
No. 15 Pour entretenir mes amours Busnoys
No. 17 Vostre bruit et vostre grant fame G. Dufay
No. 18 Fortune, par ta cruaulté Vincenet

TABLE 1 (continued)

No. 20 L'aultre d'antan Jo. Okeghem

No. 21 Le corps s'en va Busnoys

No. 23 Mercy, mon deuil Joye

No. 24 N'aray je jamais mieulx que j'ay? Morton (à 4)

No. 26 Ou doy je secours querir Vincenet

No. 29 Joye me fuit Busnoys

No. 35 Tout a par moy Frye

No. 37 O Fortune, trop tu es dure [Busnois]

No. 38 Enfermé suys je en la tour*

No. 39 Au povre par necessité [Busnois]

No. 50 Donnés l'assault Dufay (à 4)

Rondeaux cinquains layés

No. 16 Quand ce viendra [Busnois] (à 4)

No. 40 Mort ou mercy Caron

No. 48 Ou lit de pleurs (à 4)

Rondeau sizain

No. 27 Comme femme desconfortee Binchoys

Strophic oda

No. 52 Hora cridar "Oymè"

Barzelletta (incomplete)

No. 43 Triste qui sperò morendo Vincenet (à 4)

Bitextual chansons

No. 4 Petitte Camusette J. Okeghem (à 4)

No. 11 Puis que ma damme ne puis voir / Je m'en voy et mon cueur demeure
Regis (à 4)

No. 28 Mon trestout et mon assotee / Il estoit ung bonhome Petit Jan (à 4)

No. 34 Il sera pour vous conbatu / L'ome armé [Morton]

No. 54 Ma dame de nom / Sur la rive de la mer

Devotional motets

No. 19 O virgo, miserere mei Jo. Tinctoris

No. 57 Virgo Dei throno digna Jo. Tinctoris

Texts in languages other than French

Italian: Nos. 33, 43, 46 (contrafact), 52

English: Nos. 45, 47, 55

Spanish: No. 44

Latin: Nos. 19, 57

---

*Although the refrain of this rondeau consists of five lines, the rhyme scheme is not that generally used in poems of this type, and the structural division of the strophes comes after the second line rather than after the third as was usually the case (see Versification for No. 38).

first set polyphonically in the fourteenth century, although it never achieved the wide diffusion or the artistic stature of the ballade. It continued to be cultivated, more or less sporadically, into the fifteenth century but appeared more and more frequently in musical sources with only a single stanza of verse. In this reduced format the virelai came to be designated a bergerette.[23] Busnois and his immediate contemporaries were particularly attracted to this form, leading to Pierre Fabri's assertion, however erroneous, in *Le grand et vrai art de pleine rhétorique* (published in 1521), that the bergerette was Busnois's invention.[24] All three of Busnois's bergerettes in the Mellon repertory are evidently addressed—along with his rondeau *A vous sans aultre* (No. 42)—to Jacqueline d'Hacqueville. Although one could assume that they were written within a relatively brief period, the date of this musical courtship has yet to be fixed.[25] Equally indefinite are the dates for the remaining three bergerettes of the collection (Nos. 30, 31, and 36). Ockeghem and Caron are definitely men of Busnois's generation—unlike the composers of the ballades in the manuscript—and le Rouge appears to have been only slightly older if one can judge from the style of *Se je fayz dueil* (No. 31), the only piece by which he is represented in the chansonnier. However, although the latter work is indisputably a bergerette in its present form, there are indications that it may have been originally conceived as a *rondeau cinquain* to which the final section, *ouvert* and *clos*, was subsequently added,[26] perhaps in an attempt at modernizing it to some extent.

As is to be expected, the form most generously represented in the collection is the rondeau. There are 36 examples of one sort or another, more than 63 percent of the total number of pieces. Of these the majority have a refrain of five lines—20 in all as opposed to 11 with a refrain of four lines. This statistical relationship reflects a general trend in the development of the rondeau toward larger structures. In the fourteenth century, the rondeau was either *simple*, that is, based on a refrain of two lines, or *double*, with a refrain of three lines. In the fifteenth century come the *rondeaux quatrains* and *cinquains*, with refrains

---

23. See Wolfgang Marggraf, "Bergerette," and also the description of the poetic forms below (*Formes Fixes*).

24. See the edition by A. Héron (Rouen, 1889–90), 2:71 (cf. Reese, *Music in the Renaissance,* p. 15 and n. 69).

25. Concerning Busnois's chansons for Jacqueline d'Hacqueville, see Reese, ibid., p. 101; Thibault, "Busnois," pp. 516–17, and Comments and Textual Notes for Nos. 5, 12, 14, and 42.

26. See Comments for No. 31.

of four and five lines, respectively, and the *rondeaux layés*, in which the basic framework is expanded even further by means of short lines interlarded in a variety of ways between those of conventional length.[27] This procedure results in an alternation between rhyming lines of unequal length in a manner recalling the medieval *lai*, from which the form may derive its name. It also offers a wide range of possibilities for subtle formal diversity within the relatively restricted confines of the fundamental design. The manuscript contains four such poems, apparently only one of which is based on the rondeau quatrain, whereas the others seem to have been elaborated from a refrain structure of five lines.

But if the prevailing tendency from the fourteenth to the fifteenth centuries is clearly toward more extended and elaborate formal designs, it is not possible to establish a wholly reliable relative chronology for the works of the present collection on that basis. Whether quatrains, cinquains, or layés, the rondeaux of the chansonnier are attributed to a relatively small group of composers most of whom are of the generation of Busnois and Ockeghem. Some of the most significant ones— Caron, Dufay, Morton, and Busnois—are represented by works in more than one category. In addition, the one piece ascribed to Binchois[28]— hence written before 1460—is the rondeau *Comme femme desconfortee* with a refrain of six lines. Conversely, it is entirely possible that, just as Binchois's *rondeau sizain* is demonstrably among the earlier works of the second layer, some of the rondeaux quatrains may be among the more recent.

Among the most intriguing compositions of the Mellon repertory are the five that are bitextual. Four of them are based on monophonic chansons of a popular cast that have been arranged polyphonically. The borrowed melody and its text are either carried by the tenor alone or divided between the tenor and a contratenor, while the cantus presents a related but separate poem, usually with independent melodic material. The most celebrated tune so treated is *L'homme armé*, which was so frequently employed in the polyphonic masses of the fifteenth and sixteenth centuries.[29]

---

27. See below the discussion of formal structures in the verse, pp. 86–87.

28. See Comments for No. 27.

29. Concerning the character of the *L'homme armé* melody, its possible origins, and its use in polyphonic compositions, both secular and sacred, see Lewis Lockwood, "Aspects of the *L'homme armé* Tradition," Proceedings of the Royal Music Association for April 1974.

In a setting attributed to Morton (No. 34), the song of the redoubt-
able "armed man" is fitted to an ironic rondeau naming Maistre
Symonet le Breton, Morton's colleague at the Burgundian court, as
the man to conquer the fearful Turk.

The military imagery of the verse is matched musically by the short
fanfare figures of a falling fifth traded back and forth between the two
lower voices. Gentle mockery is evident not only in le Breton's non-
military status as singer and cleric but also in the ambiguity of the
expression *crocq de ache*, which can be interpreted either as "battle-
axe" or as "celery stalk."[30] Pleasantries of this sort imply that the
composer and his subject had been acquainted over a reasonably
extended period of time and that the latter's capabilities, whether
with arms or at the table, were well known to the intended audience.
It is likely that the composition dates from the period when both
Maistre Symon and Morton were at the Burgundian court, prior to
le Breton's departure for Cambrai in mid-1465. But it is also possible
that the work was written in connection with a visit made by Morton
and Hayne to Cambrai, in which case both this event and the composition would have to postdate Maistre Symon's removal to the cathedral
church.[31]

A similar spirit of lighthearted raillery permeates the anonymous
Ma dame de nom | Sur la rive de la mer (No. 54) and Petit Jan's *Mon
trestout et mon assotee | Il estoit ung bonhomme* (No. 28). In both songs the
stereotyped metaphors of courtly love poetry are placed in humorously
incongruous juxtaposition with the earthy language of the popular
theater. In fact, both are based upon chansons found in *farces* of the
fifteenth century.[32]

In spite of some noteworthy resemblances between the two pieces,
there are also some significant differences. The anonymous *Ma dame de
nom* is written for only three voices and is relatively modest in scope, like
the setting of *L'homme armé*. Petit Jan's *Mon trestout*, however, possesses
a fourth part (an untexted contratenor) and surpasses in length—by a
considerable margin—every other composition in the collection. Since
Ma dame de nom is part of the older of the two layers discernible in the

30. See the Textual Notes to No. 34.

31. See above, The Composers, vol. 1, p. 6.

32. See Comments for Nos. 28 and 54. In *Ma dame de nom* there is one such song, but in *Mon
trestout* there are two that can be traced to contemporary theatrical productions. A third song,
somewhat more courtly in character, seems to be present, but its source has yet to be identified.

manuscript, it must have been composed prior to 1465. *Mon trestout* appears to be more recent. In addition to displaying the characteristics cited, it is written in a diminished mensuration and introduces at the end a proportional change of meter rarely encountered before the end of the century.[33]

Equally sophisticated and even more forward-looking is Ockeghem's *Petitte Camusette*. The piece was clearly conceived from the outset for four voices because the second contratenor, like the first, participates (imitatively) with the tenor in the presentation of the borrowed material, both tune and text. As given in the Mellon Chansonnier the piece is very much like the compositions for four fully texted voices that were cultivated in the last decade of the fifteenth century. It was undoubtedly this stylistic similarity that caused it to be included in a collection as late as the Brussels manuscript 11239, copied at the turn of the century.[34]

Both Morton's *Il sera pour vous / L'ome armé* and Ockeghem's *Petitte Camusette* are cast in the form of a rondeau. In either case the preexistent melody is tripartite and is adapted to the formal structure of the polyphony in the same manner: the initial strain is sung with the opening section of the rondeau, the second strain and the reiteration of the first with the closing section of the fixed form. In this manner the repetitions conventional for the rondeau can be observed without violating the formal integrity of the borrowed materials. The verse provided for the cantus of Morton's piece is in fact a rondeau, as is the poem *S'elle m'amera*, found with Ockeghem's composition in three of the manuscript sources. But in the Mellon Chansonnier there is for the latter only a single strophe of a different poem (also beginning with *Petitte Camusette*), and any trace of the rondeau structure has all but disappeared (see Versification to No. 4, II). The other two works of similar character, *Ma dame de nom / Sur la rive* and Petit Jan's *Mon trestout et mon assotee / Il estoit ung bonhomme*, share a formal feature characteristic of the ballade—the repetition of the initial section of music for the second strophe of verse—but display no other traits of that poetic and musical genre.

In contrast to the light ironic humor of the bitextual chansons discussed thus far is Regis's *Puis que ma damme ne puis voir / Je m'en voy et mon cueur demeure* (No. 11). What would appear to be the refrains of

---

33. See below. Mensuration. Tempo, and Rhythm, pp. 16–19.
34. See the description of the codex in question in The Sources, pp. 153–54.

two rondeaux quatrains dealing with conventional themes of amorous torment are presented simultaneously by cantus and contratenor. Unusual is the courtly character of both poems, for most bitextual chansons exploit the humorous contrast between aristocratic and unabashedly popular poetic idioms. Also, a pair of slightly misplaced coronas suggests a workable bipartite division at the initial pitch of the second opening (the beginning of m. 16). However, because the additional strophes of the poems are absent, it is impossible to know whether the composer envisaged the concurrent presentation of two complete rondeaux. If so, an adjustment would have to be made in the text placement indicated by the manuscript in order that the first pair of lines terminate at the cadential point in both of the parts sung.[35] It is difficult to know whether musical or social factors might have prompted a combination of the sort attempted here by Regis. Nevertheless, it is interesting to note that the two texted voices begin with the same melodic figure, suggesting that the composer may have combined not only the two poems but also preexistent settings for them essentially because of the similarities between them.

Of the works outside the categories so far discussed, one has a Spanish text, two set Italian poems, and two are devotional motets in Latin. Vincenet's *La pena sin ser sabida* (No. 44) is a typical example of the *canción*, the Spanish cousin of the bergerette so assiduously cultivated during the second half of the fifteenth century. By contrast his setting of *Triste qui sperò morendo* (No. 43) poses certain problems. Structurally indistinguishable from a rondeau, it consists of two principal sections of slightly unequal length with the central point of division marked in the customary manner by a corona and a cadence on the confinal of the mode. But the lines of Italian verse written under the cantus part follow the mold of the *barzelletta* (an Italian form of the bergerette), which is incomplete in this instance because the *volta* is absent. Consequently, the only pattern of repetition possible musically —if any is to be used at all—is the one generally observed for the second and third stanzas of that poetic form without the usual return to the initial section for the *ripresa*.[36] Had it been Vincenet's task to set a complete barzelletta, one would expect him to have adopted the corre-

---

35. See below and Comments for No. 11.
36. See below, *Formes Fixes*, pp. 92–95, and Comments and Versification for No. 43.

sponding musical form. Since he did not, one must conclude either that his starting point was the poem as it is given here, for which he selected the conventional structure that appeared to him best adapted to its unusual formal requirements, or that the Italian poem is a contrafact presumably replacing a French rondeau. Although *Triste qui sperò* comports four voices, like the Spanish piece that follows, one cannot affirm unequivocally, as one can for the latter, that it was composed during Vincenet's service at the Aragonese court, apparently in the early 1470s.[37] Rather, the indication *Si placet* attached to the contratenor and the possibility (however faint) that the Italian text was not original tend to suggest that the work as transmitted by the Mellon Chansonnier was updated to flatter the tastes of his new patrons after his arrival in Naples.

Also problematic is the structure of the anonymous *Hora cridar "Oymè"* (No. 52). On the one hand a division is indicated in the music at the end of the second phrase, leaving in the somewhat longer second section three musical phrases, the last two of which have been articulated internally. The Italian text, on the other, is clearly strophic and requires no partial repetitions. Thus the structural division of the music appears to be conventional rather than functional, once again raising the possibility of a contrafact. However, the proportions between the two musical sections are not those normally found in a rondeau, and the piece has neither the length nor the alternate endings generally characterizing the ballade. In any case, since the work is included in the older layer of the present manuscript, it is to be dated prior to 1465, and the compositional style, as will be seen, is typical of the musicians trained in Franco-Burgundian regions in the first half of the century.

The pair of devotional motets attributed to Tinctoris resemble nothing so much as the contrapuntal exercises with which he illustrated his treatises. It is quite possible, as has been shown, that *O Virgo, miserere mei* (No. 19) was composed in connection with the compilation of the chansonnier. *Virgo Dei throno digna* (No. 57) may be slightly earlier but can hardly have preceded the beginnings of Tinctoris's service at the Neapolitan court early in the 1470s.[38]

---

37. See above, Italian and Spanish Elements, vol. 1, pp. 16–17.
38. See above, Tinctoris and the Compilation of the Chansonnier, vol. 1, pp. 17–18.

Mensuration, Tempo, and Rhythm

An examination of the mensural signs in the Mellon Chansonnier points to a number of noteworthy developments in the third quarter of the fifteenth century. In the older group of compositions the mensurations are rarely marked, perhaps because the uniformity of prevailing usage made it superfluous to do so. All eight pieces lacking a signature in the final two gatherings are undoubtedly written in perfect tempus (○), as are Nos. 50 and 55, where the mensural signs are given. The remaining two works (Nos. 54 and 56) carry the symbol for imperfect tempus (C) (see table 2).

By contrast, in the later repertory of 45 compositions (Nos. 1–44 and 57) 10 pieces, a much smaller proportion of the total, are written in perfect tempus, which is specified in all but one instance. The integral imperfect mensuration is relatively more frequent, occurring in six or seven pieces of the group, whereas the diminished form (¢) that first makes its appearance among these later works actually predominates, having been used for 21 or 22 of them.[39] In addition, four compositions (three bergerettes and the formally related canción) have their two principal sections written under contrasting mensurations, the first integral and the second diminished, or the first ternary and the second binary, or both.[40] Such a shift of mensuration is new to French secular music of the period. Although alternating mensurations became part of the structural organization of both mass and motet during the first half of the fifteenth century, the procedure was not generally applied to the more modest dimensions of the chanson. It is definitely significant that the change is found here only in the formal structure of the bergerette, with which Busnois and his contemporaries were apparently experimenting during the third quarter of the century.

In the compositions with contrasting mensural signs a proper interpretation governs the tempo of the two sections and the relationship between them. As is generally understood, the tempo of fifteenth-century music was regulated by the *tactus*, or beat, consisting of two motions, one ascending, the other descending. As a general indication of the rapidity with which the movements were to be made, the tactus

---

39. The apparent uncertainty is due to Vincenet's *Ou doy je secours querir* (No. 26), which carries the sign for imperfect tempus (C) in the present manuscript but has the stroke of diminutioh in the Pixérécourt Chansonnier (¢); see Collation, p. 290.

40. See table 2 and Collation for Nos. 12, 14, 36, and 44.

was compared to the regular heart beat of a person at rest, itself divided into two complementary pulses, the diastole and the systole.[41] As a result it is possible to conclude that the approximate tempo for the complete tactus was between 60 and 78 per minute (hence between 120 and 156 for the individual pulsations). Under the integral mensurations of perfect and imperfect tempus with minor prolation (here transcribed under the time signatures $\frac{3}{4}$ and $\frac{4}{4}$, respectively), the tactus was applied to the semibreve (the quarter note of the present edition). With the stroke of diminution drawn through the mensural symbol, it was related instead to the breve (the half note of the transcriptions).[42] Thus, the practical result of shifting from an integral to a diminished mensuration is to double the tempo, provided the note values remain the same.

Interestingly, in the repertory at hand, although an acceleration usually does occur, the rate of movement and of textual declamation is not suddenly doubled. Instead, the second section begins with longer values, breves and semibreves, before gradually introducing the shorter notes in the new tempo. Typical in this regard is Busnois's *Ja que li ne s'i attende* (No. 14), in which the declamation, having been tied to the semibreve in the syllabic passages of the refrain, is shifted to the breve immediately after the mensural change. Also representative is Caron's *S'il est ainsi* (No. 36), in which syllabic patterns of declamation using repeated minims (eighth notes) toward the end of the initial section give way immediately after the mensural shift to breves and semibreves. In addition, either the shortest note value used in the integral mensuration is dropped with the stroke of diminution and the next longer value added instead at the opposite end of the range, as with the latter composition, or the incidence of the shorter values is greatly reduced as in the former, where the semiminim is employed in the second section for only a single ornamental figure.

Obviously, the shortest values utilized, whether for declamation or for melodic ornamentation, are determined by both practical and

41. See, for example, Franchinus Gaffurius, *Practica musicae utriusque cantus*, Liber tertius, Cap. IV, "Quae et ubi in contrapuncto admittendae sint discordantiae," or the English translation by Clement Miller, pp. 129–30.

42. See Andreas Ornithoparchus, *Musice active micrologus*, Liber secundus, Cap. VI, "De tactu"; cf. Reese, *Music in the Renaissance*, pp. 179–80 and n. 152. (When the latter author affirms that after about 1500 the diminished sign of mensuration only "theoretically" indicated the *tactus alla breve* but "in practice" the "normal" tactus of a semibreve, he is clearly contradicting the very practical treatise by Ornithoparchus that he himself cites.)

aesthetic considerations. If the movement becomes too fast it may outrun the skill of the performers, and an excessively rapid rate of declamation can pose problems for both the singer's tongue and the listener's ear. This is undoubtedly why the rates of motion and declamation in works written wholly in diminished imperfect tempus with the tactus applied to the brevis are not radically different from those found in compositions written in an integral mensuration. The range of rhythmic values used gives a general indication of the relationship that obtains because the *fusa* (thirty-second note), occasionally employed in ornamental figures under the integral mensurations, is rarely found with the stroke of diminution. Conversely, the brevis is often the most extended value found with the unaltered mensurations whereas the long is much more common when the sign for a proportional reduction is present.[43]

More meaningful, however, is the general rapidity of movement and textual delivery. Let us compare in this respect Nos. 7 and 8 with Nos. 9 and 10, taking at random a series of pieces in contrasting mensurations. It will be observed that the first two, written in perfect and imperfect tempus, respectively, proceed most frequently in minims and semiminims (eighth and sixteenth notes in the transcriptions). In Busnois's *Est-il merchy*, where fusae also occur in the melodic figuration, repeated pitches in minim patterns (as in m. 7) indicate that the declamation is also tied at times to the same note values. By contrast Nos. 9 and 10 advance primarily by semibreves and minims with semiminims restricted almost exclusively to an occasional dotted pattern or to precadential melodic flourishes. The rhythmic character of the compositions written under a diminished mensuration is so marked in fact that it seemed necessary to construe as an error the integral mensural symbol given in the manuscript for Vincenet's *Ou doy je secours querir* (No. 26) and to accept instead, for this edition, the diminished sign under which it appears in the Pixérécourt Chansonnier. This construction seems all the more defensible in light of the striking similarity between the beginning of Vincenet's chanson and that of Busnois's *A qui vens tu tes coquilles* (No. 10), cited in the preceding comparison.[44]

If the declamation appears essentially brisker in the compositions using a diminished mensuration, this may be due in part to the light or humorous character of the text in such pieces as Nos. 9 and 10 or to

43. See table 2, Range of Rhythmic Values.
44. See Comments for No. 26, p. 290.

an interest in clear, direct declamation that appears to have been developing during the second half of the fifteenth century. This trend may conceivably have gone hand in hand with the growing preference for diminished imperfect tempus since the compositions in which the latter is used are generally shorter in terms of the total number of tactus units than those employing the integral mensurations. It may also be that the tactus tended to become gradually slower in the course of the fifteenth century, if only within the limits presumably allowed by variations in the rapidity of the pulse. Thus in the earliest pieces, none of which carries the stroke of diminution, much less use is made of semiminim patterns (sixteenth notes) than in those written under the same mensurations by the composers of Tinctoris's generation. *Or me veult* (No. 49), for example, one of the oldest pieces in the collection, has nothing smaller than a minim, and Nos. 45–47, 50, 51, and 55 in particular employ relatively few semiminims, the majority of them in cadential or ornamental figures.

In any case the increasing attention after midcentury to questions of declamation appears to have begun to alter somewhat the rhythmic dynamics of the characteristic melodic phrase. In the earlier works the line unfolds with little discernible differentiation between the rhythmic activity of opening, medial, and closing elements. In the later ones there is an ever clearer distinction between the slower-moving declamatory rhythms at the beginning of a phrase and the more rapid, energetic figures of a melismatic stamp that generally precede a well-marked cadential formula.[45] Moreover, the rate of rhythmic activity varies little from part to part within a given chanson. Even in the earliest works of the repertory there are only scattered examples of more extended values in tenor or contratenor parts, and the increasingly consistent use of imitative part writing in the second half of the fifteenth century necessarily reinforced the similarity of rhythmic profiles between the voices.

NUMBER AND RANGE OF THE VOICES

As has already been observed, three voices or parts[46] remained the rule for the secular composition of the fifteenth century until at least the final decade. It is not surprising then that the majority of the pieces

45. See below, Words and Music, pp. 59–61.

46. In the discussion that follows, as elsewhere in the edition, a "voice" may be either human or instrumental, and the term is used indifferently to designate parts that may be both sung and played.

in the Mellon Chansonnier adhere to such a format. In nine instances, however, about 16 percent of the total repertory, the manuscript provides a fourth voice. Of these compositions, three (Nos. 4, 11, and 28) are the bitextual chansons discussed above. There the fourth part, although obviously not indispensable to their special combinatorial character, may be considered a function of it.[47] In three others (Nos. 16, 24, and 43) the second contratenor part is labeled *si placet*, indicating that it is optional. It may have been added to a chanson originally conceived for three voices, possibly by a different composer. For example Busnois's *Quant ce viendra* (No. 16) has the fourth part only in this chansonnier, whereas Morton's *N'aray je jamais mieulx que j'ay?* (No. 24) is written à 3 in every other source but one.[48] Vincenet's *Triste qui sperò morendo* (No. 43) is unique to the present collection, but there is some evidence that it may be a reworking of an earlier piece provided with a contrafact text and a fourth part.[49] Also, Dufay's *Donnés l'assault* (No. 50) is written for only three voices in one of the three sources in which it has been included. The second contratenor, although constructed with admirable contrapuntal skill, does not participate in the imitative figures linking the other three parts and generally gives the impression of a later addition.

There remain Vincenet's *La pena sin ser sabida* (No. 44) and the anonymous *Ou lit de pleurs* (No. 48). Neither carries the *si placet* label nor gives any indication in its contrapuntal structure that one of the parts has been appended to a preexistent structure à 3, but since both are unique to the manuscript, there is a possibility, however slight, that one or the other first existed in a version for three voices. Aside from these two works then (one in each of the chronologically distinguishable layers of the chansonnier), only the bitextual chansons seem to have been initially conceived in their present format à 4. But the four added contratenors signal the beginnings in the secular realm of a growing preference for the fuller sonorities of the four-voice structure, which had become the rule in the sacred music of the period. By the end of the century the shift was complete; the chanson à 3 had become the slightly archaic exception rather than the rule, and four voices the indispensable foundation to which a fifth or a sixth was sometimes added.

47. See above, Formal Structures, pp. 11–14.
48. See Comments for the compositions in question.
49. See above, Formal Structures, pp. 14–15.

The three voices that were still customary in the 1470s were disposed in a variety of ranges and combinations belying the uniformity of the terminology generally used to identify them. The text-bearing voice, cantus or superius, is rarely designated in the sources of the fifteenth century. The two supporting voices, tenor and contratenor, are usually so labeled in the chansonnier. The total compass of the individual voices is not unduly variable, however, since the smallest covers the interval of a seventh (of which the sole example is the popular melody forming the tenor of No. 4) and the largest that of a thirteenth,[50] straining in no instance the practical limitations of either voices or instruments of the period. Generally speaking, for reasons apparently linked to the observance of modal norms, the range of the cantus and contratenor parts tends to be slightly wider than that of the tenor. The majority of the former encompass either a tenth or an eleventh. The remainder are divided primarily between the range of a ninth and that of a twelfth with an occasional instance of a thirteenth (Nos. 20, 24, 26, 29, 36, and 50) but only rare examples of an octave (Nos. 4, 16, 34, 46, and 47). Most of the tenors, on the other hand, span either a ninth or a tenth. A lesser number employ a compass of an octave or an eleventh. The twelfth appears in a few scattered instances (Nos. 12, 21, 37, and 50), but the thirteenth is nowhere to be found. It is perhaps noteworthy in this connection that in the compositions of the earlier layer, the range of the cantus part is inclined to be somewhat smaller than in the later works. In no case does it exceed a tenth, whereas two of the tenors (Nos. 47 and 53) and three of the contratenors (Nos. 47, 54, and 56) span an eleventh, one of each a twelfth (Nos. 48 and 50), and the contratenor of No. 50 a thirteenth.

If the size of the ambitus covered by the separate voices shows only limited diversity, that is not the case for the placement of the parts on the staff and the various combinations of high and low ranges used. The upper limit of the cantus parts spans the interval of a seventh, from a″ (above the treble staff) to b′ below and in two special instances (Nos. 1 and 31) is located a fourth lower still on f. The lower limit extends from the same f down an octave and a fourth to the C of the bass staff.[51] Nonetheless, there is an approximately standard range for

50. See table 2.
51. Concerning the manner in which the register of the pitch is indicated in the edition, see the introduction to Critical Apparatus, p. 186.

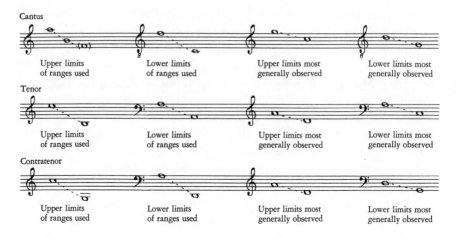

Cantus

| Upper limits of ranges used | Lower limits of ranges used | Upper limits most generally observed | Lower limits most generally observed |

Tenor

| Upper limits of ranges used | Lower limits of ranges used | Upper limits most generally observed | Lower limits most generally observed |

Contratenor

| Upper limits of ranges used | Lower limits of ranges used | Upper limits most generally observed | Lower limits most generally observed |

the cantus: in 51 pieces the upper limit of the part is situated between c′ and g′ above—40 of them between c′ (the highest pitch in 20 works) and e′ a third above—and the lower limit between G and d a fifth higher. The tenor parts have upper limits extending from e′ to the b an octave and a fourth below, and lower limits reaching from a to A an octave lower, but the greatest number have their highest pitch somewhere between d above middle c and a′ a fifth higher (50 in all), their lowest between C of the bass staff and the note a a sixth higher (53 altogether). The contratenors, with upper limits extending from c′ to G an octave and a fourth below and lower limits anywhere between a and D′ an octave and a fifth below, have them situated most frequently within the fifth between d and a′ at the top of the range (in 45 instances) and within the fifth between G′ and D at the bottom (in 48 cases).[52] To be observed in this connection is the fact that the pieces of the earlier layer of the chansonnier do not make use of the extremes of range occasionally found in the presumably later works. For example, none of the cantus parts rises above e′ of the treble staff, and all have their upper limit between this pitch and the b′ a fourth below. Similarly the lower limit in those works, whether in tenor or contratenor, is generally located within the fourth between G′ and C of the bass staff.

In the more recent layer of the present repertory the three voices of the prevailing format are most often placed in distinctive but

52. The figures given do not include the second contratenor parts of the pieces written for four voices.

overlapping ranges with the cantus predominating in the upper registers, the tenor in the middle ones, and the contratenor at the lower end of the scale.[53] The ambitus common to a pair of contiguous voices is usually approximately the interval of a fifth, but it may be as much as an octave, especially between the lower two. Moreover, there is almost invariably a small overlap between the outer voices as well. Because the type of combination just described recurs with sufficient frequency to be qualified as normative, it is instructive to compare with it the solutions found in the compositions of the earlier layer. In the majority of them although the cantus usually has exclusive possession of at least a fifth on the upper side of its range, tenor and contratenor share an almost identical range. In Nos. 45–47 and 49–53, notably, the upper and lower limits of these two voices are either precisely the same or divergent by no more than a tone. In addition the contratenor, which frequently sounds below the tenor not only in the works cited but in Nos. 48 and 54–56 as well, instead of closing a fifth or even an octave under the final pitch of the tenor (as is generally the case in the later works), climbs above it for the terminal cadence in every instance but one. The sole exception is Dufay's *Donnés l'assault* (No. 50), in which the disposition of the version à 3 has been altered to accommodate the addition of the second contratenor by doubling the last note of the presumably original contratenor at the lower twelfth.

Solely on the basis of the choice of ranges and the consequent placement of the voices that characterize representative works in each layer of the manuscript, a number of pieces in the more recent segment of the repertory appear somewhat archaic by comparison with those around them. For example, in Dufay's *Vostre bruit et vostre grant fame* (No. 17) tenor and contratenor share essentially the same ambitus, and the former not only reaches the concluding cadence a fifth below the latter but actually moves a step under the lower limit of the contratenor range. Similar relationships are to be observed in Ockeghem's *L'aultre d'antan* (No. 20), Busnois's *Le corps s'en va* (No. 21), Barbingant's *L'omme banny* (No. 25), Binchois's *Comme femme desconfortee* (No. 27), Ockeghem's *Ma bouce rit* (No. 30), Dufay's *Dona gentile* (No. 33), Morton's *Il sera pour vous conbatu / L'ome armé* (No. 34), Frye's *Tout a par moy* (No. 35), and Caron's *S'il est ainsi* (No. 36). With

---

53. See, for example, Nos. 2, 3, 5, 6, 8, 14, 15, 18, 19, 21–23, and so on.

regard to the compositions attributed to Binchois and Frye and the Italian text set by Dufay, available biographical information tends to confirm the relatively earlier dating suggested by the aspects of style under discussion that point approximately to the mid-fifteenth century. Consequently, it is possible that the other chansons mentioned may likewise stem from about the same period, twenty years or more before the compilation of the present collection.[54]

Also of interest in the more recent layer of the repertory are those pieces that depart from the norms generally observed in a manner that can apparently best be described as experimental. Especially striking are Busnois's *Bel Acueil*, the opening work of the manuscript, and le Rouge's *Se je fayz dueil* (No. 31), in both of which all three parts are confined to the same low range between the C of the bass staff and the f an octave and a fourth above. Busnois also wrote for three equal treble voices (with both cantus and tenor bearing text in this chansonnier) in setting the rondeau *A vous sans aultre* (No. 42). In *Je ne puis vivre ainsy* (No. 12) he paired cantus and tenor in a high register over the sustaining accompaniment of a comparatively low contratenor—once again with the text given to both cantus and tenor. It is possible, of course, that a number of the differences in range and voicing that have been mentioned here are simply a function of the voices and instruments available to the composer for a performance of his work, but the distinctive solutions adopted by Busnois suggest that he was less bound by tradition in this regard than any of his immediate contemporaries.

MODAL STRUCTURES

When the ranges of the separate voices of a given composition are related to one another, both with respect to the total compass and to the points of melodic reference within that basic frame, it becomes evident that they were determined to a very considerable degree by fifteenth-century concepts of mode. In fact, it seems, to use Tinctoris's own terms, that the *tonus*, or mode, was regarded as the fundamental principle of melodic organization by which "the beginning, middle,

---

54. The downward shift of the contratenor range compared to the tenor has been noted by Heinrich Besseler, *Bourdon und Fauxbourdon*, specifically with respect to Dufay, but the editor cannot agree with Besseler's interpretation of the historical developments and the significance he attaches to them.

and end of any song" was to be regulated.[55] The final and the confinal, whether regular or transposed, were taken both as pivotal
points for the unfolding of the melodic line and as cadential terminations for its articulation, thus defining the melodic movement
primarily in terms of the characteristic species of fourth and fifth
associated with a given modal pair.[56]

In the anonymous *Loing de vo tresdoulce presence* (No. 6), to take a
particularly clear example, tenor and cantus begin with the confinal
of the Dorian modes, move scalewise upward through the characteristic fourth, turning on the upper octave of the final, and return to the
point of departure. The cantus then changes direction, but the tenor
continues its downward sweep to the final before rising a second time
to the upper limit of the modal octave. Similarly, the contratenor
begins with the confinal, moves down by step to the final, by leap to
the lower A of the characteristic fourth of the mode, and back up an
octave to turn around the confinal, where it terminates that segment
of its phrase. As the composition unfolds, final and confinal continue

55. "Tonus itaque nihil aliud est quam modus per quem principium, medium, et finis cuiuslibet cantus ordinatur," *De natura ac proprietate tonorum*, capitulum i; see Coussemaker, *Scriptorum*,
4:18, or the English translation by Albert Seay, *Concerning the Nature and Propriety of Tones*, p. 4.

56. The modal system current during the fifteenth century provides the basis for the discussion
that follows. It had been formulated in the Middle Ages as a means of conceptualizing the
distinctive characteristics of liturgical plainchant. Consequently its concepts are essentially
melodic in nature; they could be used either for classification or, as began to happen in the
fifteenth century, as a guide to melodic composition. There were eight modes in the system, each
defined in terms of its final (the last pitch of any given melody) and its range or ambitus. The
four regular finals were D, E, F, and G, and each was used to close a pair of modes, one of which
was authentic, the other plagal.
The range of the authentic modes was conceived theoretically as based upon a characteristic
octave above the final, comprising the fifth between it and the confinal (which was always a
perfect fifth higher) and the fourth between the confinal and the duplication of the final at the
upper octave. The range of the plagal modes was based upon an octave centered around the final,
comprising the fifth between it and the confinal above and the fourth between the final and the
octave duplication of the confinal a fourth lower. (In practice it was possible to exceed the octave
limit by one or two pitches in either direction.) Since the underlying scale of pitches was diatonic
(that given by the white keys of a piano), to which only b-flat was regularly added, each mode
was characterized by a distinctive arrangement of whole and half steps. This arrangement was
referred to as the *species* of the scale bounded by the defining melodic intervals: the fourth, the
fifth, and the octave characteristic of the mode. The authentic modes are designated both by the
numbers I, III, V, and VII, and by the Greek terms Dorian, Phrygian, Lydian, and mixolydian;
the plagal modes by the numbers II, IV, VI, and VIII or by the Greek names hypodorian,
hypophrygian, and so on. See the treatise by Tinctoris cited in the previous note, or the *Practica
Musicae* of Gafforius as translated by Clement Miller.

to serve as the principal points of melodic orientation and cadential rest, and the characteristic species of fourth and fifth become the most conspicuous intervalic units thrown into relief by the profile of the melodic line.

A certain "tonal" coherence is imparted to the polyphonic combination of the three voices constituting this work by their common modal orientation. The range of the cantus is defined by the authentic octave of the Dorian modal pair, exceeded on the upper limit in a single precadential passage by only a step—apparently for contrapuntal reasons—and extended below the final in the concluding phrase by the addition of the characteristic fourth. The result is the combination of authentic and plagal octaves that Tinctoris designated a "mixed mode."[57] Similarly, the contratenor is confined mainly to the plagal octave of the Dorian pair, moving below it by step in only one instance (for reasons presently to be explained) and above it most of the time only by a modally acceptable half-step[58] used repeatedly in the figure, a, b♭, a, so typical of plainchants in the Dorian modes. But for the last phrase of the initial section, the part ascends to d, filling out the authentic octave and thus creating a modal mixture analogous to that of the cantus. Only the tenor appears anomalous since it climbs above the characteristic authentic octave of the mode first by a tone (m. 4) and then by a third (mm. 7, 13–21). However, it is possible to interpret these deviations as reflecting a temporary transposition of the characteristic species of fifth to the confinal, thus implying the formation of a plagal octave from E to e with the f functioning at the top of the range as does the b♮ in the contratenor below. The profile of the latter voice in the first cadential formula (mm. 4–5) seems to confirm this explanation of the melodic events,

57. *De natura ac proprietate tonorum*, Capitulum xxii, "De mixtione tonorum. . . . If the authentic mode descends below its final as much as a fourth, it is said to be mixed. . . . Similarly, if the plagal mode ascends above its final as much as an octave it will be mixed." (cf. Coussemaker, *Scriptorum* 4:28, or Seay, *Concerning the Tones*, p. 23).

58. Tinctoris, like his contemporaries, held the normal range of the modes to be a ninth, an octave plus a tone (or half tone) below the final for the authentics, an octave plus a tone (or half tone) above the confinal for the plagals, and he conceded that "by licence" the total compass could be extended to a tenth by adding yet another step (or half-step) below the characteristic octave of the authentic modes or above that of the plagals; cf. *De natura ac proprietate tonorum*, capitulum xx, "De medio tonorum," and capitulum xxi, "De gradu tam autenticis quam plagalibus ex licentia concessa," Coussemaker, *Scriptorum*, 4:27 ff., or Seay, *Concerning the Tones*, pp. 21–22.

for it outlines clearly the authentic octave of mode I with the final on A and the confinal on E.[59]

As will be seen from the Comments in table 2, each composition has been analyzed in modal terms with results analogous to those concerning No. 6. In every case the species of fourth and fifth characteristic of a single modal pair can be said to predominate, particularly in the opening and closing phrases. The final and confinal form the goals and turning points within the melodic line as well as the terminal pitches at cadences. In the earlier layer of the manuscript the overall compass tends to be somewhat narrower and the tenor and contratenor usually lie in the same range. The authentic and plagal octaves may be combined in adjacent voices, either with the cantus in the authentic octave and the supporting parts in the plagal octave below (as in No. 49 and the concluding portion of No. 53) or the other way around (as in Nos. 45, 46, and the opening of No. 53). In Bedingham's *Myn hertis lust* (No. 47), however, the cantus is confined to the plagal octave, but the tenor and contratenor encompass within their range of an eleventh not only the overlapping authentic octave but also the characteristic fourth below, thus establishing a mixed mode within each part.

Other works in the same segment of the collection are distinguished by a common octave—if not necessarily a common ambitus—for all parts, either the authentic as in No. 56, or the plagal as in No. 48. This distinctive feature is shared by a good number of the pieces in the more recent layer of the chansonnier that have a combination of voice ranges appearing unusual or archaic in comparison with the majority of the surrounding compositions.[60] However, in most of the presumably later works the overlapping voices generally occupy complementary octaves of the mode, occasionally with the tenor in the authentic octave, as in No. 2 (an arrangement also found in the older layer with No. 55) but much more frequently with the tenor in the plagal octave and the two outer voices in the authentic one.[61]

59. In the modal system of the Middle Ages, the melodies terminating on a were assimilated to the Dorian pair, those concluding on c to the Lydian pair because of the affinities between their characteristic octaves, that is, the identity of the respective species of fifth in the first instance, of the species of fourth in the second, and of the possible identity of the entire octave when b♭ is present in the modes on D and F, as it frequently is in plainchant.

60. See in table 2, Ranges; also Comments, Nos. 1, 12, 17, 25, 27, 30, 34, 35, and 42, and in the older layer of the manuscript, Nos. 51 and 52.

61. See in table 2, Ranges; also Comments, Nos. 3, 5, 14, 18, 22, 24, 32, 39–41, and 47.

TABLE 2 Summary of Mensural and Modal Data

No.	Incipit	Composer	Mensuration	Range of Rhythmic Values[1]	Primary Units of Declamation	Signed Flats	Melodic Ranges	Final Cadence	Medial Cadence(s)
1	Bel Acueil	[Busnois]	○	Br–Sm	Sb	♭ ♭ ♭	C–f D–f C–d	D	D
2	En soustenant vostre querelle	[Busnois]	₵	L–Sm	Br, Sb		a–c′ D–f A–d	A	D
3	Accueilly m'a la belle	[Caron]	○	L–Fu	Sb, M	— ♭ ♭	c–f′ G–g B♭–d	C	(b′ e) G
4	Petitte Camusette (à 4)	J. Okeghem	C	Br–Fu	Br, Sb		G–c′ F–g D–c A–a	D	(e c) a
5	A une damme	[Busnois]	C	L–Fu	Br, Sb		d–g′ a–a′ C–f	D	e c A
6	Loing de vo tresdoulce presence		C	L–Fu	Sb, M		a–c′ D–f G′–d	D	E

1. Excluding final longs. For abbreviations used, see p. 187.
2. Brackets for measures indicate a purely melodic or otherwise unusual cadential formula.

Internal Cadences	Measures	Modes I & II	Modes III & IV	Modes V & VI	Modes VII & VIII	Comments
D F	6, 21, 22 [17]²	×				To be noted are the equal ranges of the three voices—all in the authentic octave of the modal pair—and the systematic use of imitation involving all three.
D A F	5, 23, 26 9 22	×				C and CT occupy the plagal octave of the first modal pair and the T the authentic one, but in the final melisma the final of the modes is apparently transposed to A.
C G	8, 10, 20 14, 23, 26				×	The species of 4th and 5th characteristic of modes VII and VIII have been transposed to a final on C by means of the signed flats; C and CT employ the authentic octave, whereas the T is confined to the plagal.
D A	5, 21 7	×				The borrowed melody of the T, clearly in mode I, when imitated a 5th above or a 4th below by the other voices places the latter in the plagal octave of the modal pair.
D a + e A C	5, 7, 20, 22 [9] 12 11	×				Despite the imitation at the octave linking C and T, the latter is confined to the plagal octave of the modal pair, whereas the C and the CT below employ the authentic one. Also of interest are the independent cadential formulas of the imitative voices.
A D	5, 20 8, 17, [20], [21]	×				The melodic lines are oriented with unusual fidelity by the species of 4th and 5th characteristic of the first pair of modes; the T occupies the authentic octave, but C and CT add below the lower 4th of the plagal octave.

TABLE 2   (continued)

No.	Incipit	Composer	Mensuration	Range of Rhythmic Values[1]	Primary Units of Declamation	Signed Flats	Melodic Ranges	Final Cadence	Medial Cadence(s)
7	Est-il merchy	Busnoys	○	Br–Fu	Sb, M	♭	c–d'	G	D
						♭	C–d		
						—	G'–d		
•8	Ung plus que tous	Busnoys	C	Br–Sm	Sb, M	♭	G–d'	G	⎛ f ⎞ ⎝ a ⎠
						♭	D–f		
						♭	E'–G		D
9	Ce qu'on fait a quatimini	G. Joye	₵	L–Sm	Br, Sb	♭	G–c'	G	(a)
						♭	C–d		D
						♭	G'–d		
10	A qui vens tu tes coquilles	Busnoys	₵	L–Sm	Sb	—	c–f'	D	F
						—	a–d'		
						♭	C–f		
11	Puis que ma damme ne puis voir/Je ın'en voy et mon cueur demeure	Regis	C2	L–Sm	Br, Sb		f–g'	C	
							F–c'		
							G–a'		
							C–d		
12	Je ne puis vivre ainsy	[Busnois]	○ ₵	Br–Fu L–Sm	Sb Br, Sb		a–e' a–e' A–e	C	⎛ d ⎞ ⎝ b ⎠ G

Internal Cadences	Measures	Modes I & II	Modes III & IV	Modes V & VI	Modes VII & VIII	Comments
G	6, 16, [16], 21	×				The species of 4th and 5th belonging to the first pair of modes have been transposed to a G final by means of the signed flats. C and T employ the plagal octave, but the CT adds the authentic 5th below.
A	[9]					
D	20					
G	5, 15, 16, 17	×				The first modal pair is transposed to G by the signed flats; the T occupies the plagal octave, the CT the authentic one, and the C moves primarily in a plagal ambitus but drops occasionally into the 5th below.
A	9					
B♭	14					
G	6	×				The signed flats transpose to G the species of 4th and 5th belonging to the first pair of modes; the T is confined to the plagal octave, whereas C and CT add below the 5th of the authentic octave.
D	14					
D	5, 15, 16	×				Final and ambitus of the respective voices would indicate modes I and II with C and CT in the authentic octave and the T adding the plagal 4th below, but the lowered b′ of m. 10 and the melodic movement between F and C suggest a modulation to the Lydian area.
F	10					
E	19					
C	7, 25, 28			×		C, T, and CT II are written in the third pair of modes on C as a final with the latter in the authentic octave, the former two in the plagal, but CT I with its written b♭'s suggests a mixolydian melody transposed to C to facilitate combination with C, T, and CT II.
G	11, 13, 16, 18, 20, 21, [24]					
E	[6]			×		The characteristic species of 4th and 5th are those of the third pair of modes with a final on C; all three voices employ the authentic octave extended in both directions by a 3rd, and C and T share, imitatively, the same range.
C	10, 12, 25; 29, 32, 34, 35, 38					
G	18, 19					

TABLE 2   (continued)

No.	Incipit	Composer	Mensuration	Range of Rhythmic Values[1]	Primary Units of Declamation	Signed Flats	Melodic Ranges	Final Cadence	Medial Cadence(s)
13	Non pas que je veuille penser	[Joye]	₵	L–Sm	Br, Sb	♭♭ ♭♭ ♭♭	G–c′ G–g B♭–e♭	C	(b′♮ d) G
14	Ja que li ne s'i attende	[Busnois]	C ₵	L–Sm L–Sm	Sb Br, Sb		a–e′ G–g B–d	C	G|C
15	Pour entretenir mes amours	Busnoys	₵	L–Fu	Br, Sb		d–a″ a–c′ B–d	D	(c′ e) a
16	Quant ce viendra (à 4)	[Busnois]	○	(L–Fu³) Br–Sm	Sb, M	♭ ♭ ♭ ♭♭	d–d′ D–a′ D–d F′–b♭	G	(f″ a) D
17	Vostre bruit et vostre grant fame	G. Dufay	₵	L–Fu	Br, Sb		a–c′ C–e B–d	G	(e) C
18	Fortune, par ta cruaulté	Vincenet	₵	L–Sm	Br, Sb	♭♭ ♭♭ ♭♭	c–f′ G–g B♭–d	C	(d b) G

3. In CT *si placet* only.

Internal Cadences	Measures	Modes I & II	Modes III & IV	Modes V & VI	Modes VII & VIII	Comments
G C	5, 12, 16, 17, 22, 24 7, 9, 17, 23, 28	×				By means of the signed flats the species of 4th and 5th belonging to the first pair of modes have been transposed to C; the T is restricted to the plagal octave, the CT occupies the authentic, and the C combines the two.
A G C	5, 7, 17 9, 27 11, 12, 13, 15		×			The characteristic species of 4th and 5th are those of the third modal pair with a final on C; the T is confined to the plagal octave, whereas C and CT occupy the authentic one.
D E F	2, 4, 5, [7], 8, 9, 25, 28 [12] (= a, c ♯, e) 22	×				The T is largely confined to the range of the plagal mode, the CT to that of the authentic mode, whereas the C combines the two. Noteworthy is the use in m. 12 of the "interrupted" cadence, usually reserved for the midpoint of a rondeau.
D G C A	[5] (over G′, B♭) 9, 24, 25 [10] (CT *si placet* and CT II) 22	×				C and T are confined to the plagal octave of the modal pair an octave apart, leaving the space (perhaps intentionally) filled by the CT *si placet*.
G C E	6, 15 11, 22, 25 21			×		Although the final cadence is on G, suggesting the fourth pair of modes, the melodic lines turn generally around C and G, pointing to Lydian on C. The result is the kind of modal mixture Tinctoris would presumably have called *modus commixtus*.
C G	[3–4], 5, 7, 13 15	×				With a final on C and two signed flats, the characteristic species of 4th and 5th are those of the first pair of modes; the T is confined to the plagal octave whereas C′ and CT use the authentic one.

TABLE 2   (continued)

No.	Incipit	Composer	Mensuration	Range of Rhythmic Values[1]	Primary Units of Decla-mation	Signed Flats	Melodic Ranges	Final Cadence	Medial Cadence(s)
19	O Virgo, miserere mei	Jo. Tinctoris	¢	Br–Sm	Br		a–c′ D–f G′–d	A	
20	L'aultre d'antan	Jo. Okeghem	¢3	L–Sm	Br, Sb		d–e′ D–e C–a′	G	(E c A)
21	Le corps s'en va	Busnoys	¢	L–Fu	Sb		a–c′ A–e F′–b	D	A
22	Se mon service vous plaisoit		¢	L–Sm	Br, Sb	♭♭ ♭♭ ♭♭	b–e♭′ G–a′ B♭–e♭	C	(b′ d G)
23	Mercy, mon dueil	Joye	¢	L–Sm	Br, Sb	♭ ♭ ♭	b–d′ D–e G′–a	G	(f ♯ a D)
24	N'aray je jamais mieulx que j'ay? (à 4)	Morton	○	Br–Sm	Sb		d–f′ a–a′ C–d D–f	D	(e c A)

Internal Cadences	Measures	Modes I & II	Modes III & IV	Modes V & VI	Modes VII & VIII	Comments
D E G A	2, 19, 22 4 7 13	×				Melodic writing turns in general around D and A, occasionally G with B♮; the character is that of the first pair of modes, and the termination on the confinal appears irregular as a result.
C G D	3, 27, [33] 11 19				×	Both the vocal ranges and cadential pitches suggest the pair of modes on G; all three voices use primarily the plagal octave, but the tenor also employs the authentic.
D A F	6, 9, 14 10 21	×				T and CT share essentially the same range, whereas the C is just an octave above; thus all three move primarily in the plagal octave of the first pair of modes, but the tenor also ascends to the top of the authentic.
C G	4, 4, 7, 9, 10, 18 12, 15, 20	×				As in Nos. 13 and 18, the octave species of the first pair of modes have been transposed to a final on C by means of the two signed flats; C and CT employ the authentic range, the T the plagal.
G D A	4, 11 6, 21 16	×				The species of 4th and 5th characteristic of the first pair of modes are transposed to a final on G by the signed flats. This is particularly evident in the CT, which uses the authentic octave, whereas C and T employ primarily the plagal range.
D A C	6, [18] 9 11	×				CT si placet touches A only for the penultimate note; it otherwise conforms to the authentic octave of the mode, as do all voices except the T, which is confined to the plagal octave. The texture is exceptionally consonant without the CT si placet, dissonance in the other 3 voices being restricted to (cadential) suspensions.

TABLE 2 (continued)

No.	Incipit	Composer	Mensuration	Range of Rhythmic Values[1]	Primary Units of Declamation	Signed Flats	Melodic Ranges	Final Cadence	Medial Cadence(s)
25	L'omme banny	Barbingant	○	L–Sm	Sb	♭ ♭♭ ♭♭	G–c' A–d B♭–d	F	D
26	Ou doy je secours querir	Vincenet	C [¢]	L–Sm	Br, Sb	♭ ♭♭ ♭♭	a–f' F–a'♭ B♭–d	C	(d b) G
27	Comme femme desconfortee	Binchoys	○	L–Fu	M, Sb		a–c' c–f B–e	C	(f) D
28	Mon trestout et mon assotee / Il estoit ung bonhomme (à 4)	Petit Jan	¢	Maxima –Sm	Br, Sb	♭ ♭ ♭ ♭	c–e' E–F C–g F'–a	G	G
29	Joye me fuit	Busnoys	¢	L–Sm	Sb	♭ ♭ ♭/♭♭	E–b♭' D–f D'–b♭	D	(a' f♯) D
30	Ma bouce rit	Okeghem	C	L–Fu	Br, Sb		a–d' C–f C–f	E	g♯ E A

Internal Cadences	Measures	Modes I & II	Modes III & IV	Modes V & VI	Modes VII & VIII	Comments
B♭ G	4, 6, 9, 16, 17, 23, 25 13			×		The characteristic species of 4th and 5th are those of the Lydian modes transposed to b♭ by the signed flats, but following the cadence of m. 25 the composer effects an ending on the confinal.
C G G and D	6, 19 14 21	×				The two signed flats with a final on C transpose the species of 4th and 5th characteristic of the first pair of modes; the CT employs the authentic octave, the T the plagal octave, and the C combines the two.
C G D E	[2], 3, 10, 22 5, 19 14 24			×		The characteristic species of 4th and 5th are those of the Lydian modes on C; all three voices employ primarily the authentic octave. Note *fauxbourdon* approaching cadences, mm. 9, 13, 21, and 29.
G D A	5, 14, 16, 25, 31, 33, [43], 51 24 ⎱ Phry- 37 ⎰ gian	×				The range and melodic patterns characteristic of the first pair of modes transposed to G are most marked in the C, which uses the plagal octave, and CT I and II, which use the authentic octave, but are less marked in the popular melodies of the T.
D G	4 7, 8, 13, 18, 21, 27, 31, 31	×				Although the piece terminates on D, the signed flats and the orientation of the melodic lines between D and G suggest the transposition of the final to G and a close on the confinal.
C G D A	8, 10, 15 13 17, 21 18		×			This is the only chanson of the repertory closing on E, and despite a certain emphasis on A and C—melodically and harmonically—the voice ranges employed are essentially those of the second pair of modes.

TABLE 2   (continued)

No.	Incipit	Composer	Mensuration	Range of Rhythmic Values¹	Primary Units of Declamation	Signed Flats	Melodic Ranges	Final Cadence	Medial Cadence(s)
31	Se je fayz dueil	G. le Rouge	¢	L–Sm	Br	♭♭ ♭♭ ♭♭	D–f D–f C–F	G	(a f) D
32	De tous biens plaine	Heyne	¢	L–Sm	Br, Sb	♭ ♭ ♭	G–c' D–e♭ G'–b♭	G	D
33	Dona gentile	G. Dufay	○	Br–Sm	Sb, M	♭ ♭♭ ♭♭	G–c' C–d C–d	C	G
34	Il sera pour vous conbatu / L'ome armé	[Morton]	C3	Br–Sm	Sb, M		f–g' G–g G–a'	G	(b' d) G
35	Tout a par moy	Frye	[○]	Br–Sm	Sb	♭ ♭ ♭	c–d' D–f C–d	G	(e c) A
36	S'il est ainsi	Caron	○ ¢	Br–Fu L–Sm	Sb, M Sb		a–d' C–f A–f	A	e c D A
37	O Fortune, trop tu es dure	[Busnois]	¢	L–Sm	Sb	♭ ♭ ♭♭	d–g' D–a' G'–b♭	G	(a f) D

4. Resembles in structure and function the medial cadence of a *rondeau*.

Internal Cadences	Measures	Modes I & II	Modes III & IV	Modes V & VI	Modes VII & VIII	Comments
G	6, 10	×				With two signed flats and a final on G, the characteristic species of 4th and 5th become those of the first pair of modes with b consistently flatted; all voices use the plagal octave.
D	13, 29 (Phrygian), 43 (f, a)					
D (f♯, a)⁴	21					
G	3, 8, 17, 21	×				A clear example of the first modal pair transposed to G by means of b♭; T is confined to the plagal octave whereas C and CT employ primarily the authentic one.
D	11, [20], 24					
C	5, 18	×				The signed flats transpose the species of 4th and 5th characteristic of the first pair of modes; T and CT share the authentic octave and the C employs both plagal and authentic.
D (Phrygian)	8, 24					
G	3, 5			×		The melodic writing is clearly oriented around the final and confinal of the mixolydian mode, and all three voices are in the authentic octave.
D	12					
A (Phrygian)	6, 15, 17, 20	×				The characteristic species of 4th and 5th are those of the first modal pair, and all three voices are confined rather strictly to the plagal octave.
D	8, 10, 27, 33					
G	14, 19					
A	7, 18, 34, 42, 44	×				Voice ranges and melodic patterns point to the first pair of modes with a regular final on D, the T using only the authentic octave, C and CT both authentic and plagal, but after the cadence of m. 26, the final melisma closes on the confinal of the mode.
D	13, 19, 26					
F	23, 40					
A (Phrygian)		×				With the signed flats the final on G produces the species of 4th and 5th characteristic of the first modal pair; the CT uses only the authentic octave, but C and T employ both authentic and plagal.
G	6					
	8, 12, 17, [25]					
D	13, 22, 24					

TABLE 2   (continued)

No.	Incipit	Composer	Mensuration	Range of Rhythmic Values¹	Primary Units of Declamation	Signed Flats	Melodic Ranges	Final Cadence	Medial Cadence(s)
38	Enfermé suys je en la tour		¢	L–Sm	Br, Sb	♭♭ ♭♭ ♭♭	c–g′ a–d′ C–e	C	$\left(\begin{matrix} d \\ b♮ \end{matrix}\right)$ G
39	Au povre par necessité	[Busnois]	¢	Double L–Sm	Br, Sb	♭♭ ♭♭ ♭♭	b♭–e♭′ F–g C–d	C	$\left(\begin{matrix} d \\ b \end{matrix}\right)$ G
40	Mort ou mercy	Caron	¢	L–Fu	Sb	♭ ♭ ♭	G–c′ D–e G′–b♭	G	$\left(\begin{matrix} a \\ f \end{matrix}\right)$ D
41	Paracheve ton entreprise	[Morton]	○	Br–Sm	M, Sb		c–g′ G–a′ C–e	D	$\left(\begin{matrix} c \\ e \end{matrix}\right)$ A
42	A vous sans aultre	[Busnois]	C	Br–Fu	M, Sb		G–c′ a–c′ a–c′	D	$\left(\begin{matrix} e \\ c \end{matrix}\right)$ A
43	Triste qui sperò morendo (à 4)	Vincenet	C	Br–Fu	Br, Sb	♭ ♭ ♭ ♭♭	G–c′ D–f D–f G′–a	G	$\left(\begin{matrix} a \\ f♯ \end{matrix}\right)$ D

Internal Cadences	Measures	Modes I & II	Modes III & IV	Modes V & VI	Modes VII & VIII	Comments
C G D (Phry-gian)	4, 8, 13, 16, 21, 27, 28, 30 7, 12, 22 25	×				The characteristic species of 4th and 5th are those of the first pair of modes transposed to a final on C by the signed flats; all three voices employ primarily the authentic octave even though the triplum extends its range upward to g′.
G C	6, [15], 28 [8], 12, 22, [32]	×				The two signed flats transpose the species of 4th and 5th characteristic of the first pair of modes to a final on C; C and CT employ the authentic octave, whereas the T is confined to the plagal.
G D A (Phry-gian)	3, 4, 6, 8, 10, 11, 20, 24, [30] 7, 16, 20, 23, 29, 32 35	×				The characteristic species of 4th and 5th are those of the first pair of modes transposed to a final on G; C and CT employ the authentic octave, but the T is confined to the plagal one.
D A	3, 8, 13, [15], 18, 24 11, 28	×				The final is regular for the first pair of modes; C and CT employ the authentic octave, but the T is confined to the plagal one.
D A C	4, 9, 20, 21 6, 11, 15, 18 14	×				All three parts share exactly the same range and employ the plagal octave of the first pair of modes.
G D	6, 12, 16, 19 12, 18	×				The signed accidentals transpose to G the species of 4th and 5th characteristic of the first modal pair; T and CT *si placet* are confined to the plagal octave, the bassus employs the authentic one, and the C, although extending down to G on occasion, moves primarily in the plagal octave above d.

TABLE 2   (continued)

No.	Incipit	Composer	Mensuration	Range of Rhythmic Values[1]	Primary Units of Declamation	Signed Flats	Melodic Ranges	Final Cadence	Medial Cadence(s)
44	La pena sin ser sabida (à 4)	Vincenet	[○] C	Br–Fu L–Sm	Sb Sb	— — ♭ ♭	c–d' D–g D–f A–d	D	C|D
45	So ys emprentid	Walterus Fry	[○]	L–Sm	Br, Sb		a–c' C–d C–e	D	(e c) | D A
46	Gentil madona	[Bedingham]	[○]	Br–Sm	Sb, M	— ♭ ♭	c–e' E–g F–f	F	(a) | F F
47	Myn hertis lust	[Bedingham]	[○]	Br–Sm	Sb	— ♭ ♭	c–c' C–f C–f	F	(e) | F C
48	Ou lit de pleurs (à 4)		[○]	L–Sm	Br, Sb	(♭) ♭ ♭ ♭	d–e'♭ C–g F–a'♭ G–a'♭	C	(d b♮) G
49	Or me veult bien Esperance mentir		[○]	L–M	Br, Sb, M	—|♭ ♭ ♭	G–b'(♭) D–e(♭) C–e	G	f a | G D

Internal Cadences	Measures	Modes I & II	Modes III & IV	Modes V & VI	Modes VII & VIII	Comments
)	3, 13, 14, 15, 22	×				With the regular final of the first pair of modes, C, T, and CT employ the authentic octave, extended upward in the latter two, whereas the CT bassus combines the plagal and authentic octaves.
?	8					
Λ (Phry-gian)						
	12					
Λ	6, 14, [37], 42	×				The C occupies essentially the plagal octave of the first modal pair, whereas T and CT give support below in the authentic octave, and the final is the normal one.
)	7, 9, 15, 18, 41, 44, 46					
?	28					
ʒ	33					
?	4, 10, 22, 26, 33			×		The pair of modes regularly terminating on F were frequently used in the fifteen century with a signed b♭; T and CT share the authentic octave, but the C employs the plagal one.
?	6, 18, 29					
ʒ	21					
?	5, [16], 28, 32, [41]			×		Final and signed flats are as in the previous work, but in addition to the C, the CT employs primarily the plagal octave, rising into the authentic 4th only when above the T, whereas the T employs the authentic octave, except where it passes below the CT.
?	8, [34]					
Λ (Phry-gian)	13, [34]					
ʒ	15, 40					
?	11	×				Although only one flat is signed, the consistent recurrence of written E♭ in all four voices and an occasional A♭ suggest the first pair of modes transposed to C as a final. All voices employ primarily the plagal octave even though CT I drops briefly into the 5th below.
)	22 (Phry-gian), [24] (?), 27					
ʒ	31					
Λ	[24]					
ʒ	9, [19], 57	×				The species of 4th and 5th characteristic of the first pair of modes have been transposed to a final on G by the signed flats; the C employs the authentic octave whereas T and CT share the plagal one.
)	38, 43					

TABLE 2 (continued)

No.	Incipit	Composer	Mensuration	Range of Rhythmic Values[1]	Primary Units of Declamation	Signed Flats	Melodic Ranges	Final Cadence	Medial Cadence(s)
50	Donnés l'assault (à 4)	Dufay	○	L–Sm	Br, Sb	— ♭ ♭ ♭	b–d′ C–a′ C–g C–g	C	⎛ d ⎞ ⎝ b♮ ⎠ G
51	Par le regart	Dufay	[○]	Br–Sm	Sb	♭|— ♭ ♭	a–c′ D–f D–f	G	D
52	Hora cridar "Oymè"		[○]	Br–Fu	Sb, M		⎛ a–c′ ⎞ ⎝ C–e ⎠ C–d	C	(C)
53	Puis que je vis le regart		[○]	L–Sm	Sb	— ♭ —	c–e′ F–a′ E–a′	C	⎛ e ⎞ ⎝ c ⎠ A
54	Ma dame de nom / Sur la rive de la mer		C	Sb–Fu	Sb, M		a–c′ D–d A–d	D	A
55	"Alas, alas, alas" is my chief song	[Frye]	○	Br–Sm	Sb	— ♭|— —	a–b′(♭) C–e G–a	D	(C) A (e) C D

Internal Cadences	Measures	Modes I & II	Modes III & IV	Modes V & VI	Modes VII & VIII	Comments
) C 3	9 13, 15 29, 33	×				Signed B♭'s and accidentals for E♭ and A♭ suggest the transposition of the species of 4th and 5th characterizing the first pair of modes to the final of C; C employs the authentic octave, T and CTs add above the 4th of the plagal octave. However, the repeated e♮'s of the concluding fanfare introduce a mixture of modes.
) 3 A (Phry-gian)	3, 9, 20 6 19	×				The signed flats and a G final suggest the transposition of the first modal pair with the T in the plagal octave, but C and CT are clearly oriented around D and A as if they were Dorian melodies untransposed with a consistent b♮.
3 C)	4, 13 5, 21 15, 17			×		All three voices respect the ambitus and species of mode V with a final on C, but the emphasis on G and D, mm. 11–17, harmonically and melodically, suggests mode VII as well.
' C 3	7 13, 20, 29 14, 21, 23, 28				×	Initial phrase clearly oriented toward final on F with C in the plagal octave and T and CT in the authentic one, but with the second phrase, mm. 8 ff., the final is shifted to C with the C in the authentic octave and T and CT in the plagal one.
) '	6 10	×				The T is confined to the authentic octave of mode I, whereas C and CT extend their ranges downward on occasion through the lower 4th of the plagal octave as well.
) A ' 3	9, 25, 27, 38, 47 15 (Phry-gian), 17, 36 30 41	×				The T employs the authentic octave of the first modal pair, whereas C and CT use the plagal octave in a manner characteristic of mode II.

TABLE 2   (continued)

No.	Incipit	Composer	Mensuration	Range of Rhythmic Values[1]	Primary Units of Declamation	Signed Flats	Melodic Ranges	Final Cadence	Medial Cadence(s)
56	Nos amys, vous vous abusés	A. Basin	C	Br–Fu	Sb, M		c–d′ D–d C–f	A	D
57	Virgo Dei throno digna	Jo. Tinctoris	¢	M–Fu	Br, Sb	♭ ♭ ♭♭	G–c′ C–f G′–c	G	(G)

Internal Cadences	Measures	Modes I & II	Modes III & IV	Modes V & VI	Modes VII & VIII	Comments
D	2, 5, 9	×				All three voices move within the normal range of mode I until the last phrase, where both melodic contours and cadential final suggest mode II transposed to A.
A	4					
G	3, 7, 22	×				Voice ranges and signed flats suggest the first pair of modes transposed to G with C and CT in the authentic octave and T in the plagal but all three extended upward by a 4th. In mm. 14–19, however, the melodic orientation around C and G suggests a further transposition to C as a final.
D	5					
C	14, 16, 18					

More common still in the later compositions with their usually wider ranges is a combination of a regular modal ambitus with one or more voices covering the more extended compass of a mixed mode.[62]

Of particular interest are the choices not only of mode but also of final. On the one hand the species of fourth and fifth characteristic of the Dorian modes predominate to a surprising degree, but on the other, the regular final is utilized less frequently than a transposition of it.[63] Fourteen compositions of the first modal pair close on D, whereas 15 terminate on G, 9 on C, and 5 others have finals that must be considered irregular, as will soon be seen. By contrast, there is but a single chanson using the Phrygian species with a final on E— Ockeghem's *Ma bouce rit* (No. 30). Three pieces belonging to the Lydian modes conclude on F (Nos. 25, 46, and 47), all of them comparatively early pieces, and 6 others on C. The remaining 4 works can be assigned to the mixolydian modes, No. 3 with the final transposed to C, and Nos. 17, 20, and 34 (among the earliest compositions of the more recent layer) on the regular final.[64] The evidence therefore suggests that the Lydian modes with a final on F, so frequently adopted for the polyphony of the fourteenth and early fifteenth centuries, were virtually abandoned for secular music after 1450 and that the general trend was toward an increasing reliance on the Dorian pair, especially in transposition. But if the general tendency is reasonably clear, the reasons for it have yet to be probed and illuminated.

As has been observed, final or confinal were utilized in the majority of cases as the concluding pitch in cadential figures. When other degrees of the modal scale were so employed, they were generally those terminating the differentiae of the modal pair, that is, scale degrees having acquired a conventional cadential function through several centuries of use in the plainchant of the Roman rite.[65] The only note-

---

62. See in table 2, Ranges; also Comments, Nos. 6–10, 13, 15, 26, 33, 36, 38, and 57.

63. For the modal transpositions most commonly used in the fifteenth century, see Tinctoris, *De natura ac proprietate tonorum*, capitulum xlv ff.; Coussemaker, *Scriptorum*, 4:37 ff.; or Seay, *Concerning the Tones*, pp. 37 ff.

64. See table 2, Final Cadence and Modes.

65. Concerning the role of the differentiae, their terminations, and other degrees of structural and practical significance for the modal scales in the cadential formations of fifteenth- and sixteenth-century polyphony, see the editor's discussion of "Mode and Structure in the Masses of Josquin," pp. 189 ff. and Table 1, Characteristics of the Modes. The "Regular Cadential Pitches" listed there may be compared with the internal cadences of works such as Nos. 2, 12, 17, 20, 21, and so on.

worthy exception is the degree immediately above the final, which came to be used with great regularity for internal cadences in the polyphony of the fourteenth century—presumably because it allowed a cadential articulation without conveying an impression of finality— and continued to serve that purpose in the secular music of the fifteenth.[66] In the present repertory, however, the second degree of the authentic octave evidently appears cadentially on occasion in the manner described as the result of a transposition of the final to the upper fifth, in which it functions as a temporary confinal.

At the beginning of Busnois's *A une damme* (No. 5), for example, tenor and contratenor are definitely oriented around the final and the confinal of the Dorian modes, the former in the authentic octave, the latter in the plagal. The cantus is more ambiguous, giving no more emphasis to the fourth between a′ and d′ than to the fifth between a′ and e′ with its implication of a final on a′. However, the latter configuration is strengthened by the melodic figure of the contratenor in m. 9, leading to the passing cadence on e′ in m. 11 and culminating in the following measure with the more marked cadential formula on a′. *Est-il merchy* (No. 7), also by Busnois, opens with the characteristic octave of the transposed hypodorian mode. Its constituent species of fourth and fifth are clearly defined by the melodic motion between the final g at the center of the range and the confinal at either extreme. But beginning in m. 7, the tenor octave—and less noticeably that of the cantus—comes to be divided with the fifth at the bottom, thus implying a final on D, and the shift prepares a medial cadence on the latter pitch, which is reached by way of a preparatory cadence on a′ (m. 11).[67]

Variety was achieved within the framework of a single modal pair primarily by the type of transposition just described, which does not alter fundamentally the characteristic species of the mode but at times takes on unusual aspects. A surprising number of compositions (Nos. 2, 17, 19, 25, 29, 36, and 56) feature a shift in ambitus at the concluding phrase, leaving the impression of an irregular terminal cadence on the

66. An interesting example is *Loing de vo tresdoulce presence* (No. 6), in which the second degree is used for the medial cadence in a manner recalling the secular works of Machaut.

67. See, in addition to the transpositions occurring in the two compositions discussed briefly above, those preceding the cadential figures indicated in the following compositions: Nos. 10 (m. 19), 16 (m. 22), 19 (m. 4), 23 (m. 16), 33 (mm. 8, 24), 35 (mm. 6, 15, 17, 20), 42 (m. 14), 46 (m. 21), 47 (mm. 15, 40), 50 (m. 9), 51 (m. 19), and 52 (mm. 15, 17).

confinal of the mode. There are also a few instances in which the transposition of the species of fourth and fifth around which the melodic
movement is oriented produces a modification of their internal structure and, consequently, the juxtaposition of divergent modal scales that
Tinctoris designated a *tonus commixtus*.[68] To illustrate, the second phrase
of Busnois's *A qui vens tu tes coquilles* veers away from the melodic
orientation around the Dorian species of fourth and fifth, clearly
outlined at the beginning and the end, to an equally unambiguous
delineation (reinforced by the introduction of the accidental b♭) of
those characterizing the Lydian modes. This is achieved by means of
a series of figures turning between f and c, particularly in the cantus
and contratenor (mm. 5–11). As a result the initial section of the
rondeau closes in a well-established Lydian mode with a typical,
strongly marked cadence on F. A similar, if not quite so striking,
example is offered by the anonymous *Hora cridar "Oymè"* (No. 52).
There the use of c and g as the pivotal points for the construction of
the melodic lines, evident in the opening phrase, is momentarily abandoned after the corona for an unmistakable orientation around g and
d, implying a kind of modulation from the Lydian modes on C with
which the piece begins and ends, to the mixolydian on G characterizing
the inner phrases.[69] The resulting shift is not quite so conspicuous as in
the preceding instance, obviously, because the species of fifth is the
same in the two pairs of modes in question. But in *A qui vens tu* the
transposition is from a modal scale with a minor third above the final
to one with a major third. Regardless of the nature or the degree of
the transposition it is worthy of note that such procedures occur most
often in the presumably earlier compositions of the repertory, suggesting a trend toward greater modal consistency in the second half of
the fifteenth century.

Melodic Style

One of the most significant determinants of the melodic style
exemplified in the Mellon Chansonnier is the utilization of the fixed
structural points of the modal scales, final and confinal, as both axis
and goal within the horizontal line: the basic skeleton underlying any
given melodic profile is comprised primarily of the scale degrees

---

68. See his *De natura ac proprietate tonorum*, capitulum xiii, "De commixtione tonorum," and
the chapters that follow; Coussemaker *Scriptorum*, 4:24–25, or Seay, *Concerning the Tones*, pp. 15 ff.

69. An analogous situation is to be seen in Dufay's *Vostre bruit et vostre grant fame* (No. 17).

delimiting the predominant species of fourth and fifth. Within this basic framework the shape of the line is characterized by a distinct preference for stepwise movement and a most judicious control of the energy generated by a leap. If a melodic line begins from a relatively low point in its profile with an upward leap, it may continue by step in the same direction. Conversely, it may conclude with a downward leap from a descending scalewise passage, particularly in the tenor or contratenor parts. But when a leap occurs in the course of a phrase, it is almost invariably followed by a reversal of the melodic motion, either to fill in the interval left vacant by the skip or to compensate for it by a leap in the opposite direction. The larger the leap, the more likely is a corresponding turn of the line in the manner indicated. The outcome of this complementary alternation of conjunct and disjunct movement is in most cases a series of graceful arcs, now convex, now concave, that turn between and around the structural points of the modal scale, linking them in a nicely balanced succession of ascents and descents.[70]

These generalizations are valid to a greater or lesser degree for the entire repertory, but some interesting distinctions can be drawn. If the initial pieces of the collection are compared with those heading up the earlier layer, it is possible to observe that the melodic lines of the more recent pieces are more clearly defined; they meander less and proceed more directly from one point of structural reference to the next. For example, the cantus of Busnois's *Bel Acueil* (No. 1) describes its first arc from the final up to the confinal and back within the two first measures of the opening phrase. That of Frye's *So ys emprentid* (No. 45) appears more static, repeating and turning below its initial pitch before beginning its rambling descent toward the lower end of its range. Even more sharply marked and probably more significant is the degree of stylistic disparity between the cantus and the two accompanying voices in the two segments of the repertory. In the earlier pieces tenor and contratenor (especially the latter) tend to be distinctly more disjunct and haphazard in their movement than the text-bearing part above, whereas in those presumably written later, their melodic profiles are generally much more like that of the cantus. At times the contratenor of compositions such as Bedingham's *Myn hertis lust* (No. 47) proceeds

---

70. Observe that the melodic style of this secular repertory is not far removed from that of the late sixteenth century as described by Knud Jeppesen, *Counterpoint*.

more frequently by leap than by step, seemingly guided by no consideration other than the requirements of the counterpoint. This is in clear contrast to the smoothly rounded contours and carefully controlled direction evident in the lower pair of voices of a work such as Busnois's *En soustenant vostre querelle* (No. 2). Although there is still a discernible gradation in smoothness and coherence from cantus to tenor and from tenor to contratenor in this piece—as in the majority of the compositions included in the more recent layer of the manuscript—it reveals the predominant tendency in the second half of the fifteenth century toward an ever greater stylistic assimilation of the separate voices. Obviously, the rhythmic and melodic similarity of the parts is most complete and most evident when they become identified with one another through a systematic use of canonic imitation, as in Busnois's *Bel Acueil*. Therefore, it was to be expected that the equalization of the voices would be achieved with increasing frequency by means of the imitative compositional procedures discussed below.

COUNTERPOINT

The harmonic practice reflected in the repertory of the chansonnier is manifestly intervallic in character (rather than triadic). The vertical sonorities employed and the manner of their placement and treatment conform—with rare exceptions—to the precepts expounded by fifteenth-century theorists generally and by Tinctoris in particular.[71] The intervals considered concordant were grouped into two classes. Those defined as "perfect" consonances included the unison, the fifth, the octave, and in some circumstances the fourth; those designated "imperfect" consonances were the thirds and sixths, both major and minor. In the fifteenth century perfect consonances were used alone almost invariably to begin and to end a composition, and not infrequently the individual phrases as well. Nevertheless, they were not to be employed in parallel progressions, and the fourth was allowed as a consonance only when sounding above another consonant interval (except the unison); otherwise it was handled as a dissonance. Imperfect consonances, on the other hand, could be used more easily in the course of a piece because they were not subject to the same restrictions

71. The comments that follow may be compared with his *De arte contrapuncti* for definitions of consonance and dissonance and the rules to be followed in using both (see Coussemaker, *Scriptorum*, 4: 77 ff., especially liber III, "De Octo generalibus regulis," pp. 147 ff., or the English translation by Seay, 17 ff., 132).

on parallel movement. To maintain a wholly consonant texture under these conditions was not unduly difficult when only two voices were involved, but the task became more complex with the addition of a third or fourth part because a vertical sonority, to be considered consonant, had to be comprised solely of mutually concordant intervals. Differently stated, the division of a large consonance such as an octave or a fifth by an intervening pitch had to result in two smaller consonances, such as a third and a sixth, a fifth and a fourth (with the latter sounding above the former), or a pair of thirds.

The intervals considered dissonant were the seconds, the sevenths, and any of the perfect consonances altered by a semitone, such as an augmented fourth or a diminished octave. Their use in the counterpoint of the fifteenth century was much more strictly regulated than that of the concordant intervals. According to Tinctoris dissonance was simply not to be admitted when the part writing proceeded note against note; elsewhere its placement and duration were to be related to the tactus.[72] He contends that the duration of a dissonant note should be no more than half a tactus unit even though he is obliged to concede that some of the best masters had allowed a discord to sound for a full tactus.[73] He also suggests that the beginning of the tactus should be consonant as a rule unless the dissonance is preceded immediately by a perfect consonance or introduced by syncopation (i.e., in suspension), that the discordant interval should last no longer than the previous consonance, and that it should resolve whenever possible to the consonance most proximate (i.e., a step or, at the farthest, a third away).[74]

In the musical practice of the fifteenth century these rules were embodied in a limited number of rather carefully controlled figures. Most common by far was the passing tone that allowed a stepwise melodic progression from one consonant combination to the next. In the repertory at hand the duration of this type of dissonance was most often limited to a semiminim (sixteenth note) even in the diminished mensurations, although it also occurs occasionally as a minim as well, particularly in the earlier layer of the collection, where semiminims

72. De arte contrapuncti, liber II, capitulum xxiii and following; Coussemaker, Scriptorum, 4:134 ff., and Seay, The Art of Counterpoint, pp. 113 ff.

73. Ibid., capitulum xxix, "Quomodo multi nunquam supra integram partem dimidiam note secundum quam mensura cantus dirigitur immo super minorem assumunt"; Coussemaker, Scriptorum, 4:143–44, or Seay, The Art of Counterpoint, p. 126.

74. Ibid., capitulum xxxii, "De ordinatione cuiuslibet discordantie"; Coussemaker, Scriptorum 4:144 ff., or Seay, The Art of Counterpoint, pp. 128 ff.

are relatively rarer. Similar in effect, but ornamental instead of utilitarian in function and consequently less frequently used, are the neighboring tone and the anticipation. The former is reached by step either up or down from a consonant pitch to which it immediately returns, whereas the latter sounds in a dissonant context a note that is immediately repeated in a consonant one. Somewhat more sophisticated but less frequent are the dissonances left by leap, the *nota cambiata*, and the *échapée*. In the cambiata the discordant pitch is reached by step, left by a third taken in the same direction (usually descending but occasionally ascending as well), and generally, but not invariably, followed by a turn back to the scale degree that had been skipped. In the échapée the dissonance is also reached by step but left by leap in the opposite direction. There appears to be no special context for the former, but the latter occurs most often in the cadential figure ornamented by the third below the final. Also found primarily in cadential passages are the dissonances introduced by suspension, in most case in conjunction with a syncope. But whereas the ornamental discords (neighboring tones, anticipations, cambiatas, and échapées) like the passing tones tend to be restricted in the compositions of this repertory to the duration of a semiminim or a minim at most, the suspended dissonances generally last a minim or longer, perhaps because of their important functional and structural role in cadence formations.

Bearing in mind these six principal types of dissonance used more or less systematically in the secular music of the fifteenth century, it is once again instructive to compare the works of the earlier layer with those presumably written somewhat later. Striking, first of all, is the significantly lower incidence of dissonance in the older pieces, especially those attributed to English masters such as Bedingham and Frye. Some idea of the disparity to be observed in this regard may be had from a detailed examination of the treatment of dissonances in two representative works, Bedingham's *Gentil madona* (No. 46) and Busnois's *Pour entretenir mes amours* (No. 15). In the former there are only half a dozen dissonant combinations in the initial section, including the presumably unaltered augmented fourths of the cadential formulas, and no more than 17 discords in the entire length of 33 ternary breves (99 tactus units excluding the final longs). The latter, by contrast, has dissonant sonorities at 58 separate points in the space of 56 binary breves (56 tactus units under the diminished mensuration).[75] Let us also examine a relatively dissonant example among the English pieces, Frye's "*Alas, alas, alas*" *is my chief song* (No. 55). This may be one of his more mature works to judge from the voice ranges used. Nonetheless, compared with one of the more consistently consonant pieces of the later layer, such as Busnois's *Bel Acueil* (No. 1), the difference remains considerable even though this could be one of Busnois's earlier compositions in view of the mensuration signed. Frye has used only 47 dissonances for 48 ternary breves (144 tactus units), whereas Busnois wrote 38 discordant sonorities in 22 ternary breves (66 tactus units). The predominantly consonant texture of these English songs obviously has a good deal to do with the much vaunted "sweetness" characterizing the *contenance angloise* of the first half of the fifteenth century. Furthermore, the evidence of the present manuscript suggests that the Continental composers immediately contemporary with them really did emulate their style in this regard, as Tinctoris and others asserted at the time.[76] Dufay's *Par le regart* (No. 51) has only 23 dissonances for 21 ternary breves (63 tactus units), Basin's *Nos amys, vous vous abusés* (No. 56) 23 dissonances for 20 binary breves (40 tactus units), reflecting in both cases a lower incidence of dissonance than *Bel Acueil*.

In addition to the divergences between the two segments of the repertory in the frequency of dissonance, there are also discernible differences in the procedures preferred for its introduction. In the earlier works the suspension is the most commonly used, occurring more often even than passing tones. It appears not only in cadential

75. The following dissonances have been identified by the editor: No. 46, passing tones at mm. 16 (contratenor note 5), 24 (cantus 4); neighboring tones at mm. 5 (C-5), 13 (C-5), 20 (C-4), 29 (C-2), 30 (C-4), 35 (C-3); *cambiate* at mm. 9 (tenor 2), 32 (T-2); an anticipation at m. 25 (C-5); and suspensions at mm. 5 (C-4), 10 (C-1), 13 (C-4), 17 (CT-3), 22 (T-1), 26 (C-1), 29 (C-1), 32 (C-3), 35 (C-2). No. 15, passing tones at mm. 1 (CT above 3, 5), 3 (CT-2, 4), 4 (T-3, 5), 6 (C and T-2, 4) 7 (C-6), 8 (CT-5, 7), 10 (T-5), 11 (C-2, T-8), 12 (CT-4, 5), 13 (CT-3, 6), 15 (CT-2, T-4), 16 (C-6, T-5–7), 17 (CT-2), and so on; neighboring tones at mm. 11 (T-2, CT-3), 14 (CT-4), 26 (C-5, T-7), 27 (C-7); cambiate at mm. 8 (CT-2), 16 (C-2); *échapées* at mm. 7 (C-10), 8 (CT-9), 17 (C and T-4), 21 (C-5), 25 (C-3), 29 (C-6); anticipations at mm. 28 (C-2), 29 (T-6); and suspensions at mm. 2 (CT-2), 3 (CT-7), 5 (T-2), 21 (C-2), 28 (C-3). The number of neighboring tones in No. 46 is rather large due to the unusual configuration of the cadences. At the same time the suspensions at the beginning of No. 15 are of a particular kind in which the voice that strikes the dissonance also resolves it, a device not often used in this repertory.

76. Notably in the prologue to his *Proportionale musices*; Coussemaker, *Scriptorum*, 4:153–54, or as translated by Oliver Strunk, *Source Readings in Music History*, p. 195. Concerning the entire question of the *contenance angloise*, see Kenney's study, *Walter Frye*.

formulas but also in other contexts, most notably in precadential sequences employing a kind of elaborated *fauxbourdon*. Dissonant sonorities tend to become denser at a cadential approach in the more recent works as well—their function being in either case to throw into sharper relief the consonance with which the phrase concludes by an increasing level of preparatory asperity—but the choice is more varied and balanced. If the English, in particular, seem ill at ease with discordant harmonies, giving the impression of a systematic attempt to avoid them whenever possible, the Continental composers of the generation of Busnois and Ockeghem seem to handle them with confidence and pleasure. One would hardly expect to find the awkward unprepared dissonance in the tenor of *Gentil madona* (m. 24) in their works of the 1460s and 1470s.

Also of interest as a point of comparison for the contrapuntal styles of the two chronological layers of the manuscript are the cadential formulas found in each. Those used at points of structural significance correspond as a rule to one of three fundamental types. Basic to all is a framework of two voices that expand in contrary motion from a sixth to an octave. The sixth is usually reached from a seventh in suspension and is almost invariably major, even if an accidental alteration is needed.[77] The differences reside in the melodic patterns given to the unessential third voice, generally the contratenor. Two of the basic cadential formulas used in the collection predominate in the earlier compositions. Of these the more venerable is undoubtedly the so-called parallel (or double leading tone) cadence, in which the contratenor follows the cantus at the lower fourth, and both approach the final note of the pattern by a semitone even though one or both parts may require an accidental sharp to that effect.[78] This cadence is already found in the polyphony of the fourteenth century, where, especially during the second half, it comes to be used more than any other. In the fifteenth century the parallel cadence continues to occur when the position of the voices is close, particularly in the context of a precadential fauxbourdon, where it is in fact unavoidable.[79] But by

77. For fifteenth-century cadential types and the distinction between the indispensable structural voices and those utilized primarily to enrich the sonorities, see Don M. Randel, "Emerging Triadic Tonality in the Fifteenth Century," 73–86 (but cf. Perkins, "Mode and Structure," pp. 193 ff.).

78. See, for example, the two main cadences of Busnois's *Bel Acueil*, mm. 11–12, 23–24.

79. As, for instance, in Walter Frye's *So ys emprentid* (No. 45), mm. 20–21, 48–49.

midcentury it seems to have become slightly archaic, along with the parallel sonorities of the compositional device with which it became associated, even though it still appears on occasion in the polyphony of the early 1500s. Also present in the secular polyphony of the fifteenth century from the first decades on is the cadence characterized by an octave leap in the contratenor from a fifth below the tenor to a fifth above.[80] With the increasing differentiation of the individual voice ranges about midcentury there emerged the cadential formula favored in the later segment of the repertory. It is characterized by a doubling of the tenor's final pitch, either at the lower octave or, if that is not feasible technically, at the unison.[81] The consistency with which these cadential figures are employed in the respective segments of the manuscript, especially at the ends of sections, is rather striking. The doubled tenor closing is found in the earlier layer at a point of structural division only in No. 54 and internally in Nos. 47, 50, and 55. Parallel cadences, on the other hand, are to be seen in Nos. 1, 20, 34, and 42, and octave leap cadences at the close of a section in Nos. 6 and 21 (elsewhere they are used internally). Songs 17, 25, 27, 30, 33, 35, and 36, which have examples of both, are by and large the compositions that have already been pointed out as presumably earlier than the surrounding ones on the basis of the mensuration employed, the range and distributions of the voices, or both.

Implicit in many of the comparisons and observations that have been made thus far is a changing contrapuntal relationship among the three voices of secular song during the period represented in the repertory of the chansonnier. Undisguised homophony is relatively rare, occuring briefly at the beginning of the second section in the bergerettes Nos. 12, 14, and 31. In the last one it is in such striking contrast to the preceding part as to raise doubts concerning its authenticity.[82] It is found in an analogous position in the ballade *Or me veult* (No. 49) and for brief stretches in a few scattered pieces of the collection. Consequently, it provides no point of meaningful chronological reference. Somewhat more instructive are the passages written in a kind of embellished fauxbourdon in which the homophonic nature of the counterpoint is veiled rhythmically, usually by the displacement of a syncopation. Part writing of this kind appears in Nos. 25, 27, 33–35,

---

80. Illustrated in the anonymous *Or me veult* (No. 49), mm. 29–30, 66–67.

81. Examples may be seen in Busnois's *En soustenant vostre querelle* (No. 2), mm. 4–5, 15, 29–30.

82. See Comments for le Rouge's *Se je fayz dueil* (No. 31), p. 318.

and 42 of the more recent segment.[83] They are once again without exception compositions previously singled out because of other stylistic features of a relatively archaic stamp.

However, it is not in these homophonic (or quasi-homophonic) passages that a modification is to be discerned in the roles played by the individual voices and the manner of their combination in the contrapuntal fabric, but rather in the imitative ones. The majority of the pieces in the earlier layer have no trace of imitation. Thus they convey the impression of having been conceived as accompanied solo song in which the dominant text-bearing melodic line is given sonorous and rhythmic support by a pair of parts sharing a less conspicuous and less brilliant lower level. But in the few exceptional cases where imitative writing does appear (as in Nos. 50, 52, 55, and 56), it is employed generally to link cantus and tenor, placing them, however briefly, on a footing of structural equality.[84] As a result, instead of a duo of accompanying voices, tenor and contratenor, characteristic of the earliest works in the manuscript, the duo in these pieces is perceived between cantus and tenor despite the usual differences in range and mode of performance. Their relationship now appears not only in the cadential formulas where they were traditionally the structural voices but also at the beginnings of phrases in which they are identified imitatively. In this context only the contratenor is heard as a harmonic supporting part, particularly when its range is below that of the other two parts, or as a filler.[85]

That the cantus–tenor duo had come into existence as a contrapuntal conception by the 1460s is attested by its use in the earlier layer of the manuscript as well as in some of the demonstrably older compositions of the more recent one. More significantly, its increasing currency and importance in the contrapuntal structures of secular polyphony during the second half of the fifteenth century are shown by the large number of the more recent works of the collection in which it provides the

---

83. The passages based on fauxbourdon are the following: in the earlier layer, No. 45, mm. 18–20, 46–48; No. 51, mm. 4–5; No. 52, mm. 16–17, 22–23; among the more recent works, No. 27, mm. 9, 13, 20–21, 28–30; No. 33, mm. 27–28; No. 34, mm. 4–5, 16; No. 35, m. 7; and No. 42, m. 5.

84. Only in Dufay's *Donnés l'assault* (No. 50) does the imitation involve three parts, and this is probably for pictorial rather than contrapuntal reasons.

85. Concerning the cantus–tenor duo as a compositional procedure, see Kenney, *Walter Frye*, pp. 147 ff.

fundamental framework.[86] The contratenor also joins in the imitative procedures in a few chansons (most of them by Busnois[87] but as a rule only with a brief statement, often anticipatory, of the initial melodic figure. It never shares in the imitation in a systematic fashion except in the quasi-canonic chansons *Bel Acueil* (No. 1) and *A vous sans aultre* (No. 42) by Busnois, both of which are unusual works in several respects. The cantus–tenor duo with supporting contratenor retained its importance until, little by little, the imitative principle came to be applied equally and systematically to all the voices of a composition —whether three, four, or more—in the manner prefigured by Ockeghem's *Petitte Camusette*.

WORDS AND MUSIC

As will be evident already from the foregoing discussion of musical structures, the relationship between the poetic text and its setting is essentially formal in nature. The successive strophes of the poem and their structural subdivisions correspond to clearly delineated sections of the musical composition. For each line of verse to be declaimed there is a matching musical phrase, distinctly delimited by a cadence, a rest, or both. In a number of instances the caesura of the poetic line is apparently articulated musically as well, usually by a pause followed frequently by a sizable leap.[88] But if the connection between hemistich or verse and the corresponding melodic unit is highly formalistic, it is not in every case entirely mechanical.[89] On the one hand a cadential formula is sometimes either avoided or considerably attenuated when there is a continuity of sense or syntax from one line to the next. In Busnois's *Pour entretenir mes amours* (No. 15), for example, the second and third verses of all three strophes are bridged to some degree by the structure and meaning of the constituent phrases. The composer has

---

86. The compositions of the more recent layer in which the cantus-tenor duo is a significant element of the contrapuntal structure include the following: Nos. 2, 5–10, 12, 15–18, 20–22, 26, 29, 30, 33, 38, 40, and 42. It also figures more modestly in a number of other works, such as Nos. 35 and 36.

87. See, for example, Nos. 7, 12, 15, 20, 29, and 40.

88. Although the coincidence of rest and caesura is not always demonstrably irrefutable, an intention to articulate the latter musically seemed reasonably clear in the following passages: No. 3, mm. 8 ff.; No. 8, mm. 1 ff.; No. 9, mm. 1 ff.; No. 29, mm. 2 ff.; No. 35, mm. 8 ff., 22 ff.; No. 36, mm. 1 ff.; and No. 37, mm. 9 ff.

89. Contrary to the assertion to that effect by Reidemeister, *Die Chanson-Handschrift 78 C 28*, pp. 35–36.

accommodated the situation with a sort of interrupted cadence (m. 12) that serves both to mark the end of the line and to provide a link with the beginning of the next, thus subordinating the established musical conventions to the special requirements of a particular poem.[90] Even more frequent, on the other hand, are examples in which the musical development appears to depart at least momentarily from the usual formal and textual considerations. Either the melodic line comprises distinct phrases for which there is no independent text, as in the initial section of Frye's *So ys emprentid* (No. 45) and Bedingham's *Myn hertis lust* (No. 47), or it is broken into short motifs of an autonomously musical character, like the ascending sequence of Morton's *Paracheve ton entreprise* (No. 41). To such passages the verse can be fitted only with some difficulty and in an arbitrary fashion.[91]

The problems involved in attempting to match the textual syllables with the appropriate notational or rhythmic units, discussed in greater detail below,[92] are obviously inextricably tied to the identification of poetic line and musical phrase. In a large number of pieces in the repertory these relationships are reasonably evident. The phrases begin with longer values in melodic patterns that lend themselves to a syllabic declamation of the text, then terminate with more animated figures of a distinctly melismatic character and a clearly articulated cadence. In view of the declamatory relationship between word and tone that developed early in the sixteenth century, one would expect to find the text treated in such a manner primarily in the more recent compositions. However, this is not always the case. In *Or me veult* (No. 49), evidently one of the earliest pieces of the collection, melismatic and declamatory sections are plainly separated, and the text has apparently been set to allow a surprisingly consistent syllabic delivery. Of a similar stamp are the anonymous settings of *Hora cridar "Oymè"* (No. 52) and *Puis que je vis le regart* (No. 53), the successive phrases of which tend to begin with a series of repeated pitches inevitably necessitating a syllabic presentation of the corresponding verse. The compositions attributed to Dufay in both layers of the manuscript are also generally of the same type.

90. Similar instances may be seen in No. 12, mm. 13ff.; No. 14, mm. 11–13, 22–24; No. 26, mm. 8–10; No. 36, mm. 39–41; No. 43, mm. 3–4; and No. 44, mm. 8ff.

91. In this same connection see No. 18, mm. 12ff.; No. 22, mm. 14ff.; No. 31, the initial section; No. 36, mm. 19ff.; No. 38, mm. 12ff.; No. 39, mm. 20ff.; and No. 42, mm. 10ff.

92. See Text Placement in Editorial Policy, pp. 137–48.

Among the more recent works, particularly those most closely tied poetically to the courtly tradition, the relationship between text and music is often less direct, more abstract; the unambiguously syllabic passages are fewer and shorter, the melismatic ones usually longer and less distinctly differentiated from the declamatory sections. This may be seen from compositions such as Busnois's *En soustenant vostre querelle* (No. 2), his *Ja que li ne s'i attende* (No. 14), or Hayne's celebrated *De tous biens plaine* (No. 32), to cite but a few examples at random. It is in the chansons of a more popular cast included in the later segment of the repertory that one can discern once again a more immediate connection between the verse and the music, melodic writing of a more declamatory character, and melismatic passages both more contained and more sharply differentiated in style from the syllabic ones. Pieces such as Joye's *Ce qu'on fait a quatimini* (No. 9), Busnois's *A qui vens tu tes coquilles* (No. 10), and Ockeghem's *L'aultre d'antan* (No. 20) illustrate this situation well.

Also found in a number of these popular pieces are some of the earliest indications in fifteenth-century secular music of an awareness of the possibilities for textual illustration and expression by musical means that were so extensively exploited in the course of the following century. Such an assertion may seem surprising in view of the strophic nature of the fixed forms, but the evidence is most convincing. Reference has already been made to the military imagery of Morton's setting of *L'ome armé* (No. 34) and Dufay's *Donnés l'assault* (No. 50), where fanfare figures evoking the trumpet calls that sent fifteenth-century soldiers into battle are unmistakable.[93] Of a somewhat different order, but equally interesting, is the considerable extension of the third phrase (mm. 10–14) of Joye's *Ce qu'on fait* (No. 9). It seems entirely conceivable that it was intended primarily as a musical counterpart to the word *tenu*, especially since the same device is not inappropriate for the notion of the second strophe, . . . *jamais il n'est revelé*. Perhaps even more suggestive is the terminal melisma of Busnois's *A qui vens tu* (No. 10) with its sudden shift to ternary rhythms. The passage can be construed as illustrating the movement of an old man hobbling off with his sack over his shoulder, and once again the musical figure is not unsuitable for the corresponding line of the long strophe. The examples cited of possible musical interpretations of the text are

93. In No. 34, see especially mm. 3–4 and 14–15; in No. 50, mm. 34–38.

certainly few, but coupled with the more intimate relationship between line and phrase, note and syllable in the compositions in which they appear, they are perhaps enough to suggest a significant trend toward a declamatory, text-oriented compositional style. This shift, which can be perceived in the secular polyphony cultivated in territories of French culture during the closing decades of the fifteenth century, was due at least in part to an emulation of the popular songs that had penetrated the courtly tradition in arrangements such as those found in the Mellon Chansonnier.

THE VERSE

Howard Garey

THEMES

The Mellon Chansonnier, through its lyric poems, opens a door to a universe of sentiment, morals, philosophical and theological attitudes, ideas, assumptions, and myths quite different from the one in which we dwell. The time is the late fifteenth century; the locale—based on the proveniences of the several dozen concordant sources—embraces Naples, Florence, northern Italy, Burgundy, France, Germany, and the Low Countries, an area subject to Burgundian rule or influence, the world so sensitively described by Johan Huizinga in *The Waning of the Middle Ages*. We propose to inspect this world through the poems of the Mellon, to gather what light we can from this source alone, with only minimal assistance from the literary–historical context in which our songs are set. This synchronic, descriptive approach applied to a collection of fifty-seven songs remarkably representative of a fifteenth-century courtly setting will, we believe, lend to it an actuality that more general considerations cannot evoke by themselves.

A fairly sharp bifurcation between "courtly" and "popular" lyric types asserts itself upon even a cursory perusal of the Mellon songs. Both "courtly" and "popular" are equally at home in the courts in which these styles were cultivated. The terms refer not to the real world of courtiers and peasants of the fifteenth century, but to the fictive or mythical universes existing in the imaginations of the courtiers and inhabited by conventionalized "courtiers" and "peasants." These two lyric types are distinguished by formal traits while the fictive worlds to which they correspond can be identified by assumptions about love and life, men and women, social and ethical bonds characteristic of each of them, and by the specialized vocabularies, or *langages*, that reflect them.

Historically, it appears most likely that lyric verse had truly popular origins and that it had been taken over by aristocratic societies by the time such verse was first committed to writing. However, purely popular songs were not directly or completely written down; thus our literary legacy is entirely mediated through the noble classes or through those who served them. The bifurcation with which we are concerned becomes then, as early as the eleventh and twelfth centuries, a purely courtly phenomenon with a stock of images, personages, and clichés sufficient to nourish the courtly lyric for several centuries.[1]

The courtly poems are typically written in the *formes fixes* we shall describe later: the *rondeau*, the *ballade*, the *virelai* (or, in its shortened form, the *bergerette*). The favorite verse lengths in the French poems are the octosyllable and the decasyllable. They range in mood from despair through hope to a blissful fulfillment of desire or to the optimistic affirmation of control, by the will, of one's destiny. Poems written in the formes fixes and within the limits of the courtly vocabulary may express sentiments slyly contrary to the conventional courtly assumptions. Such poems are parodic and ironical, but, by the very fact of their bringing into question the basic mythology of the courtly world, they remain within the courtly tradition.

The "popular" songs too are marked by formal and lexical traits. The songs that present several poems sung simultaneously in the different voices usually consist of one poem in a courtly form, usually in the cantus, and another poem, of popular type, sung by the remaining voices. This second poem is apt to be less strict in its versification: a simple quatrain in *abba* or *abab*, a succession of repetitions of a single line followed by a last line that does not rhyme with the preceding lines, or, as in No. 28, a single repetition of the last line. Another element, associated with the lighthearted gaiety of the popular mode, is the repetition of nonsense syllables perhaps slightly suggestive of words conceptually appropriate to the subject matter of the song (in No. 54, for example: *Holà*, *duriau*, and similar exclamations).

The lines tend to be of five or seven syllables, although octosyllables and decasyllables do occur. There is one example (No. 4 in the lower three voices) of the twelve-syllable line, which had not yet become the

---

1. A reasonable hypothesis concerning the origins of medieval lyric verse is expounded by Alfred Jeanroy in *Les Origines de la Poésie Lyrique en France au Moyen Age*, 3rd ed. (Paris: Champion, 1925). Essentially, he says that the truly popular lyric verse is scarcely represented in written literature, which is a product of the courts and differs markedly from the spirit and ideas of the popular songs. The latter can be to some degree recovered in the mutilated fragments remaining in the form of the refrains accompanying dances and by a study of the similarities of the refrains with the ancient lyric poetry of other Romance languages, especially Provençal and Portuguese.

great classic alexandrine that has reigned in French verse since the sixteenth century but was used in the Middle Ages in a few long narrative poems.

Upon reading even the sampling of fifteenth-century French poetry represented by the Mellon, one comes to recognize some words as "courtly," others as "popular"—that is, as being incompatible with verse identified as courtly by nonlexical criteria. Proper names are always associated with a light or comic context (not necessarily noncourtly; see No. 34, the rondeau in the cantus). Certain names have rustic connotations. One knows what to expect on hearing *Robin et Marion* (as in No. 4): the mere mention of the names sets the stage, establishes the tone, and abolishes any universe incompatible with the pastoral world. Another identifying trait of the popular mode, though not a necessary one, is a coarse vocabulary—exemplified by *sanglantement belle, crotee,* and *musel* in No. 28. Sexual explicitness is hardly to be found in courtly verse, although the possibility that the unspecified, deeply longed-for boon is carnal is never absent from it. In the popular mode the unmistakable suggestion of the physical expression of love is frequent. Witness *Retirés vostre main* in No. 28 and, in No. 54, *Il n'est pas venu pour messe chanter,* and *Il a trop dansé le pas de Brabant,* not to mention the little fragments of what sound for all the world like the *grivois* anecdotes that are still current in France: *La femme d'un marounier | J'encontray en mi ma voye* (No. 54).

The great majority of the courtly poems of the Mellon Chansonnier are serious in that they embody an implicit acceptance of the basic spiritual, psychological, and social assumptions about life and, especially, love that give the courtly universe its peculiar reality. From a historical perspective it is evident that this moral world is directly descended from that supposed (or created) by the troubadours, but an attentive reading of our poems will show some subtle changes of emphasis.

Since we are concerned with the synchronic consideration of this fifteenth-century collection, let us put history aside and ask what we can learn about love from the unmistakably courtly poems, in the serious vein, of the present repertory. Love, as a relationship between a man and a woman, may or may not be reciprocal. The way in which a man loves a woman in these songs differs in important aspects from a woman's love for a man, although there is a large field of common ground between them and there are some poems in which the manner of loving is peculiar to neither sex. The paradigm of love, the model in comparison with which all other paradigms are "irregular," is that of a man who loves a woman; who uses a language indicative of a desire to serve; who expresses a profound need for a boon or favor from the lady, a boon not explicitly sexual in nature but one the desire for which is expressed in tones of passion, deep longing, feelings compounded of sexual desire and an attitude of great respect for the object of that desire. In these poems, then, these two basic attitudes vie for expression: the intensity of the desire and the profundity of the subservience and respect.

In the absence of the boon, the lover is sleepless (No. 12), changes color (Nos. 16, 48), is sick (Nos. 7, 16), longs for the sight of his beloved (No. 31), fears death (Nos. 7, 25), or desires it (Nos. 26, 31, 40, 55)—if his longing cannot be satisfied. Allied with the desire for the boon is the wish to serve: declarations of fidelity (Nos. 21, 47, 51), of admiration of the lady (Nos. 6, 32, 45), of a willingness to fight in her behalf (No. 2). Some of the poems, in looking toward the granting of the prize, tend to be more optimistic. They harbor a sentiment that had been the cornerstone of the whole philosophy of love as expounded by troubadour poetry: Love is ennobling; love granted by the lady is a cause of the spiritual advancement of the lover. The poems in which this notion is made explicit are exceedingly rare in the Mellon. When it does appear it is apt to be tongue-in-cheek; the "advancement" is as much social or material as it is spiritual or ethical (No. 13, *Non pas que je veuille penser*).

The typically serious poem in the current repertory, then, will stress one or two of the following ideas: the pain of unrequited or unsatisfied love, or of separation from the beloved; supplication for the boon of love; promises of fidelity to the beloved; and the celebration of the excellent qualities of the beloved—but the notion of spiritual improvement as a consequence of the boon is nearly lacking in these poems.

Although the range of basic ideas is exceedingly small, the charm of the poems is not to be found in the ideas but in the manner of expression. The technical facility of the poet, the deftness with which he manages certain sequences of images, of allegorical settings, and of clever antitheses; the skill with which he threads his sentences and clauses through the stanzas, the daring with which he rhymes words, practicing either admirable variety in his rhyming words or an audacious brinkmanship in rhyming words that are almost, but not quite, the same word; his ability to utter the name of his beloved without actually using it as a word in the poem through a cryptographic device such as an acrostic (Nos. 12, 14)—all this was more highly valued than the basic "message" of the poem because, in truth, the number of such messages was so restricted. When we think we discover in one of these songs the accents of sincerity, the expression of what we recognize as a human emotion, we feel something akin to gratitude, however much we may owe to our own culturally imposed perception of what constitutes authentic humanity.

The courtly mode has special conceptual markers that function only if they are used within the formal and lexical limits inherent in this mode. That is, if a given concept is couched in noncourtly terms, it no longer serves as a marker of the courtly mode. For example, the expression of joy, itself compatible with it, is not in itself an identifying trait if its expression includes "coarse" or "popular" words or turns of phrase. With this proviso, the concepts characteristic of the courtly mode may be enumerated as follows, with a representative sampling of its vocabulary in parentheses:

Grief and pain (*dueil, douleur, grief, anuy, mort, mal (mal = 'maladie'), pleurs, larmes, peine, desespoir; plourer, douloir, agrever, mourir, finer, trespasser, desvier, rendre l'ame*)

Supplication for mercy (*grace, mercy, secours, remede; querir, supplier, secourir, garir,*)

Offer of service and protestations of fidelity (*service, serviteur, servant, léauté* [and related words] *signour, maistresse; servir, honorer, vostre estre* ['be yours']; *tousjours, en tous lieux*)

Hope (*espoir, esperance; esperer*)

Praise (*fame, bruit, renom, beaulté* [and related adjectives], *gentillesse* [in the sense of "noblesse"], *doulceur, maintieng bel et gent, goodly port, jonesse, yowght* [= youth])

Joy and fulfillment (*joye, confort, léesse, alegance, deduit, paix, plaisance, amour; obtenir, trouver, s'esjoïr*)

Separation of the person (lover or beloved) into parts associated with certain emotions, especially the eyes and the heart. These anatomical names function in a quasi-allegorical way by governing verbs whose usual subject is a whole human being. We may include here also verbs of function, often presented as a noun or a substantified infinitive or participle (*oeil, cuer, penser, pensé, pensée, pensement, sentir, sentement, regart*). This usage is distinct from that in which visible parts of the body such as eyes, face (*yeux, face, visage*) are admired for their beauty.

Allegorical personages representing moods and faculties of the person. Again, the test that distinguishes the literal from the allegorical use of such a word is its collocation with other words in the context, such as with a verb, as subject or object, or with adjectives: if the word with which the term in question is collocated in a given context is normally collocated with animate or human terms, the term is said to be used allegorically. Many of the terms listed above are so used; here is a brief sampling (*Pitié, Courtoysie, Bel Acueil, Souvenance, Couroux*)

Allegorical toponymy, representative of emotional states or of transition from one to another (*Lac de Dueil, Chemin de Dueil, Tour de Bel Acueil*)

Hyperbole (*fondre tout en larmes de plourer, je me meurs en pleurs, je noye en plours*)

Antitheses (*Le corps s'en va et le cueur vous demeure*; *Joye me fuit et Doleur me ceurt seure*; *Ma bouce rit et ma pensée pleure*)

Military images (*Doleur me ceurt seure*; *Donnés l'assault* ... ; *Tournay n'y vault jouster, ne faire estour*)—roughly the vocabulary of the *chansons de geste*

Religion, pagan and Christian references to known divinities, relationship of worshipper to object of worship (*Dieu, haut dieu d'amour, Amour, Fortune*).

Of the themes just enumerated, that of service perhaps most reveals the doctrine of love.

The notion of service is linked to that of subservience and subordination, the feudal relationship of vassal to suzerain. Such an ordering is perceived as pervading nature, as being part of the order established by God. The poet as lover was pleased to declare his subservience to his lady and to use to this end analogies in which he figures as servant to the master/mistress personified by the lady, as vassal to lord, as patient to physician, as mortal worshiping a divine being. The mechanisms, attitudes, gestures, and symbols of these relationships were at hand in the ambient culture. The appropriate vocabulary and images evoked with automatic promptness and perfect economy the subservience, fealty, dependence, and adoration of the lover for his beloved.

There is, if not reciprocity in the relationship of inferior to superior, a kind of quid pro quo: the superior reserves certain favors, which he has the right to bestow according to his unconstrained desire or whim but which he is more likely to bestow if the inferior executes faithfully and well the duties incumbent upon him. Duties must be performed, although they may be carried out more or less well. The boon has no necessary relation to the service; if the master wishes to reward the service, he may. It is his right to withhold or grant the boon, whatever the quality of the service.

However legitimately the tradition of the male poet's subservience to his lady may be rooted in the feudal society of twelfth-century Provence, by the period of our songbook and in the social milieu in which it took form, the subordination of man to woman is so purely conventional as to be nearly a cruel joke.[2] One may say that the voluntary submissiveness of the male is a grace on his part since it is a direct contradiction of the social realities of the time. The tension between the social reality of female subordination and the conventions of courtly love is resolved as (1) the very abstract expression of the courtly tradition in the "serious" poems; (2) the parody of the same tradition; (3) the escape from that tradition into another, the pastoral, rustic, or popular; (4) the exploration of the love of a woman for a man whose expression, although not without precedent (because that is exactly the starting point for popular lyric expression, according to Jeanroy[3]), is nevertheless relatively free from the restrictions of a rigid structure; (5) escape from the whole problem of love, but within the forms of courtly verse, into allusions to the military life or to the stouthearted defiance of Fortune. The escape from love is rarely complete. For example, the defiance of Fortune, although often one is not sure why the poet rails against her, is usually couched in the language of the despondent lover before it reaches the courageous climax.

2. An excellent summary of the theories about the origin of the *fin' amor* of the Provençal poets is to be found in Pierre Bec's *Nouvelle Anthologie de la Lyrique Occitane du Moyen Age* (Avignon: Aubanel, 1970).

3. *Origines*, p. 158 and pp. 193–94. "[L]a forme préférée de la lyrique romane à ses débuts était un monologue ... de femme non mariée" (The favorite form of the romance lyric in its inception was a monologue ... of an unmarried woman). "Le dialogue entre la fille et la mère était fréquent dans l'ancienne poésie française comme en Portugal; ces deux personnages, avec celui de l'amant, étaient ... stéréotypés.... [C]'est dans ce genre ... que la poésie populaire a laissé le plus de traces" (The dialogue between the daughter and the mother was frequent in the old French poetry, as it was in Portugal; these two characters, along with the lover, were ... stereotyped.... Popular poetry left its deepest traces in such dialogues.)

For the purpose of definition, a religious element, model, or analogy is discernible in a posture of worship, prayer, or supplication to a being unconstrained in its power to grant the prayer. Formal marks consist of certain words (*dieu, prier, supplier*) and names of divinities or allegorized abstractions, especially in direct address (*Dieu, Fortune, Espérance* [as used in No. 49], *Amours*). The line between allegorized abstractions and deities has been indistinct since late Roman times. An allegorical figure approaches divinity when in a given text it receives some show of reverence from a mortal. But here another nearly impalpable distinction comes into question—the line between obeisance paid an earthly lord and the reverence paid to a divinity. The stylistic difference is largely one of vocabulary. The use of Latin is evocative of religious attitudes or postures: Nos. 19 and 57 use Latin to evoke the general feeling of adoration and thereby to express the relationship of servant to lady. In these instances the words *servant* and *lady* must be understood literally: we are speaking of musicians in their relationship to the princess Beatrice of Aragon. The servant–mistress relationship being preempted by reality, the higher relationship—that of worshipper to divinity—is left to serve a symbolic function. It is mediated through the Latin language and a vocabulary primarily liturgical. Number 19 cannot really be distinguished from a prayer to the Holy Virgin, except for the name of the mortal lady to whom it is addressed in the title. Number 57, by its specification of musicians in ll. 2 and 3, gives a clue to its secular purpose. But the tone of each is resolutely devotional. In No. 9, Latin is used, this time in parody, to establish a relationship with an unnamed ecclesiastical authority (see below for more on this poem).

The topology of the courtly universe is a landscape of the mind. The lover is near to or far from his beloved. He speaks to and about his own heart and thought, but Hope, Joy, Grief, and the like are externalized and are conceived of as acting upon him. His will is never reified or personified; in some poems not dealing specifically with love, the poet, having armed himself with "the staff of Hope," makes a declaration of intent to free himself from the tyranny of Fortune (No. 18). The only places conceived of as surrounding the speaker or as external to him are, like the allegorical figures, representations of internal states—the Lake of Grief (No. 36), the Road to Grief (No. 3), the Road to Love (No. 53). The Court of Love (that is, of the god of love, Amours) is in fact the universe of love with which we are dealing here. In No. 1 the god of love is sending his courier, well-named Fair Welcome, to summon the poet to his court. If the poet does not recognize the suzerainty of the god of love, he will be deprived of his succor in time of need. In this poem the concepts of religious and feudal allegiance are perfectly blended.

Although the first-person narrator, the poet himself, usually provides the center of action (the I-here-now), it is sometimes the beloved, addressed as *vous*, who is the focus of movement, as in No. 21: *Le corps s'en va et le cueur vous demeure.* The *en* of *s'en va* ("goes *away*") refers not to the poet as center, but to the beloved, as is made clear in the second clause.

"Real" places are mentioned in a nonsymbolic way—but never in a "serious" poem (No. 20, *Melan*; No. 4, *au bois*). Verbs of movement or location are often collocated with goals or locations that are not, strictly speaking, places at all but states of mind or feeling apart from the allegorical places mentioned above. In No. 26 the question *Ou doy je secours querir?* is answered by implication with *Sinon par vous requerir,* an expression of means rather than of place or movement. In No. 33 the poet is in *questo purgatoro*; No. 32 locates paradise *en mon cueur.* The unhappy woman of No. 27 finds *toute douleur assemblee en moy.*

Parody employs the characteristic devices of serious verse to resolve the tension between the givens of the courtly universe and the conditions of the everyday world. Some parodic poems are so subtle, so nearly imperceptible in their deviation from the courtly norm, that an occasional scribe has taken it upon himself to correct an "error," to erase a flaw in such a production (as in version J of No. 13). Other poems are courtly only in their forms. The vocabulary, although partly in context, introduces words that clash with their polite neighbors in an incongruity of comic intent (No. 28). At the extreme of silliness and, sometimes, vulgarity, the label of parody hardly applies. No longer is there mockery directed against the dogma of *fin'amors,* but sheer rollicking fun and nonsense bubble out in a more or less standard verse form. Although there are gradations between the parodic and the comic, the parodic can be understood specifically to reveal the incongruity between courtly ideal and practice.

Number 13, *Non pas que je veuille penser* is perhaps the best of this genre. It is squarely in the courtly register with respect to form and vocabulary but has a pattern of cynical surprises beautifully integrated with the rondeau form in which it is couched. A surprise is found at the end of each division: full refrain, short strophe, and long strophe (hence, of course, not at short refrain, which ends at l. 3 of R and where there is no such surprise). The expression of cynical self-interest is ambiguous the first two times (ll. 5 and 8) but the intent of the poem is made unequivocal at l. 13: "unless I can forget her."

The genre vocabulary is impeccable and trots out the full range of courtly ideas: loyalty, love, service, incomparability of the lady, desire to be in her favor, and, upon its first and apparently innocent appearance, the desire to achieve some kind of self-improvement through love and service. Service and honor for the lady appear in the next section(s), and with them the willingness to sacrifice oneself totally—as long as the reward (spiritual or material? there is still doubt) follows this self-abnegation. The self-serving nature of the lover's protestations is softened a bit by the next flood of conventional attitudes: pleasing sweetness without peer, my heart desires to live and die as her possession, and that is exactly what I'll do—unless I can forget her! It is because the mere possibility of the lover's forgetting his lady is so foreign to the courtly mode (except as contained in a passionate denial of that possibility) that the final awakening to the cynicism of this expression is so effective. For the struggles of various scribes to accommodate the unconventional point of view expressed in this poem, see Variants for No. 13 (pp. 236–38).

Pour entretenir mes amours (No. 15) is similar in mood to No. 13 but does not depend on the device of the graded surprise as its main weapon. The tone is set at the outset in the refrain, which is all that the Mellon preserves of the poem. It seems to tell the story of a courtier-in-spite-of-himself who finds himself confined to a boring court by the impossibility of financing the lordly behavior expected of him by the prevailing social code. As a consequence he cannot afford the lavish gifts his departure would impose. He feels like a pet animal, performing many an incongruously lordly gesture (*seignourie*), or, according to one variant, "monkeyshines" (*singerie*), which amounts to about the same thing. For the rest of the poem the concordant sources give us two quite different versions, which, however, have this in common: an impecunious courtier is forced into an uncomfortable parasitism.

In this poem it is the hard realism of the material situation that wakes us out of our courtly dreams, whereas in No. 13 there was a subtle inquiry into motives and character. With their realism both these poems delineate something much more like an individual than the unvarying type of person presented in the "serious" poems.

The voice of *Ce qu'on fait a quatimini* (No. 9) is no longer that of
the courtly lover. The poet does not place himself in a direct and
reciprocal relationship with the "girls" whom he addresses here; there
is no emotion but that of an amused and somewhat cynical detachment.
We seem to hear a worldly priest at the confluence of the two currents
of clerical antifeminism and of the taste for sensuous living characteristic of the fifteenth-century aristocracy.

Is *Se mon service vous plaisoit* (No. 22) ironical in intent? We shall
never know unless a lucky find someday reveals the rest of the poem,
for the extant text of this rondeau does not go beyond the short strophe.
As far as it goes, it appears to be a cool, well-controlled declaration of
willingness to serve a lady, and it includes the standard expressions of
admiration—but *de serviteur despourveue* gives us pause. It could well
lead to an ironical dénouement.

L'autre d'antan (No. 20), although a rondeau, has really left the courtly
realm. Aside from the *forme fixe*, it bears all the characteristics of
comic, popular verse. Even the form of this rondeau is provided
with a return of the first line at the end of the refrain, an anomaly
that makes of the first line a sort of strophe–final refrain like that of
the ballade and gives to the whole a childlike dance character. Furthermore, the language is resolutely popular: *l'autrier* is a cliché of the
pastourelle (a medieval dialogue poem of wooing); *d'antan* as a noun
is a grammatical oddity that could well be an imitation of rustic
speech. The suspense in which we are kept waiting for the subject of the
verbs of the first sentence is not resolved until *elle* of l. 8, thus height-
ening the excitement of the poem. The repetitions (*l'autre . . . l'autre*;
passa . . . passant; *brassin . . . brassa*); the introduction of a down-to-earth
military language more redolent of the barracks than of the *chansons de
geste*; the use of a proper noun that has reference to the real, contemporary world (*Melan*, Milan, a great industrial center even then, famed
for the skill of its armorers)—all this confers upon the poem the
popular stamp.

This poem, like those whose descriptions follow, has an essential
feature that contrasts it with the serious songs: time is treated as a
narrative flow of events. As we shall see, in the parodies of serious verse,
in the comic verse written in the *formes fixes*, and in the popular songs,
the tenses of narration (the historical present, the simple past) and of
temporal context (the imperfect) are used. Characteristically, the
serious poems refer to a sort of eternal present, a *présent figé*: the situation
or state of mind in which the poet finds himself is endless. Progress is

not part of this conception; at the most a resolution—death, say, or the granting of the boon—is envisaged. One of the rare verbs in the simple past that occur in an orthodox courtly poem establishes a beginning point for the sentimental situation of the poet (No. 53, *Puis que je vis le regart*). It may be significant that, though courtly, this poem is a happy one.

A qui vens tu tes coquilles (No. 10), a rondeau, is as popular for its seven-syllable lines and its "low" words as for the unpleasant picture of the lecherous old man and the lewd and venal girls who are the subject of the poem.

Numbers 4 (*Petitte Camusette*), 28 (*Mon trestout et mon assotee*), and 54 (*Ma dame de nom*) have many popular features in common: they are composite songs; they introduce low words, sometimes in incongruous collocation with courtly terms, for shock effect (No. 54: Se ne me donnés / De mercy le don, / Je seray *tennés*; Je vous ayme tant / Qu'en suis *rasoté*); they fall into a narrative mode in which time flows and events succeed one another within definite time frames and explicitly delimited spaces, unlike the suspension of time *sub specie aeternitatis* and vagueness of locale characteristic of the serious poems (No. 4: Robin et Marion s'en vont au bois jouer ... Ilz se sont endormis; No. 28: Il estoit ung bonhome / Qui charioit fagot ... / Il avoit une fille / Qu'on appeloit Margot; No. 54: Sur la rive de la mer [space] / L'aultre jour [time] jouer m'aloye / La femme d'un marounier / J'encontray [event] en mi ma voye [further spatial specification]); nonsense syllables spice the text, words and phrases undergo playful repetition, and suggestions of amorous play are always near the surface.

Whether serious or popular, the great majority of these songs deal with the problem of love in the relationships between men and women. We have ample opportunity to inspect the world of men—their feelings, joys, and despondencies—but what of women? The poets are probably all men; the only woman to have made a name for herself as poet, writer, or thinker in the late Middle Ages is Christine de Pisan (1364–ca. 1430). Because of the anonymity of our poets, it is impossible to determine their sex, but the presence of a woman among them would be surprising. There are a few poems, however, whose "voice" is that of a woman. Before we explore them, it would be well to examine the question of the voice—that is, the purported or fictive identity behind the first person pronouns, if any, of the poem, and whether the poem is addressed to some one (as manifested by use of the second person), or speaks of some one. Once these possibilities are recognized, they prove to have relevance to questions of style and mood.

Very few poems employ the detached, anonymous voice associated particularly with storytelling. Of the seven poems with indeterminate voice (Nos. 4 II, 9, 28 II, 34, 43, 54 III, 54 IV), all but Nos. 9 and 43 are in the narrative mode. Number 43 is a conventional lover's complaint generalized to the third-person subject; No. 9 has the voice of the worldly cleric mentioned above.

The rest of the poems are in the first person; of these, seven are apparently feminine. The remainder are either explicitly masculine or, in the absence of an indication to the contrary, may safely be considered so. In 32 poems the masculine voice uses the second person to address his beloved (23 poems) or to speak to Fortune (3 poems), various personified abstractions (such as Amours), or personified parts or faculties of persons ("mon dueil" in No. 23, "lingua maladicta" in in No. 52). The poet uses the third person in reference to similar entities (the beloved in 13 poems and Fortune, Bel Acueil, Amours, Hope in 1 each for a total of 17 poems, that is, about half as many as those in direct address). For these poems we may assume an "indeterminate ear": empty room, accidental listener, unnamed confidant.

The poem in direct address corresponds to the pragmatic function of language: the use of language to influence behavior. Thus the supplication for mercy evokes a dynamic situation, a tension to be resolved. The third-person declaration is a simple statement of fact: I am unhappy, longing for the sight of my beloved. The possessor of the indeterminate ear is not expected to intervene; resolution of the tension is not expected.

Whereas the poems with a male voice addressed to a second person are about twice as numerous as those describing the subject's feelings about a third person, the songs supposedly expressing a woman's point of view are never addressed to the beloved. In five poems a woman speaks about her beloved (Nos. 8, 14, 27, 29, and 56). In one of them (No. 29) she deals with a whole troop of personified abstractions, Joye, Douleur, and the like. When a woman does address anyone directly, it is not her beloved but rather a suitor whom she vigorously rejects (Nos, 10, 28 II, and 56, all of them with popular or anticourtly traits). Although we are dealing here with small numbers, there does appear to be a significant difference: the male poems manifest a clear preference for passionate or respectful apostrophe, the female songs of love express reflective resignation or quiet satisfaction.

This distinction provides a point of departure for considering a

primordial question about the moral world of the Mellon songs:
What is a woman? We have already glimpsed her from the point of
view of the man as male poet and male voice, man speaking for man.
At least in the present text, if she is called *dame, damoiselle, m'amour*, or
(*noble*) *femme*, she corresponds to the courtly myth of the nearly divine
lady who can grant happiness, fulfillment, even life itself to the panting
suitor by accepting him as *ami* or *servant* (or *serviteur*). Her characteristics
can be summed up in a short list: She is beautiful, young, noble,
gracious, kind, well-famed, gentle. She is also capable of being cruel,
although it is never explicit that she is deliberately so. Her right to
accept or reject a suitor is absolute; it follows that she has the right
to be cruel without impairing her value or worth as a lady. Just as she
operates with absolute freedom, so her lover is absolutely subject to
her will. He has been enslaved by her qualities (most of which are
named as the causes of his love) and has neither the wish nor the power
to free himself. Although the relationship of the lover to his lady is
likened in different poems to the vassal–lord bond or to that between
patient and physician or servant and master, the only adequate analogy
is between mortal and divinity, owing to the servitude of the one and
the freedom of the other.

In the world of realistic parody, however, neither lover nor lady
appears in this idealistic light. Usually self-centered, they are concerned
with getting the greatest possible material benefit from the situation,
which in the courtly world presented real problems. (The word *fille*,
rather than *dame*, to refer to the woman in two such poems, Nos. 9 and
10, seems to belong to the parodic mode.)

The poets who adopt the woman's perspective provide themselves
with an instrument for escaping from the abstract figure of the lady:
this goddess who is beautiful—but tall or short? With blue eyes or
perhaps hazel? Conceivably plump? Ah, no! Gracious in bearing, yes,
but quick in her movements or languid? We will never know from
these usually self-centered declarations of passion. If the poet speaks
with a man's voice, the woman must be an idealized lady, an object
of contempt, or a delightfully conventionalized little shepherdess. If
on the contrary he adopts the woman's voice, a new depth, a new note
of pathos, of dignity with tenderness can be discerned. An individuality
is hinted at that is not possible in the male mode.

It is odd that freedom from convention is found in the song of the
woman, for it is precisely here that the lyric genre began, apparently,

with the naïve lament of the girl talking to her mother, in the folk songs of the eleventh century. At least this is what the scanty literary vestiges of that remote age give us to understand. So the escape from convention is at once an innovation and a return to a more ancient convention.

Finally, the whole problem of love can simply be finessed: there are, after all, other subjects for lyric verse. There is a transitional area consisting of songs that could be about love, that is, songs whose words are applicable to a more general situation but one that certainly includes love. Some songs are probably love poems even though love is not explicitly and specifically named or described, others clearly apply to the more general situation rather than to love, and finally, some have nothing to do with love at all.

Triste qui sperò morendo (No. 43) is almost surely a love lyric. Not only does the general mood correspond to that of the despondent lover, but it is safe to say that "burning" and "fire" are practically synonymous with "loving" and "love." Similarly, *Ou lit de pleurs* (No. 48) adduces the conventionally morbid manifestations and symbols of unsatisfied love: tears, hair-tearing, wounds, pallor, darkness, a state "far from my medicine."

Moving away from love in the narrow sense, the songs dedicated to Princess Beatrice (Nos. 19 and 57) breathe the respect and submission that the poet, a musician, felt for his noble patroness. The social subordination symbolic of Love's power in the traditional courtly song is here perfectly real. So recourse is had to a symbolic level, the analogous relationship of a worshiper to the Holy Virgin.

In No. 39 (*Au povre par necessité*) although there is no first-person pronoun or verb, there is probably self-reference; it is the "povre" who is speaking. This single cinquain from a rondeau is in the mood of a supplication to an indeterminate hearer to help an unfortunate person. The full rondeau, if recovered, would no doubt provide further specification. Although unrewarded love is not excluded, the poem is just as applicable to any kind of misfortune, including, quite literally, poverty.

Songs 37, 41, and 18 are apostrophes to Fortune, or Lady Luck. In No. 37 (*O Fortune, trop tu es dure*) one cinquain of a rondeau is not sufficient to establish the "plot." We have an unmotivated complaint addressed to Fortune whose vocabulary is at least compatible with that of love. The word *aliance* is feudal and juridical; it here denotes a contract that can be renounced. The allegory's application to real life is hard to follow: If Fortune (representing the aleatory events of life) has deprived the poet of hope (that is, of reason to hope), how can the poet renounce his bond to Fortune? He can give up hope but hardly dissolve his dependence on chance, or so it seems to a twentieth-century reader.

The attitude is not so defiant in No. 41 (*Paracheve ton entreprise*). Fortune is clearly identified as a lady—a conveniently ambiguous device because it is equally possible that a "real" lady is being identified with Fortune. In any case the complaint addressed to Fortune could just as well be directed to a lady. The language represents an intersection of two sets: the language appropriate to be addressed to a cruel mistress, and that suitable for complaint to the goddess Fortune. In this way, l. 11 (*Choulle moy du tout a ta guise*) seems particularly apt as addressed to Fortune (though it is not incompatible with the concept of the cruel mistress), whereas the following sentiment, "Pour your venom on me, you will never be reproached for it," represents the compulsory submission to the lady (an optional attitude toward Lady Luck, as the other poems on Fortune show).

It is instructive to see how a song explicitly about love (No. 35) works in an allusion to Fortune. Lines 3–5 (Je me tien seul / Comme une ame esbaÿe / Faisant regret de ma dolente vye / Et de Fortune, qu'ainsi fort me guerroye) barely personify Fortune: she is an ad hoc allegorical figure of no more than one line's duration. Thus *Fortune* refers less to an active, quasi-conscious force than simply to luck, to chance brought to symbolic life as subject of a single verb.

Fortune, par ta cruaulté (No. 18) apostrophizes Fortune forthrightly and finds a courageous alternative to resignation. The poet thrives on adversity: "The more blows you shower upon me, the less fear and the more confidence I have, for I have the Staff of Hope," he says in the short strophe. In the same brave vein he ends the long strophe with another explanation of his assurance: "I have pride with which to meet your power, for everything comes to me from *loyaulté* [fidelity, reliability, frankness, candor, scrupulous observance of the obligations imposed by social relationships]." With hope and *loyaulté*, our poet is impervious to Fortune's cruelest blows. Although the vocabulary is courtly, there is little suggestion of love in this song. There is neither the despair of the rejected lover nor the joy of the successful lover. Hope and *loyaulté*, then, are the means for coming to terms with life: be honest and optimistic, and all will be well. The song is truly an anomaly in this collection.

The remaining song with no discernible reference to love is No. 34 (*Il sera pour vous conbatu / L'ome armé*), a good-natured poem that puts one who is, it seems, a musician (see Textual Notes for No. 34 1) into a mock-heroic military situation. Just the boys having some fun— and who is to say, after the tears and the anguish, the noble poses, and the occasional descent into snide cynicism, that they do not deserve it?

METRICS

In the poetical tradition of the Romance languages, verse length is measured by the number of syllables in the line. The traditional French method of syllable counting is fundamentally different from the method common to the Italian and Spanish traditions, so that what is called an eight-syllable line in one will be considered nine-syllabled in the others. Once this source of confusion is exposed and neutralized, the French and Italo–Spanish metrics are more similar than had appeared. Nevertheless, the certain real differences that remain will be discussed in this section. The principles of English metrics are somewhat different, as we shall see for the three English songs in Mellon.

The French Tradition

Since the beginnings of French literature, the dominant meters of French verse have been the ten-syllable line, especially for narratives of an epic character, the eight-syllable line for courtly romance, and both meters for lyric verse. The decasyllable has been favored for the ballade, and, for rather light or frivolous lyric verse, the seven-syllable line and occasionally the line of five syllables. Although the twelve-syllable line (the alexandrine) has been used since the twelfth century, it is only since the sixteenth century that this meter has come to dominate French verse. In principle, the number of syllables in a line is equal to the number of vowels or diphthongs, that is, to the number of syllabic nuclei. Some successions of two or more vowel letters (for example, *ou*, *ai*) represent simple vowels; others (*au*, *oi*) represent diphthongs in Old and Middle French; still others (*ie*, *ai*) may stand for two successive syllabics—for example, *lié*, the passive participle of *lier*, 'to bind', has two syllables, whereas *lié* 'happy' from Latin LAETU, has only one. We shall mark such disyllabic combinations with a diaeresis (¨): thus, *lié* will be assumed by the reader to be mono-syllabic, *lië* and *haï* as disyllabic.

Since all syllabics are either counted (whether followed by another vowel or not) or elided (that is, not pronounced at all), French verse is fundamentally different from Italian and Spanish verse, in which successive vocalic segments may be run together in what is convention-ally recognized to be a single syllable—whatever the phonetic facts may be. The Italian and Spanish traditions allow for latitude on the part of the poet in rather arbitrarily considering a sequence of vowels to constitute the same number of syllables as of vowels, or some lesser number, down to one.

The so-called mute *e* (represented here by the inverted letter *ə*) gives French metrics a certain amount of "give"; the rules for its being counted or omitted in the determination of meter are easily stated.

1. Scribal practice accounts for the occurrence in manuscripts of such sequences as *que on, que il*, especially in the form of the regular scribal abbreviation of *que*: *q̄*. See No. 7, l. 2, *q̄on*, realized in our edition as *qu'on* rather than *que on*, in accordance with metrical exi-gencies; similarly, No. 9, l. 1, *q̄ on*, No. 21, l. 4, *q̄ Jncessamment*, No. 14, l. 3, *q̄ asses*, and others. Note also No. 4, l. 3, *de acquerir* for *d'acquerir*. These scribal practices date from a period in Old French when the poet had a free choice in conserving or eliding the *ə* of such conjunc-tions as *que, se* ('if'), *ne* ('and, nor'), *de*. Although this choice continued into the late Old French period, there are no examples, buttressed by the metrics of the line, of hiatus with *ə* in the Mellon Chansonnier. Therefore, as far as we are concerned, this rule holds: A final *ə* is elided before an initial vowel in the same line.

2. In the "epic decasyllable," in which the fourth syllable always receives word stress and almost always sentence stress, the fourth syllable is usually followed by a slight pause (the caesura). An *ə* that follows this fourth syllable is not counted; it seems to "fall into" the caesura, *between* the fourth and fifth syllables. As early as the fourteenth century this rule is violated in the "lyric decasyllable"; the fourth syllable may have *ə* as nucleus, of course unaccented. In spite of the terminology, which distinguishes "lyric" and "epic" types, lyric poems exist in which the epic rule is respected.

3. If the last syllable of a line has *ə* as nucleus, that syllable is not counted; it is considered as coming *after* the "last" syllable, as falling

into the pause after a line. Thus, a line that ends with *prise* (the accented vowel, *i*, being the eighth syllabic nucleus of the line) is regarded as octosyllabic. If a line ends in ə it is "feminine"; if it does not it is "masculine." Feminine lines may also end in -*e*, -*es*, or -*ent* (the verb ending of the third person plural).

It must be mentioned, although the elision of ə is not involved, that the vowel of *la*, feminine definite article and feminine direct object pronoun, is regularly elided before an initial vowel. This is a rule of grammar rather than of versification, and admits of no exception.

Of the meters found in Mellon's French songs, only the epic decasyllable has a strict accentual requirement: the fourth syllable (as well as the tenth) must receive a word stress. In the lyric decasyllable, the caesura must come after the fourth syllable, which must be the last syllable of a word. It follows that in the decasyllable, whether epic or lyric, no word begun in the first hemistich (syllables 1–4) continues into the second hemistich (5–10).

Here is a summary of the French decasyllabic poems of Mellon:

Epic: No. 35, *Tout a par moy* (l. 5 has *fortune*, with *tu* as fourth syllable).

Probably epic: No. 3, *Accueilly m'a la belle* (no ə at fourth place). No. 30, *Ma bouce rit* (same). No. 36, *S'il est ainsi* (l. 3, *Que feray je: je* is probably accented and pronounced [žə́] because in Old French it was regularly used in much the same way as the modern disjunctive pronoun *moi*). No. 53, *Puis que je vis le regart* (no ə in the crucial position).

Lyric: No. 7, *Est-il merchy* (l. 4 has *vostre*, with ə as fourth syllabic; similarly, l. 5 has *sceusse* [süsə], l. 7 *paine*). No. 8, *Ung plus que tous* (l. 3 *termes*). No. 21, *Le corps s'en va* (l. 6 *vostre*). No. 29, *Joye me fuit* (l. 4 *cesse*; l. 11 *estre*).

In no poem in the collection is there a mixture of rules, that is, no poem has some lines with uncounted, nonelided, caesural ə, other lines with ə as fourth syllabic.

The other meters have as their only prosodic requirement that the last counted syllable bear word-stress. In a "feminine" line an uncounted syllable with ə as nucleus may follow.

The Italo–Spanish Tradition

Italian meters are differently counted from the French in two respects. In the first place, the meter is named as if the line always consisted of one more syllable after the last stressed syllable. In other words a meter that would be called *décasyllabe féminin* by the French is by the Italians called the *endecasillabo piano*—a "normal" eleven-syllable line. If the tenth, stressed syllable is not followed by another syllable, the line is still considered to be of eleven syllables, but "truncated"—*tronco*; such a line would correspond to the French *décasyllabe masculin*. And if the tenth, stressed syllable is followed by two unstressed syllables, it is called *endecasillabo sdrucciolo*—a dactylic eleven-syllable line, even though it has twelve syllables. The same procedure is followed for the other meters: a line of five syllables, that is, one whose last stress is on the fourth syllable, is called a *quinario*; a seven-syllable line is a *settenario*, one of eight syllables an *ottonario*, one of twelve a *dodecasillabo*. According to the Italian tradition, the *endecasillabo* is the most noble meter, and its effect is said to be heightened in lyric poetry by a judicious admixture of *settenari*.

The second most important difference between French and Italian metrics has to do with the counting of syllables, particularly with respect to the treatment of two or more vowels in succession. In French this is hardly a problem: final, atonic -*e* [ə] is regularly elided before a word beginning with a vowel (with the optional, pre-Mellon exceptions noted above for such monosyllables as *que, se*), whereas a stressed final vowel is never elided. The classical French usage is to avoid vocalic sequences, but medieval French poets had no qualms about *hiatus*.

Italian has more variety in its unstressed final vowels (-*i*, *e*, *a*, *o*) than French (-*ə*), and its poetic tradition affords great flexibility in dealing metrically with vowel sequences. If we start with the situation in prose as representing a kind of norm, we can examine the liberties that versifiers may take with this norm.

The vowels *a*, *e*, and *o* are customarily syllabic; the word *poeta*, then, is normally three syllables. The vowels *i* and *u*, when unstressed, are generally nonsyllabic if contiguous to a syllabic in the same word; thus, *pianti* ("plaints") consists of two syllables. The combination of unstressed *i* or *u* with a syllabic (*a*, *e*, *o*) is called a diphthong (*dittongo*).

Now, if these rules were strictly followed in versification, there would be no more flexibility for the Italian poet than for his French colleague. But two principles facilitate his task: (1) diphthongs may be expanded to two syllables, and (2) successions of two or more syllables may be reduced to as few as one syllable, simply by pronouncing them all in the time ordinarily required for one syllable.

There is a restriction on the first rule: diphthongs resulting from phonetic changes in the passage from Latin to Italian may not be expanded to two syllables. For example, the *i* that comes from Latin *l* between a preceding consonant and a following vowel is never counted as a syllable. Examples are, *pianto* < Lat. PLANCTU, *fiore* < FLORE, *più* < PLUS. Similarly, Italian *ie* < Latin E (short, tonic, and free) and *uo* < O (under the same conditions) are not expansible to two syllables; thus, *piede* < PEDE cannot be counted as three syllables. Otherwise, *i* in combination with preceding or following *a*, *e*, or *o* may be treated as syllabic or nonsyllabic, according to the exigencies of the meter. As an example, *pietà* < PIETATE may be counted as two or three syllables.

These two principles apply whether such combinations of vowels occur within a word or between words. A pause or an important syntactic boundary may occur between words; even so, the contraction of a final vowel with the initial vowel of the following word (syneresis) is permitted. In No. 52, l. 4, for example, *posso—aymè* counts *-so ay-* as one syllable. A rule of thumb is that contractions are made more often than not, whatever the prose usage may be, between a final vowel and the initial vowel of the next word in the same line. The rare examples of syllable separation in such instances will be called to the attention of the reader in the notes accompanying the separate poems, but special notice is made now of No. 33, l. 8: *salvo en* separates the sequence *-vo en* into two syllables.

In the one Spanish song of the chansonnier (No. 44, *La pena sin ser sabida*), all the lines are of eight syllables, counted in the Italo–Spanish manner: one syllable past the last stressed syllable. In this poem the *versos llanos* (Italian, *versi piani*) alternate with *versos agudos* (*versi tronchi*). This meter corresponds to the French *heptasyllabe, féminin* and *masculin*, respectively.

There are rules for the patterning of the stresses of the Italian eleven-syllable line that have been admirably analyzed and explained by Patrick Boyde.[4] Stated very briefly, they are as follows: (1) Every hendecasyllable has a strong stress on the tenth position. We may call this stress the FIXED STRESS. (2) There is another strong stress on the fourth or the sixth position that we shall call, following Boyde, the DOMINANT STRESS. The word on which the dominant stress falls is followed by a caesura, that is, a break in the line manifested by a pause, a sudden

---

4. "The hendecasyllable," in *Dante's Style in His Lyric Poetry*, chap. 5.

change of tempo, or a change in the intonation contour. Thus the dominant stress divides the line into two unequal parts. (3) There is at least one more stress, not so important as the dominant stress, in the longer part of the line, in other words, in the second part of a line whose dominant stress is on the fourth position (such a line is called *a minore* in the theoretical tradition), or in the first part of a line (*a maiore*) with dominant stress on the sixth position.

Boyde provides charts showing statistical evidence on the frequency of the various patterns of stresses.[5] He designates a stress pattern with numerals representing the position of the fixed stress (always 10), of the dominant stress (*4* or *6*, italicized in his notation), and the subsidiary stress or stresses. The commonest pattern, for example, is 2-*4*-8-10, of which there are 105 examples in Dante's lyric poems. Boyde cautions his readers against undue extrapolation from his study of Dante's verse to Italian lyric poetry in general. Yet his analysis has proved useful and reasonable and certainly worth mentioning in connection with medieval Italian lyric poems.

Formes Fixes AND THEIR RELATION TO MUSICAL FORMS

The preponderant song form in this collection is the rondeau, used in 80 percent, or 46 of the 57 songs. Its musical form is X Y X X X Y X Y, each letter corresponding to a section. The segments of the poem that is sung to this form are the full refrain (R), the short strophe (s), the short refrain (r), the long strophe (S), and the repeated full refrain (R'). The musical sections correspond to the segments of the poem as follows:

$$X\,Y \quad X\,X \quad X\,Y \quad X\,Y$$
$$R \quad\ \ s\ \ r \quad\ \ S \quad\ \ R'$$

In the music as it appears in the manuscript, the end of X is usually marked by a corona.

The rhyme scheme of the rondeau is strictly keyed to the above schema. There are two rhymes, *a* and *b*. The long segments (R and S) have the same number of lines in a given poem, usually four or five, but sometimes six or seven or more. The typical four-line segment (quatrain) has the rhyme scheme *abba*, and the most frequent rhyme scheme of the five-line segment (cinquain) is *aabba*. The scheme is keyed to the melodic sections in such a way that the first line *b* is the

---

5. Ibid., pp. 226–35.

last line of melodic section X. Thus, in a four-line segment the first two lines, rhyming *ab*, are sung to X; the last, *ba*, to Y. In a rondeau cinquain, *aab* is sung to X, *ba* to Y. Hence the pattern X (*ab* or *aab*) Y(*ba*) evolves.

The primitive form of the rondeau (called variously rondel, rondet, triolet) is represented in the Mellon Chansonnier only by the second poem of No. 4, *Petitte Camusette*. Its long segments consist of only two lines, on *ab*, so that the one-line short segments cannot include the rhyme change. Its pattern, then, would be R (*ab*) s(*a*) r(*a*) S(*ab*) R′(*ab*). The second poem of No. 4 is incomplete because it lacks the long strophe.

Song No. 1 is an example of the rondeau quatrain *abba* (*ab*):

			Line nos.	
R	*a* ⎫ *b* ⎭	X	1 2	Bel Acueil, le sergant d'Amours, En bien soit faire ses esploys,
	b ⎫ *a* ⎭	Y	3 4	M'a ja cité par pluseurs foys D'aller a l'une de ses cours,
s	*a* ⎫ *b* ⎭	X	5 6	Et m'a chargé qu'a tous les jours Mettra deffault se je n'y voys.
r	*a* ⎫ *b* ⎭	X	1′ 2′	Bel Acueil, le sergant d'Amours, En bien soit faire ses esploys.
S	*a* ⎫ *b* ⎭	X	7 8	Et que se brief je n'y accours Ou mes conseulx secrés et choys,
	b ⎫ *a* ⎭	Y	9 10	Me bannira de vive voyx Et plus ne m'y fera secours.
R′	*a* ⎫ *b* ⎭	X	1″ 2″	Bel Acueil, le sergant d'Amours, En bien soit faire ses esploys,
	b ⎫ *a* ⎭	Y	3″ 4″	M'a ja cité par pluseurs foys D'aller a l'une de ses cours.

Here and in the Critical Apparatus we use primes to number the lines of the short refrain, double primes for the repetition of the long refrain.

Mellon rondeaux quatrains, *abba*, represent 21 percent, or 12 of the 57 songs of the chansonnier.

Song No. 2 exemplifies the rondeau cinquain, *aabba* (*aab*):

R	*a* ⎫ *a* ⎬ *b* ⎭	X	1 2 3	En soustenant vostre querelle Je maintiens que vous estes celle En tous les lieuls ou je m'enbas

	b } Y	4	Qu'il n'y a partout hault ne bas
	a	5	Dame qui de vous soit plus belle.
s	a }	6	Au monde n'a tel damoiselle,
	a } X	7	Et pour ce que vous estes telle
	b }	8	Trestous les jours je m'en combas
r	a }	1′	En soustenant vostre querelle;
	a } X	2′	Je maintiens que vous estes celle
	b }	3′	En tous les lieuls ou je m'enbas.
S	a }	9	Vostre beaulté pas je ne celle,
	a } X	10	Mais affin qu'il en soit nouvelle
	b }	11	A vous fort amer je m'esbas.
	b } Y	12	J'enprendroie mille debas
	a }	13	Pour en mourir de mort cruelle
R′	a }	1″	En soustenant vostre querelle.
	a } X	2″	Je maintiens que vous estes celle
	b }	3″	En tous les lieuls ou je m'enbas
	b } Y	4″	Qu'il n'y a partout hault ne bas
	a }	5″	Dame qui de vous soit plus belle.

Mellon rondeaux cinquains, $aabba$, represent 35 percent, or 20 songs.

We may construct a general formula for the rondeau on the principle that the end of melodic section X coincides with the end of the first line b; thus, the long segment (R or S) has the form $X(a[a]b)$ $Y(ba)$. The short segments, based on melodic section X, have the rhyme scheme $a(a)b$, which corresponds to the first part of the long segment.

One elaboration of the rondeau is called the rondeau layé. Typically it has more than five lines and varying line lengths, usually two (a four-syllable and an eight-syllable line, for example). It is more or less similar to the rondeau (usually cinquain) described above, but with insertions of short lines (rhyming in a or b) at certain places in the basic strophe. There are three rondeaux layés in Mellon.

Song 16 is a rondeau of six lines per long segment: aa^abba (aa^ab). The superscript letter represents a feminine four-syllable line; the other lines in this poem are feminine octosyllables. It is evident that the long segment, as represented by the octosyllables alone, is that of a regular rondeau cinquain, $aabba$, with a tetrasyllabic insertion on rhyme a after the second line.

Number 40 presents what appears to be the full refrain of a ten-line rondeau of alternating eight- and four-syllable lines: $a^ba^bb^aa^ab^a$; the basic strophe is of the unusual form, $aabab$. One could conjecture that the short strophe would have the form $a^b a^b b$, that is, the first part of the basic strophe as far as the first octosyllabic b- rhyme. This conjecture is supported by the appearance in the music of the corona over the syllable -*me* of the last word of 1. 5, *royaume*.

Song No. 41 is also a rondeau of six lines, $aa^b ba^b$ (aa^b), the super-script letters representing feminine tetrasyllables, the rest being feminine octosyllables. Upon abstraction of the tetrasyllables we appear to have $aaba$ (ba) as the basic pattern, with tetrasyllabic insertions on rhyme b after the second and fourth lines. But the basic strophe, like its short segment, is not a conventional one.

Number 48 is a rondeau of seven lines per long segment, the text's only poem of this description. Its rhyme scheme is $aa^a bb^b a$ $(aa^a b)$; the metrical variation is between octosyllables and tetrasyllables; the a rhymes are masculine, the b rhymes feminine. The basic long segment is $aabba$, with short segment aab a perfectly conventional pattern.

Although No. 27 has more than five lines in its long segments, we do not classify it as layé, since its lines are of equal length. It is a rondeau sixain in octosyllables, with rhyme scheme $aabaab$ (aab); the a rhymes are feminine, the b rhymes masculine.

There are several ways in which the short refrain (r) and the concluding full refrain (R′) may be integrated syntactically and semantically into the poem. First, the refrain can be autonomous—that is, the short strophe ends a sentence, and the short refrain forms a complete sentence. If the short refrain is to be autonomous, the full refrain must be composed as a loose construction so that a period may follow the first b rhyme without damage to sense or grammar up to that point. Mellon poems with autonomous r and R′ are Nos. 1, 3, 7, 10, 16, 20, 23, 26, 29, 38, 41, 50. Poems with autonomous r alone are Nos. 21, 24, 32, 56. Poems with autonomous R′ alone are Nos. 15, 18, 34.

Second, the refrain (short or long) may be integrated with the preceding segment, which clearly does not end a sentence and requires the following refrain to complete it. Sometimes the first line of a refrain is a more satisfactory completion of the sentence than is the whole of r or R′; we shall discuss this case below. Mellon poems with integrated r and R′ are Nos. 6, 8, 9, 13, 25, 27, 53. Poems with integrated r alone are Nos. 15, 18, 34. Poems with integrated R′ alone are Nos. 21, 24, 32, 56.

Third, the refrain's autonomy or integration may be ambiguous. That is, the strophe (short or long) may conclude satisfactorily as a complete sentence, and the following refrain may similarly enjoy autonomy—but the refrain can be interpreted with equal plausibility as concluding a sentence begun in the preceding strophe. We shall call this a syntactically ambiguous (or, simply, ambiguous) refrain. Song 51 exemplifies this form.

In some instances the refrain (r or R') may integrate its first line very satisfactorily with the preceding strophe (s or S), leaving a remainder that is syntactically and semantically acceptable, whether as a complete sentence or main clause, or as an element (adjectival or adverbial) subordinate to what precedes it. However, from the point of view of optimum sense, neatness, style, humorous point, or another such aesthetic consideration, one would prefer to suppress the remainder. In No. 2, for example, the expressive force of the first line of the refrain, which also serves as title (*En soustenant vostre querelle*), is increased upon repetition in ll. 1' and 1" if it is not followed by the remainder of the refrain, especially, in this poem, of the short refrain. Similarly, in No. 27, although the short and long refrains make perfect sense when presented in full, the force of the line, *Comme femme desconfortee*, would be intensified by the omission of the remainder, again especially in the short refrain.

A subtype of the ambiguous refrain is the "overlapping construction." The strophe may be logically concluded by its own last line or by the first line of the following refrain, but if the first line of that refrain (1' or 1") may provide a possible completion to the preceding strophe, the rest of the refrain cannot, for semantic or syntactic reasons, participate in that conclusion; yet, in order to fit the music, the whole of the refrain must be performed. If we take as example the s + r of rondeau quatrain, this means that ll. 5–6 make sense, as do ll. 5–1', and that ll. 1'–2' make sense as an autonomous refrain, but that the sequence ll. 5–2' does not make syntactic or semantic sense. We may represent this schematically for the s + r of a rondeau quatrain and of a rondeau cinquain as follows:

$$
\text{s}
\begin{array}{ll}
5 & a \\
6 & b
\end{array}
\left.\rule{0pt}{2.5em}\right]
\qquad \text{but not} \rightarrow \qquad
\text{s}
\begin{array}{ll}
5 & a \\
6 & b
\end{array}
$$

$$
\text{r}
\begin{array}{ll}
1' & a \\
2' & b
\end{array}
\left.\rule{0pt}{2.5em}\right]
\qquad\qquad\qquad\qquad
\text{r}
\begin{array}{ll}
1' & a \\
2' & b
\end{array}
\left.\rule{0pt}{2.5em}\right]
$$

```
  s   5   a ⌉⌉              s   5   a ⌉
      6   a |                   6   a |
      7   b ⌋|                  7   b |
                but not →
  r   1'  a ⌋⌉              r   1'  a |
      2'  a  |                  2'  a |
      3'  b ⌋                   3'  b ⌋
```

Confronted by this situation we may suppose either that the words are sung only to the point where they still make sense, or that they are sung to the end of the refrain, perhaps for a comic effect (or maybe simply disregarding the semantic or syntactic anomalies so produced), proceeding beyond the sentence that begins with the preceding strophe, to conclude the overlapping sentence begun at l. 1'. Thus,

$$\overline{5, 6, 1'.} \quad \text{or} \quad \overline{5, 6, 7, 1'.}$$
$$\underline{1', 2'.} \qquad\qquad \underline{1', 2', 3'.}$$

Or, going one line further into the short refrain of a rondeau cinquain,

$$\overline{6, 7, 8, 1', 2'.}$$
$$\underline{1', 2', 3'.}$$

Mellon No. 17 affords an example of such overlapping. But this song leads us ineluctably to consider another possibility, one we have alluded to lightly but which is important in the history of the rondeau as a poetical form, independent of the music: the first line, or the first hemistich, or even the first word of the first line of the refrain is the only part of the short refrain or of the concluding refrain that the poet intended to be realized as spoken words. In this event, if the poem was subsequently set to music, the musical refrain would have to be completed, while for purposes of recitation, nothing beyond this first fragment of the refrain, which we shall here call the TAG, is pronounced.[6] Number 17 may present an example of just such a tag, or

6. For the musical execution of such a poem, several possibilities suggest themselves. The first, already mentioned, is that the words are sung to the end of the refrain, possibly by singers who are not concerned with the meaning of the words, to an audience whose concern for the poetry is no greater than that of the musicians. But it is imprudent to assume that all practitioners and amateurs of this art form were equally insensitive to a poetic device that gives free expression to the ingenuity characteristic of the epoch, and so we must mention other logical solutions to the dilemma. If the words of the rest of the refrain are not sung to the end, the music of the refrain, whose completion is required by the musical form, could conceivably have been filled

it may be an example of overlapping construction. Its l. 8 is completed by the first hemistich of l. 1' (*Vostre bruit*), in which case the rest of l. 1', with ll. 2'–3', makes autonomous sense; or l. 8 is completed by all of l. 1', in which case ll. 2'–3' do not make sense and are better suppressed; or l. 8 is completed by half of l. 1', the rest of r being suppressed. But l. 13 must be followed by l. 1" and no more, which means that ll. 2"–5" must be suppressed. Aesthetically, the best effect seems to be achieved by completing the sentence begun in the short strophe with *vostre bruit* and that begun in the long strophe with *vostre bruit et vostre grant fame.*

Gaston Raynaud distinguishes between the *refrain incomplet*, a refrain cut back to its first line, and the *rentrement*, a refrain reduced to its first hemistich or less.[7] We use the word *tag* for both types of abbreviated refrain. Raynaud makes a good case for the existence of both types in the period that interests us. He indicates, and in this is supported by Pinet and Wilkins,[8] that Christine de Pisan may have been responsible for the introduction of the shortened refrain. This innovation may well have been suggested by the invariable scribal practice of indicating r and R' not by all the words (already written out for R), but just by a word or two of the first verse, followed by *etc.* or *&c*, which, however, being redundant for whoever understands the structure of the rondeau, could well be omitted and often was.

Such a scribal practice would not have sufficed, however, to institute such an important change in the form of the rondeau as poetry if it had continued invariably to be sung. But it is clear from the testimony of Eustache Deschamps (1346–1407) that already in the fourteenth century a "song" could be played by instruments alone or simply be recited with a speaking voice.[9] Thus a song unites two distinct "sciences," called by Deschamps *musique artificielle* (music, in the usual understanding of the term) and *musique naturelle* (poetry and its techniques). It is reasonable to suppose that the full repetition of r and R', without the support of music, would tend to be boring and that

out by instruments alone; or the refrain could have been completed vocally, not through words but through a long vocalise or melisma. These considerations are as applicable to No. 27 as to No. 17.

7. *Rondeaux et autres poésies du XVe siècle.*

8. Marie-Josèphe Pinet, *Christine de Pisan (1364–1430): Etude biographique et littéraire* (Paris: Champion, 1926), p. 242. Nigel Wilkins, *One Hundred Ballades, Rondeaux and Virelais from the Late Middle Ages*, p. 136, note to poem 71, pp. 91–92, "Que me vault donc le complaindre?"

9. "L'art de dictier," in *Oeuvres complètes*, vol. 7, pp. 266–92, esp. pp. 270–72.

their abridgment would bring a welcome change to recited poetry. In this situation, the unintentional suggestion made by the purely scribal abbreviation of the refrain would be warmly accepted by poets. And so it was, by Christine de Pisan and by many of the writers of rondeaux of the fifteenth century, and its practice continued among the poets of the sixteenth century.

Modern editions of fifteenth-century rondeaux tend to presuppose one or the other type of shortened refrain, even in those poems where sense and syntax do not support this hypothesis. Our editorial principle is conservative: we shall suppose completeness of r and R′ except where meaning and grammar make the tag clearly more plausible. In this way we can conserve the subtleties of refrain integration, with its varying syntactic structures, from one realization of the refrain to another within a given song. In this consists one of the most engaging aspects of the art of making rondeaux.

There are in Mellon seven bergerettes, or songs of that general description. Such poems are often referred to as virelais, but the latter term refers strictly to a more elaborate bergerette, as we shall explain.

The musical structure of the bergerette is $X\ Y_1\ Y_2\ X\ X$, the subscript numeral referring to the possibility of first and second endings for the Y sections. The corresponding poetic segments are refrain (R), ouvert (O), clos (C), strophe (S), refrain (R′).

Segments: R O C S R′
Sections: X Y Y X X

(The true virelai, of which we have no example in Mellon, is a triple bergerette, as follows: $R\ O_1\ C_1\ S_1\ R'\ O_2\ C_2\ S_2\ R''\ O_3\ C_3\ S_3\ R'''$; here the subscript numerals represent the introduction of new verbal material, all the Rs being exactly alike. The term *virelai* is often used in a generic sense to include the bergerette and even some non-French forms, such as the Italian *ballata* and the Spanish *villancico* and *canción*.)

The strophic segments (R and S) are on rhymes *a* and *b*, and the middle segments (O and C) introduce new rhymes, *c* and *d*. With regard to metric structure and rhyme scheme, R = S and O = C. Correspondence is not necessary, whether in rhyme scheme, verse length (measured in syllables), or segment length (measured in lines) between the strophic segment and the middle segment.

The strophic segments resemble the long segments of the rondeau:

we have three instances of $abba$ and one of $aabba$ in our small sample
(see table below). The middle segments are the ouvert and the clos,
each sung to Y; if Y has two endings, O is sung to Y_1, C to Y_2. The
rhyme scheme of a middle segment is cd or $cccd$ in Mellon (and ccd
and $ccccd$ in other collections).

No.	Title	Strophic segment (R, S)	Middle segment (O, C)
5	A une dame	$abba_8$	cd_8
12	Je ne puis vivre ainsy	$a_8a_8b_1b_8a_4a_8b_4$	cd_8
14	Ja que li ne s'i attende	$abba_7$	cd_7
31	Se je fayz dueil	$abba_8$	cd_8
36	S'il est ainsi	$aabba_{10}$	$cccd_8$
43	Triste qui sperò morendo	$abba_7,$*	$cd_7,$
44	La pena sin ser sabida	$ababa_7,$	$cd_7,$

*7′ means that the seventh syllable is accented and may be followed by one or two unaccented
syllables. Such a verse is called *ottonario* in Italian, *octosílabo* in Spanish. If the seventh syllable
is followed by an unaccented syllable, the verse is *piano* (*llano*); if not, it is *tronco* (*agudo*); if followed
by two unaccented syllables, it is *sdrucciolo* (*esdrújolo*).

The strophic segment of No. 12 is reminiscent of the long segment
of a rondeau layé, but if the tetrasyllabic lines are omitted the remaining
octosyllabic lines form a pattern, $aaba$, which is not one of the dominant
patterns of our rondeaux, nor is it listed in Raynaud's *Rondeaux et Autres
Poésies du XVe Siècle* (p. xlv). He also does not list the full formula with
his seven-line rondeaux layés (p. l). Finally, under *bergerettes doubles
layés* having strophic segments of seven lines (p. liv), the rhyme scheme
of our No. 12 is not listed.

Triste qui sperò morendo (No. 43) is apparently a truncated *barzelletta*,
which is a specialized type of ballata. The ballata in its conventional
form consists of the *ripresa* (R), the first and second *mutazioni* (M_1 and
M_2), and the *volta* (V). Like the virelai, it is usually a multiple of this
basic formula. The *stanza* itself consists of the mutazioni and the volta
($S = M_1 M_2 V$), and the whole poem is apt to number a ripresa plus
three or four stanze. The ballata is bound together by a pattern of
rhymes and, in many instances, of varying line lengths, usually of
seven- and eleven-syllable lines. The ripresa may consist of one to
five lines; the only constraint that its rhyme scheme exercises on the
volta, which has the same number and metrical pattern of lines, is
that the volta's last line must rhyme with the last line of the ripresa

and have the same number of syllables. Since the volta's first line, by another rule, must rhyme with the last line of the preceding mutazione, it is manifestly impossible for the volta to reproduce the rhyme scheme of the ripresa. A typical pattern would be (using capital letters to represent eleven-syllable lines, and lowercase letters for seven-syllable lines) R *Abba*; M$_1$ *CD*; M$_2$ *CD*; V *Deea*. The second stanza would continue in this pattern but with new rhymes, except that the volta would have to end in rhyme *a*, hence, *FG FG Ghha*. Typically, two or three more stanze would complete the poem.

The characteristics of the barzelletta that define it as a subtype of the ballata are (1) it consists entirely of eight-syllable lines, and (2) to the volta is appended a repetition of the first line of the ripresa.[10] The cycle is then ordinarily repeated several times, as follows (*a* here representing the first line of the ripresa and its repetitions): *abba cdcd deea a*, followed by *fgfg ghha a*, and so on. It is hard to see how the repetitions of *a* (which, Federzoni emphasizes, must be skillfully integrated with preceding material) would correspond to the music, unless we assume that the ripresa is repeated integrally in all four lines, much like the long refrain of the French rondeau. The description in HDM, s.v. "barzelletta," confirms this view.

The musical structure of the ballata is as follows: X Y Y X, or if it consists of several stanze, X Y Y X Y Y X Y Y X, and so on that is, X corresponds to R and to V, and Y to each mutazione. Song 43 is a variation, a simplification, of this form. We call it a ballata because of the musical structure X Y Y, but it lacks the volta, not because a hypothetical original volta has been lost, but because the final cadence of the music coincides with the end of the second mutazione. The rhyme scheme is consistent with the ballata structure: the ripresa has the enclosing rhyme *abba*, and the mutazioni have the crossed rhyme *cdcd*, each pair corresponding to section Y of the musical structure. We have not been able to find another example of such a truncated ballata.

The canción, No. 44, is a development of the villancico, with influence from the Provençal *dansa* and the bergerette; in fact, the present poem differs from the bergerette in only two respects. First, the favorite rhyme scheme of the Spanish five-line strophe (*quintilla*) is

---

10. Giovanni Federzoni, *Dei versi e dei metri*, p. 82.

a b a b a (as is that of our poem), unlike the more typically French *a a b b a*. Second, the first strophe (*tema*) is not wholly repeated, as is the French refrain; rather, the last part of the tema (in our poem, the last three lines) is repeated as part of the *vuelta*, the quintilla that comes after the middle section or *mudanza*, which corresponds to the ouvert and clos of the bergerette. The fit to the music is exactly that of the bergerette, except that the X section is repeated only once at the end of the canción, instead of twice, as it is for the bergerette.

The distinctions between villancico and canción are subtle. Pierre Le Gentil treats this problem lucidly and at considerable length in *La poésie lyrique espagnole et portugaise à la fin du moyen âge; Deuxième Partie: Les Formes*. The meat of it is contained in the following comments:

> The refrain of the *canción* is longer than that of the *villancico;* it consists normally, in fact, not of three lines but of four or five. . . . The *vuelta* of the strophe is normally characterized by complete symmetry between the rhyme scheme and the melodic structure; or, to put it another way, the *vuelta* reproduces exactly the rhyme scheme of the *initial theme* [the *tema*]—and this is never true of the *villancico*. . . . The *canción* is a short piece which as a rule has *but one stanza*, rarely two or three. . . . The *canción* is an essentially *courtly* and learnèd genre, almost exclusively concerned with amorous themes.[11]

The present song corresponds to this description in every respect. The device of using the last part of the first strophe as the last part of the vuelta is a frequent one in both canción and villancico, but not at all, as we have noted, in the bergerette.

The table below shows the structural resemblances of the bergerette and the strophic forms of the Spanish canción and the Italian ballata. The rhyme structures represented here are only typical, not invariable. The italics designate repeated lines. (X) refers to that section of music that is integral to the bergerette because of the repetition of the refrain, but absent from the canción. For the ballata, the Italian

11. "Le refrain de la *canción* est plus long que celui du *villancico;* il comporte, en effet, normalement, non pas trois, mais quatre vers ou cinq. . . . La *vuelta* de la strophe est caractérisée normalement par une symétrie complète entre le schéma des rimes et le schéma mélodique; autrement dit, la *vuelta* reproduit exactement le schéma du *thème initial*, ce qui ne se produit pas dans le *villancico*. . . . La *canción* est une pièce courte qui ne comporte en règle générale *qu'un seul couplet*, rarement deux ou trois. . . . La *canción* est un genre essentiellement *courtois* et savant, presque exclusivement réservé aux thèmes amoureux" ([Rennes, France: Plihon, 1952], p. 263).

convention is followed of using capital letters for eleven-syllable lines and small letters for shorter (usually seven-syllable) lines.

Bergerette		*Ballata*		*Canción*		*Music*
Refrain	*aabba*	Ripresa	*Abba*	Tema	a b *aba*	X
Ouvert	c d	Prima mutaz.	C D	Mudanza $\begin{cases} \text{c d} \\ \text{c d} \end{cases}$		Y
Clos	c d	Seconda mut.	C D			Y
Strophe	aabba	Volta	D e e a	Vuelta	a b *aba*	X
Refrain	*aabba*	Ripresa	*Abba*	———		(X)

The *oda* (No. 52, *Hora cridar "Oymè"*) is an Italian form of the fourteenth and fifteenth centuries consisting of several quatrains, either all in *aaab* or with changing rhymes in the same pattern with a linking rhyme between the quatrains: *abbc cdde effg*. ... The last line is of a different length from the others, according to Reese, a fact that tends to corroborate our analysis of the fourth line of each strophe of No. 52 as dodecasyllabic (see Textual Notes thereto). Because it is a strophic song (each strophe is sung to the same music), the metrical pattern is the same in each strophe. In No. 52 it is apparently 11, 11, 7, 12, and its rhyme scheme conforms to the description given above.

There are approximately five *ballades* in the collection; "approximately" because No. 54 involves several poems sung simultaneously, only one of which has the complete ballade strophe. The musical structure underlying one strophe of a ballade is $X_1 X_2 Y$. The subscript numerals refer to the possibility of first and second endings for the repeated section. Ideally, a ballade consists of three or four of these strophes and often has at the end a truncated strophe, called the *envoi*, sung to Y, and having the rhyme scheme of the Y part of the full strophe. None of the Mellon ballades is complete in this sense; they are recognizable by the rhyme structure and by their fit to the music.

The rhyme scheme of the part of the strophe corresponding to each X section is *ab;* hence a ballade always begins with *abab*. The rest of the ballade, sung to Y, is subject to considerable variation from one poem to another. It usually begins with *b*, introduces *c* in various patterns of couplets, crossed rhymes (*bcbc*), and enclosing rhymes (*bccb*), and often introduces *d*, sometimes *e*, and sometimes even *f*. The last line of the strophe, called the *refrain*, is repeated verbatim as the last line of every strophe, inclusive of the envoi. Since none of our ballades seems to have more than one strophe, we cannot logically call the last line a refrain. The most frequent ballade meter is the decasyllable (in English verse better described as the pentameter), and this is borne out by our small sample. (Asterisk indicates five stresses per line.)

		$X_1 X_2$	Y
45	*So ys emprentid*	$abab_{10}$	$bcbc_{10}$
47	*Myn hertis lust*	$abab*$	$bcc*$
49	*Or me veult bien*	$abab_{10}$	$abbcbc_{10}$
54	I. *Ma dame de nom*	$abab_5$	$cdcd_5$
	II. *Sur la rive de la mer*	$efef_7$	——
	III. *Il y a un clerc en ceste cité*	ce_{10} (not repeated)	——
	IV. *Holà durié*	?	——
55	*"Alas, alas, alas" is my chief song*	$abab_{10+1}$	$bcbc_{10+1}$

English poetry of the fourteenth and fifteenth centuries—notably Chaucer's—has examples of ballade-like strophes not called *balades* in the manuscripts. The only poems termed balades are those that consist of several strophes, each of which has the same last line (the refrain); apparently the envoi is not a necessary characteristic of the balade, if we consider the contemporary usage. One of Chaucer's favorite strophic forms was the rhyme royal, in $ababbcc$ and invariably in iambic pentameter. It was used with great effect in *Troilus and Criseyde*, a narrative poem written entirely in these strophes, without refrain of course, and each strophe having its own set of rhymes. Chaucer also used as few as one strophe of rhyme royal for comic effect.[12] The avowed "balades" of Chaucer are in eight-line ($abab$ $bcbc$) and seven-line rhyme royal ($abab$ bcc) strophes, each strophe having its own rhymes. The English poems of Mellon belong to this general category of ballade-like poems. They exhibit two different structures in the second part: No. 47 bcc, and Nos. 45 and 55 $bcbc$; that is, the strophes are of seven and eight lines, respectively.

The Italian *canzone* is uniquely exemplified by No. 46. It consists musically of one through-composed melody (the *ode*), or of a melody (*ode*) that consists of two musical sections (X and Y) at least one of which is repeated, yielding the possible structures XXY, XYY, and XXYY. As a poem, the canzone consists of several *stanze*, each

12. F[red] N[orris] Robinson, ed., "Chaucer's Words unto Adam, His Owne Scriveyn," in *The Works of Geoffrey Chaucer*, p. 534.

of which is sung to the full *ode*. When the first part of the *ode* is unitary, the part of the *stanza* that is sung to it is called, in Italian, the *fronte* (in Latin, *frons*); when binary, the corresponding part of the poem is said to consist of two *piedi* (*pedes*), or "feet." When the second part is unitary, the corresponding part of the poem is called, in both Italian and Latin, the *sirima* or *sirma;* it is also called the *coda* (*cauda*). When Y is repeated, the corresponding parts of the text are called the *volte* or *giri* (*versus*).

As is true of most Italian lyric verse, a patterned mixture of long lines (usually of eleven syllables) and short lines (most often of seven syllables, sometimes of five) is favored. The rhymes of the piedi are usually three in number (*a*, *b*, *c*) but do not follow the same pattern in each piede. Using the traditional notation of Italian metrics, in which capital letters represent long lines, lowercase letters short ones, such patterns as the following are frequent: *ABbC*, *CAaB*, in which (1) both piedi have the same pattern of line lengths (XXxX) and (2) all the rhymes of the first piede are repeated in the second, but in a different order. When the piedi are followed by a sirima, the first line of the sirima rhymes with the last line of the preceding piede. When the second part of the stanza consists of two volte, each volta must have the same pattern of line lengths as the other, and all the rhymes of the first must be repeated in the second. Aside from the first line of the sirima (the *verso chiave*, or "key line"), the second part of the stanza introduces new rhymes not present in the first part.

The Language of the French Poems*

Although the dates of the beginning and the end of Middle French (MF) vary considerably from one authority to another, there is no doubt that the language of the fifteenth century represents this phase to perfection. As its name implies, it is "in the middle"—that is, a stage of transition from Old French (OF) to modern French (modF). The reason for the lack of agreement about the chronological limits of Middle French is that different scholars have used different criteria for the definition of the transitional stages. A familiarity with fifteenth-century French is essential to the understanding and pronunciation of the text of the Mellon Chansonnier. To this end, we offer below a summary of the features of Middle French in Mellon (and, when used, in the concordant sources), which will be unfamiliar to the reader whose

---

*A glossary of linguistic terms begins on p. 120.

knowledge of French language and literature is restricted to the period beginning in the seventeenth century.

The pronunciation of Middle French is impossible to determine with minute precision but can be known within certain limits. For practical purposes (singing these songs, reciting this poetry), we can pronounce like modern French (modified in ways to be specified later) words that have subsisted to modern times. For words that have not survived, we shall have to establish specific procedures by which a plausible pronunciation can be proposed according to spelling, evidence furnished by the rhyme, and knowledge of etymology.

There have been important changes in morphology (the forms of verbs, pronouns, nouns, and adjectives) and in syntax since Middle French that will be briefly discussed below. Reference to Old French will be made only when it appears to be in the best interests of the clear description of fifteenth-century French but especially when the latter appears to be inconsistent or patternless. Much of the seeming capriciousness of the language we are to explore is due to dialect mixture, which is often best understood in the light of the history of dialectal divergence since the end of the Archaic French period (up to early twelfth century) or since the Old French period. Problems of detail will be taken up in the Textual Notes to the poems.

Pronunciation

Vowels	Front	Central*	Back	
High	i	ü	u	
Mid	e, ə	ö	o	
Low		a		(Length: [:])
Nonsyllabic	y	ẅ	w	

*Also describable as front and rounded for the high and mid vowels.

The mid vowels range more or less freely between the open and close qualities of the corresponding vowels of modern French, which have been separated and redistributed according to a new set of rules in the process of development since the seventeenth century. Therefore, we shall not attempt to be more specific in our transcription. Middle French [e] in open syllables before the stressed syllable apparently had a rather lax pronunciation ranging between the [ɛ] and the [ə] of modern French, but without the lip-rounding of the latter. In the final, posttonic syllable it was probably closer to [ə], that is, with the tongue somewhat retracted, but again not rounded to the same degree as the modern vowel. We shall use this symbol, [ə], in our phonetic transcriptions for this value in final syllables. It seems probable that the slightly lengthened vowel [e:] in words that had had preconsonantal [s] had less retraction of the tongue. Thus *desconfort*, also spelled *deconfort*, had a vowel in its first syllable that tended less to [ə] and more toward [e] than the pretonic vowel of *querir*: [de:kõⁿfort], [kərir]. Thus Middle French did not have contrasting vowel patterns as in modF *répéter, relever, reléguer, jeter, céder*. Final, unaccented -*e* [ə] is pronounced except when followed without pause by a word beginning with a vowel.

Similarly, our phonetic transcription of Middle French does not distinguish open and close [o]. The diphthong spelled *au* (from OF *al* + consonant), which was pronounced [o] in Ile-de-France, still has its diphthongal pronunciation outside the central area. Furthermore, because from both internal and external evidence most of our poems appear, to have been composed in the north and east, we recommend [aw] (*ou* of English *house*) in words such as *autre* and *aultre* [awtrə].

Study of the rhymes shows apparent inconsistencies, which are due mostly to mixture of dialects. In several cases the dialect of a given poet is transcribed by a copyist who speaks another dialect and whose writing habits reflect his own speech rather than the poet's. For this reason we offer the following suggestions for the pronunciation of the graphies *o, ou, eu,* and *u*, which are particularly subject to confusions of this sort.

In words in which *o* and *ou* are used interchangeably, in different occurrences of the same word in this collection, or even in the same poem, they are both to be pronounced *ou* [u] if they occur before the word stress. For example, the first syllable of *dolour, douleur* is [du], as if spelled *dou-*.

Some poems have *ou* and/or *eu* or *ue* in the rhyming syllable. If all the words so affected correspond to modern French words with *eu* or *oeu* [ö], however they may be spelled, they are to be pronounced with [ö]. If it appears by the same criterion to be a consistent *ou*-rhyme, pronounce them all with [u]. If they are mixed between modF *ou*-types and *eu*-types rhyming together, pronounce them all [u]. In this last instance the poet's dialect is not Francian (of Ile-de-France), in which OF *ou*, accented and in an open syllable, became *eu;* in his dialect it remained *ou*. In No. 15, for example, *douleurs* rhymes with *plours* (= Francian and modF *pleurs*), as well as with *amours, tours, jours, lours* (= *lourds*), and *secours*. Despite the Francian spelling of *douleurs*, it is clear that all these words end in [-urs].

In a few poems rhyming in *eu*, the combination corresponds for some words to modF *eu* [ö], in others to *u* [ü], especially in such past participles as *peu, leu, sceu*, or preterites such as *j'eus, receus* (spelled with *x* instead of *s*, for eye rhyme, in No. 53). A solution in terms of dialect, like the solution proposed to the *ou* / *eu* problem, is again possible. These forms in Old French had endings in two syllables: [pəü], [ləü], [səü], [žəüs], [rəsəüs] (= modF *pu, lu, su, j'eus, reçus*). During the fourteenth century this combination was reduced to one syllable. The Francian solution was [ü] (for example, as in modF *lu*), while in dialects peripheral to Ile-de-France, especially in the west and northwest, it was [ö].[13] Adopting this solution for No. 53, the rhyming vowel would be [ö], even for *j'eux* and *receux*. However, this poem appears to present a pattern such that (Francian) [ü] occurs in the fourth line of each of the full quatrains, the refrain, and the long strophe. The sample is too brief to rule out the possibility of coincidence, but if there is a pattern in the distribution of [ö] and [ü], the poem has two rhyme schemes: one for the eye, *a b b a*, one for the ear, *a b b c*.

The *a*-rhyme of No. 21 is [örə] for the most part, but ll. 6–7 (that is, the two *a*-lines of the short strophe) have *seure* and *asseure*, both of which would be pronounced with [ürə] in Francian. Is this a patterned deviation from the ear rhyme, or is this non-Francian [örə]? Probably the latter, for a deviation of phonetic rhyme at the halfway point in the rondeau would probably shock the ear and seem to violate a pattern rather than to create one. We recommend [örə].

In No. 5, l. 9 *sceu* is isolated among rhyming words in [ö]; it is therefore pronounced [sö]. (See also 7.7 [No. 7, l. 7] *sceusse* and 21.12 *deusse*, for which neither [ö] nor [ü] can be confidently affirmed, since they are not involved in the rhyme.)

For a reader who is not a specialist in Old French, the recourse to modern French as a mirror of Francian is reasonably safe, but it can lead to error when an Old French or Middle French word is mistakenly identified with a modern word. For example, in No. 29, *seure* might seem, because of its semantic and formal resemblance to modF *sur*,

13. M[ildred] K. Pope, *From Latin to Modern French*, § 245.

to correspond to an OF *[səürə], later Francian *[sürə] (an asterisk is placed before a hypothetical or conjectural form). However, such an assumption is mistaken because in Francian the Old French form was [sörə].

Another instance in which recourse to modern French may lead to error is that of No. 48, l. 15 *meure* 'mulberry'. Although it corresponds to modF *mûre*, it was never *[məürə] in Old French, but [mörə]. The modern form has undergone the influence of *mûrier* 'mulberry tree', whose first syllable reflects a relatively late regular phonetic change from [ö] to [ü] in an open syllable in pretonic position. Since it never happens in Mellon that the Middle French vowel descended from OF [əü] rhymes with a simple [ü], it appears most reasonable to assume that the vowel with which it does rhyme, namely [ö], indicates its pronunciation.

Middle French differs markedly from Old French in that it no longer has falling diphthongs (that is, whose first element is syllabic and the second nonsyllabic) of the type [ey], [ow]—with the exception of the non-Francian [aw] from OF [al], to which we have referred. The graphy *oi, oy* usually represents the rising diphthong [we]. Here again we have an acute problem of dialect mixture for modern French because of mixture of dialects with respect to the products of AF [ey] and [oy] (AF = Archaic French [before the twelfth century]). Archaic French [ey] remains [ey] in Old Norman and becomes [oy] in Old Francian, joining the already existing [oy] (cf. *rei, roi* 'king'). Before nasal consonants, AF [ey] remains as such in western Old Francian and becomes [oy] in the eastern part of the central region (*fein, foin* 'hay'). Near the beginning of the Middle French period there is a generalized trend toward the monophthongization or leveling-out of falling diphthongs: [ey] becomes [e], [oy] becomes [we]. Late in the Middle French period a tendency developed to reduce [we] to [e], particularly after initial [r] or an initial cluster consisting of stop + [r]. That is why modern French shows a bewildering mixture of [wa] (the modern product of MF [we]) and [e] (in a variety of spellings) in words whose phonetic history seems about the same. Compare *veine* [ven] < VĒNA, but *avoine* [avwan] < AVĒNA; or *roide* and *raide*, which go back to the same Latin word, RIGIDUS. Modern French does not represent any particular dialectal distribution of the words as they occurred in Middle French because its vocabulary is largely borrowed from dialects neighboring Ile-de-France.

How are we to pronounce the graphy *oi* (or *oy*) in the Mellon poems?

In the first place the possibility should always be considered that *oi* is the scribe's response to *ei* or *ai* in the text he is copying. It is useful to know the etymology of the word concerned, but in most instances even with this aid the question will remain open as to the choice between [we] and [e] unless the rhyme offers clear evidence. For if the rhyme is not rich, [we] does in fact rhyme with [e]. In some cases the etymology settles the question. For example, in No. 1, l. 2 *soit* = modF *sait* (because this word was never pronounced with a diphthong, [se] imposes itself). I recommend the pronunciation of the imperfect and conditional endings *-oye, -oyes, -oit, -oyent* with [e]: [-eyə], [-eyəs], [-et], [-eyət].

A vowel followed by a nasal consonant is nasalized, even if (as is not true for modern French) the nasal consonant is followed by a vowel): *amer* [ãmer] 'to love; bitter'. When the nasal consonant is followed by another consonant, it is often not fully articulated, so that in some occurrences the nasal vowel is followed directly by a nonnasal consonant, as in modern French. Thus, for MF *plainte*, [plẽntə] varies freely with [plẽtə], the latter being the only pronunciation sanctioned by modern standard French. For details, see below the discussion of nasal consonants. The vowels [i] and [ü] retain their quality when nasalized: [ĩ], [ũ]; in modern French they have become [ẽ] and [õ], respectively.

	Labial	Dental	Palatal	Velar	Faucal
Stops	p b	t d	—	k g	—
Spirants	f v	s z	š ž	—	h
Nasals	m	n	ñ	ŋ	—
Laterals	—	l	l' *	(ł) †	—
Trill	—	r	—	(ʀ) ‡	—

* [l'] is pronounced like the *ll* of Castilian Spanish; it has since become a semivowel [y] in modF.
† Phonetically [ł] had ceased to exist in MF; it occurred in OF after a vowel and before a consonant; OF [ł] > MF [w].
‡ The velar [ʀ] of modF had not yet come into existence.

In both Old and Middle French, no word ends in a voiced stop [b d g] or spirant [v z ž] unless, by the elision of *-e* before a word beginning with a vowel the consonant thus becomes final. Put another way, the sequence *voiced stop or spirant + pause or open juncture* does not occur. A verb stem that ends in a voiced stop or spirant (that is, which has such a consonant before a verb ending, like *gard-er* or *trouv-er*) realizes that consonant as voiceless before a zero ending (OF *je gart; je truef*). Similarly, an adjective that has a voiced stop or spirant before the feminine ending *-e* (such as *longue* [loŋgə], *gratïeuse* [grasiözə], *brieve* [bryevə]) realizes that consonant as voiceless before the zero ending of the masculine (*lonc* [loŋk], *gratïeus* [grasiös], *brief* [bryef]). A final stop continues to be voiceless in "liaison," that is, in close juncture with a following word beginning with a vowel (for example, the modF pronunciation of *un grand homme*, in which *d* = [t], is a continuation of that rule). The spirants [f] and [s] of such adjectives are realized as [v] and [z] in liaison.

It may be said in general that the transition from Old French to Middle French is marked by the reduction of consonant clusters. Of particular importance for the interpretation of Middle French spellings are the transformations undergone by [l] and [s] before a consonant. In a word such as OF *altre* 'other' the *l* was pronounced rather far back in the mouth, as in the American pronunciation of *milk*, with a "dark l" [ł] having a definite *u*-coloring [miłk], or even, with total loss of consonantal articulation, that is, now fully vocalic, as [miwk]. In much the same way, after a period of free vacillation between [ałtrə] and [awtrə], the *l* was completely vocalized. The orthography kept pace with *autre*, but conservative writing habits enforced a compromise with the frequent spelling *aultre*, which combines past (*l*) with present (*u*). The *l* was absolutely without phonetic function in such a word and was often introduced where it had *never* been pronounced. An example is the use of *gratieulx* to represent a word whose suffix came from the Latin -ōsus through the influence of a more justifiable *mieulx*, from *mieus*, itself from an older *miels*, ultimately from Latin MELIUS.

Similarly, [s] disappeared before a consonant, leaving as a trace the lengthening of the preceding vowel. It is supposed that the sibilant became first an *h*, that is, a voiceless vowel of the same timbre as the preceding vowel, and then was voiced, joining with the preceding vowel as one long vowel. The total duration of the syllable was thus conserved: vowel + [s] became vowel + [h], and this [h] became a vowel of the same duration as the [h] had been. Thus OF *feste* must have gone through these stages ([*e̥*] will represent voiceless [e], or [h] with [e]-quality): [festə] > [feh̥tə] (= [fee̥tə]) > [feetə] (= [fe:tə]). The lengthening was probably less marked for an unaccented vowel. The result is that Middle French words whose spelling reflects OF preconsonantal [s] are not to be pronounced with [s]. During the sixteenth century and since, a number of words have had the [s] restored for a variety of reasons. Subsequently, even though in a given word modern French pronounces the *s*, Middle French did not. For example, *jusque* is MF [žü:kə], and even *esploys* (< OF esploiz [esployts]) is pronounced in Middle French [e:plwes]. The modF *exploits* [eksplwa] contains a cluster of consonants that would have been inconceivable in the fifteenth century.

Evidence for this change is to be found in "spelling mistakes." The omission of *s* (as in *juque*) is no less indicative than its inappropriate use: *resconfort*, probably spelled in analogy with *desconfort*, both pronounced without the *s*, the latter word having the prefix *des-*, the former *re-*. Some scholars claim that *esprit* and words formed on the root *esper-* 'hope' have always pronounced the *s*.

The reduction of the s + consonant cluster eventually had its effect at word boundaries. Whereas in Old French a final consonant was pronounced regardless of what followed it, in Middle French a final stop or spirant was dropped if another word following without pause began with a consonant. Thus in Middle French a final stop or spirant was pronounced only if succeeded by a pause, an open juncture, or an initial vowel (liaison). As a result the rhythm of Middle French came to be characterized by a succession of syllables mostly in the consonant –vowel pattern. These general tendencies make the nasal consonants subject to several observations.[14]

In Old French a nasal consonant followed in the same word by another consonant was pronounced with the same articulation as that

14. Modern French has made the following changes in the system of nasal vowels and consonants. The nasal consonant before pause or open juncture, as well as the preconsonantal nasal, are no longer articulated: [ãpriz], [tyẽdre], [mòbyẽ], and so forth. Since the sixteenth century the high vowels [i ü] have been lowered to [ẽ õ], respectively, when nasalized. A further reduction in the number of nasal vowels is now in progress in popular French of the region of Paris in that [õ] has gone to [ẽ], but the conservative pronunciation of [õ] is still widespread.

Another significant prosodic change in modern French is that a vowel preceding a nasal consonant that is itself followed by a vowel (VNV) has been denasalized. Thus (ãmi] has become [ami], [fĩnə] has become [finə], then [fin]. *Femme* [fãmə] has become [famə], then [fam]. In this way modern French has a rule very different from the old rule: A vowel followed by a nasal consonant is never nasalized (e.g., [fam]); only a vowel not followed by a nasal consonant may be nasalized: *faim* [fẽ], *plainte* [plẽt]. An exception to this rule often adduced is *emmener* [ãmne], which contrasts with *amener* [amne]. But more and more, French people fail to make the distinction and pronounce them both without the nasal vowel.

consonant (labial, dental, palatal, or velar): labial, *enprise* (also spelled *emprise* [ãmprizə]; dental, *tendray* (future of *tenir*) [tãndre]; palatal, *manche* [mãňšə]; velar, *encore* [ãŋkorə]. As the phonetic transcriptions show, every vowel preceding a nasal consonant was nasalized.

Middle French was characterized by an optional relaxation of the articulation of a nasal consonant followed by another consonant. The nasalization of the preceding vowel is a sufficient indication that the nasal consonant is "there"—and since the articulation of the nasal consonant is necessarily that of the following consonant, the full articulation of the nasal as [m n ň ŋ] has become redundant and may be omitted. Thus [ãmprizə] varies freely with [ãprizə], [tãndre] with [tãdre], and so on. In subsequent transcriptions of Middle French we shall symbolize the nasal whose articulation is predictable (when articulated) and which varies with zero by a superscript [n] and will not mark the vowel with the tilde, since any vowel followed by [n] will be understood to be nasalized: [a^{n}prizə], [ta^{n}dre], [ma^{n}šə], and so on.

A nasal consonant at the end of a word is pronounced [ŋ] if a pause or an open juncture follows, [n] if followed by an initial vowel. It is pronounced with the same articulation as a following initial consonant; or, as within the word, the articulated nasal varies freely with zero, the preceding vowel being nasalized. (Examples are 20.12 [= No. 20, 1. 12] *bon an* [bõnãŋ], 3.2 *mon bien* [mõ(m)byẽŋ], 20.12 *bon jour* [bõ(ň)žur], 13.10 *mon cueur* [mõ(ŋ)kör], or, in the simplified transcription, [bo^{n}a^n], [mo^{n}bye^n], [bo^{n}žur], [mo^{n}kör], respectively.) It is evident that the various articulations of the nasal consonant do not stand in contrast in word-final position—the differences are neutralized.

Morphology

Nouns and adjectives

Old French had a declensional system for nouns and adjectives that distinguished two cases, nominative and oblique, and whose forms, generally speaking, derived from the Latin nominative and accusative, respectively. For most masculine nouns and adjectives, the nominative was marked in the singular by the ending -*s*, and the oblique case was marked by its absence (or by a "zero" ending). In the plural, it was the converse: nominative, zero; oblique, -*s*. A typical adjective–noun combination, with the definite article to disambiguate these forms, is *li bons murs, le bon mur; li bon mur, les bons murs.* It is evident that modern written French has conserved the oblique forms. The feminines derived from the Latin first declension do not distinguish case formally: singular, *la bele rose,* plural, *les beles roses.*

During the transitional movement between Old French and Middle French (ca. 1250–ca. 1400) there were two contrary tendencies. On the one hand, the nom. sg. -*s* was extended sporadically in the manuscripts to masculine forms that did not originally have it (*pere*[*s*] < Lat. PATER). On the other hand, the declensional system was undergoing rapid decay in the spoken language. The French of the manuscripts represents a conscientious effort on the part of both authors and scribes to preserve a respected tradition in the face of contrary habits of speech. The number of violations of the Old French declensional system steadily increases in the manuscripts until the late fourteenth century and early fifteenth centuries, when by an almost universal assent the writing begins to reflect the new situation: the syntactic function of nouns is now assumed by word order; -*s* is for the most part simply the sign of the plural, and by this very important criterion Old French is surely dead.

As an example of the transitional state between the two systems, "L'art de dictier" of Eustache Deschamps, a treatise on versification dated 1392, does not exhibit the declensional system in its expository prose, whereas the illustrative poems, many of them composed by Deschamps himself, observe the Old French case system.

There are not many vestiges left of the nom. sg. -*s* in the Mellon poems. A few examples are: *Amours,* name of the god of love, in 1.1; 48.2 *plains,* .13 *attains,* and .14 *tains* are masc. sg. adjectives (see the Textual Notes to these two poems).

As for the gender of adjectives, the final -*e* (from Latin -A) and its absence are useful markers in modern written French of the feminine and masculine genders, respectively. The usefulness of this criterion is limited only by the existence of adjectives (such as *roide*) that end in -*e* in both genders. In Old and Middle French, besides this qualification there was the converse one: the existence of adjectives that ended in a consonant in both genders. These words were for the most part from (1) Latin adjectives of the third declension, especially the present participles in -ANTEM (> -*ant,* for example, 23.8 *La plus cuysant de ce royame,* where the *d-* of the following word shows that it was not in the original poem an adjective in -*ante,* whose -*e* would have been elided before a vowel; another example of a feminine is -*ant* in the adverb 21.4 *incessamment*, derived by adding -*ment* to the feminine adjective *incessant*); (2) adjectives in -*al* borrowed from Latin words in -ALEM (the following adverb consisting of the feminine form of an adjective + -*ment*: 12.6 *Léaument* < *loyal* + -*ment*); and (3) adjectives in -*el* inherited from Latin adjectives in -ALEM, such as *tel* < TALEM, *quel* < QUALEM (2.6 *tel damoiselle*). Such forms coexisted from the Old French to the end of the Middle French periods with corresponding feminines with added -*e* (7: *souffissante*, *puissante*, and so on). The resulting choice was a great metrical convenience for the poets.

Verbs

Present Stem (Present Indicative, Present Subjunctive, Infinitive, Present Participle).

Many verbs have vowel alternation in the stem (cf. modF *meur-* when the stem is stressed, *mour-* when the ending is stressed). In modern French such alternation no longer occurs in the -*er* verbs (first conjugation), but into the sixteenth century even they were not exempt.

The stressed stem of a verb with vocalic alternation is STRONG, and so is the vowel of that stem (e.g., *meur-*, *eu*); the unstressed stem and its vowel are WEAK (*mour-*, *ou*). In the poems of Mellon, only two alternations emerge: *eu/ou* and *ien/en*. By a process of leveling, here generalization of the strong (or weak) vowels to all the forms of a paradigm, a strong vowel is often found in a weak stem, and vice versa.

Examples of strong vowel in strong stem: 29.5 *meure*; 29.6 *labeure* (modF has generalized *ou*); 29.7 *pleure* (cf. 31.11 *plourant*) (modF has generalized *eu*); 29.10 *saveure* (infinitive usually *savourer* in the fifteenth century) (modF generalizes *ou*); 13.7 (je) *veuil*, 13.1 *veuille*, 40.7. *veult* (modF keeps *eu/ou*); 38.7, 12 (je) *treuve* (modF generalizes *ou*).

Weak vowel in weak stem: 15.12 *trouver*; 26.13 *flourir* (modF generalizes *eu*, probably influenced by the noun *fleur*); 49.5 *voloir* (*o* is a frequent spelling for *ou* [u]); 17.7 *tendray* (future of *tenir*):

Weak vowel in strong stem: 1.7 *accours* (but see discussion of *ceurt*, *sequeure* below).

Strong vowel in weak stem: 14.10 *tiendray* (cf. *tendray* above); 17.12 *vueillez*, 42.5 *veulliés* (both as imperative, as in modF).

It appears from this small sample that in modern French, the leveling process has gone much further since the fifteenth century, mostly in the direction of generalizing *ou* in the *-er* verbs. The one apparent case of a weak vowel in a strong stem is not a real one, because the *eu/ou* alternation found in derivatives of *courir* (OF *courre*) is not the result of normal phonetic change but of analogy. The vocalic alternation of *eu* and *ou* arose as a result of the Francian phonetic change by which an original [ǫ], which had been free and tonic in Vulgar Latin, became [ew], then [ö] in Francian. The Latin root of this verb terminated in [rr] (CURR-ERE) so that the stem vowel was not free, hence not subject to this change. The appearance of forms with *eu* is to be ascribed to the influence (analogy) of verbs of similar shape showing vocalic alternation, as in the following proportion: *mourons* : *meurt* :: *courons* : (*ceurt, queurt*). That such an analogy was at work is shown by the replacement of OF *courre* by modF *courir*, probably modeled on *mourir*. It seems more likely that the forms of this verb keeping *ou* in modern French are the result of continuous use than that they are the result of leveling (for example, 29.1 *ceurt*, 29.2 *sequeure* [subjunctive], but 1.7 *accours*).

First person singular, present indicative

The Latin ending in -ō either dropped completely from the French form or remained as *-e* [ə] if the verb stem in Vulgar Latin (VL) ended in a consonant + *l* or *r*. In the first instance, that of the zero ending, the bare stem that was left ended in Archaic French in one of the following ways: (1) in a vowel, if the VL stem ended in a vowel, or in a vowel + dental or velar stop; (2) in a sibilant (dental or palatal spirant), if the VL stem ended in *s* or in any voiceless stop, before VL -yō (< Classical Latin -ēō or - īō); (3) in a consonant in all remaining cases: VL stem ending in a trill, lateral, or nasal, or a labial stop or spirant.

By the beginning of the Middle French period these categories were exercising reciprocal influences so that in Mellon we find the following inherited and analogically altered forms (the list is illustrative, not exhaustive):

1. Inherited *-e*: 27.6 *desire* (< VL DESID'RO).

2. Analogical *-e*: 2.9 *celle* (with change in stem vowel: cf. OF *çoil*); 11 II.2 *chante*; 12.17 *noye*; 14.12 *amande*; 21.7 *asseure*; 23.1 *supplie*; 54 I.6 *ayme*, 29.13 *demeure*, 38.7 *treuve* (cf. OF *truef*).

3. Inherited stem-final vowel: 11 II.1 *voy*; passim *ay*; 26.1 *doy*, 26.7 *suy*; 29.9 *sçay*; 40.6 *mercy*.

4. Analogical stem-final vowel (by removal of original final consonant): 11 II.2 *fay*.

5. Inherited stem-final consonant: 7.9 *puis* (< VL *POTE̩O); 28 IVA.1 *veuil* (< VL VOLE̩O); 30.14 *vif* (< VĪVŌ).

6. Analogical stem-final consonant (addition of a consonant, viz., -*s*, probably in analogy with -*ir* verbs in -SCO, such as OF *fenis* < VL FINISCO): 1.7 *accours*; 2.8 *combas*; 11 II.4 *ris*; 15.6 *tiens*; 18.7 *suis*; 28 III.7 *prens*, 29.6 *dors*; 30.14 *meurs* (replacing OF *muir* < VL *MORIO < CL MORIOR).

Present subjunctive

Whereas in Old French there was a special set of endings for the present subjunctive of -*er* verbs, Middle French had generalized the set of endings still used in modern French (-e, -es, -e, -ions, -iez, -ent), which in Old French were characteristic of the other conjugations. The only survivor in Mellon of the OF -*er* subjunctive (which added zero or a consonant to a bare stem in the singular forms) is *gard* [gart], which appears in two of the songs of the combinatorial chanson, No. 28 (I.10 and III.1). In both instances *Dieu* is the subject of an optative verb, suggesting a formulaic use that tends to preserve archaisms (cf. the subjunctives of English *God bless you* and *if you please*).

The two verbs *avoir* and *estre* have preserved in Middle French an irregular pattern of endings in the singular: -*e*, -*es*, -*t*, which probably spread from *estre* to *avoir*. However, in modern French only *avoir* has kept this pattern, whereas the present subjunctive of *être* has adopted the -*s* -*s* -*t* set of endings, which are not found in the present subjunctive of any other French verb.

The special stems of the subjunctive occurring in some modern French irregular verbs (e.g., *puiss*-, *sach*-) are direct continuations of the earlier stages of the language. They are the result of the contact of stem-final consonant with the palatalizing [y] from the VL endings -YA, -YAS, and so on, from CL -EAM, -IAM, -EAS, -IAS, and so forth. Examples from Mellon are 8.5 *veulle* [völ'ə], 28 I.2 *sace* [sašə], 53.9 *puisse*, 36.12 *faille*.

Personal pronouns

The personal pronouns denoting the subject do not accompany their verbs as inevitably as they do in modern French. If a subject of a verb is ascertainable from the context, the pronoun is frequently omitted. Most often it is present when there is a change of subject; if it initiates a chain of verbs having the same subject, one pronoun usually suffices. If a pronoun beginning with a vowel is in an inversion (interrogative or otherwise) with a verb ending in a vowel, the resulting hiatus is tolerated, well into the sixteenth century (14.5 *a-il*).

The personal pronouns *je*, *tu*, and *il*, unlike those of modern French, may be stressed for emphasis: 36.3 *Que feray je*, and, by conjecture, to be sure, 38.1 *Enfermé suis je* (see textual notes on the poems in question).

There is one example of the feminine stressed pronoun of Old French, *li*, in 14.1, on which an elaborate pun depends: *Ja que li ne....* The Cop and Dij variant, *lui*, shows that the pun was not understood by all the copyists and also that *lui* and *li* were interchangeable as third person singular emphatic pronouns, regardless of gender. Until the thirteenth century they were specialized in Old French as masculine *lui* and feminine *li*. The use of *elle* (*s*) as feminine disjunctive begins in Middle French, but the modern paradigm was not stabilized before the sixteenth century.

In Old French, *li* was the conjunctive pronoun denoting the indirect object; it has since been replaced by *lui* in that function: 32.2 *ly*. In Middle French the two forms were in competition in this function, but Mellon has no other examples.

The infinitive does not take the conjunctive pronouns *me*, *te*, *le*, and so on as direct object, but the disjunctive *moy*, *toy*, and so forth.

Syntax: A Few Random Observations

The relative pronoun *qui* represents, in Middle French as in modern French, the subject of the verb of the relative clause that it introduces for persons male and female and for things. But there is a form, *que*, also used as subject, that may have a feminine or neuter antecedent but not an antecedent denoting a male being. This *que* presumably goes back to Latin *quae* and *quod*, respectively, for feminine and neuter.

The nonrelative *que* has a variety of functions, some of them no longer extant in modern French. One is in the meaning of 'because'. *Pour ce que* 'because' is more frequent than *par ce que* in Middle French; the two forms coexist in this meaning until the seventeenth century, when *parce que* wins out.

The imperfect subjunctive is used in a continuation of Old French usage, now obsolete, in the protasis (*if* clause) of a conditional sentence. In modern literary French, only the inversion provides a context for this tense of the subjunctive in a conditional sentence, although the pluperfect subjunctive is still used in both protasis and apodosis (result clause) in the literary language.

Certain constructions that would be regarded as faulty in modern Western languages were tolerated and perhaps even cultivated in Middle French. The dangling construction does not seem to the users of fifteenth-century French to "dangle" if it can be attributed to any nominal complement in the clause to which it is appended. It is not restricted as in the modern language to the qualification of the subject.

A compound subject whose members are singular nouns may govern a singular verb. In our example from Mellon (17. 1–2; see textual note thereto) this usage is convenient because it permits a refrain to be integrated with the preceding short strophe by taking the first nominal construction as object of the preceding clause, and the second as subject of the following verb, which according to the rule in question has the singular form.

The construction just alluded to is a kind of forked construction in that the verb is governed first by one subject and then by another. Another forked construction, called by the rhetoricians *syllepsis* and generally regarded in modern times as a fault, seems in Mellon to have been cultivated as a particularly elegant device. See No. 51. 1–2 and the textual note thereto, and No. 55. 4 and textual note.

A Word about Dialects

The Old French dialect from which modern French is descended, with of course some admixtures of other dialects, is Francian, the speech of Ile-de-France. By the fifteenth century Francian had sufficient prestige to impose itself as a model for an increasingly well-defined literary language, but texts composed outside the Francian-speaking region bear the unmistakable signs of their dialectal origins despite a relatively standardized spelling. We have frequent occasion, in the Textual Notes to the individual poems, to allude to Picard traits. We use this term as a kind of shorthand to refer to traits characteristic of the regions to the north and northeast of Ile-de-France. This is the area of whose cultural ferment this collection of songs is a manifestation, and it is precisely the linguistic traits of this region that are visible beneath the Francian disguise. The most characteristic features of this dialect, to which we make reference in the textual notes are the following.

To Francian *ch* [š] corresponds Picard [k]. It is the Francian sound

that represents a special development: the change of Latin [k] before
[a] to [č] and then to [š] at the time of the mid-thirteenth-century
spirantization of affricates, a general movement in which all the
dialects participated ([č] > [š], [c] > [s], [j] > [ž]). Thus, BUCCA
'mouth' > Francian [bučə], then [bušə], but [bukə] in Picard, spelled
variously *bouce, bouke, bouque,* and even *bouche* in a purely graphic
imitation of Francian. Yet in Old Francian there is a [č] of different
origin, one that brought the same sound to Picard, namely, the
product of voiceless labial [p] plus [y]. Thus, both Francian and
Picard share in the evolution of Latin SAPIAM to *sache.* So there is no
one-to-one relationship between Francian [š] and Picard [k].

Similarly, Picard [š] frequently corresponds to later Francian [s],
but not always. The correspondences from the period before the
spirantization of affricates show why. Latin palatal stop [K'] + high
or mid front vowel becomes Old Francian [c] (= [ts]), Old Picard
[č]. After the reduction of affricates to spirants, Picard [š] is left,
corresponding to Francian [s]. However, in words in which Francian
[s] goes back to an older [s] and not to [c], it does not differ from
Picard. Thus, to later Francian *sel* [sel] 'salt' corresponds an identical
Picard form, but to Francian *cel* [sel], the demonstrative adjective/
pronoun, corresponds Picard [šel], variously spelled *cel* or *chel.*

Francians desirous of exploiting Picard features for a rustic or
comic effect often used [š] to correspond to Francian [s] even where
authentic Picard also had [s]. See discussion of No. 28 I for an
illustration of this device.

Picard vowels adjacent to palatal consonants developed differently
from their Francian counterparts. Pretonic [e] before a palatal > [i]
(e.g., 32.9 *milleur*).

The phonetic interpretation of written words in texts subject to
Picard influence without being in a consistent Picard dialect is complicated and uncertain. It is especially difficult to ascertain the value
of such graphies as *c, ch,* and *s,* and even *ss,* as well as of *g.*

In authentic Picard texts, the letter *c* was adequate to represent
the sound [č], later [š], because unlike Francian, it did not need a
graphic means of distinguishing [č] from a nonexistent [c] (= [ts]).
The use of *c* grew as naturally from the exploitation of the Latin
alphabet for vernacular writing as it had in Italian, where its phonetic
value is much the same. Such written forms as *che, cheste,* and *avancher*
are really Francian spellings used to represent a Picard sound since

Francian had had to develop a special device *ch*, to represent the sound of *sache* and *bouche*, which needed to be graphically distinguished from the sound already given to the letter *c*. In Picard texts spelled à la picarde (e.g., *Aucassin et Nicolete*), *ceste* is an adequate representation of [šestə], as *sace* is of [sašə]. But *c* has another value, that of [k], not only in words such as *court* and *camp* (Francian *champ*) but also in words such as *cemin* [kəminⁿ], *cief* [kyef], *ceurt* [kört], and 38.3 *blance* [blaⁿkə], all of which are also spelled with *ch*, *qu*, and *k*.

The practical problem for the singer or reciter of these texts is acute when he is confronted by a Picard spelling (18.5 *lasceté*, 30.1 *bouce*) or a Francian representation of a Picard pronounciation (12.11 *merchy*, rhyming with 12.9 *cy*) because the spelling tells us more about the scribe than it does about the poet and the poem. The practical solution is to adopt the standard Francian pronunciation unless there is good reason to regard the poem as Picard. For example it may be necessary to adopt Picard for good, etymologically correct rhyme or if it is evident that the dialect is being exploited for comic or rustic associations.

Another feature of Picard, which brings up similar problems and requires similar solutions, is that there is no distinctive difference between voiced and voiceless sibilants, no contrast between [s] and [z], or between [š] and [ž]. Hence Picard would allow a rhyme not permitted to Francian or would consider as rich a rhyme that in Francian would be sufficient: 7.3–4 *souffissante*: *puissante* (Francian would have *souffisante* with [z]; here both the spelling and the rhyme argue Picard pronunciation [see the textual notes to the poem for more evidence]). For a triple proof of Picard rhyme see No. 10 with *harouges*: *rouges*. Since the first of these words is attested elsewhere as *harouce*, the rhyme with *rouges* is clearly not Francian; if we suppose Picard, we posit *harouches. The rhyme with *rouges* is possible in terms of the phonological identity of [ž] = [š], true of Picard and not of Francian.

When the feminine ending -*ee* [eə] (from Latin -ĀTA]) comes after a palatal consonant (including [y]), it becomes -*ïe* in Picard, corresponding to -*iee* [yeə] in Francian. This occurs most frequently in past participles of verbs with a stem-final palatal consonant, but it is also exemplified by 50.8 *lye* [liə] 'happy': CL LAETA > VL LETA > AF *liede* [lye(d)ə] > Francian *liee* [lyeə], Picard [liə]. Compare masculine *lié* [lye] in both Picard and Francian (< LAETU).

Proclitic words such as *la*, *ma*, *ta*, and *sa* occur in Picard texts as *le*, *me*, *te*, and *se*. This creates a mild confusion about the definite article: the feminine *le* differs from the masculine in that it is not necessarily subject to elision of its vowel and therefore to contraction with preceding *a* or *de* but may maintain its integrity, as in *a le*, *de le*. The Mellon texts only hint at the existence of feminine *le* (see 28 1.2 and the textual note for it).

SPELLING

The scribes of Western, Roman Catholic Europe were from the beginning trained to write in Latin. Writing in the vernacular began as an ad hoc practice, an attempt to render with the letters of the Latin alphabet the sounds of one's native language. There was no tradition, no standard of "correctness," nor was there at the time of the earliest attempts (the first was the Oath of Strassburg in 842) any precedent. The situation may be compared with occasional attempts by Americans of foreign descent whose forebears, if literate, used nonroman alphabets (for such languages as Armenian, Greek, or Yiddish) to render the ancestral tongue into letters of the roman alphabet, as that alphabet is used by speakers of English. In the absence of any standard, near-chaos in the assignment of phonetic values to letters is the result.

By the mid-twelfth century, French orthography had achieved a surprising degree of consistency and logic. Of necessity it did not conform to the ideal of the phonetic alphabet of one sound for every letter, one letter for every sound of the language. The Latin alphabet had too few letters to represent the rich variety of vowels and consonants that had come into the Romance vernaculars since their infancy in the Vulgar Latin period. There were four basic resolutions of the problem. (1) New letters could be invented (as in Germanic systems that devised letters for the voiced and voiceless *th* sounds, for [v], and for the velar spirants). (2) One letter could stand for several sounds, usually similar sounds, with the result that distinctive differences were blurred and had to be eked out by context (e.g., in French, the differences between upper mid and lower mid vowels [ẹ, ẹ; ọ, ọ], between high and mid back vowels [u, o], or between high, rounded vowels of different degrees of retraction [u, ü]). (3) Conversely, one sound could be represented by different letters ([u] by *o* or *u*; [k] by *c*, *k*, or *q*). (4) A combination of two or more letters could stand for a single sound (*ou* for [u], *qu* for [k], *ch* for [č]).

Romance scribes, particularly French ones, were not so ingenious as their Germanic colleagues in the invention of new letters, but they availed themselves freely of the other options. By the time of the earliest French texts, the regional differences in pronunciation had already begun subtly to manifest themselves in the writing system. Sometimes regional spelling differences did not reflect differences in pronunciation but simply arose from local conventions that spread through a region in much the same way that linguistic features spread. For example, the Norman and Anglo-norman use of the letter *u* to represent both [u] and [ü] affects only local writing habits but does not reflect any difference of pronunciation between regions that make a graphic distinction between [u] and [ü] and those that do not. Similarly, as narrative and lyric texts make their way from court to court, spelling conventions that make sense in the region in which they arose crop up, through multiple copying, in areas to whose speech they do not apply: for example, the use of *oi* to represent [e] in areas in which [ey] (later [e]) had not changed to [oy] (later [we]). The impact of the visible word often influences a scribe in his copying more than does his native pronunciation. For this reason a spelling such as 12.2 *mains* 'less', although it suggests a pronunciation [me^{n}s] for which it was evidently devised, may have been copied into a poetical text whose composer pronounced it [mwe^{n}s].

Alphabetic writing in most systems is lexical as well as phonetic. A sequence of letters does not represent only a succession of the sounds forming a phonetic word, it also represents the whole word as an entity with a meaning. This word has a visual shape and functions for the reader much like a Chinese character. Many maintain that the visual distinctiveness of homonyms is an aid to intelligent reading, for example, that the difference in spelling between English *mean* and *mien*, is helpful. Doubtless we do react to these written words as visual entities. The written sentence *She is a mien woman* would cause a reader to stumble and force him almost to read it aloud in order to understand it. However, such a reaction is due to reading habits: the fact that *mean* is a verb 'to signify', an adjective 'cruel, petty', and a noun 'average' and that all these words are spelled alike does not render difficult our immediate and appropriate recognition of the written or printed word in an adequate context. The phoneticists argue in this way that phonetic writing need be no harder to read than speech is to understand.

The first confrontation between the proponents of phonetic spelling and those of distinctive spellings for homonyms occurred in the sixteenth century. The opposing arguments are set forth in an elegant little book published in 1560, the *Dialogue de l'Ortografe e Prononciation Françoese, departi an deus liures par Iacques Peletier du Mans*[15] and have not changed essentially since. Théodore de Bèze, Jacques Pelletier du Mans, Louis Meigret, and the Estienne family joined vigorously in this struggle. The practice of inserting etymological letters (to be considered below) started almost imperceptibly in the thirteenth century, gained in force, and was nearly in full flower in the fifteenth. It remained for the sixteenth century to reason about the matter and for the seventeenth to crystallize the concept of "correct" spelling and to enforce it with royal and academic authority.

The distinctive physiognomy of the written word began with the coalescence of certain basic speech sounds. When [c] became [s], visual habit was remarkably effective in preventing a wholesale confusion or interchangeability of the letters representing them. The demonstrative *cel* is almost invariably spelled with *c* (cf. 15.10 *celle*); *sel* 'salt' only occasionally with *c*. It was not until the sixteenth century that *fasse* was generally accepted as the spelling for subjunctive forms of *faire*; *face* (as in 42.2) had been the prevailing spelling until then, and it was probably replaced in order to avoid confusing it with the word for 'face' (cf. 42.3). Once distinctive spelling of homonyms had materialized as an almost unconscious historical process, some element of deliberation began to play a role. A growing awareness of the Latin origin of French, coupled with the reverence paid to Latin, encouraged the adoption of those spellings that recalled the Latin origin (real or supposed) of a given word. Once the diphthong [ay] had assumed the pronunciation [ey], and then [e] (end of twelfth century), the graphy *ai* became available to represent [e] of other origin. Latin SAPIT had become French *set*, but the graphy *ai* recalled the original A and so was preferred. For the most part, the homonymous *c'est, s'est,* and *set* 'seven' are kept distinct in medieval texts. Because usage did not yet include the apostrophe, *cest*, the demonstrative, was spelled like *c'est*. *Set* 'seven' was spelled like *set* 'knows' until the latter was rather consistently replaced by forms using *sc-*: *scet* (29.7) or *scait* (cf. 29.9 *sçay*). The insertion of *c* in this verb was another reminiscence of Latin. Many modern students attribute the *c* to a mistaken belief that the French verb came from Latin SCĪRE, but it is more likely that

15. Geneva: Slatkine Reprint, 1964.

a kind of morphemic writing is involved here, a recognition of the structure of the French lexicon. On the semantic level the verb *savoir* has much the same relationship to the noun *scïence* that *conoistre* bears to *conoissance*. The fact that each pair is characterized by a common initial consonant reinforces the association. What is more natural than that the [s-] common to the first pair be reinforced (i.e., be rendered more recognizable) by the extension of the graphy *sc-* from the noun to the verb?

Another way to stabilize the spelling of lexical units is to maintain a graphic distinction that has been erased phonetically by the phonetico-grammatical process called morpho-phonemic by many American linguists. It is a general fact of Old and Middle French that the voiced–voiceless distinction of stops and spirants is neutralized at word-final. Thus, the masculine of *grande* is *grant*, the subjunctive of *garde* is *gart*. Phonetically, the *t* of these shorter words is [t]. But one may argue that on a higher level of analysis the [t] of *grant* is really a *d*, just as the [t] of *haut* is really a *t*, because the feminine *haute* shows that it is a *t* in a context (between vowels) that admits [t] and [d] in contrast. By the same reasoning, the [t] of *chaut* is virtually a *d* because of *chaude*. In spite of the modern spellings such words as *grand*, *chaud*, and *sang*, as they appear in liaison, show that the Old French pronunciation of the shorter forms is still in force; witness modF *un grand homme* and *un sang impur*, in which the *d* and the *g* are pronounced [t] and [k], respectively.

The spelling in 28 1.2 *gard* is remarkable for two reasons: its grammatical conservatism (probably due to its use in a formula, *Dieu . . . gard*), demonstrated by the extension of -*e* to most first conjugation verbs in the subjunctive, as the Mellon evidence shows; and its orthographic innovation in being the only example in Mellon of a letter generally reserved for a voiced consonant to represent a phonetically voiceless, but virtually voiced, consonant (*grant* still prevails). This is another kind of quasi-etymological spelling that, like *sc-*, takes into account levels of linguistic analysis more abstract than the phonetic.

The term "etymological spelling" refers most often to forms that contain silent letters that do not represent sounds ever heard in the French words in which they occur, such as the *b* of *doubté*—a scribal recognition of the ancestral status of DUBITARE. Even more redundant is the *p* of *recepvoir* (reminding us of RECIPERE) because the Latin P is still phonetically represented in its French descendant by the [v].

When *l* was vocalized (e.g., [myels] > [myews] > [myös]), the spelling at first was either conservative (i.e., maintained the familiar *miels*) or took the change into account, as *mieus*. Another form of this word both noted the phonetic change and retained the phonetically defunct *l*, probably as essential to the visual image: *mieuls*. Since a Latin scribal abbreviation of *-us* resembled an *x*, a real *x* came during the period of a flourishing vernacular literature to be so used, so that an alternative spelling of *mieus* was *miex*. This was soon redundantly expanded to *mieux*, and even to *mieulx* (as in 53.5). In the late fifteenth century and in the sixteenth, elaborate spelling came to be prized for its own sake, and redundant *b*'s, *l*'s, and *x*'s were used even without etymological justification. On the model of such nearly legitimate spellings as *mieulx*, the ending *-eulx* was extended to adjectives in [-ös] from the Latiu suffix *-ōsu*. Thus, spellings like *amoureulx* and *gratieulx* were favored for words that had never had an *l*.

The representation of vowels is in great disarray largely because dialectal differences complicate the picture. A spelling becomes fashionable in an area to which it is dialectally inappropriate. The verb ending *-oit* invades an area in which that ending is pronounced [et] and in which the traditional spelling is *-eit*. Or the pronunciation [we] is reduced to [e], but the *oi* that represents it is still used. *Droit* (e.g., 16.1) is pronounced [dret] or [drwet] in an irregular geographical and social pattern. In a given text its exact value—that is, the pronunciation the author would have given it—may be impossible to ascertain. Some texts contain phonetic spellings scattered among the traditional ones. A form such as *mirouer* or *miroer* is immensely helpful to the scholar but even so does not settle the question of the pronunciation of *oi* in other words of the same work. Of course, the spelling *soit* [set] 'knows' of 1.2 represents a word whose pronunciation never included [oy] or [we] in any dialect at any time. There is no need to say more than we already have on the subject of *ou* and *eu* (see pp. 99–101).

Scribal Practice

So far we have been discussing spelling as if the edited texts, as prepared by modern scholars, truly represented medieval practice. But they do not. The medieval alphabet is structurally different from that used in modern editions of medieval texts, including this one, in that there is no functional difference between the letters *u* and *v*, or between *i* and *j*. It would be more accurate to say that there is a letter, *u*, which has two shapes: one with a round bottom, the other with a pointed bottom. The one with the pointed bottom (*v*) varies more or less freely with *u* at the beginnings of words but is rarely used as other than the first letter of a word. Before the sixteenth century there is no hint of exploiting the difference between these letter forms to reflect the two functions of that letter—for it is only one letter, capable of representing a consonant or a vowel, as is stated in all the Latin treatises on grammar. Thus *vn* is transcribed as *un* by a modern editor, and *deuoir* as *devoir*.

Similarly, there are two *i*'s, the short one and the one with a tail(*j*). The latter varies more or less freely with the short one as last letter of a word; this is not the usage of the Mell scribe. But initially and medially, *j* does not occur, so *ie* is the only medieval spelling of the word transcribed as *je* by modern editors—unless the majuscule or capital letter is used, which may stand for either the consonant [ž] or for the vowel [i].

It is true that *y* is practically interchangeable with *i*; yet manuscripts in which it has the consonantal value of [ž] are exceedingly rare. The letter *y* stands for the syllabic vowel [i] and is especially favored at word-end (*icy*, 40.1 *mercy*) or as the second letter in a two-vowel digraph, *ey*, *ay*, *oy*, particularly at the end of a word (26.1 *doy*) but also medially, or for a syllabic [i] at the beginning of a word (*yver*), or for nonsyllabic [y] at the beginning of a word (*yeux*). Initial *i* can also have this value, so that out of context, a word such as 12.10 *ieux* would be ambiguous— is it *yeux* or *jeux*? Other ambiguities arise in this system: *iure* is either *jure* (or *juré*) or *ivre*. The editorial task is sometimes delicate. The medieval text has no apostrophe and no accent marks (with some exceptions in some ancient Anglo-Norman texts).

Another pair of letter-forms functions as *s*, the one long, like *f* without a crossbar, the other rounded, like our familiar lower-case *s*. The latter is used, in all but very early manuscripts, always and only as the last letter of a word.

The numerous abbreviations come from the Latin tradition. We shall mention a few here to facilitate reading the photographic repro-duction of Mellon. The commonest abbreviation, a bar over a vowel letter, stands for an appropriate nasal consonant (bō = *bon*, cōme = *comme*). A *q* with a bar over it stands for *que;* if the bar is nearly vertical, *qui* is represented. A *p* with a bar crossing its stem is *per* or *par;* with a curved line like a tilde above it, *pour;* with an extension of the lobe downward to the left of the stem and curving back to the lower part of the stem, it is *pro*. A small vowel written above a consonant implies that that vowel is preceded or followed by *r;* thus, a raised *e* represents *re* or *er*. A raised *r* at the end of a word represents *-ur*. A large letter that looks like the arabic numeral 9, at the beginning of a word, stands for *con-* or *com-*, and because *n* and *u* are often taken for each other, the initial *9* has come to represent *cou-* as well.

The short vertical strokes of which *i, n, u,* and *m* are composed are called minims in English, *jambages* in French. Sometimes the only way to decipher a word is to count the minims: one is *i;* two may be *n* or *u* or *ii;* three may be *iu, ui, in, ni, m,* or *iii,* and so on. And it does happen that a scribe miscounts the minims.

In the present edition we follow in general the practice of the Société des Anciens Textes Français (which is essentially also that of the *Classiques français du moyen âge*) with respect to the modern punctuation, resolution of abbreviations, the distinction between *u* and *v* and that between *i* and *j* (e.g., to distinguish *jure* from *ivre*). The same authority determines our restriction of accents to the use of the acute accent over the letter *e* only to mark the distinction between that letter as it appears (without accent) in the unstressed final syllable of a word or (as *é*) in the final syllable when it is stressed (e.g., to distinguish *jure* from *juré*). However, in spite of the rule just enunciated, we have decided to extend the use of the acute accent to one other case: the *e* that in the traditional Middle French spelling of a given word precedes a silent (but formerly pronounced) preconsonantal *s*, but which, in a particular instance of such a word, is not followed by *s*. (as An example in) *deconfort*, an alternate spelling to *desconfort*. We will spell such a word *déconfort* to indicate the probable phonetic difference between this vowel, formerly checked by *s*, and one that in a given word had always been free in French.

Glossary of Linguistic Terms

Articulation. The production of consonants by the play of active speech organs in the mouth (a: lower lip, b: tongue tip, c: blade of tongue, or forward hump, d: back of tongue, or rearward hump) against the passive organs (1: upper lip, 2: edge of front teeth, 3: back surface of front teeth, 4: hard palate, 5: soft palate, or velum). The combination of active and passive organs is called the place of articulation. The subdivisions may be finer than those presented below, but the present classification will suffice for the present discussion, which concerns primarily Middle French. The places of articulation are named as follows: a: LABIALS (a^1 bilabial, a^2 labio-dental); b: DENTAL ($= b^3$); c: PALATAL ($= c^4$); d: VELAR ($= d^5$). Obviously, many other articulations are possible.

The MANNER OF ARTICULATION (stop, spirant, affricate, [nasal: not properly a manner of articulation but conveniently classified here], lateral, trill) refers principally to the way in which the active or passive organs are brought together: if they stop the air flow entirely, the resulting sound is a STOP; if the closure is incomplete so that the air can be heard to leak through the constriction at the designated place, the result is a SPIRANT. A combination of stop and spirant (i.e., a consonant that begins firmly as a stop but whose release is slow enough to allow a moment of audible air leak) is an AFFRICATE (*ch* of English *chin*, *j* of *jug*). NASALITY is not strictly speaking an articulation but a concurrent quality imposed on an articulated consonant (or a **vowel**) by relaxing the velum, which when tense prevents the air from going through the nose and allows it passage only through the mouth. A sound involving the emission of air solely through the nose is NASAL; if the air goes simultaneously through the nose and the mouth, the sound is NASALIZED; if through the mouth alone, the sound is ORAL. (A vowel is nevertheless said to be nasal when it is distinctively so [see **vowel**]). A BUCCAL (pr. *buckle*) articulation is any consonant articulation, whether nasal, nasalized, or oral.

The LATERAL consonants (different kinds of *l*) are produced by obstructing the flow of air over the median line of the tongue but allowing it to escape, without audible friction, through one or both sides. The obstructions may be dental, palatal, or velar, each marked auditorily by a characteristic vowel color. A TRILL is produced by a rapid oscillation of the free end of a flexible organ (tongue tip, uvula) held at the exact degree of tension that will, in the presence of an air current of appropriate force, produce that movement. The stops and spirants are subject to another variation, called VOICING; that is, they are either VOICED (produced with simultaneous vibrations from the vocal cords) or UNVOICED (or VOICELESS). Compare the final consonants of English *peas* and *peace*, or the initial consonants of *sip* and *zip*. The nasals, laterals, and trills are almost always voiced; for these sounds voicing is non**distinctive.**

The following table shows the phonetic symbols for the articulations discussed in this book. If a pair of symbols appears in one box, the first member of the pair is voiceless, the second is voiced. The chart omits certain possibilities that will not arise in our discussion, for example, the voiced counterpart of [c].

	Labial	Dental	Palatal	Velar
Stop	p b	t d		k g
Spirant	f v	s z	š ž	
Affricate*		c —	č j	
Nasal	m	n	ñ	ŋ
Lateral		l	l'	ł
Trill		r		R

*An affricate may also be represented, depending on the point of the discussion, by the stop + spirant of which it is composed, i.e., [c] = [ts], [č] = [tš], [j] = [dž].

Most of these phonetic symbols have their traditional alphabetic value. Special symbols are:

[š] = *ch* of modF *machine*
[ž] = *j* of modF *jour*
[c] = *z* of German *zu* or of Italian *zio;* or *ts* of English *hats.*
[č] = *ch* of English *chin*
[ĵ] = *j* of English *jug.*
[l'] = *ll* of Castilian (not American Spanish) *calle*
[ł] = *l* of American English *milk.*
[ñ] = *gn* of modF *agneau*
[ŋ] = *ng* of English *sing*

Close juncture. See JUNCTURE.

Conjunctive pronoun. Especially in French, a personal pronoun, typically unstressed, in a close construction with a verb of which it is subject, direct object, indirect object, or adverbial complement (in modern French, such forms as *je, tu, il, me, te, le, la, lui, leur, y, en*). In Old and Middle French, the subject pronouns (*je, tu, . . .*) were disjunctive, that is, received the stress of an independent word.

Consonant. A speech sound articulated in such a way as to interrupt, constrict (producing **distinctively** audible noise), or divert the free flow of air over the median line of the tongue and out between the lips. See **articulation, syllable, vowel.**

Cover symbol. A phonetic symbol of general application to a category of sounds defined by their relation to other sounds in a context. For example, [y] represents any nonsyllabic VOWEL that is high, unrounded, and fronted relative to any adjacent vowel. Thus English *sky* may be transcribed as [skae̦] in a notation that attempts to capture rather precisely the timbre of the nonsyllabic vowel, whereas [skay] represents the range between [skae̦] and [skai̦] in a discussion to which the difference between [e] and [i] would be irrelevant. Similarly, [h] represents any voiceless nonsyllabic vowel having the same quality as an adjacent vowel: [fehtə] = [feetə], [hair] = [aair]. See **syllable.**

Distinctive. Perceived as functionally different by a native speaker, particularly with respect to the characteristics of speech sounds. The relationship between two speech sounds that, though similar, differ as to one or more DISTINCTIVE FEATURES can be symbolized by the sign of inequality, thus: [p] ≠ [b]. The test of distinctive difference is CONTRAST: if the sounds in question occur in (near-)identical contexts in words of different meaning, they are in contrast (with a proviso explained below). For examples, English *pit* and *bit* differ by the difference between [p] and [b], that of voicing; in French, too, [p] ≠ [b]; witness *pain* ≠ *bain*. If a phonetic difference in identical contexts is not associated with a difference of meaning, the sounds are not in contrast but in FREE VARIATION (the difference is nondistinctive). For example, the release or nonrelease (continued closure) of a final STOP in English is nondistinctive: both [kæt˺] and [kæt⁼] mean 'cat' —or signify the word *cat*—wherefore [-t˺] = [-t⁼] in English, although the difference might well be distinctive in another language.

In the medieval Picard dialect no functional distinction is made between voiced and unvoiced sibilants. The last consonant of such a word as *hommage* varies nondistinctively between [ž] and [š]; [ž] and [š] are in free variation ([ž] = [š]) in Picard, whereas Francian distinguishes the sounds: [ž] ≠ [š] in Francian. This permits a variation in Picard spelling between *hommage* and *hommache* that one would not expect to find in a Francian document.

However, it must be understood that there are some pairs of words that appear to exhibit free variation but the history of whose semantic and phonetic similarity is other than phonetic. The pair *servise–service,* words that coexisted in Old French in the Francian area and that have the same meaning, is not evidence that [z] = [s] in the context [i_ə] or even, more generally, [V_ə] (V́ = any stressed vowel). Upon examination, the two sibilants, one voiced, the other unvoiced, are clearly in contrast in Francian (though not in Picard), as shown by the pair *prise–prisse*. The explanation for such a close phonetic resemblance between two words that must now be regarded as a pair of synonyms rather than evidence of a nondistinctive phonetic alternation must be sought in the extraphonetic history of the words. *Servise* is the normal, native French outcome of an original Latin *servitium*, whereas *service* is the result either of influence of the continental way of pronouncing Latin ([ts] in such a word as this) or of the Italian word *servizio*. There was, beginning in the thirteenth century, a growing preference for the suffix *-ice* and a tendency to substitute it for *-ise*.

Diphthong. See discussion under SYLLABLE.

Juncture. The transition from one speech sound (phonetic segment) to the next. There are two sorts of juncture, open and close. OPEN JUNCTURE typically occurs at pause, at the end of a syntactic construction, at the caesura in verse, and, especially in English and other Germanic languages, between words, that is, between the last sound of the first word and the first sound of the second word of a pair. Compare *a nice man* with *an iceman;* in the first example, the transition between *n* and *i* is close; in the second example, it is open. Phonetically, open juncture consists of a slowing up of the rate at which phonetic segments are produced, up to the last segment before the open juncture; immediately after the juncture, the normal rate is resumed. CLOSE JUNCTURE is the smooth, rapid transition from sound to sound occurring normally within a word. In Romance languages there is usually close juncture between words as well, unless a pause or a syntactic boundary occurs between the words.

Open juncture. See JUNCTURE.

Rhyme. The correspondence of the last few phonetic segments of two or more lines of verse. A rhyme is SUFFICIENT if the rhyming segments are the last accented vowel and all following segments (consonants, unaccented vowels), if any; RICH if elements immediately preceding the rhyming vowel are the same. Thus the rhyme *souffisante : puissante* would not be rich in Francian, which distinguishes between [z] and [s]; but in Picard, which does not make this distinction ([z] = [s]), the rhyme is rich. See **distinctive.**

Strong. Having the stem accented rather than the verb-ending; said especially of verbs exhibiting vocalic alternation. Also applied to the vowel characteristic of such a strong stem. For example, *je meurs* has a strong stem, *nous mourons* a weak stem; *eu* is a strong vowel, *ou* is weak, with respect to such a verb.

Syllable. A unit of prosody (speech rhythm) that consists of a NUCLEUS (the SYLLABIC) and, optionally, MARGINAL, NONSYLLABIC elements. Typically the syllabic nucleus is a VOWEL, the nonsyllabic margin or margins, a **consonant**, or consonants. The difference between a syllabic and a nonsyllabic is principally a difference in duration, the nonsyllabics being perceived as being practically instantaneous; whereas vowels are perceived as having duration. The objective physical fact is that stops are indeed so much shorter than a vowel functioning as a syllabic nucleus (hereafter: a SYLLABIC VOWEL) as to belong to another order of magnitude. Spirants are somewhat longer than stops but, given a normal pronunciation, even a long spirant will be shorter than a short vowel. Nasals, laterals, and trills can approach the duration of a vowel but rarely equal or exceed it. In any case they always pattern in the Romance languages as marginal to the syllabic, never as nuclear. Therefore, we postulate that, as far as Romance languages are concerned, consonants are not syllabic.

The situation is different for vowels. In a sequence of two or more vowels, several kinds of TRANSITION may obtain between them. (1) The transition may be SMOOTH (or GRADUAL, or SLURRED); that is, the movement of the tongue up or down, forward or back, or in some combination of horizontal and vertical movements may be of steady, unchanging speed. (2) The transition may be ABRUPT (or DISCRETE); that is, the vowel is held in a steady state for the duration of a syllabic nucleus and then, in a transition whose duration is equal to or shorter than that of a consonant, the speech organs assume the position of the next steady-state vowel. (3) In the DIPHTHONGAL TRANSITION, one vowel may have the duration of a syllabic nucleus, and the vowel next preceding (or following) have a duration about as short as that of a consonant, so that the vowel is nonsyllabic. A sequence of two vowels, one of which is nonsyllabic, is a DIPHTHONG; of three, the first and third of which are nonsyllabic, a TRIPHTHONG.

The smooth transition creates ambiguities as to syllabicity. The beginning- and end-points of the several vowels in the chain are not marked by a distinct acoustic signal, and neither the number of vowels nor the number of syllables is easily ascertainable.

The abrupt or discrete transition assigns one syllable's length to each vowel in the sequence. The modF *chaos* [kaó] has two syllables, and OF *haïe* [haíə] has three.

The diphthongal transition takes place typically when one of the vowels in the sequence is unstressed and high [i ü u] and the other vowel is low or mid. The nonsyllabic vowel in such a sequence is called a SEMICONSONANT when it precedes the syllabic and a SEMI-VOWEL when it follows. In our transcription, [y ẅ w] represent the nonsyllabic varieties of [i ü u], respectively. When necessary, we shall also use the sign [ˌ] under the vowel symbol to designate nonsyllabicity.

We shall also use [y ẅ w] as **cover symbols** for any nonsyllabic vowel that is high and front unrounded, front rounded, or back rounded, respectively, relative to the syllabic vowel to which it functions as margin. Thus, [aǫ] would be less precisely but often more conveniently represented by [aw]; [ęo] by [yo]; and so on.

A diphthong whose first element is nonsyllabic (e.g., [wa]) is a RISING DIPHTHONG; with the second element nonsyllabic [aw], it is a FALLING DIPHTHONG.

In a sequence of consonants (C) bounded by vowels (V) before and after (VCCV), there are obviously two syllables, but the place of the boundary between them is often a subject of controversy and con-jecture. Every language has its own set of rules, traditional or scientific, for determining whether two (or three) consonants go with the next vowel to form a syllable (V–CCV), or whether the syllable boundary comes between them (VC–CV) or even after them (VCC–V). Generally, in the Romance languages the syllable division usually comes between two consonants or after the first of three, but a sequence of stop or spirant plus trill or lateral usually goes with the second syllable: modF *al-côve*, *es-père*, *es-prit*, *é-clat*. If a word begins with a consonant group, there is no syllable division before the first syllabic nucleus of the word.

A syllable that ends in a vowel is OPEN, and that vowel is FREE; a syllable ending in a consonant is CLOSED, and its vowel is CHECKED.

Vowel. Any speech sound the production of which allows the free flow of air over the median line of the tongue (i.e., along the longi-tudinal axis). The most important variables in the formation of vowels are TONGUE HEIGHT and TONGUE ADVANCEMENT or RETRACTION (see discussion below). Another variable is in the degree of LIP-ROUNDING or -SPREADING. Vowels may be ORAL or NASALIZED. If a vowel is

distinctively nasalized, it is said to be NASAL (see **articulation**). Vowels are usually voiced and usually SYLLABIC (see **syllable**), but are occasionally unvoiced or nonsyllabic. A vowel that is both unvoiced and nonsyllabic is traditionally considered a consonant [h]. We shall observe the tradition and use [h] as a **cover symbol** when it is not necessary to specify vowel timbre. Otherwise a voiceless nonsyllabic vowel will be represented in our phonetic transcription by the appropriate vowel symbol in italics, for example, American English *hot* [hat] or [*a*at].

TONGUE HEIGHT is inversely proportional to the distance from the most raised part of the tongue (blade or back; see **articulation**) to the passive organ (hard palate or soft palate, respectively) nearest the tongue. One distinguishes as many degrees of tongue height as are needed to describe the vowel system of a given language. For our purposes, four degrees of tongue height—HIGH, UPPER MID, LOWER MID, LOW—will amply suffice; and for the description of Middle French, three degrees—HIGH, MID, and LOW—will be enough. When required, a degree between upper mid and lower mid can be specified: MEAN MID.

TONGUE ADVANCEMENT or RETRACTION refers to that part of the tongue raised toward the roof of the mouth. When the blade of the tongue is raised toward the hard palate, a little behind the upper teeth, the resulting vowel is said to be FRONT, or FRONTED; if the back of the tongue is raised toward the soft palate, the vowel is BACK, or RETRACTED. Any degree of advancement or retraction between the extremes of front or back at a given tongue height may be designated as CENTRAL. These terms are used in a relative way rather than in an anatomically precise way. What is called a back vowel in one language (the *oo* of *food* as pronounced by Middle Westerners) may be perceived as central or fronted in another (as by a Frenchman who, when an American tries to say *tout*, perceives it as *tu*).

The vowel system we use in our discussion of Middle French and occasional excursions into the history of French is presented in this table.

	Front	Central	Back	Examples from Modern French		
High	i	ü	u	*si*	*tu*	*tout*
Mid	e	ö	ǫ	*était*	*jeu, peur*	*eau*, bloc
		Rounded				
Low		a				*patte, pâte*

In addition we use the following special symbols: [ə] to represent a variety of [e] of a particularly relaxed nature, somewhat retracted, slightly rounded, and unstressed; a dot to specify upper mid, and a hook to represent lower mid: *était* [ẹtę], *jeu* [žọ̈], *peur* [pọ̈r], *eau* [ọ], *bloc* [blǫk] (we will need no special sign to distinguish the vowel qualities of *patte* and *pâte*); and the sign [:] after the vowel affected to show length or duration of a vowel: *patte* [pat], *pâte* [pa:t], fête [fę:t]. In general, however, we use the broad symbol [e] or [ö] or [o] to stand for a vowel that may be realized in speech as anything between or including the opposites represented by the dot and the hook, or simply as a vowel range whose precise position or nuance is irrelevant to a given discussion.

The nasality of a vowel is indicated sometimes by a tilde over the vowel symbol, sometimes by a raised *n* (which represents the realization of a nasal, as with buccal articulation homorganic with the following consonant varying freely with no buccal articulation at all, i.e., as simply preceded by a nasalized vowel). Thus, the modern pronunciation of *enfant* is transcribed as [ãfã], the Middle French as [aⁿfaⁿt], the Old French as [ẽnfãnt] in a "narrow" transcription (which includes non**distinctive** traits) or, in a "broad" transcription (which excludes nondistinctive traits), as [enfant].

LENGTH is added duration. A long vowel can be perceptibly longer than another vowel of the same quality in a similar context, for example, stressed and before a final voiceless consonant, as in modF *un fait* [fęt] and *une fête* [fę:t]. The added length is simply more of the same vowel but not enough to constitute a new **syllable**. It may be more precisely symbolized as a nonsyllabic vowel of the same quality as the preceding vowel: *fête* [feęt] ([˰] = nonsyllabic).

See **diphthong.**

EDITORIAL POLICY

Leeman L. Perkins

The primary interest of an edition of this kind obviously derives from the fact that it makes readily accessible in facsimile a significant historical and artistic document that is both rare and beautiful. In this instance it is one of the most interesting sources of fifteenth-century secular music still in existence. At the same time the changes in linguistic and notational usage that have come about since the copying of the Mellon Chansonnier would severely limit the usefulness of the present publication without the adjunction of the transcriptions and a rather considerable critical apparatus. The fundamental editorial task was seen as facilitating as much as possible the interpretation and practical utilization of the song repertory offered by the collection. It seemed preferable to adopt for this purpose procedures that would not detract unduly from the visual appeal of the original since the transcriptions face the corresponding openings of the handsome facsimile. But because an attempt has also been made to establish an authoritative reading of both verse and music, the problems involved were both aesthetic and editorial and did not always lend themselves to common solutions.

Although chanson connotes both words and music, each of its constituent elements is capable of an independent existence. The secular anthologies of the fifteenth century abundantly illustrate this state of affairs. Several contain only verse,[1] whereas those in which musical notation is included frequently present the poetry in a corrupted or drastically truncated form, in some cases with nothing more than an incipit by which it can be identified.[2] Compared with other notated manuscripts generally, the Mellon Chansonnier appears some-

---

1. See, for example, in Sources the following sigla: *Roh, *Par 1719, *Par 7559, *Arn, *Chasse, and *Jar.

2. Of the collections having a reasonably significant number of concordances with the Mellon Chansonnier, the collections best illustrating incomplete and corrupt poetic texts are Flo 229 and Pix. Those having only an incipit or no indication at all include Sev 5.I.43, Flo 176, RomC 2856, CG XIII.27, and BerK 78 C 28.

what inconsistent in transmitting the verse. Some chansons are verbally complete, as in the chansonniers Dijon, Wolfenbüttel, Laborde, and Cordiforme, whereas for others only the refrain is given, or at most a portion of the additional strophes.[3] Moreover, there are patent errors not only in the poems in English, a language clearly unfamiliar to the copyist, but also in those in French, presumably his native tongue. Changes in the poetic text as given by the manuscript have been made in the transcriptions with the greatest circumspection and only as a rule when the correction seemingly demanded by sense or syntax could be supplied from a reliable concordant source. The fragmentary poems, on the other hand, have been completed whenever possible, again from the version that appeared to be either the most correct or the closest to the scribal tradition transmitted by the Mellon Chansonnier. Punctuation and capitalization have been supplied to facilitate comprehension, and the abbreviations to which the scribes of the period had constant recourse have been written out. One can easily recognize textual emendations and completions when they accompany the musical transcriptions by comparing the printed version with the juxtaposed original. Thus no attempt was made to set those changes off graphically in the modern score, and to avoid cluttering the page, all pertinent explanations have been consigned to the commentary. Recorded there are the sources drawn upon for the editorial emendations and additions, the significant variants, particularly those that seem to offer a superior reading, a brief description of the versification, and suggestions concerning problems of pronunciation, vocabulary, and interpretation.

Fortunately, the gaps that exist in the poetry of the chansonnier are virtually absent from the music. The copyist responsible for the notation was exceptionally careful, and even the slips that he occasionally made have been for the most part corrected, either by the scribe himself or by one of the first owners of the collection. As a result there is little in the music needing emendation. In those cases where both context and collation with concordant sources pointed ineluctably to an error, the reading judged most acceptable was adopted from the versions at hand. Elsewhere the transcriptions follow the original with all possible fidelity even when the reading of another

3. Chansons for which the complete poem is not given in the manuscript include Nos. 3, 6, 8, 10, 13–18, 20, 22, and so on (cf. the facsimiles and the Textual Notes).

source seemed to be preferable, if not necessarily more correct. In view of the general reliability of the manuscript, there was obviously no reason to resort to conflation except when absolutely necessary. However, unlike similar alterations in the poetic texts, the few emendations and additions deemed indispensable in the music have been set off in brackets. Although the facsimile makes a direct comparison possible in principle, it seemed wiser to assume that many readers would lack the specialized knowledge required to identify conveniently divergences between the chansonnier and the modern score. Explanations for the changes made will be found in the Critical Apparatus with those relating to the verse. An attempt has also been made to reveal briefly the manner in which the various extant versions of a given chanson appear to be related, but only the similarities and variants considered significant have been noted. The determination of what was deemed important in that connection was not done according to a systematic methodology like that developed by Allan Atlas in his study of the Medici Chansonnier.[4] The collation of concordant sources had been virtually completed before his dissertation became available, and it did not seem practical to adopt his procedures retrospectively. Nonetheless, the principles followed in the present edition are essentially similar, and it is hoped that the result, although far from exhaustive, will at least point in the right direction.

In order that the musical transcriptions be as immediately useful as possible to student, scholar, and performer alike, the editorial practices currently employed to that end have been adopted here. The original note values have been twice halved to obtain those in general use capable of suggesting a tempo approximating that presumably intended by the composer. Similarly, the signs of mensuration used—or presupposed—by the scribe have been replaced by a modern equivalent that retains the fundamental binary and ternary divisions and takes as the measure unit either the fifteenth-century *brevis* or some multiple of it. In general *tempus perfectum* (○) is represented by $\frac{3}{4}$, *tempus imperfectum* (C) by $\frac{4}{4}$ or C, and *tempus imperfectum diminutum* (₵) by its present-day analogue. The clef signs placed in the chansonnier in a variety of positions, primarily to obviate the inconvenience of adding ledger lines, have been superseded in the modern score by

---

4. "The Methodology of Relating Sources," in "Rome, Biblioteca Apostolica Vaticana, Cappella Giulia XIII.27, and the Dissemination of the Franco-Netherlandish Chanson in Italy, c. 1460–c. 1530," chap. 5.

those most apt to facilitate the perception of both horizontal and vertical relationships: the treble clef 𝄞 , the transposing treble clef 𝄞 (indicating that pitches sound an octave lower than written), and the bass clef 𝄢. In addition the sign of congruence ⌇ generally employed in the manuscript to mark the end of a section within a piece has been replaced by the more familiar corona ⌢, which is frequently used for the same purpose in the sources of the period. However, the conventional practice of indicating coloration and ligatures by means of brackets has not been followed since such details are of interest mainly to the specialist who can readily examine them in the facsimiles.

Accidentals

Considerably more troublesome to the editor than the explicit elements of the notation that require only the somewhat mechanical processes of transcription and emendation are those that must be extrapolated either from the written indications or, more often, from the structure of the music itself. Into this category fall two of the most vexing problems connected with the editorial preparation of fifteenth-century compositions: the use of sharps and flats in a manner stylistically appropriate for the period and the alignment of individual syllables of the verbal material with the notes to which they should probably be sung. Regarding the first matter the role apparently played by Tinctoris in the compilation of the collection suggested that the accidentals be supplied as much as possible in accordance with his precepts and prescriptions. There are in fact several passages in his treatises that pertain to this problem. Perhaps his clearest and most comprehensive discussion of it is in connection with the description of the sixth of the church tones or modes.[5] There, following the system of classification introduced by Hermannus Contractus, he explains that the sixth mode, the plagal member of the pair having F as a final, is usually formed by placing the third species of fifth (FGab♮c)[6] above the final and the third species of fourth (CDEF) below. This arrangement produces an octave scale from C to c with one semitone below the final and another between b and c at the top. However, it is also possible, as he asserts, to form both the plagal

5. *Liber de natura et proprietate tonorum* . . . , capitulum VIII, "De formatione sexti toni." The treatise is found in Charles E. de Coussemaker's *Scriptorum de musica medii aevi* . . . , 4:21 ff.

6. "Species" here refers to the arrangement of melodic tones and semitones within the designated intervals.

sixth mode and its authentic counterpart, the fifth mode (comprising the octave from F to f), with the fourth species of fifth (FGab♭c) above the final, shifting the semitone to fall between a and b, although this should only be done when absolutely necessary.

As explained by Tinctoris, the exigencies requiring a flat for b point to principles that can serve to regulate the use of accidentals in the music of the late fifteenth century generally. For example, a flat may be used to avoid the melodic tritone that would occur in ascending from the final F directly to the b above it. Because, as the theorist affirms, this interval is not only harsh to the ear, but virtually impossible to sing, he suggests that it is best eliminated wherever it may fall, regardless of the mode, by adding a flat to any b that is connected melodically with the f below it unless the line proceeds from b to c, thus mitigating the undesirable effect. The troublesome tritone is produced in the natural scales of the modes only by motion in either direction between an f and the b♮ above it, but the introduction of the flat needed to eliminate it immediately creates the possibility of another tritone above that b♭ by ascending from there directly to e. Such instances obviously require a simple extension of the same principle to allow the application of a flat to any e, or eventually even any a or d that would otherwise result in a melodic tritone. Tinctoris recognizes that this does become necessary in the irregular modes and in counterpoint.[7] Theoretically this process could lead through the circle of fifths to the use of a flat with every degree of the scale, but in practice nothing beyond an a♭ was required by the repertory at hand.

In the same context Tinctoris points out that it may become necessary in part writing to form modes 5 and 6 with B♭ when the latter pitch is sounded against an f in a higher register in order that the fifth so produced contain the three tones and one semitone required to make it perfect. Actually, for this theorist harmonic considerations are seemingly more important than melodic ones. When the melodic and harmonic situations just described demand contradictory solutions, he indicates that using a melodic tritone is preferable to losing the perfection of the consonance.[8] Tinctoris treats the harmonic aspects

7. Cf. Coussemaker's *Scriptorum*, 4:23, the "Tonus in exemplum evitandi tritoni" and its "Contrapunctus in exemplum usus tritoni" together with the explanations offered by Tinctoris.

8. Ibid., p. 22, "Non tamen ignorandum est quod in cantu composito . . . ," including the musical example.

of the problem in greater detail in his book on counterpoint. An entire chapter of the section dealing with dissonance is devoted to the proposition that the so-called false concords—unisons, fourths, fifths, and octaves (and their octave compounds) having one semitone more or less than their perfect counterparts—are to be avoided everywhere. He concedes that some of these intervals are to be discovered even in the works of the best composers but refuses nevertheless to condone their use.[9] In the next chapter he goes on to affirm that false or imperfect concords resulting from the chromatic alteration of a pitch by the application of a sharp are likewise to be shunned, though once again he is obliged to admit that they occur frequently.

It is only in this tangential manner that Tinctoris touches on the type of chromatic alteration most common to the music of the period, that employed in cadential formulas in order that at least one of the voices involved move into the final perfect consonance of the musical phrase by a semitone. This specific function of accidental inflection is well documented in sources of the fourteenth century, going back at least to the early works of Philippe de Vitry, and had definitely become conventional by the time of Tinctoris. It is consequently surprising that the theorist did not deal with such a significant area of musical practice in considerable depth, and the omission, in view of his systematic and exhaustive discussion of the musical theory of his day, suggests that some of his work may have been lost. This hypothesis receives some support from his own writings, for in the penultimate chapter of his exposition of the Guidonian "hand" (the hexachord system), he observes that "many other genera and species of conjunctions are found in our hand, the which are all most clearly explained in our *Speculum musices*."[10] Unfortunately, no such treatise is preserved under Tinctoris's name, and the apparent loss is all the more regrettable if, as it would seem, he there treated the important questions of cadential alteration.

Be that as it may, his injunction in the book on counterpoint to avoid denaturing perfect consonances by the introduction of sharps implies that the latter practice was generally understood and hence

---

9. "Quod discordantiae quas falsas concordantias vocant ... sunt evitandae," in *De arte contrapuncti*, liber II, capitulum XXXIII; see Coussemaker's *Scriptorum*, 4: 146, or the English translation of the treatise by Seay, *The Art of Counterpoint*, p. 130.

10. "De conjunctionibus," in *Expositio manus*, capitulum VIII; Coussemaker's *Scriptorum*, 4: 15–16.

in no need of preliminary explanations. Furthermore, the theorist's discussion would indicate that the cadential alteration was so universally applied as to take precedence over the general rule prohibiting the imperfection of perfect concords. Tinctoris has marked with an asterisk two harmonic combinations in a brief didactic composition. This first is a diminished fifth produced between superius and contratenor when the latter approaches from a written c♯, a cadence on d that it forms with the tenor. The second is even more interesting because the cadence, articulated in this case by the superius and tenor moving in contrary motion to the octave a–a′, apparently requires that the g in the higher voice be raised to within a semitone of the following a′, thus creating an augmented octave with the contratenor.[11] Significantly, the necessary sharp is not written, but the passage properly illustrates the observation only when it is assumed that the singer was expected to supply it on his own initiative in any such musical context.

What Tinctoris seems to be saying is that precisely because the singer (or player) has been trained to treat cadential formulas in this manner, it is advisable for the composer to avoid combinations that will inevitably result in the proscribed harmonic combinations when the cadential alterations are effected. But because the musicians whose works are included in the present collection were not always so careful, there are many places where the conventional use of an accidental produces the undesirable intervals. Since the realities of practice were evidently less refined than the abstract theorizing of Tinctoris, chromatic changes have been occasionally suggested in those contexts as well but never where an imperfect octave would result.

Despite the presence of censurable irregularities in the two examples given by Tinctoris, the cadential structures illustrated are wholly typical of the music of the period. The essential framework is formed by two voices moving in contrary motion. The cadential goal is a perfect consonance, usually an octave, but occasionally a fifth or a unison (or a fifth and an octave simultaneously in the so-called double leading tone cadence). The perfect consonance is reached in contrary motion, often by way of a suspended dissonance, from the imperfect consonance most proximate, usually a sixth but also a third (and

11. "De concordantiis perfectis quae vel imperfectae vel superfluae . . . ," in *De arte contrapuncti*, liber II, capitulum XXXIV; see also Coussemaker's *Scriptorum*, 4: 146ff., or the Seay translation, *The Art of Counterpoint*, p. 131.

sometimes both at once). The sensitive interval in relation to accidental alteration is the penultimate one. If there is a natural semitone preceding the cadential termination, either in the ascending voice (as in octave cadences on c and f) or in the descending voice (as in cadences of the Phrygian variety), no accidental is needed. However, in many cases the semitone is not normally present and must be introduced by an alteration. This is most commonly a sharp in the part (or parts) ascending to the last note of the cadential pattern while the other part descends by step, but it can be the other way about if a flat is indicated instead. And whether the concluding pitch of the octave cadence is the final of the mode or a related pitch, the procedure is the same.

In summary, then, four general principles for the use of accidentals can be extrapolated from the theoretical writings of Tinctoris: (1) melodic tritones should be avoided; (2) the perfect consonances should not be allowed to become imperfect or false; (3) cadential finals should be reached in one of the two structural voices by means of a semitone; and (4) should any two of the previous rules come into direct conflict, harmonic considerations generally take precedence over melodic ones.

In addition to these contexts there are a few that seem to require accidentals on somewhat more pragmatic grounds. For example, where imitation plays a significant role in the compositional process, alterations proposed for the initial statement of a given melodic line have usually been applied to iterations of it as well, even though the changes entailed could not be rationalized by the principles demonstrated above. That it is reasonable to do so is suggested not only by the natural tendencies of performing musicians but, more persuasively, by the fairly pervasive use of transposition as a compositional tool in the music of the period.

Further, in a number of the half cadences with which internal sections of some chansons are closed, a third is present in the final sonority and is signed in the manuscript with a sharp in the manner of a leading tone. This would indicate that it had already become a convention in the fifteenth century to raise the lowest third (or one of its octave duplications) within the cadential octave, and there are a number of songs in the present repertory for which such a change seems fitting even though it is not indicated in the chansonnier. Finally, it was necessary to determine the intended duration of written sharps and flats and to explore the implications (if any) of the notated symbol for other pitches that might require alteration as a result. In general it has been assumed that an accidental would remain in effect until the end of the phrase in which it is contained. As for the consequences generated by a chromatic change apparently given expressly as a signal for further alterations, the principles already discussed provided a guide for the suggestions made.

The editorial sharps and flats, as opposed to those included in the manuscript itself, have been placed in the customary manner immediately above the notes to which they apply and are valid only for that single pitch. These alterations must be regarded as suggestions only. Differing solutions are possible in a considerable number of instances without departing in any significant way from the principles adhered to in the edition; in fact, some are suggested by concordant sources. As a rule, the knottier and more intriguing problems have been cited in Comments and the performer may wish to experiment with the possibilities inherent in the relatively flexible usage of the fifteenth century. Since the general procedures to be followed can be determined with some degree of confidence, it is feasible to try a variety of interpretations without violating the currently known parameters of fifteenth-century style. It should be borne in mind that a standardized, authoritative reading would not seem to be in keeping with the spirit of the age, and that differences in performance were in fact part of the practice of the time.

Text Placement

Equally difficult are the problems encountered in attempting an intelligent and musical adaptation of the poetry of the chanson to the setting provided by the composer. Even the fundamental question as to which parts were conceived for vocal presentation cannot always be answered without ambiguity. The scribe of the Mellon Chansonnier, following a common convention of the period, usually wrote the poetry in full only once, placing the initial strophe under the notes of the cantus and grouping the remaining ones in space not occupied by the notation. In such cases he inscribed an incipit under the remaining voices, as was ordinarily done, solely for purposes of identification. This practice undoubtedly reflects one of the most prevalent traditions of fifteenth-century chanson performance, that of accompanied solo song.

Elsewhere, however, he wrote out the text for two or more of the parts. This he did not only for the polytextual pieces (Nos. 4, 11, 28, 34, and 54) and the devotional works in Latin (Nos. 19 and 57), where it could be expected, but also for a number of compositions where cantus and tenor function as a duo of essentially equal voices, frequently identified either by imitative or by homophonic writing (Nos. 18, 20, 29, 33, 38, and 42). In the face of this evidence, one can assume either that the copyist himself was enough of a musician to see the possibility of vocal performance for several of the voices or (with greater probability) that he followed faithfully the exemplar from which he worked.

In either case the result was not entirely consistent; in three songs (Nos. 14, 31, and 40) he provided words for voices other than the cantus only for a portion of the piece. In yet others, where the text is written only once, the melodic writing is at least as homogeneous as in some of those whose verse is entered under two or more of the voices. A striking example is the opening work of the collection, *Bel Acueil*, in which all three parts lend themselves almost equally well to the declamation of the poetry, which is written only for the cantus.

Given the situation, it would have been possible for the editor to evaluate independently the melodic character of each voice part and to place the text under all those deemed capable of bearing it, or even to provide for a totally vocal execution of each piece regardless of the adjustments needed to adapt the words to the music. However, it was thought preferable to follow the scribe in his provision of texts to be sung on the assumption that his indications may well reflect important aspects of contemporary performance practice.

The modern musician may wish to adapt some chansons of the present edition for voices alone, and it is conceivable that some of his fifteenth-century predecessors did so as well even though there is little corroboration for that supposition. By contrast the numerous musical anthologies, both manuscript and printed, in which poetry was simply not included clearly demonstrate that completely instrumental performances were common enough, particularly in Italy. But the overwhelming bulk of the evidence, both from the notated sources and from relevant iconography, would indicate that mixed consorts of a solo voice (or voices) and instruments—precisely the

type of combination implied by the procedures of the Mellon scribe—
were those most frequently heard, at least when the language sung
was understood.[12]

The copyist's inconsistencies required an editorial decision, of course.
Busnois's *Ja que li ne s'i attende* (No. 14) and le Rouge's *Se je fayz dueil*
(No. 31) both have the verse written only for the cantus at the beginning, but for the tenor and (with the omission of the final line) for
the contratenor as well in the final segment. Since in both instances
the passage in question is relatively short, generally syllabic, and
either completely homophonic or faithfully imitative, it would be a
simple matter to apply the text placement of the cantus to the other
part or parts if vocal performance were desired at that point, even
though some of the longer notes of the contratenor would require
subdivision. Therefore, it was not judged necessary to print the text
for the other voices in the modern score. In Caron's *Mort ou mercy*
(No. 40) the situation is much the same (the verse being written for
the tenor in the second section only) except that the segment for vocal
duo is appreciably longer and more contrapuntal in character. As a
result, it was thought preferable in that case to honor the inconsistency
of the copyist and to enter the text in the tenor part for the second
segment of the piece.

The indications given by the scribe for the distribution of the
individual syllables of a line of verse among the rhythmic units of the
corresponding musical phrase are imprecise at best. Because the
declamation of the poetry was essentially the prerogative of the singer,
it cannot be assumed that a trained calligrapher, such as the one who
penned the texts in the Mellon Chansonnier, was familiar with the
principles by which it was done. Moreover, the exigencies of his own
specialized task of writing the verse elegantly in a relatively cramped
space would have allowed him little freedom to follow the singer's
procedures of syllable distribution even if he understood them and—
what is even less likely—thought it important to do so. This may
explain why the copyists of the fifteenth century appear to have made
no attempt as a rule to specifiy the note or notes with which a given
element of the word was to be sung. The only help they consistently
offered was in observing a general (if sometimes rather rough) corres-

12. See Howard Brown, "Instruments and Voices in the Fifteenth-century Chanson," *Current
Thought in Musicology*, pp. 89–139.

pondence between the poetic line and the musical phrase to which it was apparently assumed to belong.

Unfortunately, the problems involved in distributing the syllables of text for performance are clarified only to a limited degree by the relevant didactic literature. No discussion of them was included in the theoretical writings of the period before Giovanni Maria Lanfranco's *Scintille di Musica* published in 1533.[13] Even in the second half of the sixteenth century, despite a growing sensitivity to the relationship between words and music both syntactically and semantically, music theorists did not routinely turn their attention to the questions of text placement. Only two of them, Gioseffo Zarlino and Gaspar Stocker, formulated a coherent set of rules that has attracted the notice of modern scholars, and in either case the principles exposed are clearly based on the earlier work of Lanfranco.[14]

Although Stocker's reworking of the material is the latest, dating from the 1570s, he gave his discussion a historical dimension, distinguishing between the rules that he reports were observed by the composers of the Josquin generation (five of them obligatory and five optional) and another five that were added in his own time. It cannot be demonstrated that the masters represented in this collection consciously respected Stocker's canon, but because many of his prescriptions are not only shared by Lanfranco and Zarlino but also reflect both pragmatic necessity and notational conventions derived from the plainchant of the medieval church, it seems entirely credible that they did, at least to some degree. It is those common principles that were generally observed in adapting text to music in the transcriptions and Stocker's formulation of them that served as a point of departure for the observations to follow concerning the editorial process.[15]

Stocker's obligatory rules begin with the obvious: (1) that the number of syllables should not exceed the number of notes, and (2)

13. See the article by Don Harrán, "New Light on the Question of Text Underlay Prior to Zarlino," *Acta Musicologica* 45 (1973): 24–56.

14. As Harrán shows, the rules given by Gioseffo Zarlino in his *Istitutioni Harmoniche* of 1558 (part 4, chap. 33) appear to be simply an elaboration of the earlier formulation of Lanfranco, now clarifying, now obfuscating the intended meaning. In turn, Gaspar Stocker's *De musica verbali* is evidently based on the discussion in Zarlino's celebrated and widely circulated treatise.

15. Stocker's observations on the proper joining of text and music have been summarized and provided with a commentary of customary lucidity by Edward E. Lowinsky, "A Treatise on Text Underlay by a German Disciple of Francisco de Salinas."

that a dot of addition should be counted with the preceding note as a single rhythmic unit. Nowhere in the present repertory was it necessary to seriously consider contravening either of these precepts, at least not in the parts that were clearly intended to be sung. The remaining three rules were traditionally observed in the liturgical plainsong and apparently carried over from the outset into polyphonic composition: (3) a ligature should carry only a single syllable; (4) several notes on the same pitch require each to receive a separate syllable; and (5) the first syllable is to be sung to the first note and the last to the last, an obligation that apparently applies not only to the composition as an entity but also to each individual phrase.

In his commentary, Stocker allows exceptions to the rules concerning the integrity of ligatures and dotted figures when the syllables do in fact outnumber the notational units, and in the chansonnier there are a few isolated passages in which it seemed justifiable to disregard the ligatures. For example, the opening phrase of *Petitte Camusette* (No. 4) is written in the cantus with two ligatures. If each were to carry but one syllable, the first rest would intervene in the middle of the second word. A copyist has perhaps here betrayed the intentions of the composer (if the text of the chansonnier is the original one) because the same melodic line, when taken up imitatively in the remaining three voices, is written to allow a syllabic delivery. So it appeared preferable for the cantus to declaim the verse in the same manner.

The fourth and fifth rules obviously require some interpretation as well. Although repeated pitches usually serve as a signal for syllabic declamation, there are contexts in which they are clearly not intended to be so treated. Frequently the first of two notes on the same pitch is part of a dotted figure and, at the same time, of a short duration such as a semiminim. In such cases it functions as a sort of anticipation, either melodically or harmonically, that has no positive meaning for the distribution of the text. The configuration in question occurs most commonly in the stereotyped cadential ornament on the third below the final, where it is usually best treated as a melismatic flourish. In the latter form it is to be seen in virtually every piece of the collection, but it also appears independently of the cadential formula in passages of a melismatic character, as in the melodic line with which the cantus closes Binchois's *Comme femme desconfortee* (No. 27).

There are also notational configurations in which a repeated pitch seems to have been used merely because there was no other way to achieve the total duration desired except by writing twice the note in question. An example is found in the cantus of Busnois's *Je ne puis vivre ainsy* (No. 12) at the beginning of the fourth measure. However, in other places, where a previous syllable was intoned at the beginning of a dotted figure or even earlier, the second of the iterated notes offers at times a most convenient opportunity to introduce a new syllable. Situations of the latter type are to be encountered frequently in the present repertory, but nowhere is the case illustrated more vividly than by the terminal phrase of the cantus in *Hora cridar "Oymè"* (No. 52).

It would seem self-evident in a vocal work that the first note sung should receive the initial syllable of the text, but if the same rule is applied at the lèvel of the melodic phrase in relation to the corresponding line of verse, the result can be problematical. Even more difficult is a practical realization of the corollary, that the final syllable should be borne by the concluding note. In the latter case the singer— or the editor—must first decide which is in fact the last tone of the phrase. Literally understood, of course, it would be the note preceding the beginning of a new phrase (and a new line of verse) and generally separated from it, for greater clarity, by an intervening rest. But the musical phrase is often articulated by a cadential pattern preceded by enough melodic material to permit a comfortable declamation of the entire line of poetry and followed by a shorter segment of a melismatic character.

Typical is the opening of Busnois's *Au povre par necessité* (No. 39), where a conventional cadence on g (m. 6) is extended in the cantus by a brief descending figure. Two lines later the melodic protraction is interrupted by a rest that gives a certain independence to the scalewise passage with which it concludes (mm. 16–19). Analogous examples are to be seen in *Puis que je vis le regart* (No. 53), where in two instances the cadential formula is followed directly by a rest (mm. 13 ff. and 28 ff.). It is possible in contexts of the kind described to consider the terminal note of the cadence as the last in terms of the musical syntax and to treat the ensuing melodic extension as a melismatic ornament.

This perception of the musical events seems quite justifiable in light of the melismatic tradition of the chanson in the late fourteenth and early fifteenth centuries. An especially clear reflection of it may be seen in the prolonged melodic elaboration of the initial word of *Or me veult* (No. 49). However, the resulting text placement does not leave the final syllable to be enunciated by the last note to sound. In addition, the melodic segments set off by rests but treated as an extension of the preceding line do not conform to the fifth rule, strictly speaking, at either end. Compliance could have been achieved by the simple expedient of repeating some element of the verse, as was frequently done in the sixteenth century. But there is very little evidence that such repetitions were used in the period from which the chansonnier stems, and passages such as those cited do not lend themselves well to declamation of the text. Consequently, the reiteration of words and phrases has rarely been suggested in the modern score and only when the nature of the melodic writing offered a reasonably compelling justification for it, as in Regis's *Puis que ma damme | Je m'en voy* (No. 11).

Although textual repetitions did not often seem to the editor to fall within the bounds of the musical style represented in the present collection, there are definite indications that the composers of the fifteenth century gave some thought to the aural intelligibility of the poetry they set. Musical phrases frequently begin with relatively longer values and repeated pitches, allowing—and even suggesting—a quasi-syllabic declamation of the attending line of verse before evolving into melodic writing of a more florid nature. When the composer's intentions are reasonably unequivocal, as in Busnois's *A qui vens tu* (No. 10) or Joye's *Mercy mon dueil* (No. 23), to cite two representative examples at random, the shape of the melodic lines makes it quite clear that only after a fairly rapid delivery of the text are autonomously musical ideas allowed to unfold in a melismatic extension terminated by a cadential formula. But because the end of such a phrase, like its beginning, is presumably sung, it raises the question as to which syllable should be prolonged by the melisma.

Stocker touches on this problem in his formulation of the first of five rules considered optional, according to him, by the composers of the previous generation.[16] He indicates that if a penultimate or antepenultimate syllable is accented, it may be carried over several semiminims and that when several semiminims (or shorter notes) fall together, they are all sung to the syllable of the first one. It can be

16. Cf. Lowinsky, "A Treatise on Text Underlay," pp. 238 ff.

assumed that the language to which his prescriptions refer is the Latin of his treatise, but his observation has some validity for the French vernacular as well.

Particularly when the rhymes are feminine, the penultimate syllable can usually be extended without obscuring the identity of the final word of the verse and without doing excessive violence to the natural prosody of the language. On the other hand, when the rhymes are masculine, the choice is not always so easily made. If the penultimate syllable is relatively important and not without a certain natural stress, as happens quite consistently in Busnois's *A une damme* (No. 5), it seemed reasonable to suggest a melismatic extension of the penultimate even at the risk of delaying the listener's perception of the line of poetry. In a few special instances it appeared more appropriate to prolong the antepenultimate syllable of the verse. Examples are the end of Joye's macaronic *Ce qu'on fait a quatimini* (No. 9) for the Latin word *Altissimi* and the close of the second line (mm. 10–14), where there is the possibility of an intended pictorialism in the considerable delay that precedes the introduction of the final two syllables of *tenu secré*. More often it seemed preferable to propose an uninterrupted declamation of the entire line and its prolongation on the final syllable, as in the first line of the piece just cited, the two initial verses of Busnois's *Je ne puis vivre ainsy* (No. 12), the beginning of Vincenet's *Ou doy je secours querir* (No. 26), and analogous cases. The resulting clarity of the textual declamation was thought sufficient justification for an ostensible violation of the precept concerning first and last syllables.[17]

The second of Stocker's optional rules has no significance for the repertory at hand. It states that when an isolated semiminim receives a syllable (as occurs frequently, according to the theorist), the following note should be similarly treated, especially if it is longer. But nowhere in the chansons of the collection did it prove necessary, much less desirable, to assign a syllable to such a small value (a sixteenth note of the transcriptions).

The number of contexts in which the remaining two of Stocker's

17. That some phrases were in fact terminated by a melisma on the final syllable seems to be implied by Lanfranco's eighth rule: "But when [the notes] will not ... carry [a repetition of the words], then one carries the penultimate syllable to the cadence or to the last singable note to give the last syllable of the text...." For the original Italian and a discussion of the meaning of the critical term, "singable note" (*nota cantabile*), see Harrán, "New Light on Text Underlay," pp. 44–45.

precepts are applicable is also rather limited. The third rule asserts that when two notes (minims or semiminims) follow a dot and are equal to it in durational value, neither they nor, usually, the following note should receive a syllable. The majority of such configurations did not lend themselves to precisely the treatment recommended. But some passages—as in the sixth measure of Ockeghem's *Ma bouce rit* (No. 30), the initial figure of Heyne's *De tous biens plaine* (No. 32), or the twentieth bar of Busnois's *O Fortune* (No. 37)—seem most natural and easy to sing when the rule is respected. Much less common still, it would appear, are situations inviting the application of the fourth rule. It allows that two minims or semiminims may on occasion carry a syllable that is pronounced with the first note and held over the second. But at least one instance in which the text could hardly be distributed in any other manner may be seen in the third measure of Vincenet's *La pena sin ser sabida* (No. 44).

The mention of specific notational values in Stocker's optional rules raises the crucial question of the relationship between tempo and text placement. More than half the compositions in the manuscript are written in the mensurations that predominated in the first half of the fifteenth century: tempus perfectum (○) and tempus imperfectum (C). A significant number employ the mensuration that was to become virtually ubiquitous in the sixteenth century, tempus imperfectum diminutum (₵). Two others (Nos. 20 and 34) have more esoteric proportional signatures (φ3 and C3), whereas a small group (Nos. 12, 14, and 36) combines one of the basic mensurations with a diminished form. On purely practical grounds the interpretation given the stroke of diminution obviously matters a great deal in the performance of the music. If the mensural symbols are understood literally, the tactus, or beat,[18] as applied to the integral semibrevis (the quarter note of the transcriptions), would be applied to the brevis (the half note) when the proportional indication is present. Inasmuch as the values written are usually about the same in either case, the use of the diminished mensuration would produce a consequent acceleration of movement. As a result the shortest note value upon which a singer could comfortably pronounce a syllable under the integral mensura-

---

18. If one accepts the general indication for the tactus in analogy to the human heart beat, as given by theorists from Gafforius to Zarlino, an appropriate metronome marking would be in the range of about 60–78 (see above, Mensuration, Tempo, and Rhythm in The Music, pp. 16–17).

tions would have to be doubled when the tempo is halved. In the three works in which integral and diminished mensurations are contrasted, a proportional division of the tempo by two seems intended. When syllabic writing makes it possible to judge with some confidence, the principal units of declamation under the basic signs are the semibreve and the minim (quarter and eighth notes), whereas under the stroke of diminution the brevis (half note) is also frequently used but the minim more rarely. The same tendencies are to be discerned in comparing the pieces written wholly in one of the integral mensurations with those in diminution, suggesting that a proportional interpretation of the mensural signs against a more or less steady beat is essentially valid for the entire repertory.[19]

If this conclusion is correct, it is of particular significance for those passages in which the declamatory pattern described earlier—a syllabic delivery followed by a melismatic elaboration of the melodic line—does not obtain. There are in fact numerous instances in which melodic and rhythmic considerations seem to have been more important to the composer than a regular syllabic presentation of the text set. These are passages in which musical configurations throw into relief a crucial question left unanswered by the rules cited: What principle guided the fifteenth-century singer in distributing the words of the verse over a musical phrase when the character of the melodic writing precluded a fairly consistent one-to-one relationship between notes and syllables?[20] Even if the procedures adopted did not give completely uniform results from one time to the next, as appears most likely, yet there must have been some general notions that made it possible for the average singer to place his text in performance without undue hesitation or uncertainty of the kind experienced by the modern editor.

Because the chanson grew out of the medieval tradition in which declamation was initially a somewhat mechanical matching of syllables and mensural units—nowhere more clearly exemplified than in the secular motets of the thirteenth century—it seemed reasonable to

---

19. See Mensuration, Tempo, and Rhythm in The Music, pp. 16–19.

20. That such passages were known to Lanfranco is suggested by his first rule: "It is to be noted that the division of the words is done in mensural music, but not as in plainsong. For in the latter the distinction is made according to the meaning of the words, but in the former it is determined by the order of the counterpoint and the necessity of rests . . ." (Harrán, "New Light on Text Underlay," p. 32).

suppose that the same practice may have persisted into the period of the present repertory and that it might even be found alongside the kind of word-oriented declamation that came to be more and more characteristic of the Renaissance. The basic rhythmic units (as opposed to individual note symbols) used in such cases to bear syllables were primarily the equivalents of semibreves and minims in the integral mensurations and breves and semibreves in diminution. However, the distribution of syllables was also guided by consideration for the natural rhythms of the prosody in relation to the recurring binary and ternary patterns of the mensurations present. In view of the regularity of the rhythmic figures used, it was assumed that the underlying brevis unit would be felt in most cases on some level and that its perception would create an expectation analogous to an accent or stress. Therefore an attempt was made to avoid the placement of an unstressed or unimportant syllable at the beginning of a brevis (or measure) when the result would have been to cast it unduly into relief and to do violence to present-day concepts of natural declamation. It is possible, of course, that the fifteenth-century singer may have given no attention at all to such matters, but it seemed, in the editor's view of things, much more likely that he did. For example, it was judged preferable at the opening of Busnois's *Bel Acueil* to hold the initial syllable over the two first notes in order that the third (stressed) syllable might come at the apex of the melodic figure at the beginning of a brevis unit instead of the relatively insignificant article *le*. Analogous cases have been treated in a similar manner.

Text placement using a basic mensural unit as the primary guide was found appropriate most often in pieces of a somewhat conservative or retrospective cast, such as the English ballades (Nos. 45, 47, and 49), and in those reflecting most clearly the courtly tradition, such as *Bel Acueil* or Morton's *N'aray je jamais mieulx* (No. 24). It even seemed justifiable in works of the type cited, and in passages in a comparable style, to use the changing of syllables to clarify or underline such rhythmic intricacies as the hemiolic shift back and forth between a simple and a compound division of the brevis (that is, between patterns of $\frac{3}{4}$ and $\frac{6}{8}$), syncopated interruptions of the regular mensural flow, and disjunctions of the melodic line by a sizable leap. No specific theoretical defense can be offered for these procedures, but Stocker's comments point to readily discernible rhythmic groups and natural stresses of language as the fundamental basis for the placement of syllables. The concepts proposed here provide tools for a rational approach that is neither excessively subjective nor unduly complicated.[21]

In every case the text placement of the transcriptions was tried at what was considered an appropriate tempo to find the most natural and musical solution possible within the conceptual framework just discussed. But as with the editorial accidentals, the printed text should be regarded as nothing more than a suggestion that the performer—or the scholar—is free to alter according to his understanding of the vocal style of the fifteenth century. Once again, even within the parameters adhered to here, there are a number of valid alternate solutions.

21. A complementary study of these problems is found in the author's contribution to the *Guillaume Dufay Quincentenary Conference*, held at Brooklyn College, New York, 6–7 December 1974, "Towards a Rational Approach to Text Placement in the Secular Music of Dufay's Time," pp. 102–14.

THE SOURCES

Leeman L. Perkins

The following catalogue of the sources concordant with the Mellon Chansonnier is descriptive in nature. In addition to the city and library of location, each entry includes whenever possible the material of the leaves (whether paper or parchment), their size and number, and, if it could be determined, the composition of the gatherings. If a musical collection consists of separate part books—an exception for the historical period concerned—this fact is noted. Otherwise, it may be assumed that the compositions are contained in a single volume with the different voices or parts placed side by side on the facing pages of an opening, as in the present manuscript. The distinctive scribal hands that can be identified in a given collection have also been cited in some instances, but in view of the difficulties inherent in such judgments, they are to be treated with all due reserve. It was generally assumed that the writing of text and music were separate skills in the fifteenth century executed by different artisans, but that was surely not so in every instance. Without archival or payment records to clarify any given case, the conclusions that can be drawn are necessarily speculative.

Each entry also includes, for the manuscripts, a concise summary of what is known concerning its provenance and date, and, for every collection, a brief description of its contents. In this connection existing inventories, editions, and the most pertinent bibliographical studies have been cited, but no attempt has been made to list all such items comprehensively. To have done so would have meant including a great many references of only marginal interest for the present edition. These citations were omitted all the more cheerfully since they are to be included in the *Census-catalogue of Manuscript Sources of Renaissance Polyphony, 1400–1550*, to be published soon by the Musicological Archive for Renaissance Manuscript Studies at the University of Illinois (Champaign–Urbana) under the direction of Charles Hamm.

Unfortunately, the completeness and value of the indications given vary from item to item. The editor was able to examine some of the manuscripts personally whereas he could see others only on microfilm. The secondary material is also uneven for the individual manuscript. Moreover, it seemed reasonable to take greater pains with those sources most directly related to the Mellon Chansonnier than with those having a more peripheral connection. But the copious files of the Musicological Archive for Renaissance Manuscript Studies were consulted in every case in the hope of providing the best bibliographical information and references available.

The manuscripts are listed in an alphabetical order determined by the name of the city and library in which they are currently held, prints in a chronological sequence beginning with the earliest. An asterisk preceding one or the other indicates that the collection contains verse without music. In the left margin are given the *sigla* used to identify the sources in the Critical Apparatus, which follows. Finally, compositions from the present repertory also found in the concordant source are listed by the number they carry in this edition.

Manuscripts

Glog   Berlin, Deutsche Staatsbibliothek (formerly Preussischer Kulturbesitz), mus. MS 40098 (*olim* Z.98), the *Glogauer Liederbuch* or better,
the *Glogauer Sammelhandschrift*; three part books in 8° written on paper:
Discantus, Tenor, and Contratenor, consisting of 155 ff., 1 + 163 ff.,
and 1 + 173 ff., respectively. An inscription in the tenor book,
"Catalogo Ecclesiae Colleg. Glogoviae Maj.," indicates that the collection once belonged to the cathedral church of Gross-Glogau in Polish
Silesia. The general character of the repertory and a number of
occasional texts suggest that it may have been prepared for the musical
establishment of that institution or, more likely, for one of its dignitaries.
The watermarks, the composers represented, and an allusion in a
ceremonial hymn all point to the 1480s as the period during which the
compilation and copying of the collection took place (see Heribert
Ringmann, "Das Glogauer Liederbuch . . ."). A complete inventory
with musical incipits and a partial edition of the music, also by Ringmann, have been published in *Das Glogauer Liederbuch*; references in
the Critical Apparatus to pieces in the part books are to the numbers
in Ringmann's inventory. The collection comprises a total of 294
compositions: 160 on Latin texts, 73 on German, 2 on Italian, 1 on
Slavic, 3 quodlibets, 16 dances, and 39 without text or identifying

incipit. The majority are without attribution, but the composers that can be identified include Attamasch, Bebrelyn, Barbingant, Bedingham, Brolo, Busnois, Caron, Dufay, Frye, Hayne, Martini, Ockeghem, Paulus de Broda, Queinfurt, Rubinus, Tinctoris, Touront, and Vincenet.

Concordances: Nos. 15, 17, 18, 22, 30, 38, 39, and 57 (a small segment of the total repertory but a significant portion of the secular works).

Roh Berlin, Kupferstichkabinett (Staatliche Museen der Stiftung Preussischer Kulturbesitz), MS 78 B 17 (*olim* Hamilton 674), generally known as the Rohan Chansonnier for having once belonged to the Cardinal Armand Gaston Maximilien de Rohan (1674–1749); parchment, 160 × 100 mm, 215 ff. On the first page of verse (f. 22^r) is a miniature generally attributed (without documentation) to Jean Foucquet, whose death between 1477 and 1481 would set a terminal date for the collection if that ascription is correct. Embodied in the illumination at the foot of the leaf is the coat of arms of the aristocratic Norman family Malet de Graville: three golden roses on a red field. As Martin Löpelmann pointed out in his edition of the manuscript, *Die Liederhandschrift des Cardinals de Rohan*, pp. ix ff., the poems to which approximate dates can be assigned would suggest that the collection was compiled between 1463 and 1475. Consequently, the original owner must have been Louis Malet de Graville, "amiral de France, grand-maître des eaux et forêts, grand veneur, lieutenant général en Normandie, gouverneur de Paris, etc.," a very important figure at the court of France from the time of Louis XI until Graville's death in 1518. The verse of the collection was divided by the principal scribe into two sections. The first (ff. 22^r–48^r) is given over in the main to ballades—only 5 of the 43 poems in the group are not in that form. The second (ff. 62^r–205^r) to rondeaux with only an occasional bergerette mixed in, 617 poems in all. A second hand later completed the final ballade, two lines of which had been written by the first, and added two more, leaving the collection with a total of 663 lyric poems, all in French. The opening folios contain an alphabetical table of contents, and ff. 0–3^v, 48^v–61^r, and 205^v–15^v are empty. Even though the manuscript includes no musical notation, it is frequently cited in musicological studies dealing with the fifteenth century because so many of the texts it contains were set to music that has survived in other sources of the period.

Concordances: No. 2, 5–7, 13, 16, 21, 25, 27, 30–32, 35, and 48.

BerK 78 C 28   Berlin, Kupferstichkabinett (Staatliche Museen der Stiftung
      Preussischer Kulturbesitz), MS 78 C 28 (*olim* Hamilton 451);
      parchment, 247 × 163 mm, 70 ff. disposed in 7 quinterns, of which
      only the first 5 (50 ff.) were originally filled with music. The illumina-
      tions of the initial opening have been identified as probably the work
      of the Florentine artists Gherardo and Monte di Giovanni del Fora,
      the arms carried by the escutcheon at the foot of f. 2^v as those of
      Margherita da Messer Francesco Castellani and Bernardino Niccolini,
      both representatives of prominent Tuscan families (see Peter Reide-
      meister, *Die Chanson-Handschrift 78 C 28 des Berliner Kupferstichkabinetts*,
      pp. 12 ff.). The author suggests that the collection may have been a
      gift for the wedding of the patrician couple, celebrated ca. 1465, and
      the repertory it contains, as given in Reidemeister's inventory, would
      tend to confirm the date of that hypothesis. Included in the manuscript
      are 43 compositions: a partial setting of the mass ordinary (ff. 51^v–62^r,
      a later addition) and 42 secular pieces, primarily by English and
      northern composers such as Basin, Bedingham, Binchois, Dufay,
      Dunstable, Frye, J. Legrant, Morton, and Pullois, but also some written
      on Italian texts (all without attribution and, a single exception aside,
      without either text or verbal incipit).
      Concordances: Nos. 24, 29, 45, 46, 51, 52, 54, and 56 (i.e., 18.6 percent
      of the total repertory).

Bol Q 16   Bologna, Civico Museo Bibliografico Musicale, MS Q 16 (*olim*
      109); paper, 214 × 140 mm, 155 ff. disposed irregularly in gath-
      erings of 5, 6, 7, and 8 double leaves with yet other combinations of
      double and single folios (see Knud Jeppesen, *La Frottola*, 2: 11). The
      principal scribe signed his name, "Marsilius," and the date 1487 at
      the end of the table of contents. Sarah Fuller has identified five other
      scribal hands in the collection, all of them posterior to Marsilius, and
      has suggested that the additions made to his original repertory were
      probably copied mainly in the 1490s (see "Additional Notes on the
      Fifteenth-Century Chansonnier Bologna Q 16," pp. 84 ff.). She has
      also deduced from the inclusion of pieces written on both Italian and
      Spanish texts that the manuscript may have originated in an Italian
      center with Spanish connections, such as the papal court during the
      presence of Rodrigo Borgia or the kingdom of Naples under the
      Aragonese (p. 86). However, a large number of compositions shared
      either with Pix, with Flo 229, or with both would point to links with
      Florence as well. Of the 131 pieces included in the collection, 87 carry

texts in French, 30 in Italian, and 8 in Spanish; in addition, there are 5 song-motets and a polyphonic mass. However, in every instance except three the text is restricted to a few words of the initial line. Similarly, there are no attributions, and the composers that can be identified through concordant sources are primarily those represented in the later additions to the codex: Agricola, Basin, Brolo, Busnois, Caron, Compère, Dufay, Dusart, Dux Burgensis, Giliardi, Guglielmo, Hayne, Isaac, Josquin, Juan de Leon, Lannoy, Malcort, Martini, Obrecht, Ockeghem, Tinctoris, Touront, Vincenet, Weerbecke, and Wreede. For an inventory of the contents including both verbal and musical incipits but, unfortunately, no concordances, see Edward Pease, "A Report on Codex Q 16 of the Civico Museo Bibliografico Musicale. . . ."

Concordances: Nos. 5, 6, 18, 20, and 32 (only 3.8 percent of the total repertory).

Q 18 Bologna, Civico Museo Bibliografico Musicale, MS Q 18 (*olim* 143); paper, 168 × 240 mm, 93 ff., of which those numbered 10, 47, and 56 are now missing. The collection was apparently copied in northern Italy early in the sixteenth century and contains a total of 92 compositions, of which 7 are incomplete because of the lost leaves. Grouped more or less at the beginning are 34 compositions associated in some source with an Italian text. Although linguistic distinctions are not always easily made, given the Italianizing corruptions of the scribe, the remaining works seem divided mainly between Latin motets and French chansons. But there is also a piece on a Flemish text, another on a Spanish one, a number with no text at all (moreover, those present usually consist of only an incipit), and a small group of instrumental pieces with titles such as *La Morra*, *La Spagna*, and *La Bernardina*. The one attribution in the manuscript is erroneous, but composers represented include Agricola, Brumel, Busnois, Caron, Compère, Congiet, Cara, Enrique (Wreede), Honophrius Antenoreus, Isaac, Japart, Josquin, Lurano, Malcort (?), Martini, Obrecht, Ockeghem, Pesenti, Stokhem, Tromboncino, and Vincenet. For a description of the codex with an inventory of the Italian pieces (*frottole* and *laude*), see Jeppesen, *La Frottola*, 2: 10 and 108 ff.

Concordance: No. 18.

R 11239 Brussels, Bibliothèque Royale de Belgique, MS 11239; parchment, 145 × 200 mm, 63 ff., of which only the first 34 contain music, the remainder empty staves. The leaves were originally disposed in 5 quaterns of which the third lacks 2 folios in the center and the fourth is entirely wanting. The codex carries the arms of the ducal house of Savoy, for which it was evidently copied just prior to the marriage in 1501 of Philibert II to Marguerite of Austria. It subsequently came into Margaret's possession following the death of her husband. Included in the collection are 18 French chansons, 4 Latin motets, and 2 motet-chansons, works by Agricola, Bruhier, Brumel, Compère, Hayne, Isaac, Josquin, Larue, Nino le Petit, Obrecht, and Ockeghem. A description of the manuscript and an annotated inventory with musical incipits, concordances, and comments are found in Martin Picker's study of "The Chanson Albums of Marguerite of Austria," pp. 176–84, 240–59. Also available is his edition of the musical repertory together with the bibliographical and historical findings of the earlier publication: *The Chanson Albums of Marguerite of Austria*.

Concordance: No. 4.

Cop 17   Copenhagen, Kongelige Bibliotek, MS fragment 17a (*olim* 598); a fragment of 6 double leaves (of which only 3 were originally together in the same gathering), paper, originally about 270 × 210 mm, now somewhat mutilated and unevenly cut. The volume to which the leaves once belonged is to be dated from about the middle of the fifteenth century and may have originated in Auvergne because the paper carries watermarks similar to those used by the manufacturers of that province. There survive in the fragment portions of 11 compositions including a segment of *Supremum est* and the contratenor of *Par le regart*, both by Dufay, and part of a work attributed to Zachara da Teramo (see Henrik Glahn, "Ein Kopenhagener Fragment aus dem 15. Jahrhundert," pp. 59–99).

Concordance: No. 51.

Cop 291⁸   Copenhagen, Kongelige Bibliotek, MS Thott 291⁸; parchment, 170 × 120 mm, 48 ff., originally disposed in 7 quaterns of which the fourth, fifth, and seventh are now incomplete, a total of 8 leaves having been lost (including ff. 26, 29, and 34). The collection seems to have originated in northern French or Burgundian territories in the 1470s. In this respect the Copenhagen Chansonnier is like the Dijon Chansonnier and the earlier layer of the Laborde Chansonnier, which were apparently copied by the same scribe and with which it shares similar readings and a large number of concordances (23 and 17, respectively) (see the introduction to Knud Jeppesen's edition of the manuscript, *Der Kopenhagener Chansonnier*, pp. xxv ff.). The codex is also related to the slightly later Wolfenbüttel Chansonnier, with which it shares the same style of illumination (ibid., p. xxvi). Early in the sixteenth century it belonged to Guillaume Hue, dean of the church of Paris, who died in 1522 (see Geneviève Thibault and Eugénie Droz, "Le chansonnier de la Bibliothèque Royale de Copenhague," pp. 13 ff.). A repertory of 33 French chansons was originally copied into the first 43 leaves, and the space left vacant was utilized in the sixteenth century for the addition of a number of others. No attributions were entered in the manuscript, but the composers represented include Basiron, Busnois, Convert, Hayne, Michelet, Molinet, Morton, Ockeghem, Prioris, and Symon le Breton.

Concordances: Nos. 14, 24, and 32 (the latter two being the most widely disseminated compositions included in the present collection).

p 1848-2⁰   Copenhagen, Kongelige Bibliotek, Ny Kongelige Samling, MS 1848-2⁰; paper, approximately 285 × 201 mm, 450 ff. Since the paper carries a watermark similar to one used in Lyons about 1515 and the spine the date 1520, it can be assumed that the collection was compiled in that city during the second decade of the sixteenth century. Lending support to this hypothesis is the fact that the manuscript was formerly in the possession of the Jesuit Library in Lyons (see Henrik Glahn, "Et fransk musikhåndskrift fra begyndelsen af det 16. århundrede"). The contents are mixed, consisting of masses, motets, 14 Magnificats, and about 190 secular French pieces, a total of some 270 compositions. Attributions are infrequent, but the following composers have been identified: Agricola, Barbireau, Bedingham(?), Brumel, Busnois, Compère, Dulot, A. Févin, Ghiselin (Verbonnet), Hacquinet, Hayne, Hesdin, Isaac, Janequin (C. and Tomas), Josquin, Lhéritier, Maioris(?), Margot(?), Morton, Obrecht, Ockeghem, Pietrequin, Prioris, Richafort, and Sermisy.

Concordances: Nos. 30 and 32.

517   Dijon, Bibliothèque Municipale, MS 517 (*olim* 295); parchment, 173 × 126 mm, 6 + 198 ff., including an initial gathering of 6 leaves (containing a table of contents and a brief treatise on notation)

and 25 quaterns, the first of which is lacking its first and eighth folios. A contemporaneous foliation in Roman numerals begins with the initial leaf of music. A modern one in arabic numbers starts with the first folio of the manuscript, but errors periodically alter the discrepancy between the two. The alphabetical table refers to neither but uses an ordinal system that goes only to no. 76. As Jeppesen has shown (*Der Kopenhagener Chansonnier*, pp. xxiv ff.), the distinctive notational style of the Dijon codex, characterized by long ascending stems and sharply pointed heads, is also found in the Copenhagen manuscript and in the earlier layer of the Laborde Chansonnier, indicating that all three were written by the same copyist or, at least, in the same atelier. Like the other two collections, then, the Dijon Chansonnier must have been compiled in northern French or Burgundian territories early in the 1470s. Droz and Thibault have suggested that it may have reached the Municipal Library of Dijon more or less directly from the bibliographical collections of the Dukes of Burgundy, a distinct possibility (see *Trois chansonniers français du XVe siècle*, p. ix). That the manuscript was prepared in any case for a thoroughly French milieu is demonstrated by the care with which the scribe wrote out all the strophes of the poetry, thus making the source particularly valuable from a literary point of view. Included in the collection are 160 compositions (only 152 of which are listed in the table), all French chansons with the exception of a devotional motet on a Latin text and 2 bitextual pieces combining French and Latin. With the exception of the last 5 chansons and a textless bicinium that were apparently added somewhat later (2 of them are attributed to Compère) the calligraphy and the notation each seem to be the work of a single hand. Among the composers represented are Barbingant, Bedingham or Dunstable, Binchois, Boubert, Busnois, Caron, Compère, Convert, Dufay, de la Haye, Hayne, Michelet, Molinet, Morton, Ockeghem, Symon le Breton, and Tinctoris. An inventory of the contents with musical incipits, but also with some errors and omissions and no references to foliation, was published by Stéphane Morelot, "Notices sur un manuscrit de musique ancienne," unnumbered pp. following p. 160. An alphabetical table of the chansons in the Dijon, Copenhagen, Laborde, and Wolfenbüttel chansonniers is found in Droz and Thibault, *Trois chansonniers français*, pp. xiii ff., together with an edition of the first 49 pieces of the Dijon manuscript. Also available is a reproduction in facsimile, edited by Dragan Plamenac, *Dijon, Bibliothèque Publique*

Manuscrit 517. In a brief review of the edition Martin Picker has included an inventory that is complete and correct, giving foliations, textual incipits, and attributions (see the review of *Dijon*).
Concordances: Nos. 1–5, 7, 10, 12, 14, 16, 20, 21, 24, 25, 27, 29, 30, 32, and 42 (11.9 percent of the total repertory).

c IV.a.24   El Escorial, Biblioteca del Monasterio, MS IV.a.24; paper, 145 × 210 mm, 137 ff. The original corpus of the collection, as nearly as can be determined from a juxtaposition of the contemporary table of contents (ff. 1ᵛ–3ʳ) and its present state, apparently consisted of a gathering of 8 or 10 leaves (set aside initially for the table) and 12 quinterns (120 ff.) of music. To these may have been added somewhat later a gathering of 6 or more leaves at ff. 86–91, while another gathering at the end was either subsequently appended or left empty at the first copying. Now absent, on the other hand, are at least 2 leaves from the initial gathering, one between ff. 14 and 15, 2 just after f. 82, and 2 more between ff. 127 and 128 (see Eileen Southern, "El Escorial, Monastery Library, MS IV.a.24," pp. 42–43, 58–77; cf. the schema of the structure of the MS given by Jeppesen, *La Frottola*, 2: 22–23). As is demonstrated by the watermarks, the collection was undoubtedly compiled in Italy. In view of the substantial number of concordances with the Mellon Chansonnier and the virtually complete agreement between the readings of the two sources, it is not unlikely that the Escorial codex also originated in Naples—conceivably at the royal court of Aragon—as Jeppesen has suggested (ibid. p. 19). It shares with the present collection the added distinction of having its texts, even those in French, written in a Gothic hand reasonably completely and correctly despite its Italian provenance. Moreover, judging from its contents and its relationship to other fifteenth-century sources, it is probably to be dated from the 1460s (see Martha K. Hanen, "The Chansonnier El Escorial, MS IV.a.24," pp. 9, 44–51). The original table lists 100 compositions, but in one instance two and in another three sections of the same piece are numbered separately (68–69 and 37–39) so that the actual total was only 97. Somewhat later, but during the same general period, 4 other works were entered at the beginning on leaves originally destined for the table, 9 at the end (of which four were also recorded with separate numbers in the table), and ten in the body of the collection, making a total of 120. Two of these pieces have since been lost, including a copy of Caron's *Accueilly m'a la belle* (see Collation for No. 3), leaving the manuscript with its present repertory of 118 works, 91 French chansons, 22 pieces on Italian poems, 2 on Flemish, 1 each on Spanish and English, and 1 textless piece. Composers represented include Basin, Bedingham, Binchois, Braxatoris, Busnois, Cornago, Domarto, Dufay, Dunstable, Frye, Horlay, J. Legrant, Morton, Ockeghem, and Pullois. Jeppesen (*La Frottola*, 2: 112–13) gives concordances for the compositions with Italian texts. Southern ("El Escorial," pp. 56 ff.) supplies a complete inventory with concordances and comments that shows both the original numbering (erroneously designated as a foliation) and the modern foliation now found in the manuscript; all references here are to the latter.

Concordances: Nos. 16, 24, 27, 45–47, 51–54, and 56 (about 9 percent of the total repertory).

FloC 2439   Biblioteca del Conservatorio L. Cherubini, MS 2439, the Basevi Codex; parchment, 168 × 237 mm, 101 ff. The manuscript was copied in the Netherlands, probably by Martin Bourgeois, during the first decade of the sixteenth century (see Herbert Kellman, "Josquin and the Courts of the Netherlands and France," table I; cf. Martin Staehelin, "Quellenkundliche Beiträge zum Werk von Johannes Ghiselin-Verbonnet," pp. 123–25). However, a coat of arms found on ff. iv and xli^r is that of an Italian family, the Conte Agostini della Seta from Pisa, indicating that the codex was made for one of its members. The repertory is divided between two sections, the first for compositions in four parts, the second for those in three, and comprises primarily pieces with French texts or incipits, many of which are reworkings of fifteenth-century-chanson tenors. There are also a few Latin motets, a half-dozen bitextual compositions combining Latin and French, seven Flemish songs, one piece using only solmization syllables, and another with no text at all—for a total of 87 works. Represented are Agricola, Brumel, Busnois, Compère, Ghiselin (Verbonnet), Isaac, Josquin, Lannoy, Larue, Ninot le Petit, Obrecht, Ockeghem, de Orto, Pipelare, Prioris, Cornelius Rigo de Bergis, and Weerbecke. A description of the codex and an inventory with comments and a few concordances was published by Léon de Burbure, "Etude sur un manuscrit du XVIe siècle. . . ."

Concordance: No. 4.

lo 229 Florence, Biblioteca Nazionale Centrale, MS Banco Rari 229 (*olim* Magl. XIX, 59); paper, 232 × 167 mm, 325 ff. disposed regularly in quinterns to which were added 5 illuminated parchment leaves at the beginning. The illuminations and decoration of the codex have been attributed to Gherardo and Monte di Giovanna del Fora, indicating that the collection was copied in Florence (see Anne Marie Bragard, "Un manuscrit florentin du quattrocento," p. 56). Howard Brown, in the introduction to his edition of the manuscript, has suggested convincingly that it was being prepared for King Matthias Corvinus of Hungary when news of the latter's death reached Florence early in 1491, that it was then purchased by Lorenzo the Magnificent, and finally presented as a gift to Alessandro Braccesi, whose arms are to be seen at the foot of f. iv^v. The same author also demonstrates that the miniature portrait generally believed to have been that of the composer Johannes Martini is probably instead that of Braccesi himself (see *A Florentine Chansonnier from the Time of Lorenzo the Magnificent* and the discussion above, pp. 10–12). The repertory is one of the largest of the period, comprising a total of 268 pieces the majority of which are French chansons. However, about 16 are also found with Italian texts, 1 with Flemish, 1 with Latin, and 84 with no text at all. Of the latter 5 are mass sections and 4 are motets, but the majority seem to be secular works. Exceptionally numerous are the works by Isaac (24), Agricola (27), and Martini (22); other attributions can be made to Barlem, Basin, Bosfrin, Busnois, Caron, Compère, Congiet, Dufay, Hayne, Hémart, Japart, Josquin, Joye, Lannoy, Mureau, Obrecht, Pietrequin, Planquard, Regis, Rubinet, Stokhem, Tinctoris, Vincenet, and Weerbecke. Brown's forthcoming edition will provide concordances and notes for the entire collection. A complete inventory has been published by Bianca Becherini, *Catalogo dei Manoscritti Musicali della Biblioteca Nazionale di Firenze*, pp. 22–29. For the Italian pieces alone but with concordances by Jeppesen, see *La Frottola*, 2: 53–54, 146–47.

Concordances: Nos. 8, 9, 13, 18, 22, 40, and 57 (only 2.6 percent of the total repertory despite the significant number of pieces common to both collections).

lo 121 Florence, Biblioteca Nazionale Centrale, MS Magliabecchiana XIX, 121; paper, 140 × 207 mm, 38 ff. disposed—exceptionally

for an Italian manuscript—in 4 quaterns plus a gathering of 6 double leaves at the end. The collection was undoubtedly compiled in Florence toward the beginning of the sixteenth century, certainly no earlier than 1500, and once belonged to Marietta, "filiuola di Francesco Pugi," a notary of that city (see Jeppesen, *La Frottola*, 2: 52–53). It contains a total of 37 compositions, the majority of them on Italian texts (frottole, carnival songs, and the like) with only 9 French chansons and some textless pieces that have French texts or incipits elsewhere. There are no attributions, but the few composers who have been identified include Agricola, Busnois, Coppini, Hayne, Isaac, Martini, Mureau (?), Obrecht, and Stokhem. A complete inventory of the manuscript is given by Becherini, *Catalogo dei Manoscritti Musicali*, pp. 53–54; concordances for the Italian pieces are provided by Jeppesen, *La Frottola*, 2: 144–45.
Concordance: No. 32.

Flo 176   Florence, Biblioteca Nazionale Centrale, MS Magliabecchiana XIX, 176; paper, 168 × 118 mm, 139 ff. disposed in quinterns (the first of which has a single leaf tipped in at the beginning) except for the third (which has 2 leaves tipped in) and the fifth, both of which were originally quaterns. The relationship in which this manuscript stands to sources such as the Pixérécourt Chansonnier and Florence, B.R.229, which are known to be of Florentine provenance, indicate that it too originated in the Tuscan capital (cf. Jeppesen, *La Frottola*, 2: 57–58). If so, since it includes nothing attributed to Isaac, it was probably copied prior to the latter's arrival in Florence in the mid-1480s. It contains 87 compositions, one of which is a duplication. Of these 67 are French chansons, 15 are found in some source with an Italian text, whereas two have Spanish and another Flemish as the poetic language and one has no text at all. Attributions have been made to Barbingant, Bedingham (Bellingham), Binchois, Busnois, Caron, Cornago, Domarto, Dufay, Frye, Arnolfo Giliardi, Joye, Lannoy, Lepitet basque, Michelet, Morton, Moxica, Obrecht, Ockeghem, Prioris, Raoulin, Symon le Breton, Tinctoris, and Wreede. A complete inventory of the collection is given by Becherini, "Autori minori nel codice fiorentino Magl. XIX, 176," pp. 27–31 (with concordances), and in the *Catalogo dei Manoscritti Musicali*, pp. 72–75, where two sections of the same piece are counted separately in four instances (cf. Jeppesen, *La Frottola*, 2: 57–58, who also provides concordances for the Italian works, p. 149). Joshua Rifkin has affirmed that the last two compositions in this source were copied by the principal scribe of the Florence manuscript Riccardiana 2356 (see below), with which it has a substantial number of works in common (see "Scribal Concordances for Some Renaissance Manuscripts in Florentine Libraries," pp. 313–18).

Concordances: Nos. 3, 5, 16, 17, 24, 25, 27, 29, 30, 37, 45, 47, and 53 (14 percent of the total repertory).

lo 178   Florence, Biblioteca Nazionale Centrale, MS Magliabecchiana XIX, 178; paper, 114 × 165 mm, 84 ff., of which the first 6 are unnumbered and carry only the table of contents, while the remainder are disposed primarily in quinterns. Because the watermark found in the paper of this manuscript resembles closely that of Florence, B.R.229, it would seem probable that, like the latter, it originated in the Tuscan capital. Judging from the repertory it contains, it must have been compiled at about the same time—the late 1480s or early 1490s (see Jeppesen, *La Frottola*, 2: 59). The collection comprises 73 compositions, the majority of them French chansons, with only 7 Italian pieces, 6 Latin motets, and a Flemish song. Composers represented include Agricola, Bosfrin, Caron, Compère, Dufay, Enrique (Wreede), G. Fogliano, Hayne, Isaac, Japart, Josquin, Lannoy, Martini, Molinet, Obrecht, Ockeghem, Pietrequin, Stokhem, and Weerbecke. For an inventory of the codex, see Becherini, *Catalogo dei Manoscritti Musicali*, pp. 75–77.

Concordance: No. 32.

loR 2356   Florence, Biblioteca Riccardiana, MS 2356; parchment, 230 × 172 mm, 100 ff., consisting of an initial gathering of 2 double leaves followed by 9 quinterns and a gathering of 3 double leaves. From the original foliation it is clear that when compiled, the manuscript comprised 12 quinterns (120 ff.) of which the second and the penultimate were ultimately lost along with the 2 inner double leaves of the final gathering (see Dragan Plamenac, "The 'Second' Chansonnier of the Biblioteca Riccardiana," 107–08). Dated entries in the opening leaves reveal that in the 1540s the codex belonged to Andrea Sardelli, a Florentine, suggesting that it originated in his native city. This assumption is confirmed by the relationship of its repertory with those of the Pixérécourt Chansonnier and Florence

Magl. XIX, 178. In addition Rifkin has identified the principal scribe as the one who copied the final 2 pieces into the latter collection (see "Scribal Concordances," pp. 313–18). With the exception of some later additions, the repertory would point to the late 1470s or early 1480s as the date of origin. If the collection was copied in Florence, it must have been before the arrival of Isaac in about 1484. In its present state the manuscript transmits 72 compositions, of which 56 are French chansons, 7 devotional Latin motets, 4 songs on Italian texts, 2 on Spanish, 1 that is macaronic, and 2 others with no words at all. The old table shows that 8 pieces were lost with the original second quintern, but nothing is known of the contents of the missing penultimate gathering. Among the composers to whom attributions can be made are Agricola, Bedingham, Binchois (?), Busnois (?), Caron, Cornelius (?), Dufay, Fresneau, Frye (?), Giliardi, Hayne, Japart, Josquin, Molinet, Morton, Moxica, Ockeghem, Rubinet, Simon le Breton, Touront (cecus), and Wreede. A complete inventory with musical incipits, concordances, and comments has been provided by Plamenac, "The 'Second' Chansonnier," pp. 123–72 (see also "A Postscript to the 'Second' Chansonnier of the Biblioteca Riccardiana," and Jeppesen, *La Frottola*, 2: 54–56, 148).
Concordances: Nos. 3, 24, 30, 32, 35, 42, and 53 (9.7 percent of the total repertory).

FloR 2794 Florence, Biblioteca Riccardiana, MS 2794; parchment, 240 × 166 mm, 78 ff. disposed in quaterns from which 2 leaves have now evidently been lost. The two principal scribes of this collection have been identified by Joshua Rifkin as those whose hands can be discerned, respectively, in later additions to the Dijon and Laborde chansonniers (see "Scribal Concordances," pp. 318–26 and figs. 9–12). This discovery confirms the evidence provided by the structure of the gatherings, the composition of the repertory, and the Gothic script in which the texts are written, thus pointing to an origin in northern French or Burgundian territories. The manuscript is obviously somewhat later than the main corpus of those to which it is related and is probably to be dated, like their accretions, in the late 1480s or 1490s. An inventory published by Bianca Becherini ("Alcuni canti dell' 'Odhecaton' e del codice fiorentino 2794," pp. 338–39) lists 68 works. There are 5 motets, 1 chanson-motet, and 3 Lamentation settings, and the remainder are French chansons for three and four voices.

Composers represented include Agricola, Basiron, Binchois, Busnois, Compère, Dufay, Fresneau, Frye, Hayne, Japart(?), Josquin, Ockeghem, Pietrequin, and Prioris.
Concordances: Nos. 15 and 32.

Lil 402   Lille, Bibliothèque Publique, MS 402; parchment, 267 × 183 mm, 168 ff. As Marcel Françon has shown in the introductory study to his edition of the codex, the poetry stems primarily from the reign of Louis XII, and a significant portion of it seems to have been written for the women of the Valois clan. It is possible that the manuscript was prepared for Anne de Graville, the youngest daughter of Louis de Graville, at the behest of the latter about 1510 (see *Poèmes de Transition*, pp. 71–74 and passim, and cf. the description of *Roh above). It contains exactly 600 rondeaux including works by Jean Marot, Octavien de Saint-Gelais, and Jean Picart.
Concordance: No. 8.

on 31922   London, British Museum, Additional MS 31922, Henry VIII's manuscript. The collection contains a substantial number of compositions attributed specifically to the king and generally reflects the repertory that must have been current at the royal court of England toward the beginning of his reign (about the second decade of the sixteenth century). However, it was probably not prepared for Henry himself but rather for one of his courtiers, Sir Henry Guildford of Kent, controller of the royal household (see the study by John Stevens in which the codex is examined in relation to analogous documents of the period, *Music and Poetry in the Early Tudor Court*, or the introduction to his *Music at the Court of Henry VIII*). The collection numbers 109 compositions, including songs, puzzle canons, and instrumental consort music. The majority of the composers represented are English musicians of the period: Cornish, Cooper, Daggere, Farthing, Fayrfax, Kempe, Lloyd, Pygott, and Rysbye in addition to the king; of the insular masters of the fifteenth century only Dunstable has survived. The few Continental works included can be attributed to Agricola, Barbireau, Busnois, Compère, Févin, Hayne, Isaac, and Prioris.
Concordance: No. 32.

1C 871   Montecassino, Archivio della Badia, MS 871; parchment and paper, 276 × 206 mm, 435 pp. As now constituted, the manuscript is divided between a series of religious writings, copied on parchment in the thirteenth century, and a collection of music written on paper about two centuries later (pp. 247–435 of the continuous modern pagination). The latter segment consists of 9 gatherings irregularly composed of 6 to 8 double leaves (12–16 ff.), but the combined evidence of an original foliation and the contemporary table of contents (pp. 433–34) would indicate that 3 additional gatherings, once present, have now been lost (see the forthcoming edition of the music of the codex by Isabel Pope and Masakata Kanazawa, *The Musical Manuscript Montecassino 871*, "The Manuscript". An annotation on the first folio of music reveals that the collection once belonged to the monastery of Sant' Angelo Palantano in Gaeta, a city that was part of the kingdom of Naples in the fifteenth century.

Although virtually all the copying seems to have been done by a single hand, changes in ink and notational detail suggest that the contents were compiled over a number of years. The watermarks and the composers represented imply the 1470s and early 1480s as the period of the scribe's activity. A substantial portion of the music is liturgical: settings for psalms, hymns, Lamentations of Jeremiah, the Magnificat, and the like—altogether 61 works. But secular pieces are numerous as well: 33 French chansons (one of them copied twice), 32 songs on Italian texts, 8 on Spanish texts, and 3 with none at all, making a total overall of 137 compositions. A number of the composers to whom attributions have been made were active at some time with the chapel of the royal court of Naples. Included are Bernardus (Ycart?), Johannes Cornago, Damiano, and Pietro Oriola, all of whom were employed at one point by Aragonese monarchs, as well as Franchino Gafforio, who resided for two years in the capital city (1478–80). Among the other composers represented are Antonius Janne, Antonius Piccardus, Johannes de Quadris, and a group of the most celebrated northern and English masters, Bedingham, Caron, Compère, Dufay, Dunstable, Frye, Hayne, Molinet, and Ockeghem. For a concise discussion of the manuscript and its historical significance, followed by a complete inventory giving incipits, attributions, concordances, and comments, see Isabel Pope (with the collaboration of Masakata Kanazawa), "The Musical Manuscript Montecassino N871."

Concordances: Nos. 4, 32, 36, 45, 46, 51, and 53 (approximately 9.2 percent of the 76 secular pieces included in the collection).

Sched   Munich, Bayerische Staatsbibliothek, MS Cim 351a (*olim* Cgm 810), Mus. MS 3232, the Schedel Liederbuch; paper, 150 × 105 mm, 170 ff. The collection was compiled by Hartmann Schedel of Nuremberg, mostly during his student years in Leipzig and Padua. The dates 1461, 1465, and 1467 are entered in the manuscript, but some pieces were evidently copied somewhat later as well. Besides 26 German song texts without music, the repertory includes 128 musical compositions: 70 Lieder (all but 2 polyphonic), 18 settings of Latin texts, 20 chansons, 2 Italian songs, 2 dances, and 16 textless pieces. The non-German composers represented include Bedingham, Busnois, Dufay, Dunstable, Frye, Morton, Ockeghem, Pullois, and Touront. Unfortunately, Schedel seems to have been a rather careless copyist, and the readings offered by his manuscript are frequently erroneous or unreliable. An inventory of the collection has been published by Julius J. Maier, *Die musikalischen Handschriften der königlichen Hof-und Staatsbibliothek in München*, 1: 125–30. There is an edition of selected German songs by Herbert Rosenberg, *Das Schedel'sche Liederbuch* (See also Eileen Southern, "Foreign Music in German Manuscripts of the Fifteenth Century.")
Concordances: Nos. 30, 31, 46, 53 (copied twice), and 55 (3.9 percent of the total repertory).

Mun 3232a   Munich, Bayerische Staatsbibliothek, MS Clm 14274, Mus. MS 3232a, the Emmeram codex; paper, 285 × 210 mm, 158 ff., disposed in 13 gatherings, of which 12 consist of 6 double leaves and one (the eleventh) of 7. Some of the repertory dates back to the fourteenth century and is written in black notation (the second through the seventh gatherings). However, the compilation was presumably done over an extended period because 10 different papers and 14 scribal hands can be identified in the collection, and it was completed about the middle of the fifteenth century. One can assume that the collection was prepared at the Benedictine monastery of St. Emmeram in Regensburg, whence it came to its present location, and that it served both the liturgical and the recreational needs of the monks. The repertory is large, consisting primarily of settings for the Ordinary of the mass and Latin motets. There is a considerable quantity of secular music as well, about a quarter of it with contrafact Latin texts. Dufay is exceptionally well represented with 39 attributions; also present are works by Antonio da Civitate, Arnold de

Lantins, Benet, Binchois, Blasius, Bosquel, Brassart, Dufay, Dunstable, Hermannus Edleraw, Forest, Jo. Franchois, Grossin (de Paris), Urbanus Kungsperger, Landini, Leonel, R. Liebert, Loqueville, N. Mecques, Portugal (?), Joh. Roullet, Rudolf, Sweitzl, Walonis, Joh. Waring, Petrus Wilhelmi, Wintzois, Wirquardus, and Zacharie. See the discussion of the codex and the inventory of its contents published by Karl Dèzes, "Der Mensuralcodex des Benediktiner- klosters Sancti Emmerami zu Regensburg."
Concordance: No. 49.

Mun 1516   Munich, Bayerische Staatsbibliothek, MS 1516; four paper part books in 8º, 103 × 152 mm, 96 (Discant), 95 (Tenor), 74 (Altus), and 95 (Bassus) ff. The collection may have been prepared for the ducal house of Bavaria, in whose library it was kept until 1618. Because it contains sequences of pieces that were published by Attaingnant in two separate anthologies of ca. 1530 in the same order found in the Parisian prints, one can assume that the compilation was done somewhat later. Included in the part books are 157 compositions, of which 2 were copied twice: 8 Latin motets, 8 dances, 9 lieder, 15 textless works, and 132 chansons. Although there are no attributions in the manuscript, the following composers have been identified: Jörg Blanckenmüller, Claudin, Consilium, Jacotin, C. Jannequin, Josquin, Mouton, Revertz, Richafort, and Senfl. For an inventory, see Maier, *Die musikalischen Handschriften*, pp. 114–17.
Concordance: No. 4.

Bux   Munich, Bayerische Staatsbibliothek, MS Cim 352b, Mus. MS 3725, the Buxheim Organ Book; paper, 210 × 300 mm, 174 ff. The collection was compiled in Munich during the decade 1465–75 and contains, in addition to idiomatic organ works (*Praeludia* and *Fundamenta*), keyboard intabulations of preexistent vocal music, both sacred and secular, monophonic and polyphonic. Non-German composers whose works were so arranged include Ciconia, Binchois, G. Legrant, Touront, and Viletti, to whom attributions are made in the manuscript, and Bedingham, Brassart, Bruolo, Dufay, Dunstable, Franchois, Frye, Morton, and Pullois, who have been identified from concordances. An edition of the codex in both facsimile and transcription has been published by Bertha Wallner, *Das Buxheimer Orgelbuch (Documenta Musicologica*, Zweite Reihe: Handschriften-Faksimiles 1, and

Das Erbe deutscher Musik, vols. 37–39. (See also Eileen Southern, *The Buxheim Organ Book*, and "Foreign Music in German Manuscripts," pp. 258–74.) Since an intabulation is, strictly speaking, an arrangement rather than the composition itself, the pieces from the repertory of the Mellon Chansonnier appearing in the *Buxheim Organ Book* are not listed with the concordances but are instead mentioned in Comments (Nos. 35, 46, 51, and 56).

ell   New Haven, Connecticut, Yale University, Beinecke Library for Rare Books and Manuscripts, MS 91. For particulars concerning the manuscript, see the Introduction.

h 191   Oxford, Bodleian Library, MS Ashmole 191; paper, 215 × 150 mm, a composite collection of 4 items, of which only the last (ff. 191–96) contains music. In the judgment of Anselm Hughes, *Medieval Polyphony in the Bodleian Library*, most of the leaves are to be dated from about 1445, but ff. 195ᵛ–196ʳ, because they are written in void rather than black notation, may be somewhat later (ca. 1450–60). That the collection is of English provenance is demonstrated by its contents, 7 English part songs, 1 for three voices, the rest for two. Unfortunately, there are no attributions.
Concordance: No. 45.

ar 1719   Paris, Bibliothèque Nationale, fonds français, MS 1719; paper, 293 × 200 mm, 182 ff. The watermarks depict a unicorn in a style similar to that used in northern France in the 1490s. On the penultimate folio (181ᵛ) is written "Paris," and on the last (182ᵛ) "Marbove" (Marboue?), the latter being perhaps the name of a former owner. Several hands are discernible in the collection, all of them cursive and none very elegant; moreover, lining-out, crosshatching, and general untidiness recur throughout. The contents comprise exclusively French verse of the period, primarily rondeaux and ballades.
Concordances: Nos. 1, 2, 5, 21, 25, 29, 30, and 48.

x   Paris, Bibliothèque Nationale, fonds français, MS 15123, the Pixérécourt Chansonnier; parchment, 180 × 120 mm, 203 ff. disposed regularly in quinterns. The elegant decoration of the leaves was undoubtedly executed in Florence, presumably in the atelier of Gherardo and Monte di Giovanni, whose artistic activity can be

documented from 1470 to 1495. The humanist script and numerous Italianizing corruptions of French verse indicate that the principal— and apparently only—text scribe was also Italian. (The music like- wise appears to be the work of a single hand.) Because the repertory contained in the collection is clearly earlier than that of Flo 229, which was illuminated in the same workshop about 1490, one can assume that the Pixérécourt Chansonnier was compiled early in the 1480s (see above the description of the Florence manuscript and Relationship to Concordant Sources). An escutcheon placed on the first opening to receive the arms of the owner was unfortunately left blank. Of the 170 compositions included in the manuscript the first 2 are devotional motets on Latin texts, 19 carry Italian verse, 3 use Spanish poems, and 1 is textless. The remainder are French chansons; the majority are à 3, but 24 are à 4. Among the composers represented are Agricola, Barbingant, Bedingham, Binchois, Busnois, Caron, Compère, Cornago, Dufay, Dunstable, Frye, Hayne, Joye, Legrant, Martini, Molinet, Morton, Ockeghem, Tinctoris, Touront, Vincenet, Wrede, and B. Ycart. A complete inventory with musical incipits and attributions but, unfortunately, no concordances is to be found in the edition by Edward Pease of selected pieces from the collection, *Music from the Pixérécourt Manuscript.*
Concordances: Nos. 3, 8, 9, 18, 20, 22, 24–26, 29, 30, 32, 36, 37, 39, 40, 45, 47, 51, and 53 (about 12 percent of the total repertory).

*Par 24315   Paris, Bibliothèque Nationale, fonds français, MS 24315; paper, 285 × 200 mm, 160 ff. The compilation of the manuscript may postdate the accession of François I to the throne of France in 1515 because the initial poem begins, "Les colleurs deschiffrées, du temps du roy Françoys de France, premier de ce nom." However, the hand in which the piece is written is different from that of the main scribe, and it may be a later addition. The codex carries the arms of the noble family d'Urfé, native to the former province of Forez (generally the Département du Loire), for one of whom it was pre- sumably prepared. The contents comprise a variety of French works, primarily in verse but some in prose as well, including treatises by *rhétoriqueurs* such as Molinet and Fabri. For a complete inventory citing the individual items then published, see Paris, *Bibliothèque Nationale: Catalogue général des manuscrits français: Anciens petits fonds français*, pp. 314–17.
Concordances: Nos. 17 and 35.

r 4379   Paris, Bibliothèque Nationale, nouvelle acquisition française, MS 4379; paper, a composite collection consisting of three separate sections: (1) ff. 1–42, 207 × 154 mm; (2) ff. 43–68, 210 × 143 mm; and (3) ff. 69–92, 220 × 150 mm. All concordances with the Mellon Chansonnier are in the initial segment of the manuscript, which was formerly part of the Seville Chansonnier, MS 5.I.43, and which will consequently be discussed in conjunction with it below. Of the remaining portions, the second is written both in black and in void notation, the latter having the sharp, angular heads of the first half of the fifteenth century. The third appears to be somewhat later because it is entirely in void notation, but it is of the same general period. The latter includes settings of French and Latin texts, the former of Italian poems as well. For a description of the manuscript and an inventory of its contents, see Paris, *Bibliothèque Nationale: Manuscrits latin et français ajoutés aux fonds des nouvelles acquisitions pendant les années 1875–1891, Partie 1,* pp. 127–30.

ar 7559   Paris, Bibliothèque Nationale, nouvelle acquisition française, MS 7559; paper, 195 × 135 mm, 75 ff. The collection was apparently compiled in northern France toward the end of the fifteenth century (possibly in the 1470s or 1480s) to judge from the visible watermarks, perhaps for a certain "Bucquet," whose signature appears on the initial folio. The 145 rondeaux it contains (a relatively modest collection) were published in an edition, now rare, by E. M. Bancel, *Cent quarante-cinq rondeaux d'amours. . . .*
Concordance: No. 64.

rd   Paris, Bibliothèque Nationale, fonds Rothschild 2973, the Chansonnier de Jean de Monchenu or the Chansonnier Cordiforme; parchment, in the shape of a heart that measures 175 mm along the spine, 180 mm from the tip to the center of the lobe, and 156 mm across at the widest point; 72 ff. including 4 left unnumbered for the table of contents (a single double leaf) and 68 ff. disposed in alternating gatherings of 5 and 3 double leaves with 6 more added at the end. (The foliation begins with the first opening of music.) The copying of text and music each seems to have been done by a single hand. The coat of arms appearing on the fourth (unnumbered) folio identifies the original owner as Jean de Montchenu, and the ecclesiastical symbol under which they were drawn indicates that he was a priest when the codex was prepared. From the latter circumstance it can be deduced that the songbook was copied and decorated while he was vicar-general and counselor to Jean-Louis de Savoie, Bishop of Geneva, between 1468 and 1477, and probably after 1470, when his revenues became sufficient to allow the purchase of a diminutive volume so exquisitely wrought. The style of its illuminations and the composition of its repertory suggest that the work was done by artisans attached to the ducal court of Savoy (see Edward L. Kottick, Introduction, *The Unica in the Chansonnier Cordiforme*). Included in the collection are 30 French chansons and 14 songs on Italian poems. Of the 44 compositions, 16 are unique to this source, an exceptionally large number for a secular manuscript of this type and period. Among the composers represented are Barbingant, Bedingham, Busnois, Caron, Dufay, Dunstable, Frye, Hayne, Morton, Ockeghem, and Vincenet. Besides his edition of the *unica* in the codex cited above, Kottick has published a complete inventory of its contents with attributions, concordances, and notes, "The Chansonnier Cordiforme."

Concordances: Nos. 7, 17, 18, 20, 24, 25, 27, 30, 32, 33, 35, 46, and 52 (29.5 percent of the relatively modest repertory).

Par 676   Paris, Bibliothèque Nationale, Département de Musique, Réserve Vm⁷, MS 676; paper, 240 × 170 mm, 116 ff. disposed in quaterns of which the first (ff. 1–8) has been lost, leaving ff. 9–125 (with some errors in the numbering). On f. 124ᵛ appears the note, "finis laus deo 26 octubris 1502," presumably indicating the date on which the copying was completed by the scribe who had entered all the compositions to that point. The visible watermarks are those used in papers from Bologna and Ferrara, and the repertory suggests connections with the ducal house of Este, either in Ferrara or in Mantua, where it was represented in the person of Isabella (see Nanie Bridgman, "Un manuscrit italien du début du XVIe siècle à la Bibliothèque Nationale," and cf. Jeppesen, *La Frottola*, 2: 86–87). The repertory consists of 114 compositions, of which 17 carry Latin texts, 3 French texts, 1 a Spanish poem, and another is textless, while the remainder are Italian pieces, primarily frottole and *laude*. Although there are only 12 attributions in the collection, the following composers have been identified: Agricola, Arnulphus, Cara, Caron, Filipo de Luprano, Ja. Fogliano, G. L., Gerardus, Hayne, Isaac, Josquin, L. C., Iannes

Plice, Touront (Cecus), Tromboncino, and in conflict, Congiet or Japart, and Isaac or Busnois. A complete inventory including musical incipits, concordances, and notes is found in the study by Bridgman cited above, pp. 196–259. Another inventory, also complete, but with concordances only for the Italian pieces as a rule is in Jeppesen, *La Frottola*, 2: 176–81.
Concordances: Nos. 3 and 32.

v   Paris, Bibliothèque Nationale, Chansonnier Nivelle de la Chaussée; parchment, 180 × 125 mm, 77 ff. (of which ff. 4, 5, and 8 are now lost) disposed regularly in quaterns. Although the exact provenance of the collection is currently unknown, it is obviously northern. This is suggested by the structure of its gatherings and by the style of its illuminations, which is exactly matched by that of a missal prepared in the fifteenth century for the Church of St. Martin's in Tours (Bibliothèque Municipale, MS 194). It would seem likely that both volumes were decorated either in the city itself—an important artistic center at the time—or in an area nearby in the Loire Valley. The composition of the repertory would suggest a date in the late 1460s or early 1470s and may provide an indication of the specific milieu whose tastes it reflects. The manuscript contains a considerable number of unica, especially pieces attributed to Jean Delahaye, a master rarely represented in other sources but about whom, unfortunately, little is known. It has been established only that he was in the service of the Cardinal of Luxembourg, with whom he traveled to England, and that he was in Rouen in 1443 (see the *Encyclopédie de la musique*, 1:664). Additional indications may be provided by names written in the codex: on f. 1ᵛ, "Hic liber discantus mea . . . est Jo. Cruezi de palacio," and on the last page, François Petit, Agna Brossemonoye, Jacques Bernar, Gillet Boignon, and François Rossignol, all presumably singers. The contents consist of 66 French chansons, 9 of which have been at least partially effaced for no apparent reason although erasures are to be seen rather frequently in the remaining compositions for the correction of scribal errors. Included are works by Barbingant, Binchois, Jean Boubert, Busnois, Delahaye, Dufay, Fédé, Morton, and Ockeghem in addition to a good number without attribution. A brief description of the codex that presents a complete inventory (but without concordances) is to be found in the *Catalogue*

of Sotheby and Company for 7 March 1939 (lot 358A), pp. 49–50.
An edition of the unpublished pieces in the codex has been prepared
by Geneviève Thibault and is soon to appear.
Concordances: Nos. 4, 7, 16, 21, 24, 25, 30, and 35 (12 percent of the
total repertory).

Pav 362   Pavia, Biblioteca dell'Università, MS Aldini 362 (*olim* 131.A.17);
        paper, 150 × 105 mm, 83 ff. disposed in quaterns with 3 leaves
tipped in at the end. On the initial folio stands the inscription, "Esto
libro é di Dortea Rabia," identifying one of the earliest owners of the
manuscript as a member of the noble family of that name from Cuneo
in the Piedmont. Since the French texts are generally completely and
reasonably correctly written and the group of Italian pieces small but
substantial, it would seem likely that the collection originated in that
(or a similar) region on the borders between the two cultures. The
repertory it contains implies that it was probably compiled in the 1460s.
Included, besides the theoretical treatises filling the first 16 folios, are
40 chansons, 7 songs on Italian texts, and 1 textless piece, a total of 48
compositions. There are no attributions in the codex, and many of
the concordant sources also give anonymously the pieces found in the
Pavia Chansonnier, but the following composers can be identified:
Barbingant, Bedingham, Binchois, Dufay, Dunstable, and Hayne. A
thorough up-to-date study of this manuscript is badly needed. The
only substantial discussion of it in print is that published in 1894 by
the philologist Antonio Restori, who gives the texts for the poetry
without a meaningful discussion of the music (see "Un codice musicale
Pavesi"). However, Jeppesen gives a brief description and a list of the
Italian pieces with concordances, *La Frottola*, 2: 89, 188.
Concordances: Nos. 25, 32, 33, 46, 51, and 52 (12.5 percent of the total
repertory).

Per 431   Perugia, Biblioteca Communale, MS 431 (*olim* G. 20); paper,
        213 × 143 mm, originally 163 ff. (of which the first 5 are now
missing) disposed primarily in gatherings of 6 double leaves. The bulk
of the collection appears to have been copied in the 1480s, but there
are some sixteenth-century additions such as the canon à 3 ascribed
to Leo X. As Allan Atlas has recently shown, "On the Origins of the
Manuscripts Berlin 78.C.28 and Perugia 431" (Symposium in Honor
of Gustave Reese, 1 June 1974), two of the composers to whom attribu-

tions are made in the manuscript are specifically identified as natives of Ortona, a port on the Adriatic coast of the fifteenth-century kingdom of Naples, and not of Cortona, as Jeppesen had indicated earlier (*La Frottola*, 2:190). Together with the overall parochial character of the repertory this circumstance would suggest that the compilation was probably done in a provincial center in that area rather than in the city of Naples itself. Further evidence for the same conclusion comes from the lack of significant concordances with a manuscript such as the Mellon Chansonnier, which stems in part from the repertory of the royal court, and from a demonstrably close relationship with the provincial Montecassino codex, which was copied about the same time in Gaeta, just across the peninsula from Ortona. The Perugia manuscript shares with the latter a number of leaves carrying the same watermark (see Jeppesen, p. 89), gatherings of 6 double leaves, a number of concordances—and composers—rarely found in other sources, and substantially similar readings for the compositions found in both. In addition to 26 secular pieces with Italian texts or incipits, the collection contains settings for the Ordinary of the mass and the Magnificat, hymns, motets, a litany (in Spanish), French chansons, and textless works. Among the attributions that can be made are the following: Advardus Ortonensis, Busnois, Petrus Caritatis, Cecus (Touront), Dufay, Dux Burgensis, Fra M. de Ortona, Isaac, M. Gulielmus, M. Je., Morton, Oriola, P., Seraphinus, Magister Symon, and Jo. Vrede (Wreede). For a description of the manuscript and an inventory, with concordances for the Italian pieces, see Jeppesen, pp. 89, 190–91.

Concordances: Nos. 18 and 32.

714   Porto, Biblioteca Publica Municipal MS 714; parchment, 193 × 135 mm, 81 ff. disposed primarily in quaterns and quinterns. The first 50 leaves contain theoretical treatises (one on the modes, another by Johannes de Muris) and only the last 29 musical compositions. The notation is black, implying origins in the first half of the fifteenth century, and English composers are exceptionally well represented, but with pieces on Italian texts, and are cited with the explanatory "de Anglia" that one would expect from a Continental scribe. Nino Pirrotta, in his discussion of "Two Anglo-Italian Pieces in the Manuscript Porto 714," pp. 252 ff., suggests that the collection may have originated in Ferrara and cites the following evidence: (1) the illuminations appear to be in the style cultivated there about midcentury, (2) the linguistic particularities of the Italian poems are characteristic of that region, and (3) two of the texts set are by a little-known Ferrarese poet, Girolamo Nigrisoli. The musical repertory consists of 19 secular works, 6 being settings of Italian poems, the remainder of French, with attributions to Ro. de Anglia, Bedyngham, Galfridus de Anglia, Dufay (a total of 7), and Joye. (See Bernhard Meier, "Die Handschrift Porto 714 als Quelle zur Tonartenlehre des 15. Jahrhunderts," for a description and inventory.)

Concordance: No. 51.

CG XIII. 27   Rome, Biblioteca Apostolica Vaticana, Cappella Giulia, MS XIII. 27, the Medici Chansonnier; paper, 231 × 167 mm, 119 leaves of music disposed primarily in quinterns, with 6 more leaves added both at the beginning and at the end for a total of 131 ff. From the escutcheon painted on the first opening of music, coupled with Isaac's setting of *Palle, palle, palle,* it is clear that the manuscript was prepared for one of the distinguished ecclesiastical figures of the Medici family. In the opinion of Allan Atlas, whose study is cited below, the portrait of Julius Caesar on the cover points to Giuliano, Lorenzo's youngest son (later Pope Clement VII). The repertory strongly suggests that the collection was compiled in Florence because the composers most generously represented were employed there. The inclusion of the motet by Isaac on a text by Poliziano lamenting the death of Lorenzo the Magnificent fixes the date of copying after that event, 8 April 1492, and Atlas regards it as unlikely that the compilation would have been done in Florence after the expulsion of the Medici in November 1494. The repertory comprises 108 works; the majority of them are French chansons, but 16 pieces have texts or incipits in Italian, 5 in Latin, and 1 each in Spanish and Flemish. Attributions are in conflict in a number of instances, but the following composers appear to be represented: Agricola, Baccio (Bartolomeo degli Organi), Barbireau, Basiron, Binchois, Busnois, Caron, Colinet de Lannoy, Compère, Dufay, Felice, Fresneau, Arnolfo Giliardi, Hayne, Isaac, Japart, Josquin, Martini, Molinet, Mureau, Obrecht, Ockeghem, Petrequin, Stockem, Wreede, Vincenet, Virgilius, and perhaps Congiet, Malcort, Pipelare, and / or Gaspar. An inventory is given by José M. Llorens, *Le Opere Musicali della Cappella Giulia,* pp. 43–48. A careful study of the manuscript, already cited several times, is that of

Allan Atlas, "Cappella Giulia XIII. 27 and the Chanson in Italy," published in 1975–76 by the Institute of Medieval Music in Brooklyn. *Concordances:* Nos. 5, 17, 18, 27, 30, and 32 (5.5 percent of the total repertory).

omC 2856   Rome, Biblioteca Casanatense, MS 2856 (*olim* O.V. 208); parchment, 270 × 200 mm, 163 ff. originally disposed regularly in quinterns with a bifolium added at the beginning for the table. The second of those leaves was later torn out, and eight others were also removed from gatherings here and there throughout the MS but without discernible loss of music. An escutcheon on the first notated folio (3ᵛ) carries the combined arms of the ducal houses of Gonzaga and Este, indicating that the manuscript was prepared either for the couple formed by Francesco II, Duke of Mantua, and his spouse, Isabella d'Este, or for the latter alone. It may have been conceived as a gift for the wedding that took place 11 February 1490, and its compilation could have been begun any time after Isabella's official betrothal in 1480 (see José Llorens, "El Códice Casanatense 2856 ... "). Arthur S. Wolff, "The Chansonnier Casanatense 2856," pp. 28 ff., suggests that the collection may be the "libro da canto figurato che scripse e notò Don Alessandro Signorello," commissioned for illumination by Ercole I in 1485. The contents apparently reflect to a considerable degree the repertory that was current at the court of Ferrara, judging from the exceptionally large place given to works by Johannes Martini —22 in all—who was active there continuously from 1474 until his death in 1497. That circumstance, in view of Isabella's well-known interest in the arts and particular affection for music, suggests that the codex was intended mainly for her and that her favorite compositions were included in it. Of the 123 works in the collection, 105 are French chansons while 8 pieces carry Italian texts, 4 Flemish verse, 3 Latin words or incipits, and 3 more are textless. Represented are Agricola, Barbireau, Basin, Basiron, Bosfrin, Paulus de Broda, Brumel, Busnois, Caron, Cecus (Touront?), Colinet de Lannoys, Compère, Congiet, Dufay, Dusart, Ghiselin-Verbonnet, Hayne, Isaac, Japart, Josquin, Joye, Malcort, Martini, Molinet, Morton, Obrecht, Ockeghem, Petrequin, and Souspison. A complete inventory of the manuscript is given by Llorens in the study cited above, pp. 170–73. An edition, as one of a series of volumes devoted to Ferrarese music, is currently projected by Lewis Lockwood, who kindly provided some of the bibliographical and biographical information for the present notice (see his "Music at Ferrara in the Period of Ercole I d'Este"). *Concordances:* Nos. 2, 13, 15, 20, 29, 30, 32, 34, and 41 (about 7 percent of the total repertory).

St. Gall 463   St. Gall, Stiftsbibliothek, MS 463, Egidius Tschudi's Liederbuch; paper, originally 4 part books in 4⁰, of which only the Discantus and Altus presently survive. The collection was compiled by Egidius Tschudi, as is shown by his autograph note on the title page. Judging from the preponderance of French and Netherlandish composers represented, compared to the paucity of pieces on German texts, it would seem likely that the copying was done primarily during his years as a student in Paris between 1517 and 1520 (see Arnold Geering, *Die Vokalmusik in der Schweiz zur Zeit der Reformation*, pp. 91–92). The inventory given by Geering (pp. 227–32) lists 200 compositions, the majority of them Latin motets. There are also a number of songs on German, French, and Italian texts and a few apparently instrumental pieces. Attributions in the manuscript name as composers Adam de Fulda, Antonius de Vinca, Adamus Aquamus, Thomas Aquamus, Hotinet Bara, P. Biamont, Bisqueria, A. Brumel, Compère, Craen, Andreas Crütz, Sixt Dietrich, F. Dulot, Robertus Fabri, C. Festa, Alex. Freydanck, Gaspar, Ghiselin-Verbonnet, Isaac, Japart, Josquin, Larue, Leo X, Felix Löw, Machon, Moulu, Mouton, Obrecht, Regis, Richafort, Jo. de Scandam, Senfl, Stefan Swartz, Tinctoris, Vaqueras, Vannius, and Willaert.
Concordance: No. 57.

Sev 5.I.43   Seville, Biblioteca Colombina, MS 5.I.43; paper, 209 × 170 mm, originally 188 ff. disposed in 6 gatherings of 5 double leaves (the first 4 and the second and third from the last), 10 gatherings of 6 double leaves (intercalated between the two preceding segments), and a final gathering of 4 double leaves. Of these 17 gatherings, most of the fifth and sixth, eighth, and thirteenth (a total of 42 ff.) were ripped out and bound together as a separate manuscript, today in the Bibliothèque Nationale in Paris (see above, Par 4379). Eight folios of the original manuscript have now been lost as well (5 from the second gathering and 1 each from the first, sixth, and seventh), leaving the Seville Chansonnier with its present total of 138 ff. (see Dragan Plamenac, "A Reconstruction of the French Chansonnier in the Biblioteca Colombina, Seville," vol. 37, pp. 501 ff.). According to *Regestrum B* of the catalogue compiled by Ferdinand Columbus of his bibliographical holdings (No. 2526), he acquired the volume in Rome in 1515, and it was already showing signs of age and wear at the time. There can be no doubt that it was copied in Italy, as is shown by the Italianizing corruptions practiced by the text scribes. The repertory would suggest, by its cosmopolitan character, that the codex may in fact have originated in an international center such as Rome. The calligraphy would argue that it was compiled by a number of different scribes toward the end of the 1470s or the beginning of the 1480s. The two segments of the original manuscript now contain, besides a short treatise on notation, a total of 167 works, some of which are incomplete: 123 in Seville, 38 in Paris, and 6 divided between them. The majority are French chansons, but there are also 22 Italian songs, 4 pieces on Latin texts, 3 on Flemish, 3 on German, 3 bitextual quodlibets, 3 with no known texts, and 1 using Hebrew. The composers represented include Agricola, Basin, Bedingham, Binchois, Busnois, Caron, Convert, Cornago, Dufay, Frye, Hayne, Japart, Josquin, Joye, Martini, Molinet, Morton, Ockeghem, Phillipet de Pres, Tinctoris, Touront (Cecus), Vincenet, and possibly Colinet de Lannoys, Compère, Mureau, and Gaspar. Included in Plamenac's study, cited above, is a careful inventory of the two manuscripts reconstructed as a single collection, including verbal incipits, attributions, concordances, comments, and a number of transcriptions (see ibid., pp. 530–42 and vol. 38, pp. 94–117, and 248–77). Also available is a facsimile edition of the reconstructed collection, again by Plamenac, *Facsimile Reproduction of the Manuscripts Sevilla 5.I.43 and Paris n.a.fr. 4379.*

Concordances: Nos. 8, 9, 14, 17*, 18, 22, 24*, 27*, 30*, 32, 35*, 37 (copied twice), 39, 46*, 51 (divided between the two segments), and 53 (about 10 percent of the total repertory as reconstituted by Plamenac). (The numbers marked with an asterisk are found in Par 4379.)

v 7.I.28   Seville, Biblioteca Colombina, MS 7.I.28; paper, 218 × 150 mm, 107 ff., of which those numbered 1, 6, 10, 13, 57, 59, 66, 82, and 92 are now lost (No. 74 was simply skipped in the foliation). The body of the manuscript was apparently copied in Spain by a single scribe, probably in the late 1480s or early 1490s. The collection now comprises 95 compositions, some of them incomplete because of

the missing leaves: 12 on Latin texts, 2 on French poems, and the remainder carrying Castilian verse. Attributions for the works present have been made to Belmonte, Borote (Torote?), Cornago, Enrique (Wreede?), F[ran] co de la Torre, Gijon, Hurtado de Exeres, J[uan] de Leon, Juanes, Lagarto, Madrid(?), Moxica, Rodriguez, Triana, and Jo. Urrede, but many pieces remain without ascription. For a description of the codex and a summary inventory of its contents, see Higinio Anglés, *La Musica en la Corte de los Reyes Catolicos*, vol. 1, *Polifonia Religiosa*, pp. 103–06, and cf. Robert M. Stevenson, *Spanish Music in the Age of Columbus*, pp. 196, 206–49. A partial edition, albeit not a very useful one, has been published by Gertraut Haberkamp, *Die weltliche Vokalmusik in Spanien um 1500*.
Concordance: No. 4.

Stra 222 C.22   Strasbourg, Bibliothèque Municipale, MS 222 C.22; paper, 290 × 210 mm, 11 + 143 ff. (now destroyed). The manuscript was in two layers. The first contained musical treatises from the fourteenth century (Philippe de Vitry and contemporaries) and compositions in black notation from the late fourteenth and early fifteenth centuries. The second consisted of pieces interpolated toward the middle of the fifteenth century in white notation in spaces that had been left vacant. As a result, sacred and secular works stood side by side: settings for the Ordinary of the mass, Latin motets, and (in markedly lesser numbers) songs with texts in French, Italian, and German—a total of 207 compositions, 21 of which were monophonic. Attributions in the codex combined with those that can be deduced with a reasonable degree of certainty include Alanus, Anthonius clericus apostolicus, Anthonius de Civitate, Arn. de Lantins, Binchois, Bocquet, Borlet, Cameraco (Cameracy), Jo. Carlay, J. Cesaris, J. Cornelius, Dufay, Egidius de Pusiex, Egidius de Thenis, Pierre Fontaine, Grenon, Magr. Grimache, Guillaume de Machaut, H. de libero castro, Henricus Hessman, Hubertus de Psalinis, Lampens, F. Landino, H. Laufenburg, C. Liebert, N. de Merqs, Nucella, Pellison, Philippe de Vitry, Jugis Philomena, Pierre des Moulins, Prunet, Richart, Philippe Royllart, Jacopinus Selesses, Tailhandier, Jo. Vaillant, Jacobus Vide, N. Zacharias, and Zeltenpferd. Because the collection was burned during the Franco-Prussian War of 1870, it is now known only through a reconstruction made by Charles Van den Borren from the notes of

Edmond de Coussemaker (see *Le manuscript musical M. 222 C.22 de la Bibliothèque de Strasbourg*).
Concordance: No. 49.

87 Trent, Castello del Buon Consiglio, MS 87; paper, 310 × 210 mm, 265 ff. Concerning the date, provenance, and contents of the manuscript, see below.
Concordance: No. 50.

88 Trent, Castello del Buon Consiglio, MS 88; paper, 310 × 210 mm, 412 ff. Concerning the date, provenance, and contents of the manuscript, see below.
Concordance: No. 16.

89 Trent, Castello del Buon Consiglio, MS 89; paper, 310 × 210 mm, 425 ff. Concerning the date, provenance, and contents of the manuscript, see below.
Concordances: Nos. 17 and 40.

90 Trent, Castello del Buon Consiglio, MS 90; paper, 310 × 210 mm. 465 ff. Concerning the date, provenance, and contents of the manuscript, see below.
Concordances: Nos. 45 (copied twice) and 47.

91 Trent, Castello del Buon Consiglio, MS 91; paper, 310 × 210 mm, 259 ff. Concerning the date, provenance, and contents of the manuscript, see below.
Concordances: Nos. 3 and 29.

93 Trent, Castello del Buon Consiglio, MS 93; paper, 310 × 210 mm, 382 ff. Concerning the date, provenance, and contents of the manuscript, see below.
Concordances: Nos. 50 and 51.

The earliest of the seven manuscripts known as the Trent Codices (87–93) are 87 and 92. Folios 1–218 of the former and ff. 144–239 of the latter are copied on paper with a common water mark by a single hand, identified by a signature as a Tyrolese named Puntschucherh.

Ceremonial and occasional pieces included in these two volumes refer
to events that took place between 1420 and 1440, suggesting that most
of the compilation was done in the 1440s. Notational details tend to
confirm the date because although the notes are void, the coloration is
in red as well as black ink, a holdover from the period when only black
notation was used. Manuscripts 88–91 were apparently written for
the most part by a single scribe who identifies himself at the end of
Trent 90 as Johannes Wiser, rector of the Cathedral School in Trent
from 1459 to 1465 and later (1470) chaplain to the archbishop, Johann
Hinderbach. Wiser presumably began his work in the 1460s, but
compositions continued to be added until the 1480s. Manuscript 90
is in large part a copy of 93 and must have been compiled at about the
same time. The repertory of the codices considered as a whole is
primarily sacred in nature, comprising settings for the mass and Latin
motets, both liturgical and ceremonial, but many secular works were
included as well. All told there are some 1,864 pieces (but with some
300 duplications), in which are represented composers of Italian,
German, English, and French cultures spanning three generations
from that preceding Dufay and Binchois to that of Busnois and Ockeghem. An inventory of the first six manuscripts with musical incipits
and attributions is found in the *Denkmäler der Tonkunst in Oesterreich*
7 (vol. 14), pp. 31 ff.; of Trent 93 in *Jahrgang* 31 (vol. 61), pp. vii–x.
Selected compositions are published in modern score in *Jahrgänge* 11 / 1
(vol. 22), 19 / 1 (vol. 38), 27 / 1 (vol. 53), and 40 (vol. 76) in addition
to the two volumes already cited. (See also, concerning the structure
of the manuscripts, Charles Hamm, "Manuscript Structure in the
Dufay Era"). An edition in facsimile of the entire corpus has been
published under the title *Codices Musicales Tridentini* (Trente, Museo
del Castello del Buon Consiglio) (Rome: Bibliopola, 1969–70).

TrBC 1947-4   Trent, Biblioteca Communale, MS 1947-4; paper, 225 ×
165 mm, a fragment of 5 double leaves (10 ff.), of which 3^r–4^r and
8^v–9^v are ruled but empty, apparently either a single quintern taken
from a collection that may have been substantially larger, or a fascicle
manuscript. It must have originated in Trent or the surrounding region
since the notations in the manuscript (aside from voice parts and a few
titles) are in a Tyrolese German dialect. The repertory consists of 9
compositions, 5 of them with German incipits, including the Flemish
song *Ein fröhlich Wesen* (*Een vroylic wesen*), and the remainder (including

a reworking of *J'ai prins amours*) with no indication of any kind. There are no attributions in the manuscript; those that have been established are to Larue and Caron. The kind of arrangement à 4 exemplified by the one concordance with the present manuscript would point to the late 1490s or early 1500s as a possible date. For a description of the fascicle and a summary of its contents, see Benvenuto Disertori, "Il manoscritto 1947-4 di Trento e la canzone 'i'ay prins amours.'"
Concordance: No. 3.

Im 237   Ulm, Bibliothek des Münsters (from Schermar'sche Familien Stiftung), MS 237 abcd; paper, 4 part books, 98 × 142 mm, 124 (Discantus), 130 (Altus), 124 (Tenor), and 125 ff. (Bassus). The collection carries the date 1551 in a gift inscription and is written in a German hand of the mid-sixteenth century. It comprises a repertory of some 104 compositions: 1 mass segment, 68 Latin motets, 13 chansons, 13 German lieder, 3 Italian songs, and 6 textless pieces. There are no attributions, but Josquin is represented with 9 works, Hayne with 1. See Jeppesen, *Der Kopenhagener Chansonnier*, p. lxxiii, and cf. Albert Smijers, *Werken van Josquin des Près*, 1:vii.
Concordance: No. 32.

er 757   Verona, Biblioteca Capitolare, MS Mus DCCLVII; paper, 330 × 245 mm, 67 ff. Like the majority of the manuscripts currently in the holdings of the Chapter Library in Verona, this one probably originated in the region where it is now preserved. That it is Italian in any case is suggested by the inclusion in its repertory of Vincenet's chanson, found elsewhere only in peninsular sources and in Glog. Of the 67 compositions constituting the repertory only 1 is for three voices; the remainder are for four. Unfortunately only 3 pieces have textual incipits and none has an attribution. The date of the collection is therefore problematic, but in view of the preponderance of pieces à 4, it should probably be placed late in the fifteenth or early in the sixteenth century. (See Giuseppe Turrini, *Il Patrimonio Musicale della Biblioteca Capitolare di Verona*).
Concordance: No. 18.

ıb   Washington, D.C., Library of Congress, MS M2.1 L252 Case, the Laborde Chansonnier; parchment, 130 × 90 mm, 149 ff. originally disposed in 20 quaterns, to which was added a gathering of 6 leaves at the beginning for the table of contents. Extrapolating from 4 pieces entered in the table but no longer in the manuscript and 7 others that are presently incomplete, the following losses can be determined: the initial leaf of the second gathering (the first with music); the central pair of leaves of the third; the second through the fifth leaves of the fourth; the third leaf of the eighth; a full gathering preceding the final one and the first leaf of the latter. Three scribal hands can be discerned in the musical notation dividing the repertory into three distinct but not entirely separate layers. Scribe I copied the first 9 gatherings of music (ff. 9^r–72^r, with the exception of 3 pieces, ff. 61^v–64^r) and 2 works in the final gathering (ff. 136^r and 138^v–139^r), the first of which is incomplete because of the missing leaf. Scribe II, whose hand appears to be identical with that of the Dijon and Copenhagen chansonniers, entered the music in the eleventh through thirteenth gatherings and most of the fourteenth (ff. 72^v–101^r) in addition to the small enclave of 3 pieces just cited (ff. 61^v–64^r). The remaining space was filled in by scribe III (or perhaps by two additional copyists) except for ff. 115^r–134^v and 149^v–150^r, which were ruled but left empty. The illuminations are likewise in three distinct styles, the first appearing with the work of scribe I, the other two with that of scribe II (the change in manner coming at ff. 87^v–88^r), while the remaining compositions were left without decoration. The first two copyists probably worked simultaneously, or at least within a relatively short span of time, probably in the early or mid-1470s. Their notational style, like the calligraphy of the texts and the illuminations, point to northern French or Burgundian territories. The remainder of the repertory was probably added significantly later, perhaps in the 1480s or early 1490s because it includes works by Compère and Prioris. A coat of arms consisting of a golden chevron and three silver birds on an azure background may eventually lead to a contemporary owner but has yet to be linked incontrovertibly with a single family (see Helen E. Bush, "The Laborde Chansonnier"; cf. Jeppesen, *Der Kopenhagener Chansonnier*, pp. xxv–xxvi). Of the 107 compositions once included in the codex, 96 survive as complete entities, 7 others only in part. All but 5 carry a secular text in French: 2 works are devotional motets in Latin (1 of which opens the collection), 2 others carry Italian verse, and 1 is textless. Represented are the following composers: Barbinguant, Basin, Baziron, Binchois, Busnois, Caron, Compère, Convert, Delahaye, Dufay, Frye, Hayne, Joye, Michelet, Molinet,

Morton, Ockeghem, Prioris, and Tinctoris. Bush gives a complete inventory with attributions in the study cited (pp. 77–79) and includes a few transcriptions as well, but there is no edition of the manuscript. *Concordances:* Nos. 5, 7, 13, 14, 16, 17, 21, 23–25, 27, 29, 30, 32, 35, 45, 51, and 56 (16.8 percent of the original repertory).

olf 287 Wolfenbüttel, Herzog August Bibliothek, Codex Guelf 287 Extravagantium; parchment, 148 × 104 mm, originally 80 ff. disposed regularly in 10 quaterns. Because of the loss of the initial leaf from the first gathering, 1 double leaf from the center and a single leaf from the end of the ninth gathering, and 3 double leaves from the tenth gathering, it now comprises only 70 ff., the first of which is torn. The notational style of the codex is similar to that of scribe I of the Laborde Chansonnier, whereas the illuminations most resemble those found in the Copenhagen Chansonnier. Consequently, there can be little doubt that the Wolfenbüttel manuscript originated in the same general area—northern France or Burgundian territories—in approximately the same period (see Jeppesen, *Der Kopenhagener Chansonnier*, pp. xxv ff.). The preponderance of compositions for three parts (only one is à 4) by composers of the generation of Busnois and Ockeghem points to origins in the late 1470s or early 1480s. The end of the 1480s, as suggested by Howard Brown in "Wolfenbütteler Handschriften," is probably too late in view of the repertory selected for copying. The collection opens with a devotional motet in Latin and includes the celebrated *O rosa bella* by Dunstable, but all remaining 54 compositions are French chansons. Although no attributions are given in the manuscript, the numerous concordant sources have made possible the identification of the following composers: Basiron, Bedingham, Binchois, Busnois, Caron, Convert, Dunstable, Dufay, Hayne, Michelet, Morton, Ockeghem, Philibert des Pres, and Prioris. For an inventory of the contents combined with those of the Copenhagen, Dijon, and Laborde chansonniers, see Droz and Thibault, *Trois chansonniers français*, pp. xiii–xviii. No edition of the manuscript is currently available, but 12 of its compositions are found in the Copenhagen Chansonnier, published by Jeppesen, and 9 others in the edition by Droz and Thibault, both of which are cited above.
Concordances: Nos. 4, 7, 14, 16, 21, 24, 27, 30, 32, 35, and 51 (19.6 percent of the total repertory).

Sixteenth-Century Prints

*Jar   Le Jardin de plaisance et fleur de rethoricque . . . Paris: Antoine Vérard
(ca. 1501). Because of its importance, this collection of secular
verse has been published in facsimile (Paris, 1910) with a volume
containing an introductory study and notes by Eugénie Droz and
Arthur Piaget (Paris, 1926).
Concordances: Nos. 3, 7, 8, 9, 12, 13, 15, 17, 24, 25, 27, 29, 30, 35, 41,
42, 51, 53, and 56.

Odh   *Harmonice musices odhecaton A.* Venice: Ottaviano dei Petrucci, 1501;
in 4^0, 103 ff. The collection—the first to be printed with movable
metal type—contains 96 compositions, the majority of them on secular
French texts but with 8 carrying Latin, 5 Flemish, 2 Italian, and 1 each
German and Spanish texts or incipits. (However, none of the texts
is given completely in the print.) As is to be expected, consequently,
most of the composers are northerners: Agricola, Bourdon, Bruhier,
Brumel, Busnois, Caron, Compère, Ghiselin (Verbonnet), Hayne,
Isaac, Japart, Josquin, Larue, Ninot le Petit, Mouton, Obrecht,
Ockeghem, Mabriano de Orto, Stokhem, Tadinghen, Tinctoris, and
Vincenet. For a bibliographical description, see Claudio Sartori,
Bibliografia delle Opere Musicali stampate da Ottaviano Petrucci, pp. 34–42
and passim. An edition, preceded by a careful study, has been published
by Helen Hewitt and Isabel Pope (*Harmonice Musices Odhecaton A.*).
Concordances: Nos. 18, 30, and 32.

PetA   *Motetti A numero trentatre.* Venice: Ottaviano dei Petrucci, 1502; in
4^0, 56 ff. As is indicated by the title page, the collection contains 33
Latin motets printed for the most part without attributions. However,
the composers that can be identified by concordant sources are almost
exclusively northern: Agricola, Brumel, Compère, Craen, Gaspar,
Ghiselin (Verbonnet), Josquin, Pinarol, and Tinctoris. See the description and inventory by Sartori, *Bibliografia Ottaviano Petrucci*, pp.
44–46.
Concordance: No. 57.

Canti C   *Canti C No. cento cinquanta.* Venice: Ottaviano dei Petrucci, 1504;
in 4^0, 168 ff. Although the title page announces 150 pieces, the
volume contains only 139, once again primarily French chansons but

with the inclusion of 9 pieces having texts or incipits in Italian, 8 in Latin, 6 in Flemish, and 1 each in German and Spanish. (Again, the texts are not printed with the music.) The composers represented, as in the *Odhecaton*, are mostly northerners: Agricola, Brumel, Busnois, Compère, Craen, Mathurin (Forestier), Foruila, Ghiselin (Verbonnet), Gregoire, Hanart, Infantis, Isaac, Japart, Josquin, Lapicida, Larue, Martini, Molinet, Ninot le Petit, Obrecht, Ockeghem, de Orto, Philipon, Pinarol, Regis, Reingot, van Stappen, Stokhem, Tadinghen, and C. de Vuilde. See the description and inventory by Sartori, *Bibliografia Ottaviano Petrucci*, pp. 69–74.
Concordance: No. 4.

hasse   *La chasse et le départ d'amours*, Fait et composé par révérend père en Dieu Messire Octavien de Saint Gelaiz, évesque d'Angoulesme, et par noble homme Blaise d'Auriol, bachelier en chascun droit demourant à Thoulouze. Paris: Anthoyne Vérard, 1509.
Concordance: No. 21.

rn   *S'ensuyt le Jardin de plaisance & fleur de rethoricque contenant pluiseurs* [sic] *beaulx livres* ... Lyon: Olivier Arnollet, n.d. (ca. 1525). As is suggested by the title, the contents of this collection, although not completely identical to those of the volume printed in Paris at the beginning of the century, are derived in large measure from it.
Concordances: Nos. 3, 7, 8, 13, 15, 17, 24, 25, 30, 41, 42, 51, and 56.

rm   *Trium vocum carmina a diversis musicis composita.* Nuremberg: Hieronymus Formschneider, 1538; three part books in 4°, 51 ff. (Tenor) and 52 ff. (Cantus and Bassus). The collection contains 100 compositions, all without texts and without attributions, but the following composers have been identified: Agricola, Arnoldus Brugensis, Barbireau, Bourdon, Brumel, Buchner, Compère, Craen, S. Dietrich, Finck, Ghiselin (Verbonnet), Hayne, Isaac, Josquin, Obrecht, Ockeghem, Prioris, Samson, and Senfl (see *Répertoire International des Sources Musicales*, vol. 1, *Recueils Imprimés XVIe–XVIIe Siècles*, p. 120).
Concordance: No. 30.

CRITICAL APPARATUS

The concordant sources are given below for each composition in an order corresponding to the preceding list. Consequently, although the distinction between manuscripts and prints is not specifically indicated, it continues to be observed with the latter in every case following the former. In addition the reader will recall that collections of poetry containing no music are marked with an asterisk. References to the foliation of the various collections reproduce the type of numeral found in the original whether arabic or roman. This was done primarily to avoid confusion with respect to manuscripts such as the Dijon Chansonnier, in which there are separate and conflicting foliations, one in each of the two styles of numbers. Attributions for the music, including those in the Mellon Chansonnier, are spelled here as in the sources in which they occur. If it has been possible to identify the composer, his name will appear alongside the incipit of his chanson regardless of source, but the ascriptions not entered in the present manuscript are in brackets.

In recording the musical variants the original note values have been used to facilitate direct comparisons among the sources. However, in the modern transcriptions those values have been invariably twice halved as has been indicated. Voices and note forms are identified by the abbreviations given below. Pitches are represented by their conventional letter names, and the register in which they fall by the form of the letter, following the model generally employed by medieval theorists: the octave descending from the bottom line of the bass clef by capital letters with prime, G', F', E', and so on; the principal octave of that clef only by capitals from A to G; the tenor octave by lowercase letters from a to g; the treble octave by lowercase letters and a prime from a' to g'; and the octave above the treble staff by the same lowercase letters with a double prime, a'', b'', c'', and so on. The location of the variant is given with reference to the transcription, first by measure number and then (in parentheses) by the note or notes within the measure. The first note to appear after the barline is always so numbered even when tied over from the previous measure; in contrast, rests are not counted with the notes but merely placed as to the measure in which they occur.

As will be apparent from the discussion of the relationships among the sources in the Introduction, the comments made below regarding the filiation of musical texts concern only the individual compositions and not necessarily the collections as a whole in which they are included. It is obvious, simply on the basis of the collations made for this edition, that the exemplars used in the preparation of presentation manuscripts of the kind seen here were not as a rule completed volumes of the same type, but rather working or performance copies carried about by the musicians of the period in what Charles Hamm has so aptly termed "fascicle manuscripts."*

The abbreviations listed below were selected, as much as possible, to facilitate the identification of the complete word and to avoid potential confusion with the letter names designating pitches. Except where otherwise specified, plurals are indicated by doubling the initial letter.

⌐	L	long	(= o)	MS, MSS	manuscript(s)
⊔	Br	breve	(= ♩)	C	cantus
◊	Sb	semibreve	(= ♩)	T	tenor
↓	M	minim	(= ♪)	CT	contratenor
↓	Sm	semiminim	(= ♪)	m.	measure
♪	Fu	fusa	(= ♪)	n.f.	no foliation

In the following commentary Leeman Perkins is the author of Concordant Sources, Collation, and Comments. Howard Garey has translated the songs and is the author of Variants, Versification, and Textual Notes.

1. Bel Acueil, ff. 1ᵛ–2ʳ [Busnois]

CONCORDANT SOURCES

Dij 517, ff. xixᵛ–xxʳ, Busnoys
*Par 1719, f. 91ᵛ

---

*"Manuscript Structure in the Dufay Era."

COLLATION

In the C of Dij 517 the passage, mm. 5(1)–7(1), is in exact imitation of the CT, mm. 4(1)–6(1), but the ornamental lower third at the cadence in the T of Mell is not used in either voice in Dij 517. The latter source has no flat as a signature for the T or the CT.

COMMENTS

The variant noted is undeniably significant, but curiously the two versions of the music are otherwise very similar even with respect to details such as the use of blackened notes and ligatures. Although the scribal traditions appear to be closely related in general, the reading of Mell seems preferable. In addition it gives correctly as M the G of the C, m. 11(5), erroneously written as Sb in Dij 517.

Noteworthy is the use of three voices in essentially the same range, a most unusual procedure in fifteenth-century secular compositions. The only analogous examples offered by the present collection are *Se je fayz dueil* (No. 31) and *A vous sans aultre* (No. 42).

> Bel Acueil, le sergant d'Amours,
> En bien soit faire ses esploys,
> M'a ja cité par pluseurs foys
> D'aller a l'une de ses cours, 4
>
> Et m'a chargé qu'a tous les jours
> Mettra deffault se je n'y voys. 6
> > *Bel Acueil, le sergant d'Amours,*
> > *En bien soit faire ses esploys.*
>
> Et que se brief je n'y accours
> Ou mes conseulx secrés et choys,
> Me bannira de vive voyx
> Et plus ne m'y fera [secours]. 10
> > Bel Accueil, *le sergant d'Amours,*
> > *En bien soit faire ses esploys,*
> > *M'a ja cité par pluseurs foys*
> > *D'aller a l'une de ses cours.*

Fair Welcome, the servant of Love,
Knows how to turn his deeds to good account;
He has already summoned me, and many times,
To go to one of his courts,

And has decreed that he will ever
Find me in default if I go not there.
    Fair Welcome, the servant of Love
    Knows how to turn his deeds to good account.

And if I do not soon hurry thither,
With my secret and discreet counsels,
He will banish me in the hearing of all,
And will no longer succor me.
    Fair Welcome, the servant of Love,
    Knows how to turn his deeds to good account;
    He has already summoned me, and many times,
    To go to one of his courts.

VARIANTS

1 sergent—*Dij Par.* 2 scait—*Dij*, scet—*Par.* 3 m'a cité pour aller aux ploix—*Par.* 4 A quelq'une de ses grans cours—*Par.* 5 m'a promis qu'a—*Dij*, m'a juré que—*Par.* 8 cois—*Dij*, coys—*Par.* 9 M'en—*Dij Par*; de toutes vois—*Dij*, a haulte voix—*Par.* 10 me—*Par*; sejours—*Mell*, secours—*Dij Par.*

VERSIFICATION

Rondeau quatrain in octosyllables, *a b b a.*

TEXTUAL NOTES

Line 1. **Bel Acueil**, Fair Welcome, is an allegorical figure in the *Roman de la Rose* by Guillaume de Lorris (early thirteenth century). *Bel Acueil* represents, as do many of the allegorical figures of the *Roman*, a psychological trait of the Girl (the object of the Lover's desire), a trait favorable to the Lover's purpose. **sergant** 'servant': pronounced with a soft *g* as in modern French (see Variants). **Amours**, a proper name: the god of love. The final -*s*, the mark of the nominative singular in Old French, remains in Middle and modern French as an indication of its function as a proper noun, regardless of its syntactic function. Compare, in modern French, the *-s* of such names as *Georges, Charles, Hugues*. In the present instance, the use of *-s* may have been reinforced by the fact that the noun *amour* 'love' was then feminine; since *-s* as a marker of the nominative case was frequent in the masculine and rare in the feminine, *Amours* tended to be specialized as the name of the god of love, *amour* as the abstract noun 'love'.

Line 2. **soit** = modern French *sait* 'knows' and is pronounced the same way, [se(t)].

Line 6. **Voys** [ves], i.e. [e], not [we], just as in the modern equivalent *vais* 'go'.

Line 7. **se** [sə] = modern French *si* 'if'. *Se* and *si* are practically interchangeable in this meaning from early Old French to about the sixteenth century. **brief** 'soon', in one syllable: [bryef].

Line 8. **Ou** 'with'. **choys** [kwes] 'discreet, quiet, hidden'. This is an unusual spelling; see the variants. English *coy* is a borrowing of this word from Old French.

Line 10. Mell *seiours* must be an error; Dij and Par **secours** agree against Mell and make somewhat better sense, although a case could be made for *séjour* in the sense of 'a home, a refuge'.

2. En soustenant vostre querelle, ff. 2ᵛ–3ʳ [Busnois]

CONCORDANT SOURCES

* Roh, f. 161ʳ⁻ᵛ
Dij 517, ff. cxxviiiᵛ–cxxixʳ
* Par 1719, f. 93ʳ
RomC 2856, ff. 70ᵛ–71ʳ, Busnoys

COLLATION

The readings of Mell and Dij 517 are very similar, but there are differences in the placement of the ligatures, the notation of the longer note values (occasionally divided into shorter ones repeating the pitch in one MS or the other, but usually in Dij 517), and the treatment of the cadential formula in m. 15 of the C (i.e., ornamented with a lower third in Dij 517 but not in Mell). Since none of these divergences alters the musical structure in any significant way, it seems reasonable to assume that the two MSS represent the same scribal tradition.

RomC 2856 agrees substantially with the two earlier sources, but it gives for a number of passages, particularly in the C and CT, a more "modern" reading, that is, one simplified by the elimination of melodic ornaments, especially at cadential points.

COMMENTS

The flat sign faintly visible in the MS at the beginning of the T is apparently an error imperfectly effaced; it is not found in the concordant sources and has been dropped from the transcription as well. The cross-relation between C and CT at m. 3 (1, 2) seems to be intentional and may be text inspired. The note values used and those serving as units of declamation in syllabic passages suggest that the diminished mensuration ($\cent$) should be interpreted proportionally.

En soustenant vostre querelle
Je maintiens que vous estes celle
En tous les lieuls ou je [m'enbas]
Qu'il n'y a partout hault ne bas
Dame qui de vous soit plus belle.   5

Au monde n'a tel damoiselle,
Et pour ce que vous estes [telle]
Trestous les jours je m'en combas   8
  En soustenant *vostre querelle*;
  Je maintiens que vous estes celle
  En tous les lieuls ou je m'enbas.

Vostre beaulte pas je ne celle,
Mais affin qu'il en soit nouvelle
A vous fort amer je m'esbas.
[J'enprendroie] mille debas
Pour en mourir de mort [cruelle]   13
  En soustenant *vostre querelle.*
  Je maintiens que vous estes celle
  En tous les lieuls ou je m'enbas
  Qu'il n'y a partout hault ne bas
  Dame qui de vous soit plus belle.

In taking up your defense
I maintain that you are the one
In all the places that I frequent
[Such] that there is nowhere, of high or low degree,
A lady surpassing you in beauty.

In all the world there's no such damsel,
And because you are thus
I daily enter into combat
    In taking up your defense;
    I maintain that you are the one
    In all the places that I frequent.

Your beauty I do not conceal—
Rather, in order that it be famed,
I love you with open zeal.
I would undertake a thousand quarrels
And would thereby die a cruel death
    In taking up your defense.
    I maintain that you are the one
    In all the places that I frequent
    Such that there is nowhere, of high or low degree,
    A lady surpassing you in beauty.

VARIANTS

1 soustiens—*Roh.* 3 m'enbas—*Roh*, m'esbas—*Mell Par.* 4 ny a pas
ne hault—*Par.* 5 qui soit de vous—*Roh*; nulle dame qui soit si belle—
Par. 6 Par dieu non ayt damoiselle—*Par*; non a il par dieu damoiselle
—*Roh.* 7 belle—*Mell*, celle—*Dij*, telle—*Roh Par.* 8 me—*Dij*; a tout le
monde men combas—*Par.* 11 louer—*Roh Par.* 12 Jen prendray—*Mell*,
Je Prendray—*Dij*, Jen prendroie—*Roh (Par).* 13 mort amere—*Mell*,
mort cruelle—*Par*; Ne pour mourir de mort cruelle—*Roh.*

VERSIFICATION

Rondeau cinquain in octosyllables, *a a b b a.* In the repeated refrain,
the main syntactic stop comes at the end of l. 1′ (or l. 1″) if it is interpreted as being in a construction with l. 8 (or l. 13). The rest of the short
refrain (ll. 2′–3′) is an incomplete construction and apparently is just

there to fill in the melodic structure. In the repetition of the full refrain at the end of the poem, ll. 2″–5″ make a complete sentence, although there is a sort of ellipsis: celle = 'she of whom it may be said . . .'.

Textual Notes

This is one of the few truly badly written poems of the collection; the syntax of the refrain limps, the short refrain is badly integrated, and l. 11 shows traces of desperation. The principal idea is vague and confused.

Line 3. Mell *je m'esbas* 'I spend my time, amuse myself' rhymes with itself at l. 11; if the Mell reading were authentic, the rule against homologous rhyme would be violated. Adoption of Roh **Je m'enbas** 'I go; I enter' resolves this difficulty.

Line 6. **tel** 'such a' can be either masculine or feminine, although there is also a specialized feminine form, *telle*, as in modern French.

Line 7. **Pour ce que** 'because' coexists with *parce que*, but in the fifteenth century is still considerably more frequent. Mell *belle* is isolated in the manuscript tradition and is in homologous rhyme with l. 5.

Line 8. **Trestous** 'all', with the intensive prefix *tres-*.

Line 9. **celle** 'conceal'.

Line 11. **amer**, the Old French infinitive 'to love' coexists in the fifteenth century with the modern *aimer*.

Line 12. Mell *Jen prendray* is one syllable short; the conditional ending of Roh and Par supplies the syllable and makes as much sense as the future of Mell and Dij.

3. Accueilly m'a la belle, ff. 3ᵛ–4ʳ [Caron]

Concordant Sources

Dij 517, ff. viᵛ–viiʳ (Saoulé m'a la belle)
Flo 176, ff. 59ᵛ–60ʳ, Carom
FloR 2356, ff. 55ᵛ–56ʳ
Par 676, ff. 47ᵛ–48ʳ
Pix, ff. 6ᵛ–7ʳ, Caron
TrBC 1947-4, n.f., Caron
Tr 91, f. 12ᵛ (Da pacem, Domine)
*Jar, f. lxxivᵛ

Collation

Caron's chanson was also included in Esc IV.a.24 between ff. 127
and 128 on leaves that have now been lost.[1] The relationships among
the musical sources are rather complicated. The C is essentially the
same in all the versions listed. However, Mell differs from the concordant sources in the T from mm. 15(4) to 18(2). In the other MSS the
T imitates exactly the short phrase of the C, mm. 15(2)–16(1), before
presenting that of mm. 15(4)–16(1) in the T of Mell, whereas only
the latter has the two notes of mm. 17(2) and 18(1), e-Sb and g-Br.
There are also two different CT parts for this chanson, but in this
instance that of the present MS is shared by Tr 91, TrBC 1947-4, and
Par 676 (with some divergences toward the end); a related yet distinctly
independent version is given by Dij 517, Flo 176 (which follows the
reading of Dij 517 quite closely throughout), and FloR 2356. TrBC
1947-4 has a fourth voice (altus) not found in the other sources.

Comments

The variant reading given for the T in Mell may have resulted from
a scribal error because the identical beginning of the two short phrases
cited could have led a copyist to jump from the initial notes of the
first to the final ones of the second without noticing his omission. The
two notes found only in Mell would then have been added to replace
the missing member when the gap became evident in performance.
It may be that the Mell variant represents the conscious revision of an
enterprising musician or scribe, but the possibility does not seem likely,
since the better version is clearly that of the concordant sources.
Because other variants are not significant, it would seem on the basis
of the differing CT parts that there are two distinct manuscript traditions for this composition and that Mell belongs to the tradition of
the two Trent MSS and Par 676 despite its unique variant.

The fourth voice of TrBC 1947-4 was probably added when the piece
was adapted for sacred use by the substitution of a Latin text for the
original French poem. The music was also employed with a contrafact
text in Italian, the *lauda* printed by Feo Belcari (*Laude spirituali*, No.
clxxxiv, pp. 83–84), and became the basis for a polyphonic mass

1. See James Thomson, *An Introduction to Philippe(?) Caron*, p. 6 (with note **).

setting, also attributed to Caron, in MS 51 of the Cappella Sistina in the Vatican library at Rome.[2]

Accueill[y m'a] la belle au gent atour,
Tournant mon bien en douloureux destour.
Destourné m'a son amoureulx racueil,
Cueillant / refus quant au chemin de dueil,
D'oeil et de cueur m'a banny de sa tour.   5

Tourner n'y sçay; tournant voie ne tour
Ne tourment n'est que n'aye tout autour,
Tournant en plains en lieu de bel acueil.   8
    Acueilly m'a la belle au gent atour,
    Tournant mon bien en doloreux destour :
    Destourné m'a son amoureulx recueil.

Recueillir fault tous les griefz a l'entour.
Tournay n'y vault jouster, ne faire estour.
Tourné suis la; je n'y voy autre escueil.
Escueilly suis et mis hors de son vueil.
Vueil ou non veul, il n'y a nul retour.   13
    Acueilly m'a la belle au gent atour,
    Tournant mon bien en doloureux destour.
    Destourné m'a son amoureulx racueil
    Cueillant refus quant au chemin de dueil,
    D'oeil et de cueur m'a banny de sa tour.

She has received me ill, the beauty of gentle mien,
Turning my well-being into a painful pass.
She has turned away from me her loving greeting;
Receiving refusal on the path of grief,
By her eye and heart I am banished from her tower.

I know not which way to turn; there is no twisting road,
    nor turn,
Nor torment which I find not all around
Turning into plaints instead of cordial welcome.

2. Ibid., pp. 8–9, 23, 44.

> She has received me ill, the beauty of gentle mien
> Turning my well-being into a painful pass.
> She has turned away from me her loving greeting.

> I must accept all the woes that surround me.
> Nor jousting nor combat can avail.
> I am turned thither—I see no other way out.
> I am turned out and removed from her desire.
> Whatever I may wish, there is no return.
> > She has received me ill, the beauty of gentle mien,
> > Turning my well-being into a painful pass.
> > She has turned away from me her loving greeting;
> > Receiving refusal on the path of grief,
> > By her eye and heart I am banished from her tower.

Variants

The three concordant sources with texts are Jar, Dij, and Pix.[3] Our text is taken, for most of the refrain, from Mell; after l. 4 *Cueillant*, the last word of the Mell text, we employ principally Jar, with help from Dij and Pix. Since the verse is in retrograde rhyme (see Versification), the restoration of correct readings has been facilitated.

1 Accueillez moy—*Mell*, Saoule ma—*Dij*, Acueilly m'a—*Jar* (*Pix*). 2 Pix omits en. 3 Pix omits son. 4 quant onque my de doeul—*Pix*. (Pix can be explained as a misreading of a Picard model *ou quemin > *ou quemȳ > onque my.) 5 Et de courage—*Jar*, de oeil de cueur—*Dij*, de oeul et de cor—*Pix*; et Da sa tour—*Dij*. (The correct reading of this line is assured by retrograde principle and syllable count: *D'oeil* conserves the former, Pix *et* restores the first hemistich to four syllables. Pix ends here.) 6 (Text from here on is that of Jar with corrections from Dij.) 7 Ne tournement—*Jar*, Et tourment nest —*Dij*. 8 Tourment et plus ou—*Dij*. 9 Reculer—*Dij*; ses—*Dij*; lenteur—*Dij*. 11 la ou—*Dij* (+1). 13 (This line as in Dij.) Comme banny ie ny voy nul retour—*Jar*.

---

3. The Pix text has been edited and somewhat modified by Wilhelm Meyer-Lübke in the *Denkmäler der Tonkunst in Österreich*, XI. Jahrgang (Vienna, 1904), 21:75, where the song *Da pacem* from Tr 91, f. 12ᵛ, is published. Only the Latin words appear in that manuscript with the French text established by Meyer-Lübke from Pix alone; surely if he had had access to some of the other sources, he would have established a more satisfactory text.

VERSIFICATION

Rondeau cinquain in decasyllables, *a a b b a*. Although no one version follows the rule, it is clear from an examination of all of them that we are dealing with what Eustache Deschamps calls retrograde and equivocal verse;[4] that is, the first one or two syllables of each line repeat the last one or two syllables of the preceding line (hence *retrograde*), but usually with a different meaning (hence *equivocal*). It appears that none of the copyists ever perceived this structural fact, so that the variants bearing on the beginnings and endings of lines are quickly diagnosed as good or bad according to their observance or violation of the retrograde rule. Thus, in our reconstruction of the second and third strophes we have had to go back and forth between Jar and Dij, with occasional help from Pix, to find the correct readings.

TEXTUAL NOTES

Line 2. **destour** 'plight, pass'.

Line 4. **Cueillant refus** '(me) receiving a refusal, being rejected'.

Line 5. **D'** . . . **de** 'with . . . with'.

Line 6. **tournant voie** 'twisting road'. Adjectives and participles ending in -*ant* may optionally add -*e* in the feminine; it was not added in this instance for metrical reasons.

Line 8. **Tournant en plains:** possibly a deliberate ambiguity— (a) 'turning into complaints'; (b) 'twisting on the plains'.

Line 9. **Recueillir fault** 'I must accept'; **griefz** [gryez], the [z] voiced in liaison, 'woes'.

Line 10. **Tournay** 'tourney'; cf. modern French *tournoi*.

Line 11. **escueil** 'way out'.

Line 12. **Escueilly** 'turned out'; **vueil** 'desire' (noun).

Line 13. **Vueil ou non veul** 'Whatever I may wish'. (*vueil* and *veul* are different spellings of the same word and are pronounced alike: [völ']). This is the first person singular, present indicative, of *vouloir*.

il n'y a nul retour: a magnificent pun. In the context of this poem it means, 'There is no way to return (to her favor, symbolized by the tower).' But it also refers to an insuperable difficulty in composing retrograde verse. The poem has been perfectly retrograde to this point, but the exigencies of form and the rhyme scheme have made

4. Eustache Deschamps, "L'art de dictier," in his *Oeuvres*, ed. Gaston Raynaud, 7:277.

it inevitable that the last word of the last stanza end in the syllable *tour*, whereas the first word of the refrain, which must follow the last stanza, is *Acueilly*. The refrain had to begin with the syllables *acueil* because the short strophe ended in that word. Hence the poet's complaint: Try as I might, there is no return.

4. Petitte Camusette, ff. 4ᵛ–5ʳ, J. Okeghem

CONCORDANT SOURCES

BruR 11239, f. 20ᵛ (C and T only)
Dij 517, ff. clxiᵛ–clxiiʳ (S'elle m'amera / Petite Camusette)
FloC 2439, ff. 31ᵛ–32ʳ, Ockeghem
MC 871, f. 160ᵛ (p. 392)
Mun 1516, No. 11
Niv, ff. lvᵛ–56ʳ (S'elle m'amera / Petite Camusete)
Sev 7.I.28, ff. ciᵛ–ciiʳ (De la momera / Petit le camiset)
Wolf 287, ff. 61ᵛ–62ʳ (S'elle m'aymera / Petite Camusette)
Canti C, ff. 122ᵛ–123ʳ, Okenghem

COLLATION

Because of the number of sources concerned and the complexity of the relationships among them, the variant readings will be considered voice by voice.

Cantus: The ascending figure in m. 4 (1–5) is written in FloC 2439 as M, M, M, Sm, Sm instead of with the dotted rhythms of Mell. BruR 11239, Mun 1516, and Canti C retain the dotted configuration for the first two notes (1, 2) but continue as in FloC 2439. Dij 517 gives g instead of a′ for 4 (7), surely erroneously; BruR 11239 has the same a′ as Sb instead of M but without the following M-rest. In m. 6 (4, 5) b and a are written as a dotted figure in BruR 11239 and Niv instead of as 2 MM. BruR 11239 and MC 871 give m. 10 (5) as f-Sb without the dot and the anticipatory e-Sm of Mell. At m. 11 (5) Niv has e instead of the d of Mell (perhaps a better reading); FloC 2439 and Sev 7.I.28 also fill in the third between f and d with 2 SSm, e and d, in place of d-M in Mell, m. 11 (6). At m. 22 (5ff.) one finds e-Sb, rest-M, e-M in Mun 1516 and Canti C. The final cadential formula of m. 23 is ornamented somewhat differently in a number of sources, including FloC 2439, MC 871, Mun 1516, and Canti C.

Niv alone has a b-flat signature for the entire C (but for no other part).

Tenor: The reading of Mell for m. 14 (3)–15 (2) is shared by no other source and creates a serious harmonic clash. In addition, Sev 7.I.28 erroneously gives m. 6 (2, 3) as FFu instead of SSm; Mun 1516 and Canti C have five BBr of rest in mm. 10–12 instead of the four of Mell and other sources, and (to compensate) only two of the four SSb of m. 13. BruR 11239 has a b-flat signature throughout the part; FloC 2439 gives a written flat for m. 16 (1), confirming the accidental suggested.

Contratenor I: At m. 5 (2–5) only Mell has the modest cadential ornament; all other sources have d-Sb, c-M instead. A rest-Br apparently missing in Mell, mm. 9–10, is found in all other sources except Mun 1516 and Canti C. In the latter two the part has been revised to compensate for the omission with d-Br, c-Sb, c-Sb, d-Br filling all of m. 10 and the first half of m. 11. FloC 2439 gives e at m. 16 (2) instead of the d of Mell; both FloC 2439 and Niv have a dotted figure of Sb and 2 MM for m. 16 (3–5); and MC 871 has f instead of e at m. 16 (4), probably an error. At the approach to the cadence, m. 22 (4 ff.), FloC 2439, Mun 1516, and Canti C give G-M, a-M, b-M, a-Sm, b-Sm, and the last two notes are also found in MC 871 and Niv in place of the a-M of Mell, m. 22 (7).

Contratenor II: There is a rest-Br wanting at the beginning in Dij 517. At m. 11 (1 ff.), Mun 1516 and Canti C have the variant G-dotted Sb, F-Sm, E-Sm (creating a sequence with the following m.), perhaps a revision prompted by that made in the T in those two sources at the same spot. In Sev 7.I.28, m. 24 begins with a rest-Sb followed by D-Sb and a final L divided between D and F.

There is confusion in the sources with respect to the mensuration of this chanson. In contrast to the indication for integral imperfect tempus (C) in Mell, both Dij 517 and Wolf 287 have the same sign with a stroke of diminution (₵) in CT I, and BruR 11239, Mun 1516, Sev 7.I.28, and Canti C have the diminished form in all parts.

COMMENTS

Because the variant in Mell at mm. 14 (3)–15 (2) is unique to this source and also generates totally unacceptable vertical sonorities, it seemed reasonable to assume a copyist's error and to emend the transcription to conform with the version given unanimously by the remaining collections.

Despite some differences of ornamental figuration, the musical reading most closely related to that of Mell is given by MC 871; even the placement of ligature patterns and coloration is frequently the same in both. The two MSS clearly represent a single tradition of transmission. Also closely related to the versions of these two Neapolitan collections is that of the Spanish MS Sev 7.I.28. Not far removed in turn from this group of sources are the readings given by the northern chansonniers dating from the fifteenth century (Dij 517, Wolf 287, and Niv). The notation in the first two is virtually identical, even in the use of ligatures and coloration. Somewhat more independent but definitely in the same scribal tradition is the version of Niv. These three MSS alone have a courtly rondeau as the text for the C. Of the three, the reading of Niv is closest to that of Mell. Curiously, the corrupted incipit of Sev 7.I.28 probably also derives from the rondeau of the northern sources although the musical version is more similar to those of Mell and MC 871.

The interrelationships with the later sources are even more complicated. Mun 1516 and Canti C share a common reading and are so similar in their divergences from the other sources as to suggest that the Munich MS was copied from the Petrucci print. The versions of BruR 11239 and FloC 2439 are more directly related to one another than to that of the previous pair, presumably because both derive from a northern tradition rather than from the Italian one from which Mun 1516 and Canti C emerge, but they are not without some affinities to Mell, MC 871, and Sev 7.I.28. Mun 1516 and Canti C share with Mell the missing rest in mm. 9–10 of CT I, thus establishing a clear link with the scribal tradition of the present MS, but carry a later revision made necessary by the error.

The conflicting mensural indications of the different sources may reflect the contrast between the popular melody of the T and CT parts—and the bright tempo at which it was presumably sung as a rule—and the stately movement traditionally required by the courtly rondeau with which it was combined, probably by Ockeghem himself. Either tempo may have been observed toward the end of the fifteenth century, and either could contribute in the proper context to the comic effect that was apparently intended. However, for the present version the greatest irony is perhaps to be achieved with the tempo given.

I. Petitte Camusette, j'ay
    Proposé me mettre en essay
    D'acquerir quelque peu vo grace:
    Force m'est que par la je passe.
    Ceste foys j'en feray l'essay.   5

II. Petitte Camusette, a la mort m'avés mis.
    Robin et Marïon s'en vont au boys jouer.

    Ilz s'en vont bras a bras; ilz se sont endormis.   3

    Petitte Camusette, a la mort m'avés mis.   1'

I. Little Snubnose, I have
    Proposed at least to try
    To obtain, however little, your grace;
    Needs be that I pass that way—
    This time I'll make the try.

II. Little Subnose, you've put me to death.
    Robin and Marion are going to the wood to play.

    They're going off, arm in arm; they've gone to sleep.

    Little Subnose, you've put me to death.

Variants

Of the concordant sources, the following are texted: Bru, Dij, Niv, Sev, and Wolf. Bru has only the text of II; Dij, Wolf, and Niv have the full rondeau, I, as well as the text of II. Sev, like Mell, has only the refrain of I (as well as a fragment of II); its texts have been so corrupted by a scribe evidently ignorant of French that they contribute nothing to text establishment. Aside from ll. 1–2, Mell, Dij, Niv, and Wolf are in substantial agreement as to the text of the refrain of I; ll. 1–2 according to Dij are as follows, and Niv and Wolf have no significant variations:

> S'elle mamera, Je ne scay,
> mais Je me mectray en essay.

The whole rondeau has been published by Martin Picker in his edition of *The Chanson Albums of Marguerite of Austria*.

The only important variant in II is in l. 2, Dij Niv *joly*, where Mell and Wolf have *jouer*, apparently in an attempt to provide a rhyme with *mis*, although *joly* does not have final -*s*.

VERSIFICATION

I. Refrain of a rondeau cinquain in octosyllables, *a a b b a*.

II. Probably a rondet, *a b*, in dodecasyllables (see p. 85). Although the text is skimpy, this identification is probably correct in view of the description of the form and its history by Alfred Jeanroy.[1] The imprecision of the rhyme mis: joly proposed by Dij and Niv suggests that Mell Wolf *jouer* is more likely the original word, and that ll. 1–2 represent the refrain in *A B*. The significance of the rondet in the history of the rondeau and in relationship to truly popular songs involving the use of a leader (*soliste*), who "lines out" the refrain to be repeated by a chorus and who then sings independent lines, is explained in great detail by Jeanroy. Such game-like songs originally accompanied round-dances (whence the names of verse forms based on the stems *rond*- 'round' and *bal*- 'dance').[2] Furthermore, dance-songs were "éminemment dramatiques ... par la manière dont elles étaient chantées, on pourrait presque dire jouées, et dont leur caractère n'est qu'une conséquence; ces répliques échangées entre le choeur et le soliste constituaient de véritables drames."[3] It is Jeanroy's opinion that, although it was generally accepted that the rondet was not invented before the fourteenth century, in fact it goes back much earlier and was cultivated from the twelfth century on. "La seule innovation au XIVe siècle consista à réduire cette forme à un seul couplet, que l'on fit précéder du refrain, lequel, à l'origine, n'était chanté qu'au début de la pièce, d'abord par le soliste, qui en indiquait ainsi le motif et la mélodie, ensuite par le choeur."[4]

1. Alfred Jeanroy, *Les origines de la poésie lyrique en France*, 3d ed. (Paris: Champion, 1925), especially pp. 406–07, 414–15, 419–24.

2. Ibid., p. 387.

3. Dance-songs were "[eminently dramatic] by the way in which they were sung, one might almost say *acted*, and of which their character is but one consequence; these lines exchanged between the chorus and the leader constituted real dramas" (ibid., p. 393).

4. "The only innovation of the fourteenth century consisted of reducing this form to a single stanza, which was made to follow the refrain which, originally, was only sung at the very beginning of the piece, first by the leader, who thus indicated its motif and its tune, and then by the chorus" (ibid., p. 407).

This view of the *performance* of the rondet, as a sort of dance-game-song, is applicable to the present song, which lends itself to pantomime. Robin and Marion go to the woods to play: A man takes a woman by the hand and leads her to a place designated, for the game, as the "wood." And then they come back. The refrain, probably sung by the leader and repeated by the chorus, is followed by l. 3, sung by the leader, and then l. 1′ is sung by the chorus. A complete rondet would have two new lines, sung by the leader, rhyming in *ab*, to be answered by the chorus, singing ll. 1″–2″.

5. A une damme, ff. 5ᵛ–6ʳ [Busnois]

Concordant Sources

*Roh, f. 115ʳ
Bol Q 16, ff. 31ᵛ–32ʳ
Dij 517, ff. lxivᵛ–lxvʳ, Busnoys
Flo 176, ff. 6ᵛ–8ʳ
*Par 1719, f. 113ʳ
CG XIII.27, ff. 88ᵛ–89ʳ
Lab, ff. 101ᵛ–102ʳ, Busn[ois]

Collation

The reading found in Lab is virtually identical to that of the present collection, and the versions of Dij 517 and CG XIII.27 differ from these two only slightly in details of melodic ornamentation: Dij 517 in the C at the approach to the cadence closing the first section, m. 16 (1 ff.), and in the T at the beginning of the second, m. 18 (1 ff.); CG XIII.27 in the cadential ornaments at the end of both sections, first by eliminating the lower third, m. 16 (10), then by filling it in, m. 25 (9). In the T, CG XIII.27 gives d-Sm (instead of e) at m. 14 (4)—a less euphonious reading—and replaces the rest of m. 20 with a dot for the preceding d-Sb, whereas in the CT it has a dotted figure instead of even MM at mm. 8 (6–7) and 15 (2–3), F-M instead of F-Sm, E-Sm at m. 21 (2–3), and omits the flat for b in m. 10. Otherwise it is surprisingly close to Mell even in notational particulars such as coloration and the placement of ligatures. Bol Q 16 differs from all four in a greater number of details, once again largely in ornamental melodic figures. There is no lower third in the cadential formula of the C at m. 16 (7 ff.), for example; the final cadence in the same voice, m. 25 (5 ff.), is written f'-Sm, e'-Sm, d'-dotted M, b'-Sm, c'-M; and in the CT, m. 9 (5), the descending fifth from e-Sb to a-Sb in Mell is filled in by four SSm, e, d, c, b. There is also a tendency in the reading of Bol Q 16 to fill in with notes the rests found in the three other sources: in the C at m. 21 an additional d'-Sb replaces the rest; in the T at m. 18 (4) the d-Sb is followed by a dot rather than a rest (as in Dij 517), and at m. 21 (1) the d has been extended by a Sb and the rest shortened by the same amount; and in the CT at m. 13 (5–6) both D-Sb and C-Sb appear with dots, eliminating the following rest. There is apparently an error in the CT, m. 25 (5), where D is written as M in Bol Q 16 instead of as Sb as in the other sources. Interestingly, the two late MSS have a diminished mensuration for this chanson (₵) in place of the integral symbol used in the remaining collections.

The reading of Flo 176, particularly in the C and the CT, displays more significant and extensive divergences from that of Mell than any other MS. The most notable variants in the C are at m. 16 (1 ff.), written d'-M, e'-M, g'-M, f'-dotted M, d'-Sm, d'-Sb, c'-M, and at m. 19 (3)–20 (4), written f'-M, d'-M, c'-Sb, d'-M, e'-dotted M, d'-Sm, c'-Sm, b'-Sm, c'-Sb. In the CT there is little of moment until m. 18 (5), from which point the part proceeds in a markedly different manner until the end of the section, corresponding to that of the Mellon only for the four notes of the *ouvert* ending (m. 23) and giving no indication of a repetition.

COMMENTS

The chansonniers Lab, Dij 517, CG XIII.27, and, to a lesser degree, Bol Q 16 evidently represent the same scribal tradition as Mell but in a decreasing degree of similarity to the present reading. The reading of Flo 176, on the other hand, stands clearly apart from the group, as Allan Atlas has already observed.[1] The diminished mensuration of Bol Q 16 and CG XIII.27 is probably due to their having been copied at a later date when diminished imperfect tempus

---

1. "Rome, Biblioteca Apostolica Vaticana, Cappella Giulia XIII.27 and the Dissemination of the Franco-Netherlandish Chanson in Italy, ca. 1460–1530," p. 390.

was virtually the only sign used; it would seem probable that the integral symbol was original with Busnois.

This chanson is very likely one of the group that the poet-musician addressed to Jacqueline d'Hacqueville since the colors of the lady of the vow, yellow and blue, were those featured in the escutcheon of the d'Hacqueville family.[2]

A une damme j'ay fait veu
Pour le grant bruit de sa valeur
Que je ne porteray couleur
Se ce n'est le jaune et le bleu.   4

Les deulz en ung *sans* que les mue
Je maintendray pour sa beaulté.

L'une en signe de retenue,
L'aultre en moustrant ma léaulté.   8

Car au fort quant il sera sceu
Que d'elle soy*e* serviteur,
Oncques ne m'avint tel honneur
Sans saillir l'escu tant soit [peu].   12
        A une damme j'ay fait veu
        Pour le grant bruit de sa valeur
        Que je ne porteray couleur
        Se ce n'est le jaune et le bleu.

To a lady I've made a vow,
Because of the great fame of her worth,
That I'll wear no color
Unless it be the yellow and the blue.

These two together, without change,
I shall keep for her beauty.

2. Concerning the chansons that Busnois addressed to his lady, Jacqueline d'Hacqueville, usually by means of an acrostic or an explicit mention of her name, see Reese, *Music in the Renaissance*, pp. 101–02; three of them are included in this collection (Nos. 12, 14, and 42). The arms of d'Hacqueville may be seen in Henri Jongla de Morenas, *Grand Armorial de France*, 4:265, or in Johannes Baptista Rietstap, *Armorial Général Illustré*, 3:cxxxi.

The one as sign of discretion,
The other to show my loyalty.

For, in fact, when it shall be known
That I am her servant,
Never [before] has come to me so great an honor
Without the scutcheon's being sullied, however little.
    To a lady I've made a vow,
    Because of the great fame of her worth,
    That I'll wear no color
    Unless it be the yellow and the blue.

VARIANTS

All the concordant sources except Bol Q and Flo are texted.

3 ja—*Lab Par*; porteroye—*Roh* (hypermetric). 5 Ces—*Lab Par*, Ses—*Roh Mell* (illuminator) (scribe's instruction to illuminator: les); sans que—*Lab Par Roh*; Dij omits en ung. 7 Lung—*Lab Roh* (*Par*). 8 monstrant—*Par Roh*; ta—*Dij*. 10 soy—*Mell*, soye—*Lab* (*Dij*), seray—*Par*, suis—*Roh*. 12 (fouller—*Par*, fuillir [?]—*Dij*) le sien tant soit peu—*Lab Par Dij*, Sans blecier lonneur tant soit peu—*Roh*; jeu—*Mell*.

VERSIFICATION

Octosyllabic bergerette, *a b b a c d*. In l. 9, if we assumed Francian pronunciation of *sceu* [sü], we would have an eye rhyme or, phonetically, an approximate rhyme (involving front-rounded vowels [ö : ü]). However, it is more likely that *sceu* represents the non-Francian simplification of the OF dipthong [əü] to [ö] (see p. 100). Hence, *sceu* = [sö]. In l. 6, *beaulté* has two syllables [bawte], while l. 8 *léaulté* has three [leawte]. *Au* represents [aw], the *ou* of English *house*.

TEXTUAL NOTES

Line 3. **porteray couleur** 'wear a color'; a lover would use the colors of his clothing as a sort of secret code, somewhat conventionalized but with a great deal of variation from one source to another, for gallant communication. In this poem the meanings of the colors are explicitly stated.

Line 5. **en ung** 'together'. **sans que les mue** 'without [my] changing them'.

Line 7. **L'une** (as also in Dij) 'the one', referring to the feminine noun *couleur*. *L'un(g)*, the reading of Lab, Par, and Roh, refers to *le jaune*. **retenue** 'discretion' refers to one of the characteristics of the ideal lover: his ability to keep the attachment secret.

Line 9. **au fort** 'finally, in fact'.

Line 12. **Saillir** must mean "sully' in this context. The usual meaning of Old French *saillir* 'to go forth, jump, dance' is impossible here. Furthermore, this verb is intransitive, except in expressions like *saillir une fosse* 'jump a ditch'; therefore *saillir l'escu* must be an error. It is possible that *saillir* is a combination of *salir* and *souiller* and that the scribe, thinking of both and intending to write down one of them, produced the scribal and linguistic error known as a *blend*. 'Sully a scutcheon' is not far from the meanings of the other versions: Roh *blecier l'onneur* 'wound the honor', Lab Par Dij *fouler le sien* 'trample hers [= her honor]'. The verb of Dij is hard to read: the initial letter is *s* or *f*, *ui* is fairly clear, what follows is *ll* or the abbreviation of *ser*, and *ir* is perfectly clear. It could be read as *suillir* or *fuillir*; the interpretation of these otherwise nonexistent forms remains difficult.

Lines 9–12. A highly elliptical sentence; even the translation which we propose requires some explanation. A freer rendering would be: Never before has so great an honor—that of being known to wear the colors of a great lady—come to me without an adverse effect on that lady's reputation. It is unclear whether the poet is claiming that this time it will be different, that her shield will not be sullied, or whether the poem constitutes fair warning. We lean toward the first explanation, if only because of the generally positive, optimistic tone of the poem. The poet seems to be saying that now, finally, he is worthy to serve the lady.

6. Loing de vo tresdoulce presence, ff. 7ᵛ–8ʳ

CONCORDANT SOURCES

* Roh, f. 72ʳ⁻ᵛ
Bol Q 16, ff. 124ᵛ–125ʳ

COLLATION

There are few variants for this work between the two musical MSS. The majority of them are minor differences in melodic ornamentation such as the lower third in Bol Q 16 to embellish the cadential figure of the C at m. 12 (2), or the division of rhythmic values to fill in a third in the C at m. 19 (4). There e-Sm, d-Sm replace the d-M of Mell, and by imitation in the T at m. 19 (6) a-Sm, G-Sm stand in the place of Mell's G-M. The most important divergences occur in the CT: at m. 4 (4) G-M, E-M are given instead of the E-Sb of Mell (a melodic pattern that creates an abrasive cross-relation with a raised leading tone in the C). The passage m. 12 (4)–13 (2) is written b-M, b-M, b-M, a-M, c-Sb, F-M in Bol Q 16; and at m. 24 (2) one finds C instead of B, perhaps an error. The written flats in Mell in the two lower voices are not present in Bol Q 16: in the T at m. 5 (2), and in the CT at mm. 7 (3), 11 (8), 19 (4), and 23 (7).

COMMENTS

Despite the considerable chronological gap separating the two MSS, the readings they offer for this composition differ little; only the variants of the CT can be considered significant. Consequently, it can be assumed that they represent related scribal traditions with only those divergences that might be expected from the errors and initiatives of copyists during the years between the compilation of the two collections.

> Loing de vo tresdoulce presence
> Mais par desir et souvenance
> Prochainement de vous, mon bien,
> Me couvient passer temps, combien
> Que ce n'est pas sans desplaisance.   5
>
> J'ay cuydé faire resistence,
> Maiz mon dueil croist tant plus y pense
> Et ne me pourroit plaire rien   8
> *Loing de vo tresdoulce presence—*
> *Mais par desir et souvenance*
> *Prochainement de vous, mon bien.*
>
> Car vostre gente contenance,
> Vo doulx parler, vostre prudence
> Ont tant asservy le cueur mien
> Qu'il ne seroit au pouoir sien

S'esjoÿr ou avoir plaisance
Loing de vo tresdoulce presence.
Mais par desir et souvenance
Prochainement de vous, mon bien,
Me couvient passer temps, combien
Que ce n'est pas sans desplaisance.

Far from your most sweet presence
(Yet, by desire and remembrance
Still near to you, my treasure)
I must pass my time, although
It is not without displeasure.

I had thought I could resist,
But my grief grows the more I think on it,
And nothing could please me
    Far from your most sweet presence
    (Yet, by desire and remembrance,
    Still near to you, my treasure).

For your gentle countenance,
Your soft speech, your prudence
Have so enslaved this heart of mine
That it would not be in its power
To have joy or pleasure
    Far from your most sweet presence.
    Yet, by desire and remembrance,
    Still near to you, my treasure,
    I must pass my time, although
    It is not without displeasure.

VARIANTS

Roh is the only concordant source for the poem. Mell has the refrain alone; Roh provides the rest. The only variants of any importance are the Roh reading of l. 1: vostre doulce presence, and of l. 3: Prochain de vous, m'amour, mon bien.

The first variant requires some explanation. The Francian *vostre* (pl. *vos*) is the ancestor of the standard modern French *votre* (and *vôtre*), pl.

vos. In Picard, the plural *vos* was remodeled as singular *vo* by dropping the plural *-s*. Since the literary language from the thirteenth to the fifteenth centuries was predominantly Francian with many Picard borrowings, the forms *vo* and *vostre* were both available to the poets, who were probably happy with the alternative of one- and two-syllable forms. It is therefore impossible to choose between *vostre doulce* and *vo tresdoulce* for l. 1. They are nearly identical phonetically, *s* being mute before a consonant, and they have the same syllable count. Line 10 demonstrates that *vo* and *vostre* can coexist in the same poem, as far as this poet is concerned (and in this he is typical). One could suppose a reading *Vo tresdoulx parler, vo prudence*, but there is no compelling reason to do so, except a desire to have nothing but the Picard *vo* throughout the poem. In the absence of other picardisms in this poem, the expectation of rigorous dialectal consistency for this one feature is hardly justified.

VERSIFICATION

Octosyllabic rondeau cinquain, *a a b b a*. Both r and R′ are integrated, with a syntactic pause at the end of the first line; our punctuation shows how the rest of the refrain fits the syntactic context differently each time.

TEXTUAL NOTES

Line 3. **Prochainement** 'near'; with adverbial suffix because it is taken as modifying the verb of l. 4.

Line 4. **Me couvient** = *Il me faut* 'I must'.

Line 7. **y** refers to *faire resistence* of l. 6.

Line 8. **rien** is the subject.

Line 9. **contenance** 'countenance; bearing; comportment'.

7. Est-il merchy, ff. 8ᵛ–9ʳ, Busnoys

CONCORDANT SOURCES

*Roh, ff. 100ᵛ–101ʳ
Dij 517, ff. lviᵛ–lviiʳ
Cord, ff. 36ᵛ–38ʳ
Niv, ff. xxxviiᵛ–xxxviiiʳ, Busnois
Lab, ff. 29ᵛ–30ʳ
Wolf 287, ff. 2ᵛ–3ʳ

*Arn, f. 57ʳ
*Jar, f. 66ʳ

COLLATION

With regard to the notation of this chanson all the sources except
Niv give basically the same reading with only minor differences of
melodic and rhythmic detail in the embellishment of cadential
formulas, the use of dotted figures, the indication of extended values
(either by longer notes or repetition of shorter ones on the same pitch),
and the like. Niv gives only two substantive variants, neither of which
alters significantly the musical structure. At m. 23 (3) of the T, instead
of the f-M of the other sources, there is a g-M that produces a consonant
combination as acceptable compositionally as the one seen here and
perhaps more effective in that particular context. The CT at m. 18 (5)–
19 (2) is written D-Sb, D-M, eliminating the C-M found in Mell,
m. 19 (1); the result is contrapuntally correct but less interesting than
the double suspension of Mell.

There are some minor discrepancies among the MSS in the use of
key signatures and accidentals as well. Neither Dij 517 nor Wolf 287
has a flat as a signature except at the beginning of the T; Niv and Lab
have a b-flat signature for all three voices; Cord has a flat signature
for only C and T in the first section, for only CT in the second. Most
of the b-flats occurring in the C of Mell are given in Wolf 287 as
accidentals, but in the T and CT the latter MS follows more closely
Dij 517, where the following flats are written in the CT: for E at m.
7 (4); for B at m. 19 (4); for E at m. 25 (2), the last being given also
by Niv.

COMMENTS

All the readings offered by the sources for this composition apparently derive from the same tradition of transmission. As is often the
case, however, Dij 517 and Wolf 287 are more similar to each other in
matters of detail than to other collections. Mell appears to be nearest
to the version of Cord. Niv alone possesses significant variants, but
they are so minor in substance that they could have been introduced
by a single compiler or scribe.

> Est-il merchy de quoy on pueut finer?
> Est-il pitié qu'on peust en vous trouver?
> Est-il, m'amour, nulle riens souffissante,

Est-il chose tant soit forte ou puissante
Dont je sceusse vo grace recouvrer?   5

Pour fondre tout en larmes de plourer,
Ne pour paine que je sceusse endurer,
Est-il chose dont vous fussiés contente?   8
    Est-il merchy *de quoy on pueut finer?*
    Est-il pitié qu'on peust en vous trouver?
    Est-il, m'amour, nulle riens souffissante?

Quel remede puis-je a mon fait donner,
Quant je voy bien que par tant vous amer
Il ne [s'ensuit] que ma mort evidente?
Et toutesfoys pour doleur que je sente
Je ne m'en puis tant soit peu destourner.   13
    Est-il merchi *de quoy on pueut finer?*
    Est-il pitié qu'on peust en vous trouver?
    Est-il, m'amour, nulle riens souffissante,
    Est-il chose tant soit forte ou puissante
    Dont je sceusse vo grace recouvrer?

Is there mercy that can bring an end?
Is there pity one could find in you ?
Is there, my love, something sufficient,
Is there anything at all, however strong or powerful,
With which I could regain your grace?

By melting in tears as I cry,
Or any pain that I might endure,
Is there something with which you'd be content?
    Is there mercy that can bring an end?
    Is there pity one could find in you?
    Is there, my love, something sufficient?

What remedy can I find for my plight
When I can see, by loving you so much,
The only result is clearly my death.
And yet, whatever sorrow I may feel,
I cannot turn aside from this path.

Is there mercy that can bring an end?
Is there pity one could find in you?
Is there, my love, something sufficient,
Is there anything at all, however strong or powerful,
With which I could regain your grace?

Variants

Of the concordant sources, Dij, Cord, Jar, Lab, Niv, Roh, and Wolf
are texted.

1 mercy—*all concordant sources*; puist—*Jar*, peust—*Cord Lab Niv Roh
Wolf*, sceust—*Dij*. 2 puist—*Jar*, sceust—*Dij Niv*. 3 amour—*Jar*;
souffisance—*Lab*, suffisante—*Cord Niv*. 4 fort—*Roh*; puissance—*Lab*.
5 vostre amour—*Cord*, vostre grace—*Lab* (hypermetric); Dont vostre
grace je peusse (puisse—*Löp*) recouvrer—*Roh*; recevoir—*Dij*. 6 Pour
fondre en lermes, pour gemir, pour pleurer—*Jar*. 7 Et—*Roh*; peusse—
Roh, puisse—*Lab Wolf*. 8 Ou faire chose—*Roh*; Dij omits vous. 9
Quelque remede—*Wolf* (epic caesura); puis a—*Cord*, puisse—*Lab*,
puisse mon—*Wolf*; mon cueur—*Roh*. 11 Seuffre—*Mell*, sensiue—*Roh*.
12 Quant toutesfoys—*Roh*. 13 tant peu ty—*Lab*, tant seul peu—*Wolf*;
descouvrer—*Lab Wolf*.

Versification

Decasyllabic rondeau cinquain, *a a b b a*, with lyric caesura (ll. 4, 5, 7,
8, 9, and, in original Mell reading, 11) in which the mute *e* following the
third syllable is counted as the fourth of the ten syllables (see pp. 80–81).
The Wolf variant of l. 9, *Quelque remede*, follows the epic rule (mute *e*
uncounted and after the fourth syllable). But this reading is suspect,
because in Wolf ll. 4, 5, 7, and 8 do contain the lyric caesura; and it
was not the practice to have both epic and lyric caesuras in one poem.
No poem of Mell does.

Textual Notes

Line 1. **merchy** represents the Picard pronunciation of *merci*
'mercy'. Mell **pueut** is unsupported by any other MS; all the others
call for a subjunctive. The verb **finer** 'die' is formed from the noun *fin*
'end' plus endings of the first conjugation (the -*er* verbs); it is not from
Latin fīnīre.

Line 2. **peust** is here pronounced [pü:t], like its modern counterpart
pût, or [pö:t].

Line 3. **m'amour** 'my love'. In the fifteenth century, the use of *m'*, *t'*, *s'*, as elided forms of *ma, ta, sa* before initial vowel was dying out, being replaced by *mon, ton, son* before feminine nouns and adjectives beinning with a vowel. By the time of our chansonnier, the elided forms were probably already felt as old-fashioned. Cf. No. 18, l. 11 *ton actavance*.

Line 5. **vo** is the Picard singular form corresponding to Francian *vostre*. The variant readings with *vostre* are hypermetric (Lab), or have resorted to rearrangement (Roh) with *grace* at the caesura, resulting in an epic caesura, or to a rough synonymy (Cord *amour*) that allows elision of the second syllable of *vostre*. It is reasonable to suppose that the Mell reading, **vo grace** (concurred in by the majority of MSS) represents the original; Lab's hypermetricity is then the result of an ill-considered substitution of the Francian form, and Roh and Cord are attempts to emend the hypermetric verse.

Besides **vo** and **merchy**, this poem has apparently one more Picard trait: the rhyme at ll. 3–4 **souffissante** : **puissante**. If the spelling is an accurate reflection of the pronunciation, this is a rhyme in [-$sant\partial$], that is a "rich rhyme," one in which at least one element preceding the tonic vowel participates in the phonetic correspondences between the rhyming words. If the words were pronounced as in Francian, [-$zant\partial$: -$sant\partial$], the rhyme would merely be "sufficient"; that is, with the tonic vowel and all elements following it in phonetic correspondence: [-$ant\partial$]—for in Francian [z] ≠ [s], while Picard makes no distinction between voiced and unvoiced sibilants ([z, s; ž, š]). Since there is no necessity for a rhyme to be rich, this rhyme does not constitute proof of pronunciation *à la picarde*, but it does, along with the spelling, lend weight to the general impression of a Picard tonality in this poem.

Line 9. **mon fait** 'my lot, state, condition'.

Line 11. Mell *seuffre* is unsupported by any concordant source. **S'ensuit** makes good sense and is supported by the majority of MSS.

8. Ung plus que tous, ff. 9ᵛ–10ʳ, Busnoys

Concordant Sources

Flo 229, ff. 51ᵛ–52ʳ
*Lil 402[1]

1. Marcel Françon, *Poèmes de Transition (XVᵉ–XVIᵉ Siècles), Rondeaux du Ms. 402 de Lille,* p. 631, pièce 518.

Pix, ff. 71ᵛ–72ʳ
Sev 5.I.43, ff. 17ᵛ–18ʳ
*Jar, f. lxviiiʳ

COLLATION

The three concordant sources actually contain not the composition
published here but a related one with substantial interpolations. In all
four MSS the first 7 mm. are essentially the same after which begins
a phrase not included in the present collection but terminating with
the cadential material of mm. 8–9, significantly altered only in the C.
The second section of the piece opens again in an identical manner
in all the readings, but at mm. 13 ff. there is a second insertion in the
other sources that concludes with the cadential formula of Mell, mm.
14–15, although with a number of divergences in the CT and C that
continue until the conclusion of the piece. In addition, the mensuration
in the three other musical collections is diminished imperfect tempus
(¢).

COMMENTS

The present chanson, in the form in which it is transmitted by Mell,
must be regarded for the time being as unique to the MS. Like the
rondeau quatrain upon which it is based (see below), the musical
setting can be viewed as the original work from which the version of
the remaining sources was elaborated. It can be assumed that the
expansion of the refrain structure to five lines made necessary the
musical interpolation of the initial section and prompted the reworking
of the second section as well. It is possible to see the present work as
a reduction of the more extensive version, but to do so would be to
ignore the general musical trends of the age. The diminished mensuration of the concordant sources would also suggest a later manipulation.

> Ung plus que tous est en mon souvenir
> Auquel pour rien jamais je ne [f]auldray;
> Mais telx termes et milleurs luy tendray
> Que damme puet *a son servant tenir.*   4
>
> Et si le veulle a mon gré maintenir
> Et sa faveur, pour *ma* devise prendray: 6
> > Ung plus que *tous est en mon souvenir*
> > *Auquel pour rien jamais je ne fauldray.*

Sur cest espoir l'ay voulu retenir
En actendant que trop mieulx j'en vauldray,
Et tel vouloir, se Dieu plaist, lui donray
Qu'il me fera ce mot entretenir: 10
    Ung plus que tous est en mon souvenir
    Auquel pour rien jamais je ne fauldray;
    Mais telx termes et milleurs luy tendray
    Que damme puet a son servant tenir.

One more than all others is in my thoughts
To whom I'll never be untrue.
But I will offer him such terms—and even better—
As a lady may offer to her knight.

And if I want to hold him to my liking
And keep his favor, as my motto I will choose:
    One more than all others is in my thoughts
    To whom I'll never be untrue.
On this hope I have wished to hold him,
Until I am much worthier,
And with such a will, please God, I will inspire him
That he will give me a reason to keep my word:
    One more than all others is in my thoughts
    To whom I'll never be untrue.
    But I will offer him such terms—and even better—
    As a lady may offer to her knight.

VARIANTS

All concordant sources are texted. Sev has only the incipit: Un plus
que tous. Pix and Flo have corrupt texts, by scribes ignorant of French,
which contribute practically nothing to the understanding or establishment of the text. The two principal sources, then, are Lil and Jar.

Both Lil and Jar (as well as Pix and Flo) present a rondeau cinquain,
which we suppose was based on an original rondeau quatrain, in
view of the historical trend at this period toward complication rather
than simplification. The quatrain in *abba* was expanded to a cinquain
in *aabba* by composing a new second hemistich (of six syllables in

rhyme *a*) for 1.2, and inserting a new line consisting of a new first hemistich (of four syllables) and the old second hemistich of the original line 2. For the short strophe, a new line was added between ll. 5 and 6, in rhyme *a*.

In the following listing of variants, the numerals designate the lines as they are numbered in Mell; 2a, 5a represent ll. 2, 5 in Mell; 2b, 5b represent the inserted lines; a raised 1 or 2 designates first or second hemistich.

1 L'ung—*Jar*. 2a² qui me peust (puist—*Jar*) advenir—*Lil Jar*. 2b¹ De loyaulte—*Lil Jar*, De beaulte—*Pix* (*Flo*). 2b² ne luy fauldray —*Lil*, ie ne fauldray—*Jar* (*Pix Flo*) (sauldray—*Mell*). 4 doit—*Lil Jar* (*Pix Flo*); (Mell omits second hemistich). 5a¹ Car sil se veult—*Lil Jar*. 5b A (En—*Jar*) si hault bruit le verrés parvenir—*Lil Jar*. 6 Quen sa—*Lil Jar*; mon mot je prendray—*Lil*, ma deuise auray—*Jar*.

For the long strophe, lacking in Mell, we present above the Lil text, below the Jar variants. We have shortened the cinquain by removing 8a² and 8b¹, without, as it happens, damage to sense or form. Here are the insertions of both Lil and Jar: 8 Presupposant—*Jar*. 8a² quen (que—*Jar*) brief doye obtenir—*Lil Jar*. 8b¹ Si grant renom—*Lil*, Ung tel renom—*Jar*. 8b² je vouldray—*Jar*. 9 Si hault; luy vauldray—*Jar*.

VERSIFICATION

Rondeau quatrain, *a b b a*, in decasyllables, with one lyric caesura, 1. 3.

TEXTUAL NOTES

Line 1. **mon souvenir** 'my thoughts'.

Line 2. Mell *sauldray* would be the future of *saillir* 'to go out', and is a less satisfactory reading than **fauldray** (*faudré*) of the other MSS: 'will be unfaithful (to), will fail' = modern *manquerai* (*à*).

Line 3. **termes** 'terms, conditions'; **tendray** 'will offer', future of *tenir*.

Line 5. **si** at this period and since the thirteenth century, like *se*, may mean either 'if' or 'and; so'. Here it apparently means 'if'. **veulle** could represent the subjunctive (corresponding to modern *veuille*) or, since the final *-e* is elided before the following vowel, it may be the first person singular present indicative *veuil*, still current in the fifteenth century, pronounced [völ']. Either mood is permissible in this context. The variants, which use the third person singular, are in the present indicative; they mean: 'If he wants to keep himself to my liking'.

Line 7. **cest espoir** [setepwer] 'this hope'; that is, the hope expressed in the motto.

Line 8. **trop** a simple intensive, like modern *très* 'very'; *mieulx*, the comparative, intensifies the meaning of the absolute degree: 'very well'. **trop mieulx**, then, is a double intensification of *bien*.

9. Ce qu'on fait a quatimini, ff. 10ᵛ–11ʳ, G. Joye

CONCORDANT SOURCES

Flo 229, ff. 282ᵛ–283ʳ
Pix, ff. 34ᵛ–35ʳ
Sev 5.I.43, ff. 62ᵛ–63ʳ
*Jar, f. xcviᵛ

COLLATION

There is little significant variation among the readings offered by the four musical sources for this work. Except for a written flat for E in the CT, m. 9(3), the T and CT of Sev 5.I.43 are almost identical with those of Mell. However, in the C at m. 11(1) the Seville MS has a-Sb, rest-Sb, both superfluous, preventing the three parts from fitting together as they are given by that source. In Pix the extra Sb (but not the rest) at m. 11(1) has been added in all three voices, thus obviating the difficulty of coordination in the version of Sev 5.I.43. Also the T at m. 19(6) has c—probably an error—instead of the b-flat of the other sources. The reading of Flo 229 differs from that of Mell for the most part in small melodic and rhythmic details, but at m. 19(5) of the T it gives G-M, F-M, a slight improvement in the counterpoint with respect to the other sources.

COMMENTS

The composition found in Wolf 287, ff. 48ᵛ–49ʳ, with an identical incipit is actually a completely different musical setting of a poem that also deviates markedly from the one published here.

Joye's rondeau is transmitted with surprising uniformity in the four musical MSS. Most closely related to the reading of Mell are those of Sev 5.I.43 and Pix. Because it is possible that the repeated SSb at the beginning of m. 11 in all voices of the latter represent a revision that resulted from the obvious scribal error in the C of the Seville collection, there is good reason to believe that the two MSS belong to the same scribal tradition. In substance Flo 229 is also very close to Mell for this work, and the differences between the readings in ornamental detail may be due in part to the later date of the Florence MS.

The written E-flat in the CT of Sev 5.I.43, m. 9(3), suggests the possibility of accidental flats for all parts in mm. 9–10, a fully defensible solution that would have the advantage of avoiding the cross-relation between b-flat and e in T and CT in that short passage, but would also require lowering the a, m. 9(2), thus producing a diminished fifth with the CT.

> Ce qu'on fait a quatimini
> Touchant multiplicamini,
> Mais qu'il soit bien tenu secre,
> Sera tenu pour excusé
> In conspectu Altissimi. 5
>
> Et pourtant operamini,
> Mes fillez, et letatimini,
> Car jamais il n'est revelé 8
> > Ce qu'on fait *a quatimini*
> > *Touchant multiplicamini—*
> > *Mais qu'il soit bien tenu secré*!
>
> Et se vous engrossemini,
> Soit in nomine Domini:
> Vous avés a proufit ouvré,
> Qui vous sera tout pardonné—
> Mais que vous confitemini 13
> > Ce qu'on fait *a quatimini*
> > *Touchant multiplicamini;*
> > *Mais qu'il soit bien tenu secré,*
> > *Sera tenu pour excusé*
> > *In conspectu Altissimi.*

What you do on the sly
About "be fruitful and multiply"—
As long as it's kept secret—
Will be deemed forgiven
In the sight of the Most High.

And so, go to it,
Girls, and be of good cheer,
For it is never revealed
      What you do on the sly
      About "be fruitful and multiply"—
      As long as it's kept secret.

And if you should find yourself with child,
Let it be in the name of the Lord;
You will have engaged in good works,
And all will be pardoned you—
Provided you confess
      What you do on the sly
      About "be fruitful and multiply."
      As long as it's kept secret,
      It will be deemed forgiven
      In the sight of the Most High.

Variants

3 tenu bien—*Pix Flo*; soit fait secretement—*Wolf*, bien fait en privé
—*Jar*. 4 por excuser—*Sev*; Est excusé legerement—*Wolf*. 5 domini—
—*Pix Flo* (−1 syll.). (Pix, Flo, and Sev end here.) 6–8 (Lacking in
Jar). 8 Ce n'est que tout esbatement—*Wolf*. 9 ingrossamini—*Wolf
Jar*. 11 Vous aurés—*Jar*; Endurez le tout doulcement—*Wolf*. 12 Et
vous—*Jar*; Ja n'en perdrez vo saulvement—*Wolf*.

Versification

Mell and Wolf present the entire text of an octosyllabic rondeau
cinquain, *a a b b a*. The rhyme varies in richness from -*imini* to -*(a/e)mini*
and even to -*ini* : -*imi*, in which [n] and [m] belong to the same
"rhymeme," that is, they are both nasal consonants. Wolf is alone
in having, as rhyme *b*, -*ment*; all the others have -*et* (spelled *e* in Mell).
Jar omits the short strophe.

Textual Notes

In a farce of the late fifteenth or early sixteenth century, the general theme of this poem is reasserted and the same biblical text is quoted.[1] The "moral lesson" of the piece is that it is better to have a loving, affectionate wife who may well, with requisite discretion, "lend" herself to others than her husband, than to have a wife who, though virtuous, is also ugly, scolding, intolerant, never ceasing to belabor her husband with invective, curses, and threats of violence. The former wife advises the latter in these terms:

> Le péché est tout pardonné
> Quand on ne le faict qu'en cachettes;
> Ung tas de menues tendrettes
> Ce n'est que chose naturelle.
> Par mon serment, m'amye belle,
> L'eaue benoiste efface tout.

> A sin is entirely forgiven
> Only when it's done in secret;
> A heap of tender little attentions
> Is only natural.
> On my oath, fair friend,
> Holy water erases everything.

(11. 232–37). And, a little further on:

> J'ouys dire a nostre curé
> Que Dieu dit en cathimini:
> "*Eva, multiplicamini,*
> *Crescite, replete terram.*"

> I heard our priest say
> That God said on the sly:
> "*Eve, multiply,*
> *Increase, fill the earth.*"

1. "Farce moralisée a quatre personnaiges, C'est assavoir: Deux hommes et leurs deux femmes dont l'une a malle teste et l'autre est tendre au cul," Farce V of Emile Picot and Christophe Nyrop, *Nouveau recueil de farces françaises des XVe et XVIe siècles, publié d'après un volume unique appartenant à la Bibliothèque Royale de Copenhague* (Paris: Damascène Morgand et Charles Fatout, 1880). The quoted passage is on pp. 131–32. Information on dates, origins, and editions is on pp. lvii–lx.

(11. 239–42).

Line 1. **a quatimini** = modern French *en catimini* 'in secret'. This expression goes back to Greek *kataménios* 'monthly', whence *tà kataménia* 'the monthlies' i.e., 'menstrual period', borrowed by French in this meaning in familiar style, at least as early as the late fourteenth century, at which time the new meaning, '"in secret, privately', is already attested.[2] The semantic development probably followed this path: 'menstruating' > 'in seclusion' > 'secretly'.

Line 2. 'concerning [the divine command] *multiplicamini*'—multiply (Gen. 1:28).

Line 3. **Mais que** 'provided that, as long as'; on the second appearance of this line (3′) it could be translated, 'But, let it . . . '.

Line 7. **fillez** [fil'ɔz] = modern French *filles* 'girls'. **letatimini** 'enjoy yourselves'—apparently a frequentative derivation of *laetari* 'be joyful', in the sense of 'have lots of fun'.

Line 9. **engrossemini:** The Wolf and Jar variant is more correct as to Latinity. DuCange lists *ingrossārī* with the meaning 'crassum fieri, inflare, tumescere'; in the examples which he gives, it refers to the swelling of the sea or to a man's becoming fat. In the same article, the Old French *engrosser* is cited in the meaning 'become pregnant'. My search has failed to discover this meaning of the Latin word in any Latin text. The Mell spelling as well as the use of this word in what appears, therefore, to be a French meaning points to a macaronic creation, that is, a French word disguised as Latin. It is possible that the variant *ingrossamini* is a learned correction of an original form represented by Mell.

Line 12. **Qui** = modF *ce qui* 'and it'.

Line 13. 'As long as you confess.' Note that, although the construction with *mais que* most often takes the subjunctive in French, the poet has not sought the corresponding mood in Latin, which would have given *confiteamini*—possibly for metrical reasons, and because *mais que* is sometimes constructed with the indicative. The corresponding Latin construction is *Dum (modo, dummodo)* + subjunctive.

Lines 1″–2″ form the direct object of the verb of l. 13.

Line 4″. **sera** 'it will be'; it is not necessary to repeat *il*, which is the subject of the preceding clause (in 1. 3″). This rondeau represents

2. Walter von Wartburg, *Französisches Etymologisches Wörterbuch*, s.v. *katamenia* (Gr.) menstruation.

one of the best examples in Mell of a refrain whose syntactic structure changes from one repetition to the next. In the first statement of the refrain, the subject of l. 3 **sera** was the noun expression of l. 1.

10. A qui vens tu tes coquilles, ff. 11ᵛ–12ʳ, Busnoys

Concordant Source

Dij 517, ff. cliiiᵛ–clivʳ

Collation

In the C at m. 4 (4), Dij 517 has c′-Sm, a′-M in place of the a′-Sm of Mell; at m. 9 (3, 4) it gives only one e′-M. At m. 22 (5) of the T, Dij 517 has g-M instead of the a-M of Mell, probably erroneously since the g-M clashes sharply with both C and CT.

Comments

The two readings extant for this work obviously belong to the same tradition of transmission; the only variants are the apparent scribal errors in Dij 517 noted above. Those of mm. 4 and 9 may be connected since the a′-M of m. 4 is clearly superfluous (it dislocates the C in the cadence of mm. 4–5 and on into the beginning of the following phrase), and the three voices mesh properly again only with the omission of the e′-M in m. 9.

The written flat in the C of Mell at m. 10 (8) is apparently confirmed by a flat faintly visible at the beginning of the line in Dij 517, but it creates problems. The flatted b′ should perhaps be allowed to sound a diminished fifth against the E of the CT, for if the fifth is made perfect (as Tinctoris suggests it should be in such a context) by flatting the E, there will be cross-relations with the e heard in the T just before and immediately after. These pitches cannot easily be lowered because they function as the leading tone in the cadence.

The final melisma of the piece, from the second half of m. 19 to the last cadential formula, is definitely cast in a ternary rhythm that cuts across the binary units of the mensuration in a most characteristic manner. It is entirely possible that the writing at that point is illustrative in intention since the hobbling movement of the music presents a clear analogy with the limping walk of an old man.

A qui vens tu tes coquilles,
Viellart aux paupier*es* rouges?
Trousse ton sac et tes bouges
Et si porte ailleurs tes quilles.   4

Car pour le deduit des filles
Faut bien galans plus harouges.   6
    A qui vens tu tes coquilles,
    Viellart aux paupieres rouges?

Tu sces que, quant pour tes pilles
T'ont festoié fines gouges,
Qu'elles crient, quant tu bouges,
"Adieu, Clais!" ou "Adieu, Gilles!"   10
    A qui vens tu tes coquilles,
    Viellart aux paupieres rouges?
    Trousse ton sac et tes bouges
    Et si porte ailleurs tes quilles.

Who are you selling your shells to,
Old man with the red eyelids?
Truss up your bags and your bundles
And move your shanks away from here.

To make the girls happy,
It takes lustier young fellows.
    Who are you selling your shells to,
    Old man with the red eyelids?

You know that, for your loot,
You've been well-treated by fancy tarts
Who cry out as you move,
"Goodbye, Clais!" or "Goodbye, Gilles!"
    Who are you selling your shells to,
    Old man with the red eyelids?
    Truss up your bags and your bundles
    And move your shanks away from here.

Variants

The long strophe, lacking in Mell, is supplied from Dij.
2 paupiers—*Mell* (− 1 syll.). 6 galant—Dij.

Rondeau quatrain in heptasyllables, *a b b a*.

Line 2. **Viellart**, pronounced with palatalized *l* [l'].

Line 3. **Trousse** 'truss up'; **bouges** 'bags, pouches'.

Line 4. **Et si** 'and'; **quilles** 'bowling pins'; here: 'legs'.

Line 6. **harouges**: This could be the same word as the *harouce* of Godefroy, *Dictionnaire de l'ancienne langue française*, or *haroce* of Tobler and Lommatzsch, *Altfranzösisches Wörterbuch*, defined by them respectively as 'orgueilleux, chicaneur, qui veut avoir la préférence' and 'anmassend'. The meaning is a little strong for the present context, which would be more easily satisfied by 'enterprising, aggressive'. The problem of the difference between *harouce* and *harouge* is not too difficult. Most of these poems show a northern dialectal coloring. Francian *-ce* corresponds to Picard *-che*. Moreover, Picard does not distinguish between voiced and voiceless spirants, so that *-ge* and *-che* are often found in rhyme with each other.

Line 7–8. A reference to venal girls (**fines gouges**), who show you a good time for your 'loot'.

Lines 9–10. 'When you move, they cry out, Goodbye, Clais or Gilles, i.e., I've found a better boy friend.'

The whole poem is a parody on a comic-erotic rondeau quatrain by Charles d'Orléans:

> A qui vendez vous voz coquilles
> Entre vous, amans pelerins?
> Vous cuidez bien, par voz engins,
> A tous pertuis trouver chevilles.
>
> Sont ce coups d'esteufs ou de billes
> Que ferez, tesmoing voz voisins?
> A qui [vendez vous voz coquilles
> Entre vous, amans pelerins?]
>
> On congnoist tous voz tours d'estrilles
> Et bien clerement voz latins;
> Trotés, reprenés voz patins,
> Et troussés voz sacs et voz quilles;
> A qui [vendez vous voz coquilles?]

Who are you selling your shells to,
You lovers on pilgrimage?
You really think that with your tricks
You can find pegs to fit all holes!

Are they strokes of balls or of cues
That you will make while neighbors watch?
Who are you selling your shells to,
You lovers on pilgrimage?

We're on to all your sly deceptions
And see right through your patter;
Trot along now, put on your shoes,
Bundle up your bags and your skittles.
Who are you selling your shells to?

Several idioms are exploited for their erotic imagery. *Autant de trous,
autant de chevilles*, still current, describes someone who is fertile in
excuses or expedients for all occasions. *Trousser son sac et ses quilles* is
also still used in modern French in the sense of 'decamp; leave hastily'.
Used in isolation these idioms have no sexual reference, but the
accumulation of such images as ball, cue, bag, bowling pin, pegs,
holes, makes its point irresistibly. The peg–hole expression resembles
the idiom *Trouver chaussure à son pied*, literally 'find a shoe to one's foot'
meaning 'find what one is looking for' or 'find one's match'.

In this poem, Charles likens lovers to false or suspect pilgrims.
People who had returned from the pilgrimage to the shrine of St.
James of Compostella announced the fact by wearing shells on their
hats, and some who had not made the pilgrimage sported the shells
in the hope that this evidence of piety would turn aside suspicious
glances from their criminal activities.[1]

Pierre Champion says that this poem likens faithless lovers to false
pilgrims wearing the shells of St. James on their hats. But Pierre
Guiraud claims that Champion's explanation is based on an incorrect
etymology of *coquille, coquillard*, and related words.[2] They come, he says,
from *coq* 'cock', which, in Middle French as in modern English, has

1. *Charles d'Orléans: Poésies*, ed. Pierre Champion (Paris: Champion, 1923), vol. 2, *Rondeaux*,
no. 77, pp. 333–34, and note on p. 579.
2. Pierre Guiraud, *Le jargon de Villon ou le gai savoir de la coquille* (Paris, 1968).

both zoological and, in slang, anatomical meanings. *La coquille* refers to the underworld, the world of thieves, gamblers, and pederasts, and the *coquillards* are its denizens.

Guiraud denies the meaning 'shell' to *coquille* in these terms: "A vrai dire, cette conjecture est mal soutenue par les faits. On n'a aucun exemple de *Coquille* en picardo-wallon et dans les dialectes modernes le *F.E.W.* [the *Französisches Etymologisches Wörterbuch* of Wartburg] ne mentionne qu'un seul *Coquille* wallon; dans toute cette région le mot couramment employé est *écaille.*" [3]

There is no doubt that the word does occur as an erotic symbol, as the following verses from Dij 517, f. 184^v indicate:

> Lors se dresse ma coquille
> Preste d'avoir le butin.

But Guiraud, in denying the existence of the word *coquille* in Picardo-walloon, surprisingly fails to mention Francian, although he is discussing a poem by Charles d'Orléans. Is it not probable that Charles knew this word in the sense of 'shell'? If so, he could very well have been making a pun, in which he uses the word with all the meanings attributed to it by Guiraud in addition to the literal one of 'shell.' If not what, then, is the connection with pilgrims, in the second line of his poem?

Whereas in the poem by Charles d'Orléans, the suspect suitors are told to peddle their doubtful wares elsewhere, Mell's poem is addressed to a would-be lover who is too old to be credible in his role.

11. Puis que ma damme ne puis voir / Je m'en voy et mon cueur demeure, ff. 12^v–14^r, Regis

COMMENTS

This bitextual chanson is the only secular composition attributed to Regis and is also unique to the present collection.

Judging from the rhyme scheme of the poems carried by the C and

---

3. "To tell the truth, this conjecture is hardly supported by the facts. There is not a single example of *Coquille* in Picardo-waloon, and in the modern dialects the *FEW* just mentions one Waloon *Coquille*; in this whole region the word commonly used [for 'shell'] is *écaille*" (ibid., p. 282).

CT I, each is the refrain of a rondeau quatrain, suggesting the possibility that the composer combined, along with the verse, the melodies of two preexistent polyphonic settings. However, since even the poetry is known only in this MS, such an eventuality remains purely speculative. In any case it is not clear whether Regis intended all strophes of the two rondeaux to be sung. At the midpoint of the piece (the cadence of mm. 15–16) only two lines of *Puis que ma damme* have been sung as opposed to three of *Je m'en voy*; consequently, to sing the poems as rondeaux would require a major revision of the text placement. The coronas at the end of the CT I and T parts on f. 13 (the second half of m. 15) seem to indicate the division of the piece into two quasi-equal sections in the manner traditional for the rondeau. But if that is their purpose, they are misplaced; in such a context the formal articulation usually coincides with the resolution of the cadence. In the present instance it may be that the coronas were meant only to mark the congruence of those two parts at that particular point. Because they serve no real function in the modern score, they were simply omitted from it.

It was assumed that the mensural sign used for this work has the value of diminished imperfect tempus. The flat for the f′ in the C, m. 28 (2), shows only that the pitch lies outside the Guidonian hand.

I. Puis que ma damme ne puis voir
Ne d'elle ouïr quelque nouvelle,
Et se ne puis aultre amer qu'elle,
Annoy et dueil me fault avoir.   4

II. Je m'en voy et mon cueur demeure;
Je chante et fay larmes *de l'euil*;
Je m'esbas et si n'ay que dueil;
Je ris, et mon euil *pleure*.   4

I. Since I cannot see my lady
Or hear any news of her,
And if I can love none but her,
Gloom and grief must be my lot.

II. I go away, and my heart remains;
I sing, and tears flow from my eyes;

I frolic, and yet have naught but grief;
I laugh, and my eye weeps.

Versification

Two different poems sung simultaneously, the first by cantus, tenor, and contratenor II, the second by contratenor I. Both poems have the same form: octosyllabic quatrain, *a b b a* (but the rhymes are not the same in the two poems).

Textual Notes

I. Line 1. **voir** 'see': note the modern spelling of this word, which has been monosyllabic since the mid-fourteenth century. It was usually spelled conservatively, in reminiscence of its bisyllabicity, as *veoir*, even in the fifteenth century.

Line 3. **se** 'if'; **amer** 'love'.

II. Line 1. **Je m'en voy** means *Je m'en vais* and is pronounced as it is in modern French. **cueur** is represented by the picture of a heart in the MS.

Lines 2 and 4. The words in italics represent our conjectural readings where omissions appear in the MS.

The poem represents a popular conceit in which each verse contains an antithesis. When this device is undertaken, it is usually carried through the whole poem. Therefore, it is doubtful that poems I and II have any essential relationship, apart from their use in this song.

12. Je ne puis vivre ainsy, ff. 14ᵛ–16ʳ [Busnois]

Concordant Sources

Dij 517, ff. xxxiiii ᵛ–xxxvi ʳ, Busnoys
*Jar, f. 84 ʳ

Collation

Instead of the five BBr of rest preceding the entry of the T in Mell, Dij 517 gives eight BBr of rest, surely an error. In the CT at m. 12 (1)–13 (1) the Dijon MS has C-Br (imperfected), F-Sb, E-M, C-M instead of the repeated C of Mell. The second section begins in the same

manner in both MSS, but after 2 mm. the reading of Dij 517 departs
fundamentally from that given by Mell. From that point to the end
correspondences between the two versions are limited to the melodic
figures seen in the C of Mell at mm. 33 (1 ff.) and 35 (2 ff.).[1]

COMMENTS

One of the two versions of this piece obviously represents a thoroughgoing reworking of the other in the second section, but one can only
speculate as to the arrangement that was original with Busnois, the
reasons for the changes made, and the person responsible for them.

The placement of the text was especially troublesome for this work.
For example, if the distribution of syllables used for the first short
strophe (mm. 28 ff.) is retained for the second, the adjective *chauldes*
is broken in the C by the rest of m. 30. This unorthodoxy may be
justifiable if one assumes the pictorial intent of a sigh. Otherwise, the
line can be divided after *plourant* with syllables placed on beats 1, 2,
and 4 of m. 31. Similarly, the cadential formula of mm. 24–25 seems
to justify the breaking of *Amours* by the rest in the T, but the second
syllable of the word could also be placed with the e or d of m. 24 and
Jus- immediately after the rest of m. 25. Elsewhere, extended melismatic passages again pose problems of interpretation.

There are also some vexing questions in the use of accidentals. The
first comes with the clearly outlined melodic tritone in T and C in
mm. 20–21. If the troublesome interval is avoided by the application
of a flat to b′, cross-relations and a diminished fifth are generated
with the CT, and these can only be corrected with flats for b and E
in that part as well. Such a solution may be acceptable, but it seemed
preferable to retain the sharp of the preceding cadential formula,
particularly since the melodic figure in question evolves as in a
cadence. In addition, the written flats for E and B in the CT at m. 36
are apparently to be interpreted as a signal calling for b-flat and e-flat
in all three voices from the second quarter-note of m. 35 to the fourth
quarter-note of m. 37 even though the result is a sharp, if short, shift
of the modal orientation at that point.

The change in mensuration from perfect tempus (O) in the initial

---

1. An edition of this composition from Dij 517 has been published by Droz and Thibault,
Trois chansonniers français du XVe siècle, No. 33, pp. 64–66.

section to diminished imperfect tempus (₵) in the second seems to
warrant a literal interpretation of the proportion indicated.

> **J**e ne puis vivre ainsy tousjou*r*s
> **A**u mains que j'aye en mes dolours
> **Q**uelque confort
> **U**ne seulle heure, ou mains ou fort;
> **E**t tous les jours
> **L**é*aument* serviray Amours
> **J**usqu'a la mort.   7
>
> **N**oble femme de nom et d'armes,
> **E**script vous ay ce dittier-cy,   9
>
> **D**es [jeulx] plourant a chauldes larmes
> **A**ffin qu'ayés de moy merchy.   11
>
> **Q**uant a moy, je *me* meurs [bon cours],
> **V**ellant les nuytz, faisant cent tours,
> **E**n criant fort:
> "**V**engance!" a Dieu, car a grant tort
> **J**e noye en plours
> **L**orsqu'au besoing me fault secours—
> **E**t Pitié dort.   18

> Je ne puis *vivre ainsy tousjours*
> *Au mains que j'aye en mes dolours*
> *Quelque confort*
> *Une seulle heure, ou mains ou fort;*
> *Et tous les jours*
> *Léaument servirary Amours*
> *Jusqu'a la mort.*

> I cannot live like this forever
> Unless I have in my distress
> Some comfort,
> Just an hour, or less—or more,
> And every day

Faithfully I'll serve the god of Love
Unto death.

Woman, noble in name and in arms,
I have written you this ditty

Weeping from my eyes hot tears
That you may have mercy on me.

As to me, I waste away apace,
Awake at night, walking in a hundred circles,
Crying aloud
"Vengeance!" to God, for, most unjustly,
I'm drowning in tears.
Just when I need it, I get no help,
And Pity—sleeps.

I cannot live like this forever
Unless I have in my distress
Some comfort,
Just an hour, or less—or more,
And every day
Faithfully I'll serve the god of Love
Unto death.

VARIANTS

Emendations of our text are from Dij. Jar omits ll. 8–11; see
Versification.

1 tousjous—*Mell.* 2 Amours que j'aye pour mes—*Jar.* 4 ai mains—
Jar; au fort—*Dij Jar.* 6 Leaument—*Dij*, Mell omits. 9 Estripuez a
ce dicté cy—*Dij* (see Textual Notes). 10 Des xx—*Mell* (see Textual
Notes). 12 je meurs le cours—*Jar* (thus, like Mell, hypometric; see
Textual Notes), je me meurs bon cours—*Dij.* 14 Et criant—*Jar.* 16
n'aye—*Dij.*

VERSIFICATION

A bergerette layée with seven-line strophes and a four-line *ouvert*
and *clos*, the long strophes of eight- and four-syllable lines as follows
(the raised letters representing the tetrasyllables): $aa^bb^aa^b$; the ouvert

and clos of octosyllables rhyming *cdcd*. *Dittier-cy* and *merchy* (ll. 9, 11) make a good rhyme, with spellings representing different dialects; if the orthography were dialectally consistent we would have both words with *c* (Francian) or with *ch* (Picard). The form Mell gives us, *dittier*, gives us a richer rhyme with *merchy* than would *dictié*.

The Jar version transforms this bergerette into a rondeau by the following alterations: (1) It omits the ouvert and clos (ll. 8–11). (2) It takes the first five lines to form the refrain of a rondeau cinquain. (3) Lines 6, 7, and 12 form the short stanza, followed by the short refrain. (4) Lines 13–18 form an overlong strophe, followed by the long refrain.

The resulting rondeau deviates from the classical form in several respects: (a) As indicated in (4) above, its last strophe is too long by one line. (b) It mixes verse lengths in an irregular pattern such that the long strophe does not structurally resemble the long refrain. (c) The rhyme schemes are irregular in that the short strophe does not follow the pattern of the short refrain (*aba* and *aab* respectively), and no five-line sequence of the long strophe has the same rhyme scheme as the long refrain (*abbaab* and *aabba* respectively).

Even if these anomalies were not sufficient to demonstrate the primacy of the bergerette version of Dij and Mell over Jar's rondeau, the acrostic formed by the initials of the verses (JAQUELINE DAQUEVILLE) would in itself suffice, since it makes the ouvert and clos indispensable. Busnoys has several other songs in this book in which he pays cryptographic homage to Jaqueline (see Mell Nos. 14 and 42).

TEXTUAL NOTES

Line 2. **Au mains que** 'unless'.

Line 4. **ou mains ou fort** 'or less, or more'.

Line 6. **Léaument:** provided from Dij for metrical reasons and to provide a letter for the acrostic.

Line 8. **de nom et d'armes** '[noble] by name (or family) and by arms.' (This may be a pun on armorial bearings and the "weapons" of ladies—feminine charms.

Line 9. The Dij reading could be interpreted as *Estrivez* (the *p* being a pseudoetymological letter imitated from the *p* of *escripvre*). *Estriver a* means 'work at, strive at'. The Mell version seems quite clear: 'I have written you this ditty, weeping hot tears from my eyes, that you may take pity on me'. But the Dij reading also has a plausible interpretation: 'Pay close attention to this ditty, that, crying . . . tears, you may take pity on me'.

Line 10. Mell **Des xx** = *Des ieus*, the name of the letter X being *ieus* in Old French.[2]

Line 12. Apparently Dij has the best reading: that of Jar does not make very good sense, and Mell has *plours* in rhyme with itself (l. 16). **bon cours** 'rapidly'.

Line 13. **Vellant** [vel'ã] 'being awake'.

Line 15. **vengance** with soft g: [vãžãs] as in modern French.

13. Non pas que je veuille penser, ff. 16ᵛ–17ʳ [Joye]

CONCORDANT SOURCES

*Roh, f. 163ᵛ
Flo 229, ff. 255ᵛ–256ʳ
RomC 2856, ff. 111ᵛ–112ʳ, Joye
Lab, ff. 17ᵛ–17ᵃ (cantus only)
*Jar, f. lxviᵛ

COLLATION

All three concordant sources have b'-L in the C at m. 19 without either the written accidental of Mell or the following rest. The readings of Flo 229 and RomC 2856 reflect the later date at which they were copied by a general tendency to simplify the melodic writing; repeated pitches are combined into longer values and the melodic ornament of the lower third is eliminated at cadences. (An exception is m. 21 of the C, where RomC 2856 has such an ornament whereas there is none in Mell.)

There are very few variants of substance in either source. Flo 229 has a sign of congruence above the b-L of the T in m. 13, but the symbol seems to serve no purpose and may be a scribal slip. At m. 17 (2) of the CT the same MS gives a-M instead of the c-Sb of Mell and is obviously in error since the result would be not only a rhythmic insufficiency but also parallel octaves with the T. At m. 27 (3) of the CT, instead of the E-M of Mell and Flo 229, RomC 2856 has D-M,

2. See Huon le Roi de Cambrai, *Li abecés par Ekivoche*, ed. Artur Långfors (Paris: Champion, 1913), pp. v, vi, viii.

thus avoiding the dissonance of the other sources, but it gives the corona for the T in m. 19 with g instead of d, clearly not as good.

Although Lab preserves only the C of the chanson, it gives several substantial variants: at m. 3 (4–6), b′-M, b′-M, a′-M (in the manner of a cadential ornament); at m. 7 (2), d instead of c, producing a rather sharp dissonance with the T; at m. 28 (2), a instead of b, making parallel unisons with the T; and at m. 28 (8, 9), e-Sm and f-Sm have been omitted, certainly erroneously.

COMMENTS

Despite the fact that both Flo 229 and RomC 2856 are considerably later than Mell, their readings seem to reflect essentially the same tradition of transmission, but that of the Florence MS appears to be the closer to the version of Mell. With only the C present it is difficult to judge the relationship of the version in Lab to the remaining sources, but it would seem to be rather independent.

The key signature of two flats, given by all the musical sources, is unusual for the period. Since the final is on C and internal cadences are exclusively on C and G, one can regard the work as a straightforward example of the Dorian mode twice transposed. It is perhaps not too surprising, then, that Joye was able to handle the counterpoint so as to avoid unusual problems in the application of accidentals.

The units of declamation used in syllabic passages and the lighthearted mockery of the poetry would suggest that the diminished mensuration, although used exclusively throughout the chanson, is to be taken as literally proportional to the integral one.

Non pas que je veuille penser
Qu'a bien et léaulment amer
Celle qui toutes aultres passe
Et ung petit estre en sa grace
Pour avoir bruit et m'avancher.   5

De la servir et honorer
Du tout me vueil habandonner—
Maiz qu'autre chose g'y pourchasse,   8
   Non pas que je veuille penser
   Qu'a bien et léaulment amer
   Celle qui toutes aultres passe.

Sa plaisant doulceur, qui n'a per,
Plaist tant a mon cueur sans cesser
Qu'il veult que sien vive et trespasse;
Si le feray, quoy que je face,
Maiz que je la puisse oublïer—   13
    Non pas que je veuille penser
    Qu'a bien et léaulment amer
    Celle qui toutes aultres passe
    Et ung petit estre en sa grace
    Pour avoir bruit et m'avancher.

Not that I'd want to think
Of anything but well and faithfully loving
Her who surpasses all others
And be just a bit in her favor,
To have a name and improve my lot.

To her service and honor
I would dedicate myself completely,
As long as I gain something by it—
    Not that I'd want to think
    Of anything but well and faithfully loving
    Her who surpasses all others.

Her gentle sweetness, which has no peer,
Pleases my heart unceasingly, and so much
That it wants to live and die as hers;
And I will do so, whatever else I may accomplish,
Unless I manage to forget her—
    Not that I'd want to think
    Of anything but well and faithfully loving
    Her who surpasses all others
    And be just a bit in her favor,
    To have a name and improve my lot.

Variants

4 ung bien peu—*Lab.* 5 m'avancer—*Flo Roh Jar* (here Mell is alone in the picardism of -*cher*). (Mell and Flo end here; we adopt Roh for

ll. 6–13.) 6 Lab omits la (− 1 syll.); A la—*Jar*. 8 J'en prochasse—*Lab*;
Autre chose je n'y pourchasse—*Jar*. 9 Sa grande—*Jar*, Se plaisir
—*Lab*. 10 Lab omits cueur (− 1 syll.); sens—*Lab*. 11 Qui veult que
s'amye trespasse—*Lab*. 12 fera—*Lab*; (Jar omits whole line). 13 Et
que ne la puisse oublier—*Lab*, Sans point la vouloir oublier—*Jar*.

Some of these variants alter fundamentally the meaning of the poem;
they seem, in fact, to point to three different redactions: R, represented
in our MSS by Roh; L, by Lab; and J, Jar. The filiation among these
three redactions is not necessarily the same as that among the three
MSS, Roh, Lab, and Jar; thus, the relative ages of the three MSS has
no bearing on the problem of the genetic relationship among the three
redactions. It seems most likely that R is the common ancestor of L and
J. R is a slyly satirical poem, a sort of monologue in which an oppor-
tunistic lover expresses in conventional terms his fidelity toward a
rich, powerful lady; but the last line of each strophe is ambiguous, in
that it can, with a little forcing, express an irreproachable courtly
sentiment, but can also, and more easily, be interpreted as a cynical
insight into the lover's real attitudes.

L and J seem to be two independent revisions of R. L moves in the
direction of more explicit revelation of the lover's venal motives, in the
form of a confidential monologue that is perfectly frank about the
lover's hypocrisy. It is a little like the monologue in the *Roman de la
Rose* in which an allegorical figure, Faux Semblant (False Seeming),
casts aside his insincerity to allow a clear view into the dynamics of
double dealing. J takes the opposite tack; it converts the double
meanings, every expression of doubtful conventionality, into a thoroughly respectable courtly sentiment. Since the original poem used
conventional expressions in the body of each stanza to lead with great
effect to the ironical ambiguity with which each stanza ends, all J
had to do to make of R a perfectly acceptable courtly lyric was to
render the last lines inoffensive.

It will be evident on studying the variants that R is indeed the
common ancestor of L and J, and that the chronological order cannot
be other. We know that R precedes J, since J somehow has not been
able to rid the poem of the pious disclaimer of the first line: *Non pas
que je veuille*. ... It is impossible to understand this line without seeing
its ironical intention. This is the basic flaw of J, but, as I shall point
out in the Textual Notes, not the only flaw; the weakness of the last line
of J, in my opinion, rules out J as first redaction.

If we accept J as a second redaction of a poem whose first redaction is either L or R, we are impelled to conclude that R, not L, is the source of J, for J could not have altered lines of L in such a way that they would be identical with the corresponding lines of R: see the variants, especially for ll. 9–11.

VERSIFICATION

Rondeau cinquain in octosyllables, *aabba*.

TEXTUAL NOTES

Line 3. **passe** 'surpass'.

Line 5. 'to enhance my reputation and advance myself'. This line can be interpreted in a noncynical sense as referring to the ennobling effect of true love; the advancement would be spiritual or moral. Its cynical meaning becomes increasingly apparent as the poem goes on.

Line 7. **Du tout** 'completely'. This idiom remains in modern French only in the negative, as in *pas du tout*.

Line 8. It is at this point that the difference between the parodic (R, L) and the serious (J) versions begins to make itself felt. This line, like the last line of each stanza of R, is ambiguous. It may be read either as (1) 'But may I enjoy another benefit (that of spiritual improvement) from my service to you'—the serious interpretation, or (2) 'As long as I get something out of it', the something being either social or material advantage (or possibly the achievement of an erotic goal; but, since the tone of the poem in general is not *grivois*, this interpretation is doubtful)—the parodic or comic possibility. The ambiguity of the verse depends on the ambiguity of some of its key words. *Maiz* can mean 'but', but *maiz que* can also mean 'provided that, as long as'. *Autre chose* is vague enough to mean anything.

The double meaning is the principal comic device of R. L, however, depends for its effect on the shock value of its cynical and unconventional sentiments, and so can dispense with ambiguity. J shuns ambiguity by rewriting the line so as to exclude a possible comic meaning: 'I have no other desire [than to serve you faithfully]'. It almost seems as if J does protest too much, as if explicitly denying the possible implication of R's l. 8.

Line 9. Roh and Jar agree in giving an adjective modifier to *doulceur*; Roh and Lab agree on the base *plais*-. The Lab verse may be translated, 'If pleasure—sweetness without peer!—...'.

Line 10. It is possible that the model Lab's scribe was following already lacked *cueur*; the scribe, then, not noticing that the verse was short by one syllable, and trying to make sense out of the line, rewrote *sans* as *sens*, so that ll. 9–10 came to mean, 'If to pleasure (that sweetness without peer!) it is so pleasing to cease [with respect] to the senses . . . ,' or, paraphrased, 'If pleasure should ever begin to cloy. . . . ' This translation reflects the function of *plaisir* as dative object to the impersonal verb, *plaist*. RJ: 'Is so unceasingly pleasant to my heart.'

Line 11. The difference between L and RJ is fundamental. L 'If one wants his mistress to die', R 'That it [my heart] wants to belong ever to her, in life and in death'.

Line 12. If the Lab verse is read in the context of the preceding Lab verses, it means 'So she *will* [die], whatever I may do'; but if one were to regard the differences in Lab as being due to errors rather than to a parodic intention, and take this line in the context of the poem as we receive it from Roh and Jar, then it could be read as follows: 'And so it [my heart] will, whatever I may do'. Roh: 'And so will I be [ever hers], whatever I may do'. It is clear from the structure of the poem that Jar lacks a line here—whether with *feray* or *fera* we cannot know.

Line 13. Roh 'Unless I can forget her'; Jar 'Without wanting to forget her'; Lab (depends on the preceding *quoy que je face*) 'to keep her memory alive'. Roh appears here to have given up the pretense of a possible serious reading, so that J had to rewrite the line to make it acceptable; the result is nearly ridiculous, for what lover would *want* to forget his lady?

14. Ja que li ne s'i attende, ff. 17ᵛ–18ʳ [Busnois]

Concordant Sources

Cop 291⁸, ff. 37ᵛ–39ʳ
Dij 517, ff. lviiiᵛ–lixʳ, Busnoys
Sev 5.I.43, ff. 57ᵛ–58ʳ
Lab, ff. 52ᵛ–53ʳ
Wolf 287, ff. 5ᵛ–6ʳ

Collation

Compared with the reading of Mell, Wolf 287 presents no significant variants, only a relatively improbable written flat for B in the CT at

m. 14 (3). Cop 291⁸ and Lab also differ from Mell in giving a b-flat signature for the T, the former up through m. 12, the latter for the entire part. The written flat for b′ in m. 25 (2) of the C in Mell is also present in Wolf 287 and Cop 291⁸, but not in the remaining three MSS.

Cop 291⁸, Dij 517, and Lab share a few small melodic details that differ from the corresponding portions of Mell: in the T at m. 10 (5) those sources give a dissonant d-M instead of the consonant c-M of the present collection; at m. 13 (6) of the T they have d-Sm instead of c (a rather inconsequential change). In addition, Dij 517 and Lab have the sign of congruence in the CT over the D-Br, m. 26 (1), instead of with the following E (probably an error), and Cop 291⁸ and Dij 517 omit the rest-Sb, C-Sb preceding the final L of the CT (a rhythmic variant that does not alter the musical substance). Only Cop 291⁸ has a slightly different cadential ornament at mm. 4 (6) and 26 (2) of the C, and a′ instead of g at m. 12 (1) of the T (technically correct but less interesting than in Mell), whereas Dij 517 has no indication of the change of mensuration at m. 20 in either T or CT.

In Sev 5.I.43 the rest at m. 11 of the C is erroneously given as Sb. At m. 3 (4) is written b-M, followed in m. 4 (3) by c-Sb, giving a different but entirely possible reading. In the CT from m. 28 (1) to the end are given G-Sb, rest-Sb, C-Sb, rest-Sb, C-Sb, G-Br, leaving the passage considerably weaker than in the other sources.

Comments

It would appear that the reading for this composition most closely related to that of Mell is given by Wolf 287, followed at no great distance by Cop 291⁸, Dij 517, and Lab, and that the latter three can be considered as an interrelated group belonging to the same basic tradition of transmission. Sev 5.I.43, by contrast, gives a distinctly independent version of several (notable) details, and in this regard stands apart from all the remaining sources.

In the second section of this bergerette (f. 18ᵛ of the MS) the text is copied for the T as if it were intended to be sung. But because the words were not written for the T in the initial section and the syllables cannot be placed beneath the notes of the second without breaking ligatures, the situation is anomalous. It may have arisen when a scribe, reacting to the homophonic character and unusual brevity of the writing in the second section, simply wrote the two couplets in full instead of limiting himself to an incipit. He did nearly as much for the CT as well. However, for the purposes of the edition it did not seem necessary to give the text for only that portion of the T. Should a vocal performance be desired, the T can readily adapt the text placement of the C.

Given the melodic configuration in which it appears, the written accidental in the CT of Wolf 287 at m. 14 (3) would fundamentally alter the modal orientation of the entire passage in all three parts and create some thorny problems in the process. Thus, it was thought better omitted from the transcription altogether.

Ja que li ne s'i attende,
Car tous aultres sont cassés,
Et je l'aime plus qu'assés
Affin que chescun l'entende.   4

Ainsi a-il le renon
De porter sur une *manche*   6

[Deulx des] lettres de mon nom:
L'une persse et l'aultre blance.   8

Plus que jamais de sa bande
Me tiendray, et de si pres
Qu'on verra bien par expres
Que tousjours son fait amande.   12
      Ja que li ne s'i attende,
      Car tous aultres sont cassés,
      Et je l'aime plus qu'assés
      Affin que chescun l'entende.

Although *he* does not expect it,*
For all others have been driven to despair,
Yet I love him more than enough
For everyone to perceive it.

Thus he has the reputation
Of wearing on one sleeve

*Or: Let Jacqueline wait.

Two of the letters of my name:
One blue and the other white.

More than ever to his band
I will adhere, and so closely
That it will be clearly seen†
That I do ever improve his lot.
  Although he does not expect it,
  For all others have been driven to despair,
  Yet I love him more than enough
  For every one to perceive it.

Variants

The song title *Jaqueline* figures in the list of songs in Rabelais' *Le cinquiesme livre*, chap. 33. All five concordant sources are texted. Lines 9–12, lacking in Mell, are supplied from Lab.

1 lui—*Cop Dij*. 2 si sont—*Lab*, en sont—*Wolf* (both have an eight-syllable line here). 3 Et je l'ame trop plus que assez—*Lab Wolf* (even if one supposes *qu'assez*, this is eight syllables). 5 Aussi—*Cop Dij Lab Wolf*; il a—*Cop Dij*. 6 (Mell incomplete); a sa plaisance—*Cop Dij*, a sa devise—*Lab Wolf*. 7 Des deulx—*Mell*, deux des—*Cop Dij Lab Wolf*. 8 blanche—*Cop Dij Wolf*, grise—Lab. 11 qu'il voirra—*Dij*. 12 son fait tous les jours—*Cop* (+1 syll.), son fait tousjours—*Dij*; s'amande—*Wolf*.

Versification

Bergerette in heptasyllables, *abba cdcd*.

Textual Notes

Line 1. **Ja que** 'although'; **li** = modern French *lui*, *elle*, i.e., masculine or feminine singular disjunctive pronoun. In early Old French *lui* was clearly masculine and *li* feminine as disjunctive pronouns; but in later Old French and Middle French the two were used interchangeably in either gender. The substitution of *lui* for *li* (as in Cop Dij) does not bear on the question of gender, but does blur the cryptographic reference to Jaqueline (see Nos. 12 and 42 for other

---

†Or, with Dij: That he will clearly see.

cryptograms on her name). This line is deliberately ambiguous, with the readings *Ja que li ne s'i attende* 'Although *he* does not expect it' and *Jaqueline si attende* 'Let Jaqueline wait'. We shall comment further on the meaning of this line as the poem develops.

Line 3. This—that she, the poet, loves him—is what he does not expect; or, alternatively, this is what Jaqueline is told, in l. 1, to wait for.

Line 4. **Affin que** = modern French *pour que* 'so that' in the sense of result rather than purpose; this clause completes *plus qu'assés* of l. 3; 'more than enough'.

Line 5. Mell is alone in having **Ainsi;** all the others have *Aussi.* Only Cop and Dij do not have the inversion.

Line 8. **persse** 'blue'. Only Lab has *grise* to rhyme with *devise.* Wolf has *blanche*, which does not rhyme with *devise!* Apparently a proto-LabWolf had changed something in *-anche* to *devise;* Lab corrected the now-faulty rhyme by changing *blanche* to *grise.* Therefore it would seem that the rhyme *plaisance : blanche* would be closer to the source than *devise : grise.* However, *plaisance* and *blanche* do not make a dialectally consistent rhyme: in a Francian type of dialect, *plaisance* does not rhyme with *blanche;* in a Picard type of dialect, *plaisanche* does not rhyme with *blanke.* The following alternative explanations suggest themselves: (1) to accept a dialectally mixed *plaisanche : blanche* as being in the original poem (this is not too implausible, since dialect mixture is a fact of life); or (2) building on Mell's defective l. 6, to posit . . . *sur une manche*, which would have the double merit of making sense and of being a good rhyme in either dialect: *manke : blanke* in Picard, or *manche : blanche* in Francian. As to the sense, detachable sleeves of varying colors were sign-vehicles in the courtly communication system (cf. No. 5).

Line 11. The only variant bearing on the sense is Dij *il* against **on** in all the others.

15. Pour entretenir mes amours, ff. 19ᵛ–20ʳ, Busnoys

Concordant Sources

Glog, No. 271 (capital *M* only text given)
FloR 2794, ff. 57ᵛ–58ʳ
RomC 2856, ff. 21ᵛ–22ʳ, Busnoys
*Jar, f. lxxᵛ

COLLATION

Of the four musical sources in which this composition is found, only Mell and FloR 2794 have the initial entry of the CT in two parts. On the other hand the latter differs from the former only in reversing the rhythmic values of the T in m. 12 to C-Br, rest-Sb, C-Sb, and in giving at m. 27 (8) of the CT (instead of the G-M of Mell) a-M, a variant also found in RomC 2856. A third melodic divergence is found in Glog at m. 24 (5) of the C, where b'-Sm is given instead of the a' of the other sources, producing a very minor change that is entirely correct contrapuntally.

The remaining variants relate only to the use of accidentals: the T of Glog has b-flat as a signature at the beginning of the part; the written sharp for c in the T at m. 12 is given only by Mell; the written flat in the CT at m. 8 (1) is not given by Glog or by RomC 2856; that at m. 10 (1) is given only by Mell; and RomC 2856 is alone in providing a written accidental for the CT at m. 14 (3, 5) (thus providing an additional justification for the editorial suggestions made).

COMMENTS

A chanson found in Niv, ff. lix^v–lx^r, based on another poem that also begins *Pour entretenir*, has in common with Busnois's composition only those two words.

None of the concordant sources for this work presents substantial differences with the reading of Mell. However, that of FloR 2794 is clearly the one most closely related to the version published here because it shares with it not only the additional counterpoint at the beginning but also a large number of notational details such as the placement of ligatures and the use of coloration. The reading of FloR 2794 and RomC 2856 at m. 27 (8) of the CT is certainly preferable to that of Mell since it avoids the open fourth between the two lower voices, a combination frowned upon by the theorists of the period. The evidence was judged sufficient to assume a scribal error in Mell, and the transcription was emended in accordance with the other two MSS.

It is interesting to note that the added line at the beginning of the CT is merely an inversion at the upper octave of the counterpoint heard in the CT, mm. 2 (2)–4 (1), and in the T, mm. 4 (1)–5 (4), against the principal melody as it is passed imitatively from CT to T to C.

Because the position of the caesura is shifted, the text placement suggested for the third line of the refrain cannot be used for the two remaining strophes without breaking a word over the rest of m. 14 in the C. As a result it would be preferable in performance to divide the corresponding line of the short strophe after *couvient* and, similarly, that of the long strophe after *souffrir*, and to redistribute the syllables of the verse accordingly.

Pour entretenir mes amours
Trouver me fault le jour cent tours
Et faire mainte seignourie;
Et puis, ma bourse mal garnie,
Me fault demourer tous les jours.   5

Je tiens bien du prince des lours
Quant en paines et en douleurs
Il me couvient user ma vie   8
    Pour entretenir mes amours;
    Trouver me fault le jour cent tours
    Et faire mainte seignourie.

Se j'eusse a mains aucun secours
De celle qui griefves douleurs
Me fait souff[r]ir jour et nuytie,
J'auroye, je vous certefie,
Joye et soulas en lieu de plours.   13
    Pour entretenir mes amours
    Trouver me fault le jour cent tours
    Et faire mainte seignourie;
    Et puis, ma bourse mal garnie,
    Me fault demourer tous les jours.

Mell and FloR:
To keep up my love affairs
I must find every day a hundred tricks
And perform many a lordly deed (FloR: ridiculous antic),
And then, my purse depleted,
I must remain forever.

I'm really like the Prince of Oafs
When in pain and in grief
I must wear away my life
    To keep up my love affairs;
    I must find every day a hundred tricks
    And perform many a lordly deed.

If I had at least some help
From her who makes me suffer
Night and day these grievous pains,
I would have, I promise you,
Joy and solace instead of tears.
    To keep up my love affairs
    I must find every day a hundred tricks
    And perform many a lordly deed.
    And then, my purse depleted,
    I must remain forever.

VARIANTS

RomC has incipit only. Mell ends with l. 5; the rest is supplied from FloR.

2 Colorer me fault mains fins tours—*Jar.* 3 singerie—*FloR.* (Jar omits this line.) 4 Car ma bourse est tres mal garnie—*Jar.* 5 Me fault deslier—*FloR;* Pour fourrer le poignet tousjours—*Jar.*

The Jar version of lines 6–13 is so different from FloR that we reproduce it here:

Ung jour demande haulx atours
Et l'autre ung grant bort de veloux,
Et je respons, "Or bien, m'amye,   8
    Pour entretenir *mes amours*
    Colorer me fault mains fins tours."

"Veez vous ce donneur de 'bons jours'?
Il a," fet ele, "en tant de cours
Pratiqué l'art de baverie
Qu'il scet moult bien, sans qu'il rie
Dire sa pensee a rebours."   13

> Pour entretenir *mes amours*
> *Colorer me fault mains fins tours,*
> *Car ma bourse est tresmal garnie*
> *Pour fourrer le poignet tousjours.*

> One day she asks for fancy clothes,
> The next, for a wide velvet ribbon,
> And I answer, "Come now, sweet friend,
>   To keep up my love affairs
>   I must think up many a sly trick."

> "Look at him, so free with his hellos!
> He has," says she, "in so many courts
> Practiced the art of small talk
> That he knows very well, with a straight face,
> How to say the opposite of what he thinks."
>   To keep up my love affairs
>   I must think up many a sly trick,
>   For my purse is very badly furnished
>   From being forever poked into by a wrist.

Versification

An octosyllabic rondeau cinquain, *aabba*. It is evident that this description applies to the Jar version, in spite of its omission of l. 3, since the three-line short strophe and the five-line long strophe, with their appropriate rhyme schemes, conform to the structure of the rondeau cinquain.

Textual Notes

We have adopted FloR as our model for ll. 6–13 because of the greater resemblance of its refrain to that of Mell. The two versions (FloR and Jar) are somewhat different in character. FloR gives the courtly complaint of an impecunious lover; Jar a lively dialogue recalling the comic realism of the fifteenth-century farce. The refrain (all that Mell gives) can go in either direction.

Line 2. Jar's *colorer* already seems to point up the deceitful character of the narrator, as does the word *fins*.

Line 3. **seignourie** 'gracious, lordly, generous act'. FloR's *singerie* 'monkeyshines, idiotic, demeaning act', in spite of the difference, is just as apt, describing the antics of the courtier.

Lines 4–5. Two interpretations of these lines as they appear in Mell are possible: (1) With commas in l. 3, as we have printed it, "I must stay here because my purse is empty." (2) Without commas, the expression **ma bourse mal garnie** is a complement to **demourer**, that is, "I must be forever with empty purse." The versions of FloR and Jar are in essential accord with each other in explaining in l. 5 why, in l. 4, the purse is badly furnished.

Lines 6–13. In FloR we have essentially a continuation of complaint, self-reproach, and similar expressions of feeling, while Jar embarks upon a lively dialogue.

Line 9. **a mains** = modF *au moins* 'at least'. **secours** 'help'— amorous or financial?

Line 11. FloR **nuytie** [nẅitiə] 'night, space of a night' is formed like those Picard past participles based on a root ending in a palatal or palatalized consonant. It corresponds to the Francian *nuitiee*.

Lines 1″–5″. In the Jar version, if the repetition of the refrain is considered part of the lady's speech, the first person pronouns should be changed to third person, as follows: . . . Trouver *lui* fault,' and so on. If not part of her speech, it is a mechanical repetition of the refrain according to the rule—which is just as plausible.

16. **Quant ce viendra, ff. 20ᵛ–22ʳ [Busnois]**

CONCORDANT SOURCES

*Roh, f. 157ʳ
Dij 517, ff. iiᵛ–iiiʳ, Busnoys
Esc IV.a.24, ff. 121ᵛ–122ʳ, Hockenghem
Flo 176, ff. 69ᵛ–71ʳ
Niv, ff. viᵛ–viiʳ (with the exception of the end of the CT and part of the text, erased from the MS)
Tr 88, f. 411ʳ (Gaude mater)
Lab, ff. 27ᵛ–28ʳ, Busnoys
Wolf 287, ff. 32ᵛ–33ʳ

COLLATION

Because most of this chanson was effaced in Niv, it was not possible to include that MS in the comparison of the sources.

Mell is alone in including the CT *si placet*, but the concordant sources vary in few significant details from the reading given here for the three voices common to all. Dij 517, Esc IV.a.24, Flo 176, and Tr 88 all begin with a rest-Br not found in the other sources and share the lower third as a cadential ornament in the C at mm. 8 and 32. There are divergences at m. 22 that affect all three parts in one source or another: in the C, Lab and Wolf 287 give a′ as a blackened Br whereas in Tr 88 that note is imperfected by the following rest; in the T, Dij 517, Flo 176, Tr 88, and Wolf 287 have a-Sb instead of a-Br; and in the CT, Dij 517, Tr 88, and Wolf 287 give only one D-Sb instead of two. Also, in the C of Dij 517 the rest was omitted at m. 25, and c′, m. 26 (2), made Sb instead of M to compensate, while at the beginning of m. 28 in the CT a rest-Sb has been added. Conversely, there is only one rest-Sb for the C of Flo 176 at m. 23. In Tr 88 a c-clef is mistakenly written on the second and third staves of the part instead of the F-clef.

As for accidentals, only Mell and Tr 88 have a written sharp for f in the C at m. 16 (1), but in Tr 88 it is placed before the preceding f, m. 15 (1). The E-flat seen here as a signature for the CT is also found in Esc IV.a.24 up to m. 28 but in no other source.

COMMENTS

Although the variants between the sources are few and of relatively minor importance, the readings of Dij 517, Esc IV.a.24, Flo 176, and Tr 88 can be grouped on the basis of the additional rest-Br with which the composition begins in those sources. The discrepancies at m. 22 (and perhaps some of the neighboring ones as well) apparently spring from an error in the interpretation of the notation that was eventually ratified as an emendation, adding an entire beat (Sb) to the piece. The original version is probably that given by Tr 88 and Wolf 287, where the composition is one Sb shorter in all three parts than it is in Mell. Dij 517 and Flo 176 share with Tr 88 and Wolf 287 the note values of the T at m. 22. Dij 517 also has the same reading for the CT at that point whereas Flo 176 maintains the original length of the C by dropping one of the Sb rests from m. 23, having lost the blackening for the Br of m. 22. However, Dij 517 adds Sb to the CT at m. 28, making that voice as long as its C without necessarily providing the proper alignment of consonances in the counterpoint. Lab retains of the shorter version only the blackened Br of the C at m. 22, whereas Esc IV.a.24 and Mell have the added beat in all parts, with the result that the final cadence falls on the second Sb of the mensural unit rather than at the beginning as is usually the case. Nevertheless, it would seem that the reading of the present collection is most closely related to that of Lab with regard both to the rests used at the beginning of the piece and to the details of melodic ornamentation and usage in general.

The placement of the text in Mell is more approximate than usual; even the customary correspondence between the musical phrase and the poetic line was not observed by the scribe. Consequently, for the transcription the indications of Lab were followed when those of Mell were clearly insufficient or ambiguous. The reader will also note that the b-flat signature for the C appears in the MS only at the beginning of the second line. However, because the flat is present for the entire part in the other sources and because the only note not explicitly lowered in the notation of Mell requires a flat to avoid a melodic tritone, the accidental was simply given as a signature throughout in the modern score.

Although the attributions for this work do not agree, they decidedly favor Busnois not only numerically but also by virtue of the central nature and general reliability of the MSS giving the piece to him. It is possible that Ockeghem was responsible for the optional CT, however, since he is known to have made similar additions to the chansons of others. It may be in this manner that his name became connected with the composition in Esc IV.a.24 even though the fourth voice was not included in that source.

Quant ce viendra au droit destraindre,
Comment veray mon oeil contraindre
    Et mon cuer faindre
A mon douloureux partement
De vous, mon loyal pensement,
A qui nulle ne puet attaindre?   6

Lermes et pleurs, gemir et plaindre,
Feront mes yeulx pallir et taindre
    Sans rien en faindre
Et lesser tout esbatement.   10
    Quant ce viendra au droit destraindre,
    Comment veray mon oeil contraindre

Et mon cuer faindre
A mon douloureux partement?

Soupirs engoisseux pour refraindre
Ma joye et ma plaisance estaindre—
    Ou les reffaindre—
Sourdront en moy si largement
Que ne pourray lors bonnement
A grace et a mercy avaindre.   16
        Quant ce viendra au droit destraindre,
        Comment veray mon oeil contraindre
            Et mon cuer faindre
        A mon douloureux partement
        De vous, mon loyal pensement,
        A qui nulle ne puet attaindre?

When it comes to the true torment
How will I see my eye constrained
        And my heart falter
At my unhappy separation
From you, object of my constant thought,
To which no other can attain?

Tears and cries, groans and plaints,
Will make my eyes colorless and dull
        Without feigning,
And [make them] forsake all pleasures.
        When it comes to the true torment
        How will I see my eye constrained
                And my heart falter
        At my unhappy separation?

Anguished sighs to restrain
My joy and extinguish my delight—
        Or [make me] feign them—
Will surge up in me so abundantly
That I will not then by any means
        Attain to grace and mercy.

> When it comes to the true torment
> How will I see my eye constrained
>   And my heart falter
> At my unhappy separation
> From you, object of my constant thought,
> To which no other can attain?

Variants

Flo and Niv are without text.

1 vendra—*Esc Wolf.* 2 pourray—*Dij (Esc) Lab Wolf;* veul—*Dij,* voel—*Esc,* vueil—*Lab Roh,* dueil—*Wolf.* 5 seul—*Esc* (− 1 syll.); Mon loyal cueur et pensement—*Lab (Wolf),* Nesloingner celle aucunement—*Roh.* 6 Esc omits A; nulluy—*Dij,* nul—*Esc Lab.* (Lab −1 syll., Esc −2 syll. Mell omits ll. 7–13, which we supply from Lab. Esc ends here.) 11 Sourrir—*Dij.* 13 refraindre—*Dij Wolf,* restraindre—*Roh.* The Mell text is resumed, ll. 14–16. 14 Saudront sur—*Lab;* tant largement—*Dij Lab.* 16 A gré—*Dij Wolf;* A grace ne mercy—*Roh.*

Versification

Rondeau cinquain layé in octosyllables, except for a tetrasyllabic insertion after the second line: $a a^a b b a$. The short strophe and the short refrain have four lines each: $a a^a b$.

Textual Notes

Line 1. **droit** 'real, true'; **destraindre**, infinitive used as noun: 'torment'.

Line 2. Mell **oeil** as against such readings as *veul, voel, vueil* (see Variants) suggests that the prototype may have had *ueil*, which, because of the ambiguity of the letter *u* (which could stand for the consonant *v* or the vowel *u*), could have represented either 'eye' or 'will', and which subsequent scribes copied as one or the other in a nonambiguous form. Since its use parallels l. 3 **cuer**, it should have a similar meaning—but either 'eye' or 'will' can serve this purpose.

Mell **veray** 'I will see' has a plausibility which, if it were not for the overwhelming testimony of the concordant sources supporting *pourray*, could conceivably justify attributing it to the prototype.

It can, unlike *pourray*, be followed by infinitives with either active or passive sense. Thus, ll. 2–3 can be interpreted as 'How will I see (= be able to stand seeing) my eye constrained and my heart faint . . . ?' With *pourray* we have 'How will I be able to compel my will (to resignation) and conceal my heart (= inner feeling) . . . ?'

Up to the eighteenth century *feindre* (**faindre**) had meanings which it does not have today. Besides its current meaning ('to feign', i.e., to pretend to have, falsely manifest [an emotion]), it meant (2) 'to conceal', (3) 'to hesitate before undertaking an action' (cf. English *faint heart*, in which the adjective has been borrowed from the past participle of the French verb), (4) 'to dissimulate' in an absolute construction, i.e., without a direct object or a necessary adverbial complement.' It is not, although such an interpetation would be tempting in l. 3, a transitive verb meaning 'deceive'.[1]

Paleographically, *veray* and *poray* are possible sources each for the other. In the handwriting of this manuscript—very typical of the period—a *p* with a short downstroke and an elaborate head resembles significantly a frequent type of *v*, examples of which occur as the initial letter of l. 1 **viendra** and l. 2 **veray**.

Line 6. **nulle**, feminine, also in Wolf; all the other versions have the masculine *nul* (or, in Dij, *nulluy*). Redactors who use the feminine express the notion that 'no other woman can so occupy my thoughts'; the masculine means that no one can attain 'you, the constant object of my thoughts'.

As to the immediate prototype underlying the extant readings, it probably had *nul*, but was hypometric due to its failure to copy a monosyllabic word, possibly *ja* or *oncque* (. . . *nul ja ne puet* . . . or . . . *ne puet oncque attaindre*). Such readings as *nulle* and *nulluy* presumably represent attempts to recapture the missing syllable. We posit *nul* as belonging to the prototype because it is supported by MSS which are relatively distant from each other, Esc and Lab, which agree with Dij as to gender.

Line 7. **gemir et plaindre** 'groaning and complaining'; infinitives used as nouns.

Line 8. **taindre** 'change color'; here, 'grow dull'.

---

1. Lexicographic sources, s.v. *feindre, faindre*: Godefroy, Tobler and Lommatzsch, Grandsaignes d'Hauterive, Greimas, Huguet, Robert, Littré, *Le Dictionnaire de l'Académie Française*, 1798, the last three for now archaic usages lasting into the eighteenth century.

Line 9. 'Without the least pretense'.

Line 10. **esbatement** 'amusement, diversion'.

Lines 1'–4'. Independent short refrain.

Line 11. **engoisseux pour** 'anguished enough to'.

Line 13. 'Or to feign them (joy and pleasure)', i.e., to make it necessary to feign them. The prefix *re-* does not mean 'again' as it does in the modern language; it means 'in return, in its turn, in reaction, contrariwise'; here it refers to the alternative to showing no more joy and pleasure, namely, feigning them. The variant *refraindre* is rejected, as this word occurs in the rhyme at l. 11.

Line 14. 'Will surge up in me so abundantly'. The variant Lab *saudront sur moy* 'will issue forth to attack me' is not in keeping with the tone of this poem, which has no military images.

Line 16. **avaindre** (à) 'attain, arrive (at)'.

17. Vostre bruit et vostre grant fame, ff. 22ᵛ–23ʳ, G. Dufay

Concordant Sources

Glog, No. 273 (capital *O* only text given)
Flo 176, ff. 36ᵛ–38ʳ, Duffay
*Par 24315, f. 30ᵛ
Par 4379, f. 20ᵛ (C only)
Cord, ff. 28ᵛ–29ʳ
CG XIII.27, ff. 85ᵛ–86ʳ (Votre brut, marionete)
Tr 89, ff. 415ᵛ–416ʳ
Lab, ff. 22ᵛ–23ʳ, Dufay
*Arn, f. 63ʳ
*Jar, f. lxxvᵛ

Collation

Although the isolated C transmitted by Par 4379 presents no variants of substance with respect to the reading of Mell, there are a number of differences of notational detail such as the combining of repeated pitches into a single note of longer value. The mensuration given by Flo 176 is imperfect tempus (C) in all parts without the stroke of diminution found in the remaining sources, and Tr 89 gives an unlikely written flat for e at m. 19(3) of the CT, but neither source differs otherwise from Mell except in minor matters of melodic ornamentation. Cord and CG XIII.27 share a significant variant in the CT, m. 14(1), where G-M is preceded by rest-M instead of the opposite as in the other sources. But—like the Florence and Trent MSS—they vary from Mell elsewhere only in minor matters of melodic ornamentation, CG XIII.27 to a greater degree than Cord. Lab is very similar to Mell in all respects except for the passage in the T, mm. 19(3)–20(5), which reads a-M, c-M, b-M, a-Sb, G-M, a-M, F-M, G-M, producing some sharp dissonances with the other voices in marked contrast to the smooth euphony of the present version. In the C of Glog, m. 10(7–10), the SSm of Mell are replaced, undoubtedly erroneously, by four FFu barred together (the dot is nonetheless present). In the CT d-M is written instead of c at m. 10(3), and b-M instead of c at m. 11(4), both of which produce irregular discordant clashes.

COMMENTS

In view of the number of sources involved and the geographical and chronological spans covered by them, the manuscript tradition for this composition is surprisingly uniform. The readings to which that of Mell appears most closely related are in Tr 89 and Flo 176, but that of Cord is also very close, particularly in the notational detail, despite the small but distinctive variant of the CT.

The accidental e-flat given by Tr 89 at m. 19(3) of the CT seems inappropriate, as much because of the mixolydian modality of the piece as because of the melodic and harmonic context in which it occurs. The units of declamation used in the syllabic passages that dominate the melodic writing again suggest that the diminished mensuration is to be interpreted as literally proportional to its integral counterpart.

> Vostre bruit et vostre grant fame
> Me fait vous amer plus que fame
> Qui de tous biens soit assouvie;
> Ne ja d'aultre servir envye
> N'aray, ne que de rendre l'ame.   5
>
> En riens ne crains reproche d'ame.
> Je vous tiens et tendray, ma dame,
> En acroissant toutte ma vie   8
>   Vostre bruit; *et vostre grant fame*

Me fait vous amer plus que fame
Qui de tous biens soit assouvie.

Et pour ce doncques, noble dame,
De vostre grace, sans nul blasme,
Au moins se je l'ay desservye,
Ne vueillez pas que je desvie,
Car vous perdriez par le *royame*   13
    Vostre bruit et vostre grant fame.
    [*Me fait vous amer plus que fame,*
    Qui de tous biens soit assouvie :
    Ne ja d'aultre servir envye
    N'aray, ne que de rendre l'ame.]

Your renown and your great fame
Make me love you more than any woman
Endowed with all that's good;
Nor would I wish to serve another
Any more than to give up my life.

I do not fear any one's reproach.
I hold you and will keep you, my lady,
Devoting my whole life to increasing
    Your renown; and your great fame
    Makes me love you more than any woman
    Endowed with all that's good.

And therefore, noble lady,
Without any blame, from your favor,
At least if I have deserved it,
Do not wish that I depart,
For you would lose throughout the realm
    Your renown and your great fame.
    [*Makes me love you more than any woman*
    Endowed with all that's good—
    Nor would I wish to serve another
    Any more than to give up my life.]

The texted sources are Flo, Cord, Lab, and Jar. (Par 4379 has just the first line.) Mell ends with l. 8; our text is completed with Jar.

2 femme—*Flo Jar Lab.* 4 Jamais d'autre servir envie—*Lab.* 5 plus que—*Cord;* jucquez que rende l'ame—*Lab.* 7 C'est vostre grace sans nul blasme—*Lab* (corresponds to l. 10 in all other versions). 9 Et pourtant ce que je clame—*Cord,* Et pource dont ce que te clame—*Lab.* 10 C'est vostre—*Cord;* En vous priant plus que nul ame—*Lab.* 11 Au moins je ne l'ay deservie—*Cord.* 13 royaulme—*Jar;* part du royaulme —*Cord,* et corps et ame—*Lab.*

Translation of ll. 9–13 in Cord and Lab.

Cord: And yet what I require
        Is your favor, without any blame;
        At least I have not deserved it.
        Do not wish that I may die,
        For you would lose your share in the Kingdom.   13

Lab: And so what I request of thee,
        Praying to you more than any soul,
        At least if I have deserved it:
        Do not wish that I may die,
        For you would lose both body and soul.   13

VERSIFICATION

Rondeau cinquain in octosyllables, *aabba.*

TEXTUAL NOTES

Line 2. **fait**, singular verb with a compound subject consisting of singular nouns; Old French offers the choice between the singular and the plural verb in this situation. The choice of the singular supports the punctuation we have given to the short refrain (ll. 1′–3′). **fame** = *femme* (see Variants).

Line 5. 'any more than to give up the ghost.'

Line 8 and short refrain (ll. 1′–3′). This can be interpreted either as an overlapping construction of short strophe and short refrain or as a normal syntactic integration of the two. In the former case, the first part (here, the first line) of the refrain completes a grammatical construction begun in the short strophe, the rest of the refrain not entering into the construction (see pp. 88–91). If, however, we insert a punctuation mark after **vostre bruit**, the direct object of **accroissant**, a new clause begins whose subject is **vostre grant fame**.

Lines 9–13. The Jar reading is probably faulty, since it reintroduces *dame* at the rhyme (see l. 7). It is, however, perfectly sensible.

In Cord it appears that the redactor did not observe that the gender of **deservie** shows that **grace** and not **blasme** is the antecedent of l. 11 **l'**. He could not have intended to say, 'At least I have not deserved your favor'.

Apparently Lab's redactor was writing from memory: he used l. 10 as his l. 7, thus requiring a new l. 10, which has the defect of *ame* as a rhyme word, already used in the same sense ('person') at l. 6 (cf. its use at l. 5: 'life'). The word *grace* having been lost from Lab's l. 10, there is no longer any feminine noun to serve as antecedent to l. 11 *je l'ay desservye*. Lab's redactor was probably thinking of l. 9 *ce que te clame* as the direct object; as in the case of Cord, the exigencies of rhyme have prevailed over the grammatical rule. The phonetic similarity of the masculine and feminine participles may explain this negligence. In the Lab version, *te* is inconsistent with the *vous* of the rest of the poem.

Line 12. **desvie** 'leave (the way), stray, deviate', in construction with l. 10 **De vostre grace**; by extension, 'depart; lose sanity; die'— as it was no doubt understood by the redactors of Cord and Lab.

Line 13. In spite of the spelling of all the sources that use this word, we here adopt the spelling **royame**, for the sake of the rhyme. *Royau(l)-me*, which coexisted with *royame* and which has survived into modern French, is the result of a blend of *réame* with *royal*. *Réame* comes from *régíminem, an incorrect accusative of régimen, which, because it is neuter, has in Classical Latin an accusative of the same form as the nominative. We have written these Latin words with accents to show that the French word comes from a Latin word that bore stress on the second syllable. It occurs in the form *royame* in No. 23, l. 8. There is apparently no clear relationship between rĕg-ō (from which regimen is derived) and rēx, rēg-is 'king'.[1]

---

1. Alfred Ernout and Antoine Meillet, *Dictionnaire étymologique de la langue Latine*, s. vv. *rego* and *rēx*. See also Albert Dauzat, Jean Dubois, and Henri Mitterand, *Nouveau dictionnaire étymologique et historique*, s.v. *royaume*, and Wilhelm Meyer-Lübke, *Romanisches etymologisches Wörterbuch*, §7170.

Lab uses *ame* for the third time—for the second time with the meaning 'life' (cf. l. 5). Jar's l. 13 makes the best sense of the three.

Lines 1″–5″. Jar necessarily integrates the first line, for its l. 13 **perdriez** requires a direct object. Placing a mark of punctuation after **vostre bruit**, as was done for the short refrain, weakens the rest of the refrain. The greatest concision and elegance result from placing a period at the end of l. 1″, in which event we must regard the long refrain as participating in an overlapping construction, since ll. 2″–5″ make neither syntactic nor semantic sense.

18. Fortune, par ta cruaulté, ff. 23ᵛ–24ʳ, Vincenet

CONCORDANT SOURCES

Glog, No. 275 (capital Q only text given)
Bol Q 16, ff. 132ᵛ–133ʳ (cxviᵛ–cxviiʳ), (à 4)
Bol Q 18, ff. 37ᵛ–38ʳ, (à 4)
Flo 229, ff. 50ᵛ–51ʳ
Pix, ff. 166ᵛ–167ʳ
Cord, ff. 34ᵛ–36ʳ
Per 431, No. 104, ff. 94ᵛ–95ʳ (Fortuna vincinecta)
CG XIII.27, ff. 40ʳ–41ᵛ, Vincinet
Sev 5.I.43, ff. 61ᵛ–62ʳ
Ver 757, ff. 66ᵛ–67ʳ
Odh, ff. 65ᵛ–66ʳ, Vincinet

COLLATION

There is a sizable group of sources that differ from Mell in their readings for this composition only in details of melodic ornamentation and in the accidentals specified: Cord, Pix, Flo 229, CG XIII.27, and, to a lesser degree, Odh. Although the version of Bol Q 16 includes an optional added voice, it is virtually identical to that of Flo 229 with respect to the other three. Somewhat further removed is the reading of Glog, in which one finds at m. 10 (3) of the CT a-M instead of G (creating a dissonance with the other two voices) and at m. 13 (1) G-M, a-M, c-M (leaving the mensural unit a Br short).

Also à 4, but with a different added voice than that found in Bol Q 16, is the version of Bol Q 18, differentiated also by two significant variants in the CT: at m. 4, C-L instead of the four different pitches of Mell, and at m. 25 (5), G-M, rest-M instead of G-Sb. It shares the

latter variant with Sev 5.I.43 and Ver 757, each of which has yet
another reading at m. 4 (1 ff.): a-flat Br, C-Br, E-flat M, F-M, G-Sb
in the former and a-flat Sb, C-Sb, E-flat dotted Sb, f-M, G-Br in the
latter. However, the same two sources virtually agree on another
significant variant in the CT at m. 23 (1–5): a-M, G-M, a-M, F-M,
C-M (and no rest-M) in Sev 5.I.43, altered in Ver 757 only by the
substitution of a dotted figure for the first two MM of the Seville MS,
a reading that works much less consonantly with the other two voices
than does that of Mell. In addition, Ver 757 has in the T, also at m.
23 (1 ff.), c-M, b-M, c-dotted M, b-Sm, a-Sm, a divergence that
hardly affects the musical substance.

Characteristic of Per 431 is the inaccuracy of the CT for this work:
at m. 4 (1 ff.) it reads a-flat Br (blackened), G-Sm, F-Sm, D-dotted
Sb, E-M (probably an error); mm. 7 (4)–16 (2) have been omitted
(perhaps because the scribe skipped a line of his exemplar); and mm.
19 (2)–22 (3) have been written a third too low.

The written accidental at m. 3 of the C is not given by Cord (which
also does not have e-flat as a signature until m. 11 [4] although it is
given as an accidental in m. 6), Sev 5.I.43, Flo 229, Glog, CG XIII.27,
or Per 431. Conversely, a natural is given for the b-L of the T at m. 18
in both Cord and Flo 229. In the CT no flat is given for a at mm. 8 (3)
or 16 (3) in Cord, Pix, Flo 229, or Bol Q 16; none is given at m. 26 (1)
in Flo 229, CG XIII.27, Bol Q 16, or Per 431; and Bol Q 18 has no
E-flat in the signature.

COMMENTS

This chanson also exists in an intabulation for lute found in Bologna,
Biblioteca dell' Università, MS 596 H. H. 24 with the title *Fortuna
vincinecta*.[1]

Two primary traditions of transmission emerge from the sources for
Vincenet's rondeau. One includes Mell, Cord, Pix, Flo 229, CG
XIII.27, Odh, and even Bol Q 16 (despite the added voice) and the
other Sev 5.I.43 and Ver 757. Bol Q 18 may also be related to the
latter two, but both Glog and Per 431 seem to have independent
variants. Mell is closest to Cord (which also has the text written out
for both C and T) and to Pix and Flo 229, which agree with Mell to

---

1. This indication was kindly supplied by Professor Allan Atlas of Brooklyn College.

a surprising degree even in the graphic details of the notation, the placement of ligatures, the use of coloration, and so forth.

Because the caesura falls differently in the first line of the long strophe than in the refrain, the text placement suggested in the C of the transcription would result in breaking the word *malgré* over the rest of m. 3. Consequently, it would be desirable in performance to divide the line differently, preferably at the point indicated by the comma. A similar problem occurs in the T at m. 20 with the word *contre* of the same strophe. There the adjustment will be more difficult but should be accomplished by dividing the line after *fierté*.

The key signature of two flats given for this chanson has already been seen in No. 13, *Non pas que je veuille penser*, and the mode is again simply Dorian twice transposed. However, in this instance the extreme use of accidentals is probably text inspired, an early example of the connection that began to be made in the thinking of the late fifteenth century between the mutable nature of Lady Fortune and the mutations of mode that could be accomplished within a given range or scale by the simple expedient of introducing accidentals. Although an a-flat occasionally becomes desirable in the melodic figures and vertical combinations employed, there seems to be no intention on Vincenet's part to generate from the written accidentals, through the application of the common rules relating to their use, others even further removed, as Josquin is thought to have done in his *Fortuna desperata*.[2] To the contrary, every flat needed is apparently carefully specified in at least some of the sources.

<blockquote>
Fortune, par ta cruaulté,
Pour dueil ou pour adversité
Ne pour douleur que tu m'avance,
Je ne perdray ma pacïence
Et ne penseray lasceté.   5

Plus tu as contre moy heurté,
Moins suis doubteux, plus ay seurté,
Car j'ay le baston d'esperance,   8
  Fortune, par ta cruauté,
</blockquote>

---

2. See Edward E. Lowinsky, "The Goddess Fortuna in Music," *MQ* 29 (1943): 45 ff.

Pour dueil ou pour adversité
Ne pour douleur que tu m'avance.

J'ay bien, malgré ta maleurté,
J'ay ris de ta diversité,
J'ay plaisir de ton actavance,
J'ay fierté contre ta puissance,
Car tout me vient de loyaulté.   13
    Fortune, par ta cruaulté,
    Pour dueil ou pour adversité,
    Ne pour douleur que tu m'avance,
    Je ne perdray ma paciënce
    Et ne penseray lasceté.

Fortune, by reason of thy cruelty,
Whatever grief, adversity
Or pain thou mayst offer me,
I will not lose my patience
Nor think of cowardly retreat.

The more the blows with which thou smitest me,
The less my fear, the greater my security,
For I have the Staff of Hope,
    Fortune, despite thy cruelty,
    Whatever grief, adversity
    Or pain thou mayst offer me.

I am well, despite thy malice,
I laugh at thy caprice,
I take pleasure in thy persistence,
I oppose pride to thy power,
For everything comes to me from loyalty.
    Fortune, by reason of thy cruelty,
    Whatever grief, adversity
    Or pain thou mayst offer me,
    I will not lose my patience
    Nor think of cowardly retreat.

VARIANTS

The texted sources are Flo, Pix, and Cord. Lines 6–13, lacking in Flo, Pix, and Mell, are taken from Cord.

2 ne pour—*Flo Pix.* 3 m'avanches—*Cord.* 5 lascheté—*Cord.*

VERSIFICATION

Rondeau cinquain in octosyllables, *aabba.*

TEXTUAL NOTES

Line 1. **par** 'by reason of'.

Line 2. **adversité** [aversite].

Line 3. **ne** 'or, nor'. Mell, Flo, Pix: **tu m'avance** without -*s*, an encumbrance to the rhyme.

Line 5. **lasceté** 'cowardly desertion,' in Picard [la:kəte], Francian [la:šəte].

Line 7. **doubteux** [dutö] 'fearful'; **ay seurté** [sürte] or [sörte] according to dialect 'feel safe, am safe'.

Line 1'. **par** 'through, during' hence 'in spite of'.

Lines 8, 1'–3'. This is one of the few poems in this collection in which the return of the refrain, both long and short, may most plausibly be read as not keyed in semantically and syntactically with the strophes that precede them. The first three lines do not form a sentence, and yet are not easily connected to the preceding short strophe. The form, then, seems to be purely musical. However, with a little forcing, l. 8 taken with ll. 1'–3' can be interpreted as we propose in our translation.

Line 9. **J'ay bien** 'I am well'; **maleurté** [malürte] or [malörte] 'malice'.

Line 10. **J'ay ris de** 'I laugh at'; **diversité** 'fickleness'.

Line 11. **actavance** 'persistence'; Note that *ton* is used, just as in modern French, before a feminine noun beginning with a vowel—Old French usage required *t'*. Cf. No. 7, l. 3 *m'amour.* The option was metrically convenient for Middle French poets. The pronunciation could have been with [akta-] or [ata-]; the former because this neologism may bear the phonetic mark of Latin influence, the latter because such consonant clusters were still foreign to the speech patterns of fifteenth-century French.

Lines 1″–5″. The long refrain is independent of the preceding strophe.

19. O Virgo, miserere mei, ff. 24ᵛ–25ʳ, Jo. Tinctoris
Dedication: Beatissime virgini domine Beatrici de
Aragonia

COMMENTS

This devotional motet is evidently unique to the present MS. It may have been intended as an introductory dedication for the entire collection addressed by Johannes Tinctoris, who may have compiled it, to Beatrice of Aragon, the patron for whom it appears to have been intended.[1]

In his article on Tinctoris[2] Heinrich Hüschen indicates that both this composition and No. 57 of the present edition are included in Sev 5.I.43. This information is incorrect; the folios designated contain in either case secular works by Tinctoris: *Helas le bon tempo* (ff. 44ᵛ–45ʳ) and *Votre regart si tresfort* (ff. 85ᵛ–86ʳ).

O Virgo, miserere mei,
Miserere meorum,
Effice me meritis
Tempus in omne tuum.

To the Most Blessed Virgin, Lady Beatrice of Aragon
John Tinctoris
O Virgin, have pity on me,
Have pity on my people;
Make me through [my] merits
Thine, for all time.

A courtly expression of fealty to a highborn lady, couched in religious language. If it were not for *meorum*, it might well be considered a love poem. The use of a love song for devotion either to the Holy Virgin or to a mortal lady is illustrated by pièce XXIII of Molinet, which has

---

1. See Introduction, Tinctoris and the Compilation of the Chansonnier, vol. 1, p. 17.
2. *MGG* 13, col. 421.

this title, in one manuscript: *Dictier qui se poeult adreschier soit a la viergé Marie ou pour un amant a sa dame.*[3]

For the light which this work sheds on the history of the Mellon Chansonnier, and for details about Lady Beatrice and Tinctoris, see vol. 1, pp. 19–20.

20. L'aultre d'antan, ff. 25ᵛ–26ʳ, Jo. Okeghem

CONCORDANT SOURCES

Bol Q 16, ff. 95ᵛ–96ʳ (La trentana)
Dij 517, ff. xviiᵛ–xviiiʳ
Pix, ff. 32ᵛ–35ʳ
Cord, ff. 24ᵛ–25ʳ
RomC 2856, ff. 52ᵛ–53ʳ, Okeghem

COLLATION

Bol Q 16 has the same mensuration sign as Mell; in RomC 2856 it is ₵ 3, whereas Cord and Pix give O3 and Dij 517 C3. At m. 11 of the C, Dij 517 and Bol Q 16 give g as a ternary breve, filling out the measure and continuing to sound against d and f in the other two voices. At m. 36(1) of the T, Dij 517 gives a-Sb (probably a scribal slip) instead of b as in the other sources. However, the only significant variants are those of Bol Q 16 and RomC 2856. After the first eight measures both have an essentially different CT until the end of the composition. In addition RomC 2856 has the following divergent reading in the T at mm. 33(1)–35(2): c-Br, d-Sb, c-blackened Sb, a-blackened Sb, G-blackened Br.

COMMENTS

For this work there are clearly two separate traditions of transmission distinguished by the divergent CT parts. Mell seems most nearly related to Dij 517, with which it shares details of coloration and ligature placement, and to Cord, which has the text partially written for the T as it is in Mell. Cord and Pix are linked by a common mensuration, and Bol Q 16, although it has the same CT as RomC 2856, follows very closely the reading of the other three MSS in C and T.

---

3. Noël Dupire, ed., *Les Faicts et Dictz de Jean Molinet* (Paris: Société des Anciens Textes Français, 1937), 2:531.

If the imitative play between C and T is maintained with respect to the declamation, in order to avoid breaking the word *gaiges* over the rest of m. 20 in the T, it will be necessary in singing the short strophe to divide the D of m. 19 and to sing the final syllable with the third beat. Similarly, at mm. 15–16 there are not enough notes in the T to accommodate all the syllables of the verse without dividing one of the blackened BBr into two parts.

The divergent mensuration signs apparently denote uncertainty on the part of Ockeghem's contemporaries as to the proper interpretation of the indications given by him and, consequently, the tempo he considered appropriate. Even the theorists of the fifteenth century who generally have only praise for the composer comment upon the ambiguity of the mensural signs employed in this piece. Tinctoris, who gives the opening phrase of the work under the mensuration found in Pix and Cord, taxes Ockeghem with an "inexcusable error" for having affixed a sign that could be interpreted either as a triple or as a sesquialteral proportion.[1] He goes on to observe that in his opinion the composer used the sign to indicate that the chanson should be sung rapidly, in the manner of a sesquialteral proportion: "ut carmen suum concite instar sesquialtere cantaretur." For such an acceleration of the mensuration he recommends, instead of an "improper" application of a proportional indication, the stroke of diminution as it is found in the reading of Mell.[2] Consequently, it is most tempting to see the mensural sign that figures in the present chansonnier as an emendation made by Tinctoris himself. When Gafforius cited the same composition somewhat later in his discussion of proportions,[3] it was with the mensuration seen here, suggesting that he may have acquired it while in Naples in the version "improved" by Tinctoris. But his brief comments on the mensuration come in the section on duple proportion with the resultant implication that the Sb should move twice as quickly as in the integral

1. *Proportionales musices*, capitulum iii, "Divisio proportionum" (see Charles Coussemaker, *Scriptorum de musica*, 4:156).

2. Tinctoris's criticism is based on the assumption that the only real proportion in *L'aultre d'antan* is equal because all the voices appear under the same sign using essentially the same values, and that it is therefore incorrect to attribute to the sign used by Ockeghem the significance of an unequal proportion such as sesquialtera or tripla. Hence his recommendation that the stroke of diminution be used, rather than an implied proportion, to signal a more rapid tempo.

3. *Practica musicae utriusque cantus*, Liber Quartus, "De genere multiplici & eius speciebus," caput tertium (cf. the English translation by Clement Miller, *Franchinus Gaffurius, Practica Musicae*, pp. 159–60).

mensuration (in either perfect or imperfect tempus). Of course the symbol suggested by Tinctoris would normally have the same meaning.

At the very least the modern performer can assume the acceleration of a sesquialteral proportion with respect to the tactus of the integral mensuration, that is, three quarter notes of *L'aultre d'antan* in the place of two in chansons such as *Bel Acueil* (No. 1) or Ockeghem's *Ma bouce rit* (No. 30). However, it seems more likely, in view of the light irony and the military imagery of the text, that an even more rapid movement was intended. In the editor's opinion it would be entirely appropriate to adopt the same quarter-note motion as that suggested for the compositions written in diminished imperfect tempus. Furthermore, it is conceivable that Ockeghem desired the even more accelerated motion of a triple proportion with respect to the integral mensuration, that is, three quarter-notes in the present work in the place of one in pieces such as those just cited (Nos. 1 and 30).

L'aultre d'antan presents one of three instances in which a composition copied in some sources with its poetic text is identified in another only by an adjectival name such as "La Trentana" serving as a title. The procedure is of special interest here since it was generally reserved for compositions that seem to have been instrumental in conception.[4]

The metaphors of soldiery employed by the poet may have prompted Ockeghem to extract some of his melodic material from the traditional tune of *L'homme armé*, a setting of which is included in the collection (No. 34). Dragan Plamenac has shown that the points of resemblance between the two works are extensive enough to be intentional.[5]

> L'aultre d'antan, l'autrier passa,
> Et en passant me trespercha
> D'ung regard forgié a Melan
> Qui me mist en l'arriere ban,
> Tant malvais brassin me brassa.   5
>
> Par tel fachon me fricassa
> Que de ses gaiges me cassa;
> Mais, par Dieu, elle fist son dan.   8
>   *L'autre d'antan, l'autrier passa,*

4. See also Nos. 41 and 49, and cf. Helen Hewitt and Isabel Pope, eds., *Harmonice musices Odhecaton A*, pp. 74 ff.

5. See *ZfMw* 11 (1929) : 381–83.

Et en passant me trespercha
D'un regard forgié a Melan.

Puis aprés nostre amour cessa,
Car, oncques puis qu'elle dansa
L'autre d'antan, l'autre [d'antan],
Je n'eus ne bon jour ne bon an,
Tant de mal enuy amassa.   13
  L'aultre d'antan, l'autrier passa,
  Et en passant me trespercha
  D'ung regard forgié a Melan
  Qui me mist en l'arriere ban
  Tant malvais brassin me brassa.

The other year, the other day, she passed by
And, in passing, pierced me through
With a glance forged in Milan
That knocked me into the rear ranks
So rude a blow she dealt me.

She destroyed me so thoroughly
That she dismissed me from her troops;
But, by God, she did her damage.
  The other year, the other day, she passed by
  And, in passing, pierced me through
  With a glance forged in Milan.

And then our love ended,
For, ever since she did her dance,
The other year, the other year,
I've had neither good day nor good year,
So much bad luck has piled up.
  The other year, the other day, she passed by
  And, in passing, pierced me through
  With a glance forged in Milan
  That knocked me into the rear ranks
  So rude a blow she dealt me.

Variants

The texted sources are Dij, Pix, Cord; Molinet D113 (L'autre d'antan par la passa), and RomC (L'auter danta) give incipits only. 2 trespassa—*Dij*. 4 m'a mis—*Dij*, ana ainst—*Pix*; (Cord omits line). 5 ane brassa—*Pix*. 6 mespicassa—*Cord*, ane fricassa—*Pix*. 8 (Mell ends here; remainder from Dij.) 10 (Pix ends here.) 11 l'antredantan l'autredantan—*Cord*, . . . d'anta—*Dij*. 13 mal en moy—*Cord*.

Versification

Octosyllabic rondeau cinquain *a a b b a*, but with the first line repeated at the end of the first full refrain (after l. 5), at the end of the long strophe (after l. 13), and again at the end of the long refrain repeated (after l. 5″). In this way the verse is used somewhat like the refrain of a ballade. But since this verse is never integrated well, semantically or syntactically, with the strophe that precedes it, we have preferred to see it as a formal device by which the first line is repeated, textually as well as musically (but with a final cadence), rather than as an organic part of the poem as connected discourse, and have not numbered it or included it in our establishment of the poetical text. Of course we have included it in the text that accompanies the song, for the execution of which it is indispensable.

Textual Notes

Line 1. **d'antan**, a nominalization of an adjectival expression meaning 'of yesteryear', from *antan* 'yesteryear' < Vulgar Latin *ANT'- ANNU, preceded by DE. *D'antan*, used nominally, may well be a nonce- form, based on the analogy of **l'autr'ier**, literally 'the other yesterday' = 'the other day', which follows immediately in l. 1. For the association of 'day' and 'year' in the sense of an imprecise unit of time, see l. 12 **ne bon jour ne bon an**. L. 1 may, then, be translated, 'The other year, the other day . . .'. **passa** 'she passed'. We posit 'she', although *elle* does not occur until l. 10; but obviously the poem is about *her*.

Line 2. **me trespercha** 'pierced me through'. The spelling with *-cha* reflects the Picard pronunciation, which is that of the scribe, not of the poet, since in Picard *-cha* will not rhyme with *passa*, *brassa*, and so forth. Hence we recommend the pronunciation [trepersa] (see Dij variant).

Line 3. **Melan** = Milan; famous for manufacture of swords.

Line 4. **arriere ban** 'final levy of troops'.

Line 5. **malvais** [mawve] ([aw] = *ou* of English *house*); do not pronounce the *l*. **brassin** 'brew' (noun); **brassa** 'brewed, stirred up'.

Line 6. **fachon**, Picard form of *façon*; but since we know (see textual note on l. 2) that the poet did not use the Picard dialect, pronounce [fasõ]. **fricassa** 'utterly destroyed'.

Line 7. 'That she struck me from her payroll'–that is, dismissed me from her retinue.

Line 8. **dan** 'damage'.

Line 9. **aprés** 'afterward'.

Line 11. Dij has *l'autre d'antan l'autre d'anta*, but this does not fit the rhyme scheme.

Line 12. See textual note on l. 1.

21. Le corps s'en va, ff. 26ᵛ–27ʳ, Busnoys

Concordant Sources

    *Roh, f. 154ʳ⁻ᵛ
    Dij 517, ff. cxxᵛ–cxxiʳ
    Niv, ff. livᵛ–lvʳ, Busnois
    Lab, ff. 25ᵛ–26ʳ, Busnoys
    Wolf 287, ff. 45ᵛ–46ʳ
    *Par 1719, ff. 3ʳ, 74ᵛ, 182ʳ
    *Chasse, f. Piiʳ

Collation

Most of the divergences among the musical sources concern unimportant details of melodic ornamentation, but differences in the key signatures and accidentals are also to be noted. Neither Dij 517 nor Niv has a flat as a signature for the T; Lab has a b-flat not only for the second line of the T (mm. 7–17) but for the first two lines of the C as well (up to m. 12), whereas Wolf 287 has the flat signature for the entire C part. Flats explicitly written in Mell are not always given in the other sources: in the T, the flat for b at m. 20 (4) is not found in Dij 517 or Lab; in the CT, the flats for B at mm. 12 (3) and 20 (3) are not given by either Dij 517 or Niv; and at m. 18 (2) no flat is seen in Lab or Wolf 287.

In addition there are a few errors and variants of substance in the notation. In Lab two notes have been omitted from the T at m. 15 (4, 6), and at m. 24 (7) the D-Sb is written as M; in the CT, the C-M at m. 9 (5) was omitted, and the final note, m. 26, is divided between a and D' a twelfth below. In Dij 517 at m. 9 (6) of the CT one reads an irregularly dissonant G'-M instead of the consonant A of the remaining MSS, and at m. 19 (2) the C-M seen here has been replaced with a rest. Finally, in Niv there is no rest in the C at m. 14 but instead d-Sb as the final note of the measure; in the T the E-Sb at m. 12 (1) has been erroneously omitted.

COMMENTS

All the musical sources apparently represent the same scribal tradition, but on the rather shaky basis of key signatures and accidentals alone, Dij 517 and Niv would seem to be closer to each other than to the rest of the group, whereas Mell seems more nearly related to Lab and Wolf 287.

Because of the rests interrupting the first and third phrases, the text placement suggested for the refrain cannot be used for the remaining strophes without breaking words. It is preferable to divide the first line of the short strophe after *poués*, using the final two quarters of m. 3 for *vostre*, and to divide the third line of the long strophe after *sans*, employing each of the three quarters of m. 14 to bear a syllable.

The units of declamation and the notational values used generally again suggest that the diminished mensuration is to be taken as an indication for a proportionately accelerated tempo.

> Le corps s'en va et le [cueur] *vous* demeure,
> Lequel veult *faire* aveuc vous sa demeure
> Pour vous voloir amer tant et si fort
> Qu'incessamment veult mettre son effort
> De vous servir jusqu'a ce que je meure.   5
>
> Qu'il est vostre poués estre *bien* seure
> Et le sera tousjours, je vous asseure,
> Combien qu'attende de mon mal confort.   8
> > *Le corps s'en va et le cueur vous demeure,*
> > *Lequel veult faire aveuc vous sa demeure*
> > *Pour vous voloir amer tant et si fort.*

Il n'est doleur ne deuil qu'a moy n'acqueure
Quant il couvient que ces maulx assaveure
Et m'en aller sans avoir resconfort
En la saison que vous deusse au plus fort
Mon cas compter; et si voy qu'a ceste heure   13
 Le corps s'en va et le cueur vous demeure,
 Lequel veult faire aveuc vous sa demeure
 Pour vous voloir amer tant et si fort
 Qu'incessamment veult mettre son effort
 De vous servir jusqu'a ce que je meure.

My body departs but my heart remains with you;
With you it wants to make its dwelling-place
Because it desires to love you so much and so steadfastly
That unceasingly it bends its will
To serving you until I die.

That it is yours, you may be very sure,
And always will be, I assure you,
However long I may await relief from my pain.
 My body departs but my heart remains with you;
 It wants to make its dwelling-place with you
 Because it desires to love you so much and so steadfastly.

There is no pain or grief that does not come to me
When I must taste of these misfortunes
And leave you without receiving comfort
At the very time when I most need
To plead my case; and so I see that, at this moment,
 My body departs but my heart stays with you;
 It wants to make its dwelling-place with you
 Because it desires to love you so much and so steadfastly
 That unceasingly it bends its will
 To serving you until I die.

VARIANTS

The texted sources are Dij, Lab, Wolf, Roh, Niv, Par 1719 (which

presents the poem three times: A = f. 3r, B = f. 74ᵛ, C = f. 182ʳ),
and Chasse. Paris 24315 has the incipit alone: Le corps s'en va et le
cueur vous demeure.

1 Mell (picture of heart); Mell omits vous (supplied from all other
versions). 2 vult—*ParB*, Lequel fera—*Chasse*; Mell omits faire (supplied from all other versions); avec—*Dij Lab Roh Wolf Niv ParABC*.
3 Par vous—*Roh Wolf*; tant amer—*Roh*; Pour vous aymer tousjours—
Chasse (ParABC). 4 Lab omits Qu'. 5 A vous—*Dij Lab Wolf ParABC
Niv Chasse*; Jusques a ce qu'il meure—*Niv*; amer ains que je meure—
Lab; belle devant qu'il meure—*Roh*, Juc a ce que je meure—*ParAC*.
6 Il est vostre—*Dij Niv*, Et qu'il soit vostre—*Roh*, Qu'il soit le vostre
—*Chasse*; Mell omits bien; Q'il est bien pouez estre bien seure—*ParB*;
pouoir—*Lab*; bien pouez estre seure—*Niv*. 7 Car de cela sur ma foy
vous asseure—*Lab Roh Wolf ParABC (Chasse)* (Dij = Mell). 8 (Dij =
Mell), Non obstant ce que sans avoir confort—*Lab Roh Wolf*, Non
obstant ce sans autre reconfort—*ParAB(C)*, Combien qu'atende de
mon mal ung confort—*Niv* (+1 syll.), Nonobstant que sans aultre
reconfort—*Chasse*.·(Dij = Mell). 9 payne ne deul—*ParA(BC) (Chasse)*.
10 Quant il fault—*Niv*, Quant il quiert—*ParB*; ses maulx—*Dij*, tel
mal—*Lab Roh Wolf*, ce mal—*ParABC*, ses griefs maulx—*Niv*; je
saveure—*Dij ParABC*, j'assaveure—*Lab Niv Roh* (Wolf = Mell);
convient que ce mal je saveure—*Chasse*. 11 Que m'en—*Lab Wolf*,
De m'en—*Roh ParBC Chasse* (ParA Et/De? Hard to read); sans
quelque reconfort—*Roh*, sans autre confort—*ParB* (ParC omits: corner
torn out of page). (Mell ends here, last two lines supplied from Lab.)
12 A l'eure que deusse venir au fort—*Dij*, A l'eure que deusse vivre
acort—*Niv*. 13 mon mal—*Dij Wolf*; que je voy—*Dij*, et se voy—*ParA*
(ruled out with one line and not replaced), compter maintenant a
ceste heure—*ParB Chasse*; Mon cas co . . .—*ParC* (rest of line missing
at torn-out page corner); Vous voyez en quel point suis a toute heure
—*Niv*.

VERSIFICATION

Decasyllabic rondeau cinquain *a a b b a* with epic caesura at ll. 1
(with *faire* supplied from other MSS) and 2; but l. 6 has lyric caesura
in Mell, Dij, Niv, epic caesura in Roh, Chasse. In view of the rare
occurrence of lyric and epic caesura in the same poem, the lyric
caesura of l. 6 probably does not go back to the original text.

Textual Notes

Line 2. **aveuc**, older spelling of *avec*, possibly still pronounced [avök]. **Demeure**, a noun, rhymes legitimately with the verb **demeure** of l. 1.

Line 5. Both Lab and Roh have 'before I die', as if the lover were begging for the privilege of serving the lady, if only once, before he dies; in the other versions, he promises to serve until he dies. The variant readings of ParAC are interesting as corroboration of the general loss of *s* before a consonant, even in words in which the *s* is conserved or preserved in modern French.

Line 6–7. Although the Francian pronunciation of *seure* and *asseure* was like that of modF *sûre*, *assure*, with [ü], the rhyme calls for the non-Francian resolution of OF [əü] as [ö] (see p. 100).

Line 8. 'However long I may have to wait for comfort of my pain'. Lab Roh Wolf: 'In spite of the fact that, without having comfort, . . .' This line is hard to integrate, semantically or syntactically, with either the preceding or following line. Perhaps the reading of all three versions found in Par 1719 (our ParABC) represents better the original form of this version of the line: 'In spite of this, without any other relief'.

Line 9. **acqueure**, third person singular present subjunctive of *acourir* 'happen (to some one)'.

Line 10. **il couvient** = *il faut*; here it is followed by two constructions: subjunctive in l. 10, infinitive in l. 11.

Line 13. **et si voy qu'a ceste heure** leads directly into the refrain; the short refrain was not so connected with the preceding short strophe. **et si** 'and (so)'.

22. Se mon service vous plaisoit, ff. 27ᵛ–28ʳ

Concordant Sources

Glog, No. 270 (capital *L* only text given)
Flo 229, ff. 287ᵛ–288ʳ
Pix, ff. 150ᵛ–151ʳ
Sev 5.I.43, ff. 87ᵛ–88ʳ

Collation

In Pix the entire composition is written a fourth lower with only b-flat in the key signature. Aside from minor differences of melodic ornamentation (e.g., the lower third figures in the final cadential formula only in Mell), there are also several relatively significant differences of pitch in that MS, particularly in the CT. The reading of Flo 229 has a discordant d-M at m. 3 (4) of the C instead of the consonant c-M of the other sources, but the dissonance is both introduced and resolved in a perfectly acceptable manner. At the beginning of m. 14 of the T is written e-flat M, f-Sb, but there is no rest as in the remaining MSS. All other discrepancies are confined to the CT: at m. 6 (3), Sev 5.I.43 has D-M (probably an error) instead of C-M; at m. 10 (2), E-flat M is found in Flo 229, Pix, and Sev 5.I.43 instead of the D-M of Glog and Mell; at m. 18 (5), instead of C-M, Glog has D-M, which clashes sharply with both C and T; at m. 18 (6), both Glog and Sev 5.I.43 have G-M in place of Mell's F-M (the two pitches work equally well contrapuntally); and at m. 20 (1), all sources except Mell give D-M instead of E-M. Considering the version of Pix as if it were transposed to the pitch level of the other sources, the following variants in the CT are noteworthy: at m. 11 (1), F-Sb (probably an error) instead of G-Sb as elsewhere, and at mm. 18 (4)– 20 (2), E-flat dotted M, D-Sm, F-M, C-M, F-M, E-flat M, D-M, C-Sb, E-flat M, D-Sb, F-M.

COMMENTS

The reading of Pix obviously stands apart from the tradition of transmission reflected in the remaining sources, both by virtue of the pitch level at which it is written and because of the extensive variant beginning at m. 18 (4) of the CT. The version of Mell appears most closely related to that of Glog, which can be linked in turn to that of Sev 5.I.43 by the common reading of m. 18 (6) in the CT. Here once again Flo 229 gives an indication of its later redaction in a tendency toward melodic simplification.

In most cases of conflicting pitches the variant was offered by only one other MS, and the version of the remaining concordances seemed clearly preferable. Conversely, at mm. 10 (2) and 20 (1) of the CT the reading of Mell is alone against the unified evidence of all other MSS. In the former case the original D of Mell clashed sharply with the c of the T, suggesting a scribal error, and an appropriate emendation was made. But in the latter the E-flat of Mell is entirely correct in contrapuntal terms because it effects with the two upper voices a dissonant double suspension that is regularly resolved at least in the C (but only by implication in the T since to do otherwise would produce parallel fifths), and the result is probably more interesting than that produced by the majority of the sources.

A b-flat is introduced into the signature of the C in Mell only in m. 11 (6), but it is present in the other MSS from the beginning of the part and in Mell by implication because of the presence of e-flat. *Se mon service*, with its signature of two flats and a final on C, offers yet another example of a composition in the Dorian mode twice transposed. In this instance the nature of the transposition is made more explicit by the version of Pix written at the fourth below with a final on G and a single flat as a signature.

> Se mon service vous plaisoit,
> Vous, de serviteur despourveue,
> Vous estes celle soubz la nue
> A qui mon cuer plus se tendroit. 4
>
> Et aussy tant qu'il vous plairoit
> Ja tendroye ma retenue, 6
>   Se mon service *vous plaisoit,*
>   *Vous, de serviteur despourveue.*
>
> If my service should please you,
> You, who have no suitor,
> You are the one under heaven
> To whom my heart would soonest turn.
>
> And so, for as long as it would please you,
> I would promptly offer my fealty,
>   If my service should please you,
>   You who have no suitor.

VARIANTS

1 (Flo Pix omit plaisoit.) (Flo Pix end here.) 2 (Sev omits whole line.) 4 corps—*Sev*; si—*Sev*. (Sev ends here.)

VERSIFICATION

Octosyllabic rondeau quatrain, *abba*. All versions are incomplete, but only Mell has enough—the refrain, the short strophe, and the catchword indicating the onset of the short refrain—to assure us that this is a rondeau. For performance, we can only recommend singing the long refrain right after the short strophe.

TEXTUAL NOTES

Line 1. **Se** 'if'.

Line 2. **despourveue** [depurvüɔ] 'deprived'.

Line 3. **la nue** 'the sky'. This is hard to read in Mell, but it is supported by Sev. It makes sense, and it rhymes with l. 2.

Line 1'. The short refrain links neatly with the preceding short strophe, although the latter, loosely constructed, does not need the short refrain to complete the sense. This creates a very pleasant relationship between verse and music, in that the refrain represents simultaneously a completion and a new beginning.

23. Mercy, mon dueil, ff. 28ᵛ–29ʳ, Joye

CONCORDANT SOURCE

Lab, ff. 58ᵛ–59ʳ

COLLATION

The only difference in the notation of pitches is in the T, m. 8 (4), where Lab gives a instead of the b of Mell, but the latter reading is definitely preferable. Otherwise there are only minor discrepancies in the use of accidentals. Lab has no b-flat signature for the C and does not specify the sharp at m. 16 (2) (which is undoubtedly valid for the two following notes as well). In the CT also Lab fails to give a written flat at m. 2 (2) (where it is really superfluous) but by contrast provides them where Mell does not at m. 24 (1) of the T and m. 22 (1) of the CT.

COMMENTS

The two MSS unquestionably represent the same tradition of transmission, there being no substantial variants between them and many points of similarity in the notational detail.

Because the treatment of the text is essentially syllabic, the placement of the text presents exceptionally few problems, and the units of declamation, together with the rhythmic activity of the composition generally, provide one of the most convincing examples of a work in which the diminished mensuration can be convincingly interpreted only as a proportional acceleration of the tactus.

The signs of congruence marking the division of the piece into two sections were not present in either source and had to be supplied by the editor.

Mercy, mon dueil, je te supplie,
Mon dueil plain de melancolie,
Mercy cent mille foys te clame,
Et vieng mettre fin a mon ame,
Qui mort requiert, et si m'oublie.   5

Mon dueil, quant sera acomplie
Ma dure fortune enfeblie,
La plus cuysant de ce royame?   8
　　Mercy, *mon dueil, je te supplie,*
　　Mon dueil plain de melancolie,
　　Mercy cent mille foys te clame.

Plus va avant, plus multiplie
Mon mal, que point je ne publie
De peur de moy chëoir en blasme
Dont, se ce n'est en Nostre Damme,
Toute esperance *m*'est faillie.   13
　　Mercy, mon dueil, je te supplie,
　　Mon dueil plain de melancolie,
　　Mercy cent mille foys te clame,
　　Et vieng mettre fin a mon ame,
　　Qui mort requiert, et si m'oublie.

Have mercy, my grief, I beg of thee,
O grief, full of melancholy,
Have mercy, a hundred thousand times I entreat thee,
And come put an end to my soul,
That longs for death, and then forget me.

O my grief, when will be accomplished
My harsh, enfeebled destiny,
The most tormenting of this realm?

Have mercy, my grief, I beg of thee,
O grief, full of melancholy,
Have mercy, a hundred thousand times I entreat thee.

The longer it endures, the greater is
My woe, which I make not known
Lest I fall into blame,
Wherefore, unless it be in Our Lady,
All hope has failed me.
    Have mercy, my grief, I beg of thee,
    O grief, full of melancholy,
    Have mercy, a hundred thousand times I entreat thee,
    And come put an end to my soul,
    That longs for death, and then forget me.

VARIANTS

All the variants noted below are from Lab.
5 requiers. 7 enfellie. 9 voy avant. 11 paour; non cheoir. 12 se seul n'est et. 13 Mell omits m'.

VERSIFICATION

Octosyllabic rondeau cinquain, *aabba*.

TEXTUAL NOTES

Line 1. **Mercy** 'Have pity'; **mon dueil** is in direct address throughout the poem and is the antecedent of **te** and the subject of imperative verbs.

Line 4. **vieng** 'come' (imperative).

Line 5. **et si m'oublie** 'and then forget me'. Lab *requiers*, first person singular, is less acceptable than Mell **requiert**, whose subject, **qui**, has **mon ame** as antecedent.

Lines 6–8. **Ma dure fortune** is the subject.

Line 8. **cuysant** 'tormenting'; it is a feminine adjective, coming from a Latin present participle, hence of the third declension (see p. 106). **Royame** coexists with *royaume;* its original form is *reame* (*reamme, reemme*) (cf. No. 17, l. 13).

Lines 9–10. **Mon mal** is subject of **multiplie**; also of **va** in the Mell version. In Lab, *voy* 'I go', the two verbs have different subjects, although it would not be indefensible to construe *mon mal* as object of *multiplie* (first person singular).

Line 11. **chëoir** in two syllables [šəwer]; an archaism, since the first vowel had by the fifteenth century generally been absorbed when immediately followed by a vowel. In normal speech of the epoch this would have been pronounced [šwer] for more than a century. The construction is not of a reflexive verb **se cheoir*, but a Latinizing infinitive construction, with **moy** representing the accusative subject.

Line 13. Mell lacks **m'**. It could be read as *esperancë est*, but it is highly unlikely that such a hiatus would be original in a poem of such late origin. We supply **m'** from Lab.

24. N'aray je jamais mieulx que j'ay? ff. 29ᵛ–30ʳ, Morton

CONCORDANT SOURCES

BerK 78 C 28, ff. 17ᵛ–18ʳ
Cop 291⁸, ff. 2ᵛ–3ʳ
Dij 517, ff. cxiiiᵛ–cxivʳ
Esc IV.a.24, ff. 130ᵛ–131ʳ
Flo 176, ff. 53ᵛ–54ʳ, Mortom
FloR 2356, ff. 63ᵛ–64ʳ
Niv, ff. 1ᵛ–2ʳ
Pix, ff. 109ᵛ–110ʳ
Par 4379, ff. 14ᵛ–15ʳ, Morton
Cord, ff. 32ᵛ–33ʳ (à 4)
Lab, ff. 57ᵛ–58ʳ
Wolf 287, ff. 6ᵛ–7ʳ
*Arn, f. lxiiᵛ
*Jar, f. 72ʳ

COLLATION

In view of the large number of concordances for this work, it seemed preferable to ignore isolated variants; none is either extensive or particularly significant. All those mentioned here are shared by two or more sources and thus capable of giving some indication of the affiliations among scribal traditions.

Of all the collections in which Morton's chanson was included, only Cord has the CT *si placet* found in Mell; elsewhere the piece is invariably written à 3. In the C at m. 8 (4), instead of a'-Sb as in Mell, one finds a'-dotted M, f-Sm in BerK 78 C 28, Flo 176, FloR 2356, Niv, Lab, and Wolf 287. In the T, m. 13 (5), instead of d-M as in Mell, e-M (a perfectly possible alternative) is given by BerK 78 C 28 and Flo 176; and at m. 22 (2, 3), instead of a-M, f-M as in Mell, f-M, d-Sb (forming parallel octaves with the CT of Mell) is written in Cop 291[8], Dij 517, and Flo 176. In the CT, m. 1 (2), instead of c-M as in Mell, b-M is found in Cop 291[8], Dij 517, Par 4379, Lab, and Wolf 287; at m. 2 (1), instead of D-Sb as in Mell, one finds b-Sb in Lab and Wolf 287; at m. 3 (2), instead of F-dotted Sb as in Mell, F-dotted M, E-Sm, F-Sm, G-Sm is offered by Dij 517 and Par 4379.

At mm. 16–17 of the CT the range of deviation is extremely wide: at m. 16 (2), Cord has F-Sb, D-M, instead of the F-dotted Sb of the other sources; at m. 16 (3), Dij 517 gives D-M instead of c-M; at 16 (4 ff.), one finds F-Sm, E-Sm, D-M, E-M in Lab and Wolf 287 (resulting in parallel octaves with the T, as it is written in Mell); the same pattern occurs up to the D-M of m. 17 (1), but it is followed by C-dotted Sb (as in Mell) in Berk 78 C 28, Flo 176, and FloR 2356, and F-Sb, E-M, C-Sb (somewhat obscured) in Cord; at m. 20 (2–4), b-M, d-M in Cop 291[8] and Dij 517; at 20 (3), d-M in BerK 78 C 28, Flo 176, and Pix (and, of course, in Cop 291[8] and Dij 517); and at m. 22 (2), instead of F-M as in Mell, D in Cop 291[8], Dij 517, and Par 4379.

The written flat for b at m. 11 (4) of the C is not given by Cop 291[8], Dij 517, Esc IV.a.24, FloR 2356, or Par 4379. BerK 78 C 28 has a b-flat signature for the entire CT, Esc IV.a.24 for the T and the first line of the CT (mm. 1–8), and Flo 176 also for the T. The result is a comparatively insignificant change because there are so few notes on that pitch in either voice. Pix has a written flat in the T for the e at m. 11 (2) and for the b at m. 12 (1).

COMMENTS

Despite some confusing cross references, it seems that the readings for Morton's rondeau fall into two main traditions of transmission with some discernible interrelationships of affinity within each. On the one hand are the primarily northern sources (Cop 291[8], Dij 517, Lab, and Wolf 287) with which must be grouped, surprisingly, the version of this piece in Par 4379. In fact the latter also shows special affinities with Cop 291[8] and Dij 517. A second subgroup is formed by the readings of Lab and Wolf 287, which share several variants not found elsewhere.

On the other hand are the mainly peninsular MSS. The readings to which that of Mell is most closely related are given by Cord, Esc IV.a.24, and Pix in that order, with Niv—unexpectedly—and the subgroup formed by Flo 176, BerK 78 C 28, and FloR 2356 but a step away. The anomalous resemblance of Par 4379 to a group of northern MSS for this composition is reversed for Niv, which contains a reading more like that of the Italian sources. The situation is perhaps to be at least partially explained in the latter instance by the fact that *N'aray je jamais mieulx* is obviously a later addition to the Nivelle de la Chaussée Chansonnier. It appears there in a different hand at the beginning of the collection on pages that were presumably left blank when the MS was originally copied since they were not illuminated like those of the rest of the collection.

In the majority of the MSS there is no rest after the final note of the section in m. 14, but in Cord one is present in all four parts. The inconsistency of Mell in this respect is of no great consequence, but it did seem preferable to adopt the uniformity seen in the other sources from the one most nearly related to it. Of the various alternatives for mm. 16–17 of the CT, the one offered by the present collection is apparently an error midway between the reading of Cord on the one hand and that of the group BerK 78 C 28, Flo 179, and FloR 2356 on the other. It was judged unacceptable as it stands because of the sharp dissonance the written e would make with the d of the T and the F of the CT *si placet*. Had the reading of Cord not been partially conjectural because of an ink smudge on the page, it would have been adopted as an emendation, but because that of the other three MSS was equally correct and not appreciably different, it was followed in the transcription. It may not be entirely without import that Nos. 24 and 25 of this collection also follow each other in that same order in Flo 176.

> N'aray je jamais mieulx que j'ay?
> Suy je la ou je demeuré,
> M'amour et toutte ma plaisance?
> N'arés vous jamais cognoissance
> Que je suy vostre et demouray? 5

Ne faictes sur moy plus d'assay,
Car vous cognoissiés bien de vray
Que je suy mené a [oultrance].   8
    N'aray je jamais mieulx que j'ay?
    Suy je la ou je demeuré,
    M'amour et toutte ma plaisance?

Je me rens et *si* me rendray;
Aultre deffense n'y mettray,
Car vous avés trop de puissance
Et pouoir de prendre vengance—
Mais dites moy, si le sçauray:
    N'aray je jamais mieulx que j'ay?
    Suy je la ou je demeuré,
    M'amour et toutte ma plaisance?
    N'arés vous jamais cognoissance
    Que je suy vostre et demouray?

Will I never have better than I have?
Am I where I've always been,
O my love and all my delight?
Will you never realize
That I am yours and will so remain?

Do not test me any longer,
For you know full truly
That I am tried to my utmost.
    Will I never have better than I have?
    Am I where I've always been,
    O my love and all my delight?

I surrender now and will surrender;
I'll offer no other defense,
For you have too much strength
And power to take vengeance—
But tell me, and then I'll know:
    Will I never have better than I have?
    Am I where I've always been,

> O my love and all my delight?
> Will you never realize
> That I am yours and will so remain?

Variants

The texted sources are Dij, Esc, Niv, Pix, Par 4379, Cord, Lab, Wolf, Jar; the first line is cited in Molinet D204.

2 demourray—*Dij Jar Niv*. 4 souvenance—*Lab Wolf*. 5 tout vostre et seray—*Dij Pix*; Lab Pix omit je (−1 syll.); et le seray—*Cord Jar Lab Niv*; demoray—*Esc Wolf*. 6 sus—*Cord*; de moi—*Dij*; plus sur moy d'aissay—*Wolf*. 7 -sses, -ssez—*Cord Dij Niv*; sçavez bien que je say—*Wolf*. 8 oubliance—*Mell* (+1 syll.); naure—*Dij Lab*, naurez—*Pix*, esmeu—*Niv*; Durement nauray a oultrance—*Wolf*. 9 et si—*Dij Lab* (Cord = Mell, hence −1 syll.); renderay—*Pix* (lacking *si*, Pix is orthometric); Vostre suis a vous me tendray—*Niv*. 11 trop grant puissance—*Lab*. (Mell ends here; ll. 12–13 supplied from Cord.) 12 Et pour de—*Dij*, et pooir de—*Pix*, et si pouez—*Lab*. 13 que je seray—*Dij*, que je feray—*Lab Niv*. (The short and long strophes of Jar are entirely different from those of the other sources and so contribute neither to the establishment nor to the understanding of the text.)

Versification

Octosyllabic rondeau cinquain, *a a b b a*.

Textual Notes

Line 2. **demeuré** = *demeurai*, preterite, which in Old French can be used as the present perfect.

Line 4. **cognoissance** [konwesa^{n}sə].

Line 5. **demouray** = *demeurerai*, first person singular future; usually with *-rr-* in Old French, as in Dij, Jar, and Niv.

Line 8. It seems likely that the original poem had *navré a oultrance* 'wounded to an extreme degree (mortally)'; that *navré* was copied (miscopied? emended?) as *mené*, as in Cord and Mell; and that *oultrance* was either misread or "emended" as *oubliance* (3 syllables + [ə]), as in Mell, with these steps in meaning: 'led to extremes (in speech and behavior)', 'led to forgetfulness', i.e., to being forgotten, to oblivion.

Line 12. **vengance** with "soft g" as in modern French: [va^{n}ža^{n}sə].
Line 13. **si** 'and, as a result, then'.

25. L'omme banny, ff. 30^v–31^r, Barbingant

CONCORDANT SOURCES

*Roh, f. 118^v
Dij 517, ff. xciv^v–xcv^r
Flo 176, ff. 54^v–55^r, Fede
Niv, ff. xxiv^v–xxv^r
*Par 1719, f. 87^v
Pix, ff. 29^v–30^r
Cord, ff. 31^v–32^r
Pav 362, ff. 21^v–22^r
Lab, ff. 66^v–67^r
*Arn, f. lvi
*Jar, f. 62^v.

COLLATION

The use of signed accidentals without clefs was evidently unusual enough to have caused the various scribes some difficulty, and the sources are neither uniform nor entirely correct in the signatures given. Niv and Cord have a g-clef on the second line for the C (the former with no flats in the signature, the latter with e-flat alone) and a c-clef on the third line for T and CT with only b-flat as the signature. Since the notes remain in the same position on the staff as in the other sources, the result is to transpose the composition up a fifth to a final on c. Pav 362 also has a g-clef for the C with no signed flats, like Niv, but T and CT are written as in Mell with no clef other than the two flats placed in the second and fourth spaces. Dij 517, Flo 176, Pix, and Lab all have b-flat and e-flat as signatures—without a clef—in all three parts, but in the C of Dij 517 they are placed as in the T and CT, implying erroneously the same pitch equivalences. In the C of Flo 176 b-flat and e-flat are located in the first and third spaces (and on the top line), that is, applying to b and f instead of b and e.

There are no significant variants for the C. In the T at m. 8(1), Pix has F-M, G-M (hardly an improvement) instead of F-Sb as in Mell; at m. 8(2, 3), Niv and Cord give E-M, D-M instead of the inverted order found elsewhere; and at m. 21(1), Cord and Pav

362 have F-Sb (instead of F-M) and no rest. In the CT at m. 4 (4, 5)
Flo 176 and Pix have E-flat M, D-M, a distinctly poorer reading than
the D, E-flat of the other sources; in mm. 9 and 10, all MSS except
Mell have the following: F-Sb, G-dotted M, F-Sm, D-dotted M,
E-Sm, F-Br, F-Sb; at m. 13 (2), instead of D-Sb as in Mell, c-Sb is
found in Flo 176, Niv, Pix, and Cord; and in m. 24, there is a rest-Sb
(instead of rest-M) and no dot for the following B-Sb in Dij 517,
Niv, Cord, and Pav 362.

The written flat for a in the CT at m. 8 (1) also appears in Dij 517,
Flo 176, and Pix; the one at m. 25 (3) is given only by Flo 176 in
addition to Mell. The reading of Flo 176 is characterized by an even
greater number of dotted figures than are already found in the work
in other sources, for example at mm. 14 (1, 2), 19 (1, 2), and 21 (5, 6)
in the C, mm. 18 (1, 2) and 21 (4) in the T, and so on.

COMMENTS

The simplified reading given by Mell for mm. 9–10 of the CT is a
fairly typical example of the independence not infrequently shown by
the present collection with respect to the concordant sources, but it
must be allowed in this instance that the version of the other MSS
has greater rhythmic and contrapuntal interest. That divergence
aside, Mell appears most closely related to Lab with respect to this
particular work and seems to follow the tradition of transmission also
represented by Dij 517, Flo 176, and Pix. Within this group Flo 176
and Pix are further linked by small variants not shared with other
MSS. A somewhat different if related tradition is reflected in the
similar readings of Niv and Cord. Pav 362 seems to stand between
the two traditions, following the latter two sources in the C but showing
affinities with the former group in T and CT.

Although the reading of Mell at m. 8 (2, 3) of the T is found in the
majority of the MSS, it is apparently an error. The passage in which
the two notes occur is in all respects analogous to that of m. 22, which
is obviously a precadential formula based on an embellished fauxbourdon. The version given by Mell at m. 8 not only disturbs the
essentially parallel motion of that type of writing, as exemplified at
m. 22, but also produces the unacceptable intervals of a fourth and
second between the two lower voices. As a result it was thought
justifiable to emend the transcription in accordance with the more
correct alternate reading.

The attribution of this chanson to Barbingant in the present MS coincides with that given by Tinctoris in his treatise, *De imperfectionis notarum*,[1] but since the theorist may have been responsible for the compilation of the chansonnier, the two ascriptions may stem from the same source. Tinctoris is probably more reliable than Flo 176, where the name Fede appears to have been entered—uncharacteristically on the recto side of the opening—by a later hand. Too little is known about the works of these two composers to permit an evaluation of the attributions from a stylistic point of view, but some rather archaic characteristics are to be observed in this composition, especially the passages in fauxbourdon and the use (hardly to be avoided in that context) of double leading-tone cadences.

It is interesting that the notational fault imputed to the composer of this chanson by Tinctoris in the passage cited—the partial imperfection of a dotted L (with which the T begins in some sources) by the following Sb—has been eliminated from Mell by the substitution of a separate Br in place of the dot. Together with the correspondence of attributions between the chansonnier and the treatise, this detail offers yet another shred of evidence that Tinctoris had a hand in the preparation of the present repertory.

If the significance of the key signatures has been correctly interpreted as to the pitch levels implied, the composition would appear to offer an example of a decidedly unusual transposition, that of the mixolydian mode twice removed to a final on F. As was observed in Comments for the previous chanson, Nos. 24 and 25 of the present collection occur together in the same order in Flo 176.

> L'omme banny de sa plaisance,
> Vuidié de joye et de lÿesse,
> Comblé de dueil et de tristesse
> *Suis*, sans nul espoir d'alegance.   4
>
> Aprés rigeur ma mort avance,
> Car desespoir jamais ne lesse   6
> > L'omme banny *de sa plaisance*,
> > *Vuidié de joye et de lÿesse.*

---

1. Liber I, "Duodecime regula," in Coussemaker, *Scriptorum*, 4:60.

Fortune m'a sans [ordonnance]
Mis en exil par grant rudesse;
Tousjours m'a fait du mal sans cesse.
Pourtant m'appelle par outrance   10
L'omme banny *de sa plaisance,*
  Vuidié de joye et de lÿesse,
  Comblé de dueil et de tristesse;
  Suis sans nul espoir d'alegance.

The man banished from his pleasure,
Emptied of joy and delight,
Laden with grief and sadness,
Am I, with no hope of relief.

On the heels of rigor my death advances
For despair never leaves
  The man banished from his pleasure,
  Emptied of joy and delight.

Fortune has without warrant
Exiled me with great rudeness;
She has always done me ill unceasingly.
Therefore she calls me, in her excess,
  The man banished from his pleasure,
  Emptied of joy and delight,
  Laden with grief and sadness.
  I am with no hope of relief.

VARIANTS

The texted sources are Cord, Dij, Par 1719, Lab, Jar, Roh.
2 Widie—*Mell*, Vide—*Dij*, Vuide—*Lab Jar Roh*, Voide—*Par*. 3 et
de destresse—*Par*. 4 Mell Dij omit Suis (− 1 syll.). 5 A seroie rigueur—
Par (+ 2 sylls.); Rigueur aprés—*Roh*; m'amour t'avance—*Cord*. 6 Et
desespoir point ne me lesse—*Par*. 7 alegance—*Mell*. 8 par sa rudesse—
Roh. 9 me fait des maulx—*Cord Par*, me font des maulx—*Lab*, des
maulx me fait—*Dij Jar*. 10 Partout—*Cord*, Pour tout—*Lab*;
m'appellon—*Dij*; m'apelle a toute oultrance—*Roh*; Pour ce me juge
on a oultrance—*Jar*.

VERSIFICATION

Octosyllabic rondeau quatrain, *abba*.

TEXTUAL NOTES

Line 2. **Vuidié** 'emptied'. Mell alone uses an unequivocally participial form. The variant forms could point to an adjective, *vuide*, as well as to the participle *vuidé*. The spelling we have adopted here takes *W* as a ligature of *Uu* or *Vu*. It corresponds to the Old French spelling and pronunciation [vẅidye] of this word, somewhat archaic for the epoch.

Line 4. **Suis** is the only finite verb of the sentence which constitutes the first strophe; hence the punctuation. **alegance** 'relief'; g = [ž] (soft).

Line 5. **Aprés** 'after, as a result of'. **Rigeur** g = [g] (hard).

Line 6. **lesse** has as direct object the short refrain, ll. 1′–2′. Par *point ne me lesse* puts the short refrain in the autonomous category, whereas the other versions treat it as integrated with the preceding short strophe (ll. 5–6). Possibly the redactor of the Par version failed to perceive the integration and felt it necessary to supply a direct object for *lesse*.

Line 7. Mell *alegance* is in error; it rhymes with itself in l. 4, and all the other MSS testify against it.

Line 9. The majority reading of this line is *Tousjours me fait des maulx (des maulx me fait) sans cesse*, which is probably the original version. The Mell version continues the compound past of ll. 7–8 **Fortune m'a ... mis en exil**; the others, by using the present **me fait** and the plural **des maulx**, express the notion of the continuing onslaught of Fortune.

Line 10, lines 1″–4″. The long refrain is integrated with l. 10 in such a way that ll. 1″–3″ form the complement to **m'appelle. Suis**, then, is no longer the main verb of the preceding sentence but begins a new main clause. Another possibility is that the first main clause is ll. 10–2″ **Pourtant m'appelle ... l'omme ... lÿesse**, and that the second clause consists of ll. 3″–4″. In this event the punctuation would be ... **plaisance**, ... **lÿesse**; ... **tristesse**, ... **alegance**. In any case, the structure of the integrated refrain ll. 1″–4″ is different from that of the autonomous ll. 1–4.

26. Ou doy je secours querir, ff. 31ᵛ–32ʳ, Vincenet

Concordant Source

Pix, ff. 168ᵛ–169ʳ

Collation

There are no substantial differences of pitch or rhythm between
the two MSS. However, Pix places all three parts under the mensuration of diminished imperfect tempus (₵) and is less explicit in indicating accidentals. The C carries no key signature in that source, the T
but one flat, and only the CT has both B-flat and E-flat as in Mell.
But some of the accidentals given here, either as a signature or within
the line, are nonetheless specified in Pix by written signs: in the C,
flats for b at mm. 2 (3), 7 (3), and 12 (5); in the T, flats for e at mm. 5 (1),
10 (3), and 20 (4), plus the natural for b at m. 21 (1); but no flat is
given for a at m. 20 (3) of the CT.

Comments

The units of declamation employed in syllabic passages and the
rhythmic motion of the music generally suggest that the diminished
mensuration given in Pix is the proper one for this composition, and
that it should be sung roughly twice as fast as under the integral sign.

Particularly noteworthy is the unusual care with which the accidentals have been signed in the present work; virtually nothing
except cadential alterations has been left to the singer. The scale
structure is once again that of the Dorian mode twice transposed to a
final on C.

Ou doy je secours querir
Sinon par vous requerir,
Ma seulle damme et maistresse?
Aultrement ne puis lÿesse
Ne resconfort acquerir.   5

Sans vous je ne puis garir
Et suy content de mourir
En angoisseuse destresse.   8
  Ou doy je secours querir
  Sinon par vous requerir,
  Ma seulle damme et maistresse?

Faictes vers moy accourir
Grace pour moy secourir
Et moustrés vostre noblesse,
Puisque vous estes princesse,
Pour faire ung monde flourir.   13
  Ou doy je secours querir
  Sinon par vous requerir,
  Ma seulle damme et maistresse?
  Aultrement ne puis lyesse
  Ne resconfort acquerir.

Where am I to find succor
If not by wooing you,
My only lady and mistress?
Otherwise I can neither joy
Nor comfort obtain.

Without you I cannot be cured
And am content to die
In anguishing distress.
  Where am I to find succor
  If not by wooing you,
  My only lady and mistress?

Send hastening to me
Grace, to succor me,
And show your nobility,
Since you are a princess
To make a world blossom.
  Where am I to find succor
  If not by wooing you,
  My only lady and mistress?
  Otherwise I can neither joy
  Nor comfort obtain.

VARIANTS

1 Ou doye seccours (T and CT: Ou doyge). 2 Senon. 5 (Pix ends here.)

Versification

Heptasyllabic rondeau cinquain, *a a b b a*. The refrain is fully autonomous. It consists of two complete sentences, the first of which ends with the third line and is thus easily converted into the short refrain.

Textual Notes

This poem is at best mediocre. The long strophe is particularly labored.

Line 2. **par vous requerir** 'by wooing you'; the full idiom, of which this is an ellipsis, is *requerir d'amour* 'ask for love'. In this instance, it is, rather, *requerir de secours*. The second line can also be interpreted simply as 'except by asking you (for succor)'.

Line 10. **moy secourir**; in Old French, and still in Middle French, it was the rule to use the disjunctive pronoun as object of an infinitive. In modern French one would use *me* rather than *moi*.

27. Comme femme desconfortee, ff. 32ᵛ–33ʳ, Binchoys

Concordant Sources

* Roh, f. 117ʳ⁻ᵛ
Dij 517, ff. xxxviiiᵛ–xxxixʳ
Esc IV.a.24, ff. 131ᵛ–132ʳ
Flo 176, ff. 123ᵛ–125ʳ
Par 4379, ff. 13ᵛ–14ʳ
Cord, ff. 38ᵛ–40ʳ
CG XIII.27, ff. 88ᵛ–89ʳ
Lab, f. 17bʳ
Wolf 287, ff. 31ᵛ–32ʳ
*Jar, f. 93ʳ.

Collation

The C of this chanson is lacking in Lab, and the CT of Cord, although corresponding to that found in the other sources at the ends of the two principal sections, is essentially a different part. In addition, the following variants, given voice by voice, appeared to be the most important:

Cantus: At m. 8 (2 ff.), e-Sb, f-Sm, e-Sm, d-Sm, c-Sm, (an only slightly different and wholly possible alternative reading) is given by

Flo 176 and CG XIII.27; in m. 11 the ternary Br of Mell is divided into three SSb (facilitating the declamation) in Dij 517, Cord, and Wolf 287; at m. 19 (3), instead of e-M as in Mell, d-M (an equally good solution) is found in Dij 517, Flo 176, Cord, and Wolf 287; at m. 27 (1), instead of the dotted figure in Mell, e-Sb, e-Sb is written in Par 4379, Cord, and Wolf 287.

Tenor: At m. 21 (2), all sources except Mell and E̦sc IV.a.24 give F-Sb instead of F-M, G-M.

Contratenor: At m. 1 (1 ff.), Flo 176 and CG XIII.27 give G-Sb, F-M, E-M, D-Sb, perhaps a more effective counterpoint to the T melody than that offered by the other sources; at m. 12 (2), instead of b-Sm as in Mell, Par 4379 and Flo 176 have d-Sm, which clashes sharply with the C; at m. 12 (4), Flo 176, CG XIII.27, Lab, and Wolf 287 read a-M, b-M instead of b-Sb as in Mell (which is probably better harmonically); at m. 14 (3), one finds G-M, F-M, E-Sb in Dij 517, Par 4379, CG XIII.27, Lab, and Wolf 287 (eliminating the parallel octaves of Mell); at m. 22 (2), Flo 176, Par 4379, Lab, and Wolf 287 have c-Sb, b-Sm, c-Sm (a slight change); at m. 27 (2), Flo 176 and Wolf 287 give a dissonant c-M instead of a-M as in Mell; and at m. 30 (2–5), Flo 176 and CG XIII.27 have G-Br, eliminating the ornamental figure found in the other MSS.

COMMENTS

Plamenac mentions a lute transcription—apparently now lost—of this chanson in his facsimile edition of Par 4379.[1] The composition found in Par 1597, ff. 29ᵛ–30ʳ, is a later setting of Binchois's T, retained at pitch under the original mensuration, with a new C and CT written under the sign for diminished imperfect tempus (₵). Yet another reworking of the T, in this instance à 4, is found in the part books at Munich, Universitätsbibliothek, MSS 328–331 (ff. 68, 43, 120ᵛ, and 56ᵛ, respectively). There the borrowed melody is transposed up a fourth with b-flat, and the surrounding voices are again written in diminished imperfect tempus. In both works the Br of the added voices is equivalent in length to the Sb of the original melody, providing a tangible demonstration of the proportional relationship that obtained between integral and diminished mensurations in the late fifteenth and early sixteenth centuries.

1. *Facsimile Reproduction of the Manuscripts Sevilla 5–1–43 and Paris N.A.Fr. 4379*, No. 40, p. 5.

Atlas, in his discussion of this piece,[2] posits two principal traditions
of transmission, one represented by Cord alone, the other by the
remaining sources, which he divides into three subfamilies: (1) a
northern group including Dij 517, Lab, and Wolf 287; (2) a "Neapolitan" group comprising Esc IV.a.24, Par 4379, and Mell; and (3)
a "Florentine" group composed of Flo 176 and CG XIII.27. However,
Cord agrees primarily with the northern MSS in C and CT, suggesting
a further ramification to the interrelationships among the MSS. In a
significant number of notational details that are otherwise relatively
unimportant, Par 4379 follows more closely the reading of the Florentine collections than that of Mell and Esc IV.a.24.

At the same time Atlas casts doubt on the authenticity of the
attribution to Binchois (pp. 364–65), but from the stylistic viewpoint
there is little reason to do so. Both the melodic writing and the contrapuntal structure, with its reliance on a basic framework of fauxbourdon,
are essentially those to be expected from that composer.

A rest-Sb has been added to T and CT at m. 15 of the transcription
in order to achieve the consistent relationship among the three parts
to be seen in MSS such as Dij 517, Lab, and Wolf 287.

Comme femme desconfortee,
Sur toutes aultres esgaree,
Qui n'ay jour de ma vye espoir
D'*en* estre en mon temps consolee,
Mais en mon mal plus agrevee
Desire la mort main et soir.   6

Je l'ay tant de foys regretee
Puisqu'elle m'a ma joye ostee;
Doy je dont icy remanoir   9
     Comme femme desconfortee,
     Sur toutes aultres esgaree,
     Qui n'ay jour de ma vie espoir?

Bien doy mauldire la journee
Que ma mere fist la portee
De moy pour tant deul recepvoir,
Car toute douleur assemblee

2. "Cappella Giulia XIII.27 and the Chanson in Italy," p. 367.

Est en moy, femme maleuree!
Donc j'ay bien cause de douloir   15
  Comme femme desconfortee,
  Sur toutes aultres esgaree,
  Qui n'ay jour de ma vie espoir
  D'en estre en mon temps consolee;
  Mais en mon mal plus agrevee
  Desire la mort main et soir.

As a woman in great distress,
More than all others distraught,
Who have not on any day of my life hope
Of being consoled while I still live;
But evermore oppressed by my misfortune
I desire death morning and night.

I have yearned for it many times
Since it took my joy from me;
Must I then remain here
  As a woman in great distress,
  More than all others distraught,
  Who have no hope on any day of my life?

Well may I curse the day
That my mother bore me
To receive so much grief,
For all pain is gathered
In me, unfortunate woman!
Whence I have real cause to grieve
  As a woman in great distress,
  More than all others distraught,
  Who have not on any day of my life hope
  Of being consoled while I still live—
  But evermore oppressed by my misfortune,
  I desire death morning and night.

VARIANTS

The texted sources are Roh (Löp No. 289), Esc, Cord, Wolf, and Jar.

2 Et plus que nulle autre esgaree—*Jar*. 3 Je n'ay—*Jar*. 4 D'estre
a nulle heure—*Jar*; Mell and Esc omit en; Löp reads Roh as De
nestre (n'estre?); jamais jour consolee—*Esc*; (Mell −1 syll.). 5 Mais
a—*Cord*; agrauee—*Roh Cord Wolf*. 6 (Esc ends here.) 7 maintes foys
—*Jar*. 8 Puisque ma joye m'est ostee—*Wolf*. 9 donc—*Cord Roh Wolf*;
ainsy—*Roh*, ainsi—*Wolf*; ainsi demourer [does not rhyme]—*Jar*
(Mell ends; the text is supplied from Cord). 11 Qu'a—*Jar*; fit—*Roh*.
12 Pour tant de douleur recevoir—*Jar*; tel dueil—*Roh*, tant mal—
Wolf. 14 malluree—*Roh*, malheuree—*Wolf*. 15 Dont—*Roh Wolf*.

Versification

Rondeau sixain in octosyllables, *aabaab*. From the poetical point
of view, the short refrain would be neater if, in the manner of the
rondeaux of Christine de Pisan, it consisted only of the first line.
However, the musical form requires the repetition of ll. 1′–3′. Similarly,
l. 15 could logically be followed by l. 1″ alone. Since the whole refrain,
ll. 1″–6″, is sung, it can be regarded either as independent (with a
period after l. 15, and the punctuation of ll. 1″–6″ like that of ll. 1–6),
or as syntactically bound to l. 15, in which case we have no punctuation
after l. 15 and a semicolon after l. 4″.

Textual Notes

Line 6. **Desire** 'I desire' is the principal verb of this strophe-long
sentence. **main** 'morning'.

Line 7. **Je l'ay . . . regretee** 'I have yearned for it (death)'.

Line 8. **Puis qu'** 'since (the time that)'; in modern French *Depuis
que*. The Wolf reading is obviously an attempt to repair a line from
which one *ma* had been dropped, by haplology, in what might have
been a misguided effort to correct a dittology!

Line 9. **Dont** and *donc* (see Variants) are interchangeable in the
meaning that each has in modern French. Here it clearly means
'therefore'. **icy** and *ainsi* (see Variants) make equally good sense;
ainsi can be understood as explicated in l. 1′ of the integrated refrain.
remanoir 'remain'.

Lines 11–12. **Que ma mere fist la portee / De moy** 'That my
mother gave birth to me'; **fist** (var. Roh *fit*) shows the complete
confusion between the third person singular forms of the preterite and
of the imperfect subjunctive. In this context it is clearly the former.
The confusion between *fit* and *fît* continues, unofficially, in modern
French. **deul** [döl′].

Line 13. 'For all the pain (in the world) gathered together'.

Line 14. The variants, Cord *maleuree*, Wolf *malheuree*, and Roh *malluree* are interesting, particularly that of Roh, which indicates a Francian pronunciation (see pp. 100, 101). The modern pronunciation of *malheur*, *malheureux*, with [ö] rather than the [ü] that would be normal for Francian, is due to the influence of spelling, to its resemblance to the word *heure*, with its astrological connotations, or to the introduction of a dialectal words.[3] Since we have no evidence that any poem in Mell has [ü] from OF [əü], we assume [ö] here, as we do at Nos. 5 (*sceu*), 21 (*seure, asseure*), and 53 (*j'eux, receux*) at the rhyme and 7 (*sceusse*) and 21 (*deusse*) before the rhyme. *Heur* comes from Latin AUGŪRIUM, as follows: > Imperial Latin AGŪRIUM > OF [əür] > MF [ü : r], [ö : r].

Line 15. **Donc** (variants: *dont*) can mean either 'whence' or 'therefore'; in fact, this is the kind of crucial context that contributed to the phonological, orthographic, and semantic confusion of *dont* and *donc*. **douloir** 'to grieve'.

28. **Mon trestout et mon assotee /**
Il estoit ung bonhomme, ff. 33ᵛ–36ʳ, Petit Jan

COMMENTS

The second pair of couplets written separately on f. 33ᵛ is obviously to be sung to the same music as the initial pair entered beneath the notes although some slight adjustments will have to be made in the text placement in order to do so without undue awkwardness. Two modes of performance are possible. The second section of the piece can either be sung through to the end a first time after the first pair of couplets and then repeated following the second pair (a, a', B; a, a', B) or be held in reserve until both pairs of couplets have been heard (a, a', a, a', B). (The schema represents the repetition patterns of the musical sections with a and a' for the ouvert and clos forms of the initial one and B for the remainder of the piece with its unchanging text.) In the latter case it would be possible to repeat the first line of text in T and CT ı before proceeding with a dual statement of the second line, as is suggested by the numbering of lines in the transcription.

---

3. The different pronunciations of the *heur* of *malheur* with [ọ̈] and that of *malheureux* with [ọ̈] are predictable from the position of that vowel, whose cover symbol is [ö], in the word.

   The composition apparently combines musical and poetic elements
from three different chansons, but the source of the borrowings have
been discovered for only two of these. Both tune and text carried by
the T in the initial section, mm. 1–19, are derived from a popular
song that figured in the fifteenth-century farce entitled *Un Chauldronnier*;[1] CT 1 anticipates imitatively the preexistent tune and shares
with the T the text as well. That the middle segment of the piece is
also a quotation can be inferred from the pattern of melodic repetition
that can be diagrammed as follows:

> z   (T, mm. 20–25)
>
> z   (CT 1, mm. 26–31)
>
> ẏ   (T, mm. 32–37)
>
> z   (T, mm. 38–43).

The most convincing reconstruction of the presumably borrowed poem
likewise emerges when this sequence is taken for the poetic elements
(see Textual Notes below). However, the chanson from which these
citations were taken has yet to be identified. (The melody found in
the present MS is different from that of the Bayeux Chansonnier and
that of MS f. fr. 12744 of the Bibliothèque Nationale, both of which
contain a related poem; see p. 299.) The third work quoted is clearly
of popular origin, like the first, and appears to be related to a song
heard in the farce of the *Savetier nommé Calbain*.[2] Characteristically,
the T carries both the derived melody and its text while CT 1 anticipates the tune and shares the poem. Evidence for the borrowing
derives not only from the character of the melodic writing and the
repetition of the musical phrases but also from unmistakable similarities with a sixteenth-century setting of a related chanson by Pierre
Moulu. The relationship between the two songs is illustrated below
by juxtaposing the relevant excerpts from the tenor parts.[3] (To
facilitate the comparison, the first three segments of the present
chanson have been transposed down a fourth.) The affinities between
the two poems are even clearer when the line *Si vous m'y blessés* is given
as *Si m'y touchez* as it is in the play.

   1. See Howard Mayer Brown, "A Catalogue of Theatrical Chansons, No. 169," *Music in the
French Secular Theater*; see also Textual Notes.
   2. Ibid., No. 111; the farce was published by Edouard Fournier, *Le théâtre français avant la
Renaissance*, p. 282.
   3. A transcription of Moulu's composition has been published by Howard Mayer Brown,
Theatrical Chansons of the Fifteenth and Early Sixteenth Centuries, No. 21; the present excerpts are
from that transcription.

Madame Lucette

Pierre Moulu

Although the CT primus is provided with text somewhat erratically in the MS, it seemed preferable to prepare the transcription for a wholly vocal performance of the part despite the fact that it was often necessary to ignore ligatures in order to do so. Because the mensural change at mm. 43 ff. does not begin in all four parts simultaneously, it is self-evident that the proportion intended is a sesquialteral one.

Four separate lyric texts are interwoven among the voices. Although it is four-part music, we may speak of three voices in reference to the distribution of the texts among the voices since either CT II says the same words as C, or its music is performed by instruments.
The first song is carried by the cantus:

  I. Mon trestout et mon assotee,
    [La] plus gratïeuse qu'on sace,
    Sanglantement belle et crotee,
    Habille a faire une grimace.   4

Autant saige en dit [*qu'*]en pensee,
Que rechevés mainte souffrage;
Quant je vous aray espousee,
Je craind[*ray*] fort la cyceface.   8

Riant et brunette en la face
—Dieu me gard de dire musel!—
Mon cuer double maintenant, tel
Que fort vous ayme et amasse.   12

My very all, my fool,
The most gracious known to man,
Bloody beautiful and becrudded,
Clever at making funny faces,

So wise in word—as in thought—
That you receive many an approving smile;
When I marry you,
I shall greatly fear the bogey-man, devourer of
    good women.

Smiling and brown in the face
—God keep me from saying mug!—
My heart doubles its beat, so
Much do I love you and hath loved you.

VERSIFICATION

Three octosyllabic quatrains, *abab abab bccb*. The *b*-rhyme, variously spelled -*ace*, -*age*, and -*asse*, presents problems, for not all the
rhymes are dialectally or etymologically consistent. If one takes the
poem as originally Picard, the following rhymes are "good": **sace** :
grimace : **face** : **souffrage** : **cyceface**, all ending in [-ašə] in Picard;
but **amasse** is pronounced [amasə], even in Picard. If, alternatively,
we assume a Francian origin, they group as follows: **grimace** : **face** :
amasse : **chicheface**, all ending in [-asə], and **sache** and **souffrage**,
which rhyme with nothing in the poem, not even with each other.
Picard, then, seems indicated, not only by the rhyme evidence, but
also by certain spellings in words not at the rhyme (**rechevés, aray**).

Such spellings could always be due to a picardizing scribe and thus prove nothing about origins, but they gain importance if one considers that Picard traits (on nonorthographic evidence) are apparent in other poems in this collection; that there is evidence as to the northern origins of much of this collection; and that this poem is found only in Mell and is therefore likely to have originated in the region from which come so many of the other Mell poems.

If a Picard pronunciation was intended, the inclusion of **amasse** in the *b*-rhyme can be explained as exploitation of dialectal traits for comic effect without regard for scientific precision, as is often done. If the poem makes fun of what is, from the Francian point of view, an excessive use of the shibilant [š], one can easily imagine the pronunciation of **amasse** as [amašə] to bring it into line with the comic and dialectally authentic [-ašə] of the other *b*-rhyme words.

In conformity with this explanation, it would solve the singer's problem to adopt the pronunciations *sache, grimache, souffrache, chiche-fache, fache,* and *amache*. Or, if the humor of the northern peasant bending over backward to sound Francian was intended, all the words in the *b*-rhyme should end in [-asə], even *sace* and *souffrace*.

Textual Notes

The poem depends for its comic effects on the mingling of conventional love sentiments and coarse expressions and images, seasoned with a rustic accent.

Line 1. **trestout**: **tres-** is an intensive prefix: 'My very all'. **assotee** 'foolish, doltish'.

Line 2. Mell *De* is either a miscopying of **La** (**plus gratieuse**) or of the Picard feminine *le*, or it is an overlapping construction: *De plus, plus gratieuse* ... becoming *De plus gratieuse*. The first explanation seems more plausible. **sace** = modern *sache*, present subjunctive of *savoir*.

Line 4. **habille** [abil] = modern *habile* 'clever'.

Line 5. Mell *et en pensee* is hypermetric by one syllable.

Line 6. **recheves** = *recevez*; a Picard spelling. **souffrage** = modern *suffrage* in the sense of 'approval'. Picard, which makes no distinction between voiced and voiceless sibilants, allows this rhyme in [-ašə].

Line 7. **aray** = *aurai*; a Picard verb form.

Line 8. Mell *crains* is hypometric by one syllable; **craindray** is in

a better sequence of tenses with l. 7. **cyceface** = *chicheface*, defined
as "qui mange toutes les bonnes femmes."[4] This legend is based on
the rarity of virtuous women noted in Proverbs 31 : 10; the *chicheface*
is depicted as gaunt and tormented by hunger. A good woman being
thrifty, the etymology of *chichephage*, if we may so respell it, would
seem to be: *chiche* 'thrifty, stingy' (attested since 1175) + *-phage* '-eater'.
This etymology also helps our Picard rhyme, for in Picard, as we
have noted, *-age* rhymes with *-ache*.[5]

Line 9. **brunette**: a reminder of the bucolic character of this
beauty; the idealized noblewoman was almost always fair.

Line 10. **gard** [gar(t)], third person present subjunctive of *garder*
'keep'.

Line 11. **double** 'doubles (its beat)'.

Line 12. **amasse** = modern *aimasse*. This could be a subjunctive
construction modeled on the Latin usage in result clauses (after **tel
que** 'so that')—a device characteristic of the fifteenth century; or it
could be the foreshadowing of the humorous effect produced in modern
spoken French of imperfect subjunctives containing *-ass-*, *-iss-*, *-uss-*.
This would be especially true in a poem that makes sport of the
singeries of peasants attempting an elevated style.

The "Farce d'ung savetier nommé Calbain" quotes a song using
this verb form in a strikingly similar context:

> Je ne sçay pas comment
> En mon entendement
> Plus fort je vous aymasse[6]

In this instance the imperfect subjunctive is used in a very specific
sense: "I don't know how . . . I could love you more."
The second poem is sung by T and CT I, simultaneously with the
first quatrain in the cantus.

> II.   Il estoit ung bonhomme
>   Qui charïoit fagot.   (CT I: carioit)

4. Anatole de Montaiglon and James de Rothschild, *Recueil de poésies françoises des XIVe et
XVe siècles* . . . , 2:277.

5. For a different etymology, see Frédéric Godefroy, *Dictionnaire de l'ancienne langue française*
. . . , s.v.

6. Edouard Fournier, *Le théâtre français avant la Renaissance*, p. 281.

Il avoit une fille
Qu'on appelloit Margot.[7]   4

There was a simple man
Who carted fagots,
And he did have a daughter
Whose name was Maggie.

VERSIFICATION

A hexasyllabic quatrain *abcb*, which could also be described as an
alexandrine couplet *aa*, with epic caesura after the sixth syllable.
There are at least five songs in Par 12744 (see the variants of song
III) consisting of twelve-syllable lines with epic caesura; so evidently
this meter survived the period of the early epics (*Roman d'Alexandre*;
Pèlerinage de Charlemagne) into the popular songs of the fifteenth century.

TEXTUAL NOTE

Line 2. **carioit** of CT 1 is a Picardism.

The third poem is carried by T at m. 20, is picked up by CT 1 at m.
26, and finished by T, mm. 32–43.

III.   T: Dieu gard celle de deshoneur
             Que j'ay longtamps amee;   2

       CT: Ou j'ay lontemps par bon amour
             Ma lÿesse finee.   4

       T: Or voy je bien que c'est falour
             D'y plus avoir pensee   6

             Pour tant prens congié sans retour;
             Adieu, ma desiree!   8

7. There is an echo of this song in the "Farce d'un Chauldronnier" (ibid., pp. 340 ff.). See
also the "Farce d'un Chauldronnier" (Emmanuel L. N. Viollet le Duc, *Ancien théâtre françois*,
2:105 ff.), which begins with "the man" singing

> *Il estoit un homme,*
> *Qui charrioit fagotz;*

the song goes no further.

God keep her from dishonor
Whom I long have loved,
And in whom, through true love, I have long since
Ended my happiness.
Now I see that it is folly
To fix my thought there.

Therefore I take leave, without return—
Adieu, my desired one!

VARIANTS

Paris 12744 f. 29^r (A); Paris 9346, ff. 32^v–33^r (B); the "Vire manuscript" (V).[8]

The MSS present a poem in two (B and V) or three (A) huitains, in alternating eight- and six-syllable lines, of whose first strophe only ll. 1, 2, 5, and 6 correspond to Mell ll. 1, 2, 5, and 6 respectively. Lines 3, 4, 7, and 8 correspond to nothing in Mell, and we have found no concordant readings for Mell ll. 3, 4, 7, and 8. The line numbers below refer to those of the Mell poem. A adds two huitains, B and V only one, quite different from A.

5 folleur—*A B V* (Gaston Paris says: follye—*B*, but he has misread). 6 d'y avoir ma pensee—*A*, d'y mectre sa pencee—*B*, mettre plus ma pensee—*V*. 7 Puisqu'elle m'a dit par rigueur—*A*, Quant elle m'a dict en plorant—*B* (no rhyme), Puis qu'elle a faict amy ailleurs—*V*. 8 Vostre amour est Ja finee—*A* (+1 syll.), Nos amours sont finees—*B*, De moy s'est esloingnee—*V*.

VERSIFICATION

A huitain in alternating octo- and hexasyllabic lines, *abababab*. -*eur* and -*our* rhyme.

8. B.N. f. fr. 12744 has been edited in its entirety by Gaston Paris in *Chansons du XVe siècle* as the first publication of the *Société des Anciens Textes Français*; the present song is No. 33, on pp. 35–36 of that edition.

B.N. f. fr. 9346 is the "Bayeux manuscript," published by Théodore Gérold, *Le manuscrit de Bayeux, texte et musique d'un recueil de chansons du XVe siècle*. The present song is No. 32, on p. 36 of Gérold's edition.

The "Vire manuscript" has been edited by Armand Gasté in *Chansons normandes du XVe siècle* (Caen, 1866); both Paris and Gérold rely on this edition for their variants. We have not been able to secure a copy of this edition, and the variants we record are those listed by Paris and Gérold in their editions.

TEXTUAL NOTES

Line 1. There is an echo between the voices and the poems: in the present poem, III, tenor m. 20 *Dieu gard celle* anticipates cantus mm. 24–25 *Dieu me gard* of poem I. We shall observe in poem IV a similar play between the voices.

Line 5. **falour** 'error, oversight'; by extension, 'folly'.

Line 6. **pensee** is a noun, object of **avoir**.

In the last part we have two simultaneous poems, one (IVA) in the cantus, mm. 38–65: *Mais celler le veuil*; the other (IVB) in the tenor and contratenor, T mm. 44–65, CT mm. 43–65: *N'atouchiés a moy*.

IVA.   Mais celler le veuil, plaisant socque,
       Et mauldit soit [..] qui le dira
       Que vous ayés nom Nicque Nocque.   3

VERSIFICATION

Three octosyllables, *a b a*. Mell *il* omitted from hypermetric l. 2.

IVB.   N'atouchiés a moy, je suy trop mygnotte;
       Retires vostre main tost, Nicque Nocque.
       Vous my froissiés tous les os, tricque trocque.   3

VERSIFICATION

A decasyllable with caesura after the fifth syllable (a meter found in popular songs of the time[9]), followed by two decasyllables with caesura after the seventh syllable, with approximate rhyme [t] : [k].

These poems must be treated together because there is method and meaning in the interweaving of IVA and IVB that go beyond the purely formal. It can be seen as one poem, a ribald one, spoken by a girl defending herself from the attentions of one who calls himself **Nicque Nocque**. At the same time, we are spectators at the game called *niquenoque* (the *nicnoque* in the list of games in Rabelais's *Gargantua*, chap. 22),[10] in which the loser is thumped by the winner's vigorous

9. See, for example, song No. 142 in Gaston Paris, *Chansons du XVᵉ siècle*, "En baisant m'amye j'ay cueilly la fleur."

10. P. 65 of the Pléiade edition of Rabelais's *Oeuvres complètes*, ed. Jacques Boulenger (Paris: Gallimard, 1959).

fingersnaps.[11] The first line, **Mais celler le veuil** 'I want to hide it'
may plausibly refer to an object that the game requires to be hidden.
Nicque Nocque refers to the game and to the fingerflip; and the
first part, *nicque* to an article of little value (cf. English *I don't care a
snap of my finger*).[12]

It is possible, then, to see IVA and IVB presenting one total situation
in which the girl, at one level, protests the silly lie told her about the
boy's name, and at another is engaged in a game that threatens to
become excessively physical. If we arrange the lines in the order of
their starting points, this is what comes out:

C, CT 38–43	Mais celler le veuil, plaisant socque,
T, CT 43–50	N'atouchiés à moy, je suy trop mygnotte
C 45–51	—Et mauldit soit [. .] qui le dira—
T, CT 48–56, T 57–65	Retirés vostre main tost, Nicque Nocque!
C 53–56	—Que vous ayés nom Nicque Nocque—
CT 56–65	Vous my froissiés tous les os, tricque trocque.

But I want to hide it, old sock.
Don't touch me, I'm too little and cute.
—Besides, to heck with any one who'll say—
Get your hand off me, Nickie Nack!
—That your name is Nickie Nack.—
You're breaking all my bones, trickie track.

The third and fifth lines of the above arrangement, set off between
dashes, constitute the expression of disbelief in the boy's name; the
other lines refer directly to the activity of the game. The solo cantus

11. In the "Farce du savetier Calbain" (Fournier, *Théâtre français avant la Renaissance*, p. 282),
a wife responds to her husband's threat to beat her by saying (or singing):

Si m'y touchez, je vous feray mettre
A la prison du chasteau, nicque, nicque, nocque,
A la prison du chasteau, nicque, nocqueau.

Fournier furnishes the following note: "C'est ce qu'on chantait au jeu de la *nique noque* mis par
Rabelais parmi ceux de Gargantua . . . : à chaque retour du refrain on s'accablait de chique-
naudes. C'est pour cela qu'elles s'appellent *niquenoques* en Poitou."

12. Godefroy, *Dictionnaire* and *Lexique de l'ancien français*, s.v. *niquenoque*; also *niquet*, 'a coin of
little value; a dirty trick'; *niqueter, niquenoquer* 'behave like an idiot'; *niquier* 'strike a violent blow'.
In modern French, *faire la nique* 'make a contemptuous, insulting gesture' goes back, according
to Dauzat, Dubois, and Mitterand, *Nouveau dictionnaire étymologique et historique*, to the end of the
fourteenth century.

stands out from the other voices to carry through the thread of its argument, while the other two voices, with their overlapping verses, represent the scurrying, coy resistance of the girl to her playful partner in the game.[13]

29. Joye me fuit, ff. 36ᵛ–38ʳ, Busnoys

CONCORDANT SOURCES

Dij 517, ff. xxviᵛ–xxviiʳ, Busnoys
Flo 176, ff. 13ᵛ–15ʳ
Pix, ff. 163ᵛ–164ʳ, Busnoys
*Par 1719, f. 33ᵛ
*Par 7559, f. 64ʳ
RomC 2856, ff. 13ᵛ–14ʳ, Busnoys
Tr 91, ff. 258ᵛ–259ʳ (Je me sans)
Lab, ff. 100ᵛ–101ʳ
*Jar, f. 98ʳ

COLLATION

With the exception of RomC 2856, the concordant sources present mostly minor variants. For example, in the C at m. 11 (4), Dij 517 and Lab have e-M, f-M, g-M, a′-M (creating parallel octaves with the CT at the beginning of the figure); at m. 12 (3), one finds a′-M (instead of g-M as in Mell) in Pix, RomC 2856, Tr 91, and Lab. But RomC 2856 has g-Br, f-Sb, g-Sb, a′-Sb, b′-dotted Sb, a′-Sm, g-Sm, f-Sb at m. 9 (4 ff.), and at m. 15 (1 ff.), b′-flat dotted Sb, a′-M, g-Sb, f-Sb.

In the T, Flo 176 gives E-Sb at m. 14 (2) (as good a reading as the F-Sb of Mell), and at m. 15 (4) D-dotted Sb, E-M, F-Sb (with questionable results contrapuntally), whereas Pix has G-Sb instead of a-Sb at m. 33 (8), probably an error.

---

13. Again, a song quoted in the "Farce de Calbain" (Fournier, p. 279; see n. 11 above) has one of our words:

> Et trique devant, et trique derrière
> Trique devant, trique derrière.

The shoemaker Calbain responds to his wife's entreaties for a new dress by singing popular songs of the day. Fournier dates the farce, printed in 1548, in the reign of Louis XII (1498–1515), largely through the many songs quoted in it.

As usual, the greatest number of divergences are found in the CT: at m. 6 (1), RomC 2856 has F-Br, D-Br, G'-Br; at m. 10 (1), the dot is absent for G'-Br in Pix and Lab, whereas RomC 2856 has G'-Sb, B-flat-Sb, G'-Sb; at m. 18 (2), RomC 2856 gives F'-Sb, B-Br, whereas at m. 18 (3), Pix has D'-Sm (a good reading) instead of E'-Sm as in Mell; at m. 21 (7), Pix gives C-M (probably an error) instead of D-M as elsewhere; at m. 22 (4), Dij 517 has E'-Sb combined with the G'-Sb of the other sources; at m. 27 (1), both Dij 517 and Lab have E'-Sb, a less happy solution harmonically than D'-Sb as in Mell; and at m. 31 (1), RomC 2856 has G'-Sb, G'-M, F'-Sb, eliminating the cadential figure found in Mell.

Neither Dij 517 nor Flo 176 carries b flat as a signature for the CT, and the sharp at m. 19 (1) of the T is not found in RomC 2856 or Tr 91.

COMMENTS

Apparently the reading most closely related to that of Mell is found in Tr 91. Also, Flo 176 and Pix represent essentially the same scribal tradition, as do Dij 517 and Lab, which are virtually identical to each other for this particular composition, even with respect to the details of the notation and the style of the calligraphy. By contrast, the version of RomC 2856 stands distinctly apart.

There can be little doubt that the T of Busnois's rondeau was conceived for vocal performance, as is suggested in the MS by the text entered under the notation of that part, but the distribution of syllables that was judged most preferable occasionally required the breaking of a ligature.

Joye me fuit et Doleur me ceurt seure;
Couroux me sieut sans riens qui me sequeure.
Ce qui me tue, ellas! c'est Souvenance.
Je ne cesse, loins de mon esperance,
Mon seul desir, *et* que briefment je [meure].   5

Quant je me dors mon esperit labeure;
Au resveillier Dieu scet comment il pleure!
Lors demande de mes maulx alegance.   8
  Joye me fuit et Doleur me ceurt seure;
  Couroux me sieut sans riens qui me sequeure.
  Ce qui me tue, ellas! c'est Souvenance.

Je ne sçay tour, sinon mauldire l'eure
Que vis celuy par qui ce mal saveure;
Mais peut estre qu'il n'a pas congnoissance
De mon annuy ne de ma desplaisance.
Pourquoy couvient qu'en ce point je demeure?   13
    Joye me fuit et Doleur me ceurt seure;
    Couroux me sieut sans riens qui me sequeure.
    Ce qui me tue, ellas! c'est Souvenance.
    Je ne cesse, loins de mon esperance,
    Mon seul desir, et que briefment je meure.

Joy flees me, and Pain charges against me,
Wrath follows me, and nothing comes to my rescue.
What kills me—alas!—is Memory.
I do not renounce, far from [the object of] my hope,
My sole desire, and [that is] that I may shortly die.

When I fall asleep, my mind is in travail;
Upon awaking, God knows how it weeps!
Then I ask that my woes be lightened.
    Joy flees me, and Pain charges against me,
    Wrath follows me, and nothing comes to my rescue.
    What kills me—alas!—is Memory.

I know not what to do save curse the hour
When I saw him because of whom I taste this woe;
But perhaps he has no knowledge
Of my unease, nor of my displeasure.
Why needs must I remain in this pass?
    Joy flees me, and Pain charges against me,
    Wrath follows me, and nothing comes to my rescue.
    What kills me—alas!—is Memory.
    I do not renounce, far from [the object of] my hope,
    My sole desire, and [that is] that I may shortly die.

Variants

The texted sources are Dij, Lab, Par 1719, Par 7559, and Jar.   Roh
f. 86ʳ (Löp No. 152) has a similar first line, but the rest of the poem
is entirely different.

1 queurt—*Dij Lab*, court—*Jar Par 1719 Par 7559*; Joie me fuit et
desespoir me chasse—*Roh*. 2 suit/suyt—*All but Mell*; sans que riens—
Dij. 3 Sans qu'il me tue—*Jar*. 4 Je me chasse—*Lab*, qui me laisse—
Par 1719 Par 7559. 5 Mon seul desir que briefment je demeure—*Mell*,
Mon seul desir et que briefment je meure—*Dij*, Mon seul plaisir est
que briefment je meure—*Jar*, Mon seul desir qui longuement demeure
—*Lab*, mon seul desir est que briefment je meure—*Par 1719*, mon
seul desir est que brief je me meure—*Par 7559*. (Par 1719 ends here.)
6 Las quant je dors—*Lab*; Lors mon esperit—*Dij* (+1 syll.), lors
mon esprit—*Jar*. 7 comme je pleure—*Dij Lab*. 8 En demandant—*Dij
Jar Lab Par 7559*. (Mell ends here. Remainder from Dij.) 9 Je n'en
puis plus—*Lab*. 10 Que je vis celle par qui je plains et pleure—*Jar*.
11 Mais bien peut estre que—*Jar* (+1 syll.? See discussion under
Versification). 13 Par quoy—*Lab Par 7559*.

VERSIFICATION

Decasyllabic rondeau cinquain, *a a b b a*. Lines 4, 8, and 11 have the
lyric caesura (*-e* as fourth syllable). This is true of every version of
l. 4, unique to Mell's version of l. 8 (*Lors demande* vs. *En demandant* in
all other sources), and, for l. 11, true of all but Jar (*Mais bien peut
estre*, plus six syllables beginning with a consonant), which has an
-e, uncounted, after the fourth syllable. But since this poem is clearly
not composed according to the epic rule, Jar's l. 11 is probably best
regarded as not belonging to the original poem.

TEXTUAL NOTES

Droz and Piaget (in their edition of Jar, vol. 2, p. 200) see in this
poem an imitation of a poem by Alain Chartier that begins

> *Joye me fuit et desespoir me chasse,*
> *Je n'ay plaisir ne je ne le pourchasse.*

It occurs in Roh, f. 86ʳ (Löpelmann's No. 152; Löpelmann calls it
anonymous). *Imitation* is too strong, for the themes are quite different,
and there is no particular structural similarity. In Chartier's poem,
a lover mourns his deceased mistress; in the Busnois song, a woman
expresses her unhappiness at being unable to communicate her love
to the man. The only resemblance between the poems appears in the
first line.

Line 1. **ceurt** [kör]; **seure** [sörə].

Line 2. Although **sieut** is more archaic than *suit* (see Variants), *suit* points up more effectively the contrast with *fuit* of l. 1 and may therefore belong to the original poem.

Line 5. Mell and Lab, both ending in *demeure*, are guilty of homologous rhyme since all sources agree that l. 13 ends in that word. If we correct *demeure* to the **meure** of the other sources, we can make up the syllable by adopting the *et* or *est* (phonetically identical in this context: [e]) of all versions but Mell and Lab. Our choice of **et** is dictated by the necessity of interpreting l. 5 in such a way that l. 4 will make sense. With *est*, l. 5 becomes an independent clause whose subject is **mon desir**; but this leaves l. 4 **Je ne cesse** without a complement. The Mell version means: "Far from [the object of] my hope, I do not give up my sole desire—that my sojourn on earth be brief."

In **briefment**, the *f* is silent, and *ie* is monosyllabic: [bryema^n].

Line 7. **il**, that is, **mon esperit**. All other sources, including Lab, have *je*, which would indicate that Mell is the starting point of a new reading. *Je* goes better with the first person of ll. 8 ff.

Line 8. **Lors demande**, against *En demandant* in all the other sources, indicates once more a new reading in Mell. **alegance** [aleža^{n}sə] 'relief'.

Line 9. Dij: 'I don't know what to do except curse the hour'; Lab: 'I can do nothing but curse the hour'.

Line 10. **Que** = modern *où* 'when'. Jar *celle* shows that the redactor of this version was thinking in terms of a male subject, and so found this correction necessary. He follows this through in the next line.

Line 11. The reason for Jar's change from **qu'il** to *que* is apparent from the preceding note. *qu'elle* would have been hypermetric and in any case the pronoun is not essential. **congnoissance** [konwesa^{n}sə].

Line 13. Dij and Lab divide on **Pourquoy** ... ? 'Why ... ?' and *Par quoy* 'Wherefore', the latter declarative, not interrogative. **couvient** = *il faut*.

30. **Ma bouce rit, ff. 38ᵛ–40ʳ, Okeghem**

CONCORDANT SOURCES

Glog, No. 267 (capital *H* only text given)
*Roh, ff. 83ᵛ–84ʳ

Cop 1848-2⁰, p. 401 (first section only)
Dij 517, ff. iv^v–vi^r
Flo 176, ff. 32^v–34^r, Ocheghem
FloR 2356, ff. 34^v–35^r
Sched, ff. 62^v–64^r, Ockegheim
Niv, ff. lii^v–liv^r, Okeghem
*Par 1719, ff. 61^r, 132^r
Pix, ff. 30^v–32^r
Par 4379, ff. 4^v–6^r
Cord, ff. 42^v–44^r
CG XIII.27, ff. 76^v–77^r
RomC 2856, ff. 61^v–63^r, Okeghem
Lab, ff. 32^v–34^r
Wolf 287, ff. 29^v–31^r
Form, No. 86
*Jar, ff. 61^r, 71^v
*Arn, ff. liv^v, lxi^v
Odh, ff. 59^v–60^r, Okenhem

COLLATION

Variants among the sources for this composition involve primarily isolated errors and details of melodic ornamentation that are rarely shared by more than two or three sources. All concordances are unanimous, however, in giving b′-M at m. 12(1) of the C, making it possible to correct the error in Mell, where the note is Sm. Although there are no differences of substance with respect to Mell in Dij 517, Niv, Cord, Lab, and Wolf 287, the latter display a tendency to give as repeated pitches notes that are written as extended values in this collection. The few variants capable of suggesting a distinctive filiation among readings are the following:

In the T at m. 4(1, 2), Flo 176, FloR 2356, and Par 4379 have two MM instead of the dotted figure seen here; at m. 8(4), Niv and RomC 2856 give a-Sb with no dotted figure; at m. 27, the rest is erroneously Sb in Flo 176 and CG XIII.27 instead of Br as elsewhere. In the CT at m. 18(6), Pix gives C-Sb instead of D-M, C-M, and Flo 176 and CG XIII.27 have D-Sb, surely an error.

In addition, Lab has a b-flat signature for both T and CT of this work and a diminished mensuration (₵) for the second section, whereas Par 4379 and Form use the stroke of diminution for the entire composition and Glog the symbol C2. The written sharps in the C at mm. 21 (4) and 35–36 are found only in Mell.

COMMENTS

For a work as widely disseminated as this popular bergerette by Ockeghem, the tradition of transmission is remarkably consistent. Moreover, because the divergences are for the most part isolated errors or minor differences in melodic ornamentation peculiar to one or two collections, it is very difficult to group the readings into families and to trace scribal traditions. However, the northern MSS Dij 517, Niv, Lab, and Wolf 287, to which may be added the Savoyard collection Cord, share many of the same notational details and seem to reflect a common parent source. The same is true of Flo 176 and CG XIII.27, which have the same distinctive error in the CT at m. 18 (6). Pix seems to belong to the same family, and Mell is apparently more closely related to that tradition than to any other. Of the two printed collections, the reading of Odh is not far removed from that of the present MS whereas Form stands distinctly apart. Cop 1848-2⁰ is evidently closer to the northern group of MSS in general than to any other, whereas FloR 2356 is very close to Mell in its version of this work. Par 4379, although more independent, would also seem to follow the version of the Italian group.

That the proper movement for this chanson is to be derived from the integral mensuration is argued not only by the preponderance of the sources giving that indication, but also by the character of the poetry and the rhythmic activity of the music in general. The accidentals specifically given by Mell, although not numerous for this work, are particularly interesting because they are required neither by cadential formulations nor by melodic configurations or harmonic combinations in the counterpoint.

> Ma bouce rit et ma pensee pleure;
> Mon oeil s'esjoye et mon cuer mauldit l'eure
> Qu'il eut le bien qui sa santé déchasse
> Et le plaisir qui la mort me pourchasse
> Sans resconfort qui m'ayde ne sequeure.   5
>
> Ha! cuer pervers, faussaire et [mensongier],
> Dittes comment avés ozé songier
> Que de faulser ce que m'avés promis;   8

Puis qu'en ce point vous vous voulés vengier
Pensés bien tost de ma vie abregier—
Vivre ne puis ou point ou m'avés mis.   11

Vostre pitié veult doncques que je meure,
Mais rigueur veult que vivant je demeure.
Ainsi meurs vif, et en vivant trespasse.
Mais pour celer le mal qui ne se passe
Et pour couvrir le dueil ou je labeure,   16
      Ma bouce rit et ma pensee pleure,
      Mon oeil s'esjoye et mon cuer mauldit l'eure
      Qu'il eut le bien qui sa santé déchasse
      Et le plaisir qui la mort me pourchasse
      Sans resconfort qui m'ayde ne sequeure.

My lips laugh and my thoughts weep,
My eye is gay, and my heart curses the hour
When it had the good which drives away its health
And the pleasure which brings me death
Without comfort that might aid or succor me.

Ah, perverse heart, false and lying,
Tell how you have dared to dream
Of breaking the promise you made to me;

Since you will avenge yourself to that degree,
Consider soon cutting short my life—
I cannot live in the plight in which you've placed me.

Your pity then, wants me to die,
But sternness wants me to survive.
So alive I die, and in living pass away.
But, to hide the ill which has no end
And to cover the grief in which I struggle,
      My lips laugh and my thoughts weep,
      My eye is gay, and my heart curses the hour
      When it had the good which drives away its health
      And the pleasure which brings me death
      Without comfort that might aid or succor me.

Variants

The texted concordant sources are Roh (=Löp No. 142), Dij, Niv, Par 1719, f. 61ʳ (Par 1719a), Par 1719, f. 132ʳ (Par 1719b), Pix, Par 4379, Cord, Lab, Jar, f. 61ʳ, Dictié et chançon magistrale (JarD), Jar, f. 71ᵛ, Motet magistral (JarM).

1 bouche—*All MSS but Mell and Par 4379.* 2 s'esjoÿt—*Par 1719b (Wolf)* (+1 syll.), s'esjoue—*Par 4379.* 3 Qui scet le bien—*Par 4379*; le bien que—*Dij Par 1719a Par 1719b Pix Par 4379 Lab Wolf* (7 × que : 6 × qui). 4 (*Par 4379* omits line); que—*Dij Niv Par 1719a Par 1719b Lab Wolf JarD* (7 × que : 5 × qui); la mon—*Par 1719a*, ma mort—*Par 1719b*; luy—*Par 1719a Cord Wolf JarD JarM* (5 × luy : 7 × me); prochasse—*Lab.* 5 l'aide—*Wolf*, n'aide—*JarD.* 6 A—*Par 1719a Par 1719b*, O—*Pix*; cueurs—*Par 1719b*; parvers—*Lab Wolf*; faulseres—*Par 1719b*, faulx yeux—*Pix*, faussart—*Par 4379*; messongier—*Mell Pix*, messonger—*Lab*, menchongnier—*Par 4379.* 7 avez oser—*Par 1719a Par 1719b.* 8 Vouloir faulcer—*Roh*, De ainsi faulser—*Cord*; m'avyez promis—*Par 1719a*; permis—*Roh.* (Pix ends here.) 9 point vous voulez—*Wolf* (−1 syll.). (JarD omits ll. 9–11.) 10 Pancer—*Niv*; Pensez bien brief—*Wolf.* 11 (Mell ends here. Remainder from JarM.) 12 Vostre rigueur—*Niv Cord.* 13 Mais pitié—*Niv Cord Wolf*; Dij omits veult (−1 syll.) 14 Aussi muir—*Par 4379.* 15 qu'il ne se passe—*Par 1719a*, qu'il me se passe—*Par 1719b.* 16 lameure—*Par 1719a.*

Versification

Decasyllabic bergerette, *a a b b a c c d.* JarD omits the clos and places the incipit, *Ma bouche rit &c*, after the ouvert; this gives the poem the form of a rondeau cinquain, but with an anomalous rhyme scheme: where a rondeau would have a short strophe, *a a b*, JarD has *c c d*, to be followed, apparently, by the short refrain, *a a b.* JarM has the full bergerette, i.e., the clos as well as the ouvert.

Mell omits the last strophe, but, with its clos and ouvert, identifies itself unambiguously as a bergerette.

Textual Notes

A series of contrasts, each of which emphasizes the appearance of joy and the inner reality of despondency.

Line 1. **bouce**, a Picard spelling; but pronounce *bouche*, as in Francian.

Line 3. Although the readings *qui/que* (*sa santé déchasse*) are almost equally well represented, Mell's *qui* is more plausible: 'the good which drives away its [the heart's] health' rather than 'the good which its health drives away'. Thus the running paradox is maintained.

Line 4. The variants of l. 4 with respect to *qui/que* are not distributed in the same way as in l. 3. With *qui* it means 'which obtains death for me/him'; with *que*, 'which death obtains for me/him'. The distribution of *me/luy* is different again.

Line 2–4, according to the Mell version:

> ... and my heart curses the hour
> when it had the good which drives away its health,
> and the pleasure which obtains death for me.

Line 5. With a three-way split, *m'ayde/n'aide/l'aide*, in which the first reading is supported by the great majority of MSS, we have an indication as to the correct reading in l. 4 *me/luy*. Wolf is the only scribe who seems to have tried to bring l. 5 into conformity with his l. 4 (which has *luy*) by changing *m* to *l*. The fact that the others have not done so may only mean that they did not notice the inconsistency between l. 4 *luy* and l. 5 *m'*. If we read ll. 4–5 in that way, we have: 'my heart curses the hour when it had ... the pleasure which brought death *to it*, without comfort to aid or help *me*'. The near unanimity of l. 5 *m'* would, then, tend to support *me* (as against *luy*) in l. 4.

Line 12–13. Great paradoxes involving two antinomies: *pitié* : *rigueur* and *meure* : *vivant demeure*.

Wolf has committed an obvious error in these lines; the paradox has become a contradiction:

> *Vostre pitié veult doncques que je meure,*
> *Maiz pitié veult que vivant je demeure.*

We are left with the choice between

> ... *rigueur* ... *meure*
> ... *pitié* ... *vivant demeure*
>   (Niv Cord)

and

> ... *pitie* ... *meure*
> ... *rigueur* ... *vivant demeure*
>   (all other sources).

The Niv Cord reading has a surface plausibility (Sternness wants me to die, Pity to live); but it lacks the very paradox on which this poem depends (Pity wants me to die, Sternness to live)—in this case, death is a mercy and being condemned to live a stern punishment. The agreement of the great majority of MSS against one obvious error and one variant worth taking seriously, manifested in only two MSS, strengthens the case for the paradox.

31. Se je fayz dueil, ff. 40ᵛ–42ʳ, G. le Rouge

Concordant Sources

*Roh, f. 74ʳ⁻ᵛ
Sched, ff. 103ᵛ–105ʳ (initial section); f. 24ᵛ (final section, "Qui plus est")

Collation

Most of the variants between the two musical sources apparently mirror scribal errors, primarily in Sched. For example the latter gives a sharply dissonant f at m. 2(4) of the C instead of e-flat as in Mell. The relationship between the T and CT parts of the initial section is confusing in the two MSS. The T of Mell is labeled CT in Sched and vice versa, but at m. 4(4) of Mell's T, the CT of Sched gives e-flat M, d-Sb, c-M, and so on, becoming identical to the CT of Mell at m. 7(1), where, conversely, the T of Sched follows the T of Mell. The correspondence continues until m. 13(2) of Mell's T, where the T of Sched again becomes Mell's CT, and until m. 17(2) of Mell's CT, where the CT of Sched again follows Mell's T. For the final section of the composition (mm. 37 ff.) the voices are identified in the same manner in both sources.

With reference to the T of Mell, the flats of the key signature are mistakenly placed in Sched on the first and third lines instead of in the first and third spaces. Further errors in Sched are in the T at m. 31(3), where F-Sb is given instead of G-Sb; at m. 45(1), where f-Br is given instead of d-Br; and in the CT at m. 33(4), where b-Sb is given instead of a-Sb. The reading of Sched also eliminates the rest-L in all voices at mm. 39–40 and the final Br in the C. By contrast, entirely possible alternate readings are found at the beginning of Mell's CT, where Sched gives G-L instead of G-Sb, b-Sb, and at m. 16(3) of Mell's T and 17(2) of Mell's CT, where Sched has b-flat M instead of c-M. At m. 17(7) of Mell's CT, Sched is once again in error, giving c-SB instead of c-M as required by the context, but at m. 19 (5, 6), Sched has D-M, C-M, definitely a much better reading than E-M, D-M as in Mell.

COMMENTS

The reading in Sched for m. 19 (5, 6) of Mell's CT is so clearly superior to the discordant pitches of the present MS that a scribal error was assumed and the consequent emendation made in the transcription.

There is a thorny problem in the choice of accidentals at mm. 20–21. The melodic line of the C rises from E-flat to a, creating a tritone that is difficult to avoid. If the flat is canceled for E, it forms a diminished fifth with the b-flat above. If the a is lowered, it engenders both melodic problems in the following descent to a written f-sharp and a cross-relation with a of the T, m. 21 (1). Applicable in this instance, obviously, is Tinctoris's explicit recommendation that harmonic considerations be given preference over melodic ones when the two come into conflict.

The placement of the text also proved troublesome in the initial section of the piece because of the melismatic character of the melodic writing. Since the first line of the long strophe has its caesura a syllable later than that of the refrain, it should be divided after *languir*, and the necessary adjustments can easily be made. In the MS the text has been written out under the T for the short strophes (mm. 37 ff.), but because the T carries no text for the refrain, the text was not printed separately for that voice in the second section of the transcription. It is really unnecessary to do so because the homophonic writing throughout the passage makes it possible for the T to follow the text placement of the C if a vocal performance is desired. However, since the T duplicates the C imitatively through much of the refrain section, it would also be possible to place the verse under the T for the whole composition.

The presence of a sign of congruence in all three parts at m. 21 raises the possibility that Rouge's *Se je fayz dueil* was conceived originally as a rondeau cinquain and subsequently transformed as a bergerette by the addition of the short strophes and a modest musical setting to accommodate them. This impression is only strengthened by the sharp stylistic contrast between the imitative, contrapuntal character of the initial section and the declamatory homophony of the second, the unusual brevity of the latter, and the manner in which the two are

physically separated in Sched. If such a modification could be documented, it would be of exceptional interest since the general tendency
in the collections without music was instead to reduce the bergerette
to the formal structure of the rondeau. An example of the latter is
cited in the Versification for No. 12.

Also unusual is the signature of two flats in lieu of clefs, a device seen
thus far only in No. 25, *L'omme banny*, and nowhere else in the chansonnier. However, in this case the transposition is unusual because the
resulting scale structure is that found with a final on A when no accidentals are present. Although A is not a regular modal termination,
in the fifteenth century it was assimilated—as it had been all through
the Middle Ages—to the first pair of modes because of the affinities
between the scales formed with D and A as the primary point of
orientation; both have the same species of fifth above the final. The
first pair of modes was frequently transposed to a final on G in the
period, as the examples published here would indicate, but it is
surprising that the modal area should seem to refer to an irregular
final twice removed rather than to the traditional one just a fourth
below, as it would with a single flat as a signature. Since b-flat is often
used in the Dorian modes (it is in fact indispensable in melodic configurations such as that with which C and T begin this chanson), the
final of G with two flats may represent in this case a simple transposition of the D final with a regularly recurring b-flat. Whatever the
interpretation, the modal framework is clearly that of the Dorian
modal pair.

Finally, the combination of three voices of equal range in this work
is extraordinary for the rarity with which it occurs in the chanson
repertory. In the present collection only Busnois's *Bel Acueil* (No. 1)
and *A vous sans aultre* (No. 42) are similarly disposed.

> Se je fayz dueil, je n'en puis mais,
> Ne nul ne m'en doibt donner blasme,
> Car je ne crois pas qu'il fut ame
> Plus desplaisant que moy jamais.   4
>
> Qui plus est, ne me doibt souffire
> De faire dueil tant seullement,   6
>
> Car par droit je me deusse occire
> Pour mettre fin a mon tourment.   8

Aultrement languir desormais
Me fauldra, jusqu'a rendre l'ame,
Plourant les maulx qu'ay pour ma damme,
Puis que seul sans la voir remays.   12
  Se je fayz dueil, *je n'en puis mais,*
  Ne nul ne m'en doibt donner blasme,
  Car je ne crois pas qu'il fut ame
  Plus desplaisant que moy jamais.

If I make dole, I can do no other,
And none ought give me blame,
For I don't believe there's been a soul
More unhappy than I, ever.

What's more, it cannot be enough
To make dole, just that alone,

For by right I ought to kill myself
To put an end to my torment.

Otherwise to languish long
I am doomed, until I breathe my last,
Bewailing the pain I suffer for my lady,
Since I am left alone and cannot see her.
  If I make dole, I can do no other,
  And none ought give me blame,
  For I don't believe there's been a soul
  More unhappy than I, ever.

Variants

12 Puys que suys sans la veoir jamaiz—*Roh.*

Versification

Octosyllabic bergerette, *a b b a c d.*

Textual Notes

Line 1. **Je n'en puis mais** 'I cannot do otherwise'.
Line 3. **fut**: probably an imperfect subjunctive; since the *s* of *fust*

was no longer sounded, and the increased length of the vowel was probably not realized in an unstressed position in the sentence, the confusion between *fut* and *fust* was already well launched.

Line 4. **desplaisant** 'unhappy'.

Line 7. **je me deusse occire** 'I should kill myself'; deusse [düs] or [dös] according to dialect (see p. 100).

Line 12. **remays**: a respelling, for visual rhyme, of *remés*, the first person singular preterite of *remaindre* (or *remanoir*) 'to remain'.

32. De tous biens plaine, ff. 42ᵛ–43ʳ, Heyne

CONCORDANT SOURCES

* Roh, ff. 184ʳ⁻ᵛ
Bol Q 16, ff. 134ᵛ–135ʳ
Cop 291⁸, ff. 5ᵛ–6ʳ
Cop 1848-2⁰, p. 201 (T only)
Dij 517, ff. xiᵛ–xiiʳ, Hayne
Flo 121, ff. 24ᵛ–25ʳ
Flo 178, ff. 34ᵛ–35ʳ, Hayne
FloR 2356, ff. 32ᵛ–33ʳ
FloR 2794, ff. 18ᵛ–19ʳ
Lon 31922, ff. 40ᵛ–41ʳ (No. xxxi)
MC 871, f. 102aᵛ (p. 344)
Pix, ff. 105ᵛ–106ʳ
Par 676, ff. 42ᵛ–43ʳ
Cord, ff. 25ᵛ–26ʳ
Pav 362, ff. 34bisᵛ–35ʳ, Heyne
Per 431, ff. 70ᵛ–71ʳ (No. 80)
CG XIII.27, ff. 64ᵛ–65ʳ (à 5)
RomC 2856, ff. 66ᵛ–67ʳ, Haine
Sev 5.I.43, f. 39ʳ (T and TC only)
Ulm 237, ff. 17ʳ (C), 15ʳ (T), 16ʳ (CT)
Lab, ff. 62ᵛ–63ʳ
Wolf 287, ff. 52ᵛ–53ʳ
Odh, ff. 22ᵛ–23ʳ (à 4)

COLLATION

All the sources were checked in order to verify the identification and location of the concordances, but because of the number involved, a detailed collation was made only with those having the greatest number of works in common with Mell. Significant variants are not numerous in view of the wide dissemination this chanson achieved, but only those seeming to provide an indication of the filiation among the readings compared have been reported here. Omitted entirely from consideration, however, is the C of the third of the collections printed by Christian Egenolff in the early 1530s (No. 16). As Martin Staehelin has shown, even though the C is identical to that of Hayne's chanson, the matching bassus in the Heilbronn MS identifies the piece in question as a reworking by Ghiselin.[1]

Cantus: At m. 7 (2) the cadential formula is embellished with a'-Sm, g-Sm in Cop 291[8], Dij 517, Lab, and FloR 2356, with g-M in FloR 2794, Cord, and Wolf 287, in both instances without the lower third following the a'-M of Mell; at m. 14 (2) Dij 517 and Lab give c-M, b-M instead of c-Sb as in Mell; at m. 18 (2), instead of c-Br as in Mell, c-Sb, rest-Sb is found in Cop 291[8], Dij 517, Lab, and Wolf 287; at m. 19 (1), instead of e-M, d-M as in Mell, e-Sb is given by Cop 291[8], Dij 517, Lab, Bol Q 16, and Pav 362; at m. 25 (4), Dij 517 and Lab have c'-M, a'-M, b-Sb, a'-M, g-M.

Contratenor: The initial pitch is an octave lower than in the present collection in Cord, FloR 2356, and RomC 2856 among the sources collated, and in Flo 121, Flo 178, Lon 31922, Ulm 237, and Odh among those that were cursorily checked; at m. 6 (2), instead of a rest and b-flat M as here, Cop 291[8], Dij 517, and Lab have b-flat Sb, whereas FloR 2794 and Wolf 287 have the rest with a-M; at m. 8 (5), Bol Q 16 and Cord have a dissonant A-M instead of B-M as here; at m. 20 (1), instead of D-Sb as in Mell, all sources collated give B-flat Sb instead of D-Sb as in Mell except Pix, CG XIII.27, Pav 362, Per 461, and FloR 2356; at m. 21 (1), B-flat Sb, G'-Sb are given (instead of the G'-Br of Mell) by Cop 291[8], Dij 517, Lab, Wolf 287, Bol Q 16, Cord, FloR 2794, FloR 2356, MC 871, RomC 2856, and Sev; at m. 21 (2), Bol Q 16, Cord, FloR 2794, FloR 2356, and MC 871 give G-dotted Br instead of G-Sb, G-Sb, b-Sb as in Mell.

The T of Cord carries e-flat as a signature (but not E-flat), affecting only the two pitches with written flats in Mell. Cop 291[8] has no signed flat for the C, but like Dij 517, Lab, and Lon 31922, it gives both

---

1. See "Zum Egenolff-Diskantband der Bibliothèque Nationale in Paris," p. 101; concerning the print, its contents, and its date, see Nanie Bridgman, "Christian Egenolff, Imprimeur de musique."

B-flat and E-flat as a signature for the CT in place of the written accidentals of Mell. Cord, MC 871, and Pav 362, on the other hand, have no signed flats for the CT at all. Surprisingly, Lon 31922 gives the mensural sign without the stroke of diminution.

COMMENTS

Some of the variants cited represent little more than differences of cadential ornamentation that would not generally be considered significant. However, the scribal tradition is so consistent with regard to the musical substance of Heyne's chanson that melodic details of this nature assume greater importance. There is considerable crossing and mixing of variant readings, but there seem to be three principal traditions of transmission. One is northern and includes the MSS Cop 291[8], Dij 517, Lab, and Wolf 287; Dij 517 and Lab in particular give almost identical readings for this work. The other two groups are Italian. The one to which Mell belongs comprises, in a descending order of affinity with the present version, Pix, Per 431, Pav 362, and (despite the fact that it has five voice parts for this composition, including two that are simply alternates for Heyne's CT) CG XIII.27, which follows closely the reading of Mell for the voices common to both. The other Italian tradition is apparently related to the reading of Wolf 287 and includes Cord, Flo 2794, FloR 2356, MC 871, and Bol Q 16.

Unfortunately, the scribe of Mell, having filled all the space available at the bottom of f. 43[r] before the CT was completely copied, evidently forgot to enter the remainder of the part on the empty staves of the facing page as he customarily did. The missing segment was supplied from Pix but with the written E-flat of the northern MSS.

If, as has been surmised,[2] Compère's *Omnium bonorum plena*, which uses Hayne's tenor as a *cantus firmus*, was written between 1470 and 1474, the composition of the chanson could not have been completed much later than the end of the 1460s.

> De tous biens plaine est ma maistresse,
> Chescun ly [doibt] tribut [d'onneur],

---

2. See Otto Gombosi, *Jacob Obrecht: eine stilkritische Studie* (Leipzig: Breitkopf und Härtel, 1925), p. 35; cf. Ludwig Finscher, *Loyset Compère (c. 1450–1518) Life and Works*, pp. 14–15, 131.

Car assouvye est en valeur
Autant que jamais fu déesse.   4

En la véant j'ay tel léesse
Que c'est paradis en mon cueur.   6
 De tous biens plaine est ma maistresse,
 Chescun ly doibt tribut d'onneur.

Je n'ay cure d'autre richesse
Sinon d'estre son serviteur;
Et pour ce qu'il n'est chois milleur
En mon mot porteray sans cesse: 10
 De tous biens plaine est ma maistresse,
 Chescun ly doibt tribut d'onneur,
 Car assouvye est en valeur
 Autant que fu jamais déesse.

Full of all good is my mistress,
Everyone owes her the tribute of honor,
For she is as perfect in virtue
As was ever any goddess.

Seeing her I have such joy
That there is paradise in my heart.
 Full of all good is my mistress,
 Everyone owes her the tribute of honor.

I care for no other riches
Except to be her servant;
And because there is no better choice,
I will ever carry as my motto:
 Full of all good is my mistress,
 Everyone owes her the tribute of honor,
 For she is as perfect in virtue
 As was ever any goddess.

Variants

The texted concordant sources are Cord, Dij, Lab, Roh (= Löp
No. 575), Wolf, Pix (first line only). The poem in Chasse, f. Piiʳ, begin-

ning *De tous biens pleine*, has nothing in common with the present poem except the initial line. Mell goes to l. 4; our text is completed with Dij.

2 lui (luy)—*all MSS but Mell*; veult—*Mell*; donner—*Mell*, de honneur—*Cord Roh*, donneur—*Dij Lab Wolf*. 3 accomplie—*Wolf*. 4 Autant qu'oncques maiz déesse—*Wolf*, Autant que fut oncques déesse—*Roh*. 9 rien meilleur—*Cord*; Et affin qu'ung chascun soyt seure—*Wolf*, Pour ce doncques pour le meilleur—*Roh*.

VERSIFICATION

Octosyllabic rondeau quatrain, *abba*. Autonomous short refrain, integrated long refrain.

TEXTUAL NOTES

Line 2. Mell is obviously corrupt. If a previous scribe has changed a hypothetical *donne^r* (the raised *r* being a normal abbreviation of *-ur*) to *donner*, then *doibt* would be semantically and grammatically interchangeable with *veult*. However, the rhyme rules out *donner*, and *veult* is no longer acceptable. **ly** is the Old French third person singular dative (indirect object) conjunctive pronoun, interchangeable with *lui* in Middle French, completely replaced by *lui* in modern French.

Line 3. **assouvye** [asuviə] 'accomplished, perfect'.

Line 5. **tel**, feminine (as well as masculine), interchangeable when feminine with *telle* in Old and Middle French (see p. 107).

Line 9. The variants for this line abound, possibly because scribes felt that, taken together, ll. 7–9 seem a little crass, out of keeping with a serious (noncomic) poem. We have put a semicolon after l. 8 and read ll. 9–10 together, for an entirely acceptable sentiment.

33. **Dona gentile, ff. 43ᵛ–44ʳ, G. Dufay**

CONCORDANT SOURCES

Cord, ff. 2ᵛ–3ʳ
Pav 362, ff. 52ᵛ–53ʳ

COLLATION

Variants of substance are indeed few between Mell and the two concordant sources. Nevertheless, there are two errors in the T of Pav 362: at m. 27 (2) a-flat is written as Sb instead of M, and at m. 28 (3), C-Sb was omitted. In the CT at m. 1 (2), both MSS have F-M (a perfectly possible if dissonant reading) instead of E-M as in

Mell; and at m. 10 (1), Cord has E-M, apparently an error of rhythm, instead of E-Sb as elsewhere. In addition, the cadential formula of the C is embellished with the lower third at m. 4 in Cord and at m. 11 in Pav 362.

There are some slight inconsistencies in the use of written accidentals: the flat for e at m. 3 (5) of the C is found only in Mell (and is scarcely necessary even there); in the C, Pav 362 gives no flat for e at m. 13 (1) and no natural for b at m. 25 (1), but in the CT the same MS has a flat for a at m. 4 (1) (where it hardly seems possible harmonically) and a natural for e at m. 26 (3)—apparently in a later hand —where its effect would be problematical at best because of the progression in the C from a-(flat?) to b-flat.

Comments

All three MSS appear to belong to the same tradition of transmission, but Cord is demonstrably closer to Mell than Pav 362.

Although the text written under the T in the present MS is incomplete, the imitative relationship identifying the part with the C makes it equally apt for a vocal performance. The lacunae of the fifteenth-century scribe were consequently filled out in the transcription.

The melodic configuration of the CT in mm. 10–11 raises a problem regarding accidentals. The a at the top of the line, m. 11 (2), would normally be lowered to avoid the tritone with the E-flat below, but since the C sings a′ at that point, it is necessary either to lower both parts or to cancel the flat for the preceding and following E in the CT. The latter solution was chosen because it also eliminates a cross-relation with the T at m. 10 (3–4).

Particularly noteworthy is the written natural for b at m. 25 of the C since the pitch in question is introduced against a sounding F in the CT and hence creates an unmistakable tritone vertically. It is tempting to assume that the carefully indicated accidental is quite intentional and that its use in this specific harmonic context was an attempt to underline the pathetic sentiment of the final line of the refrain.

> Dona gentile, bella come l'oro,
> Que supra le altre portate corona
> Como par l'universo se rasona,
> Datime secorso, Stella, que moro.

4

Que piu ne stago in questo purgatoro,
Tranquillata*te* enver di me, Fortuna,   6
    Dona gentile, bella come l'oro,
    Que supra le altre portate corona.

Lasso ja sono di tale martiro,
Que viver non posso salvo | en una;
Qui me trovo chom*e* voy, chara luna,
Por sempre servire quella qu'adoro.   10
    Dona gentile, bella come l'oro,
    Que supra le altre portate corona
    Come par l'universo se rasona,
    Datime secorso, Stella, que moro.

Gentle Lady, lovely as gold,
Who above all others wear the crown,
As is known throughout the world;
Help me, O Star! for I am dying.

Because I am ever in this purgatory,
Be kind to me, O Fortune,
    Gentle Lady, lovely as gold,
    Who above all others carry the crown.

I am so weary of such martyrdom
That I cannot live, save in one alone;
Here I am, like you, bright Moon,
Ever to serve the one whom I adore.
    Gentle Lady, lovely as gold,
    Who above all others wear the crown,
    As is known throughout the world;
    Help me, O Star! for I am dying.

VARIANTS

Cord and Pav.

1 gentile he belle—*Cord,* gentille belle—*Pav.* 2 Che—*Cord,* Quy—
Pav, Qui—*Mell (T);* li altre—*Pav;* porti—*Cord.* 3 Come per—*Cord*
Pav; se razone—*Pav.* 4 Stela—*Cord.* 5 non stago—*Cord,* non estago—
Pav; chesto purgatorio—*Cord,* questo plogatoro—*Pav.* 6 Tranquilitate

enver dima fortuna—*Cord*, Transquillata en vers de my fortuna—*Pav*.
7 Lasso yo sono—*Cord;* di talle—*Pav;* martyrio—*Cord (Pav)*. 8 Che—
Cord; Che vivie non posso en una—*Pav*. 9 Che my . . . [illegible] . . .
voy clara luna—*Cord*, Qui me [blank space for two or three words]
voy chera luna—*Pav*. 10 chello che yo adoro—*Cord*, quello qu'adoro
— *Pav*.

Versification

Hendecasyllabic rondeau quatrain, *abba* (see pp. 81–82, 85). In two
instances in which a final vowel precedes an initial vowel (ll. 2 and 5),
the two vowels are counted as one syllable, but in l. 8 there is a hiatus
following *salvo*.

Textual Notes

Line 1. **Dona**: Double consonants are not always written as such
(cf. No. 46 *madona*). There are northern dialects of Italian in which the
geminate consonants have been reduced, but it is unlikely that this
trait applies to the redactor of this poem, since all the other doublings
are respected (e.g., l. 1 *bella*, l. 4 *Stella*, l. 5 *lasso*) and there are no
examples of incorrectly doubled consonants.

Line 2. **Que** [ke] = standard Italian *che*. The phonetic ambiguity
of the graph *qu* (= [k, kw]) was characteristic of Italian spelling until
recent times. **supra** = standard Italian *sopra;* it can be either the
resolution of a common Latin abbreviation (ŝ, sᵃ, Cappelli, pp. 336,
337), a process that is the source of many Latinisms, or it can represent
a pronunciation of the south, in many dialects of which Romance
[ǫ] > [u].

Lines 2–3. **Corona**, **rasona** rhyme with l. 5 **Fortuna**, ll. 8–9 **una**,
luna. Since there is no dialect in which Latin ū > *o*, but many in
which Romance tonic *ǫ* (Classical Latin u, ō) > *u*, we may posit the
latter value for this rhyme, hence the pronunciations *coruna, ragiuna*
(see textual note on this word, l. 3, below). This phonetic development
is characteristic of southern Italy. Or this may be an instance of
assonanza atona (Federzoni, p. 46) (cf. No. 46, Versification).

Line 3. **Como** = standard Italian *come*. *Como, comu*, and the like
are found in various dialects. But this text is not dialectally consistent,
as l. 1 **come** shows. **par** might well be a French-influenced *per*, or a
resolution by a French scribe of the abbreviation of *per*.

se rasona 'is said, is well known' = standard Italian *si ragiona*. The use of *-s-* as a reflex of Vulgar Latin (VL) *-ty-* (we are supposing an underlying *RATYONARE) argues a northern, western dialect of Italian. But since the rhyme is indicative of a southern origin for this poem (see note on ll. 2–3), we may assume that the present text is a northern copy (probably made by a Frenchman more familiar with northern Italian than with the southern variety) of a southern poem, in which such forms as *coruna* and *ragiuna* have been "corrected" to the spellings we have here. Forms of the lexical family of *ragione*, *ragionare*, when they appear in the south, seem more often to be borrowed from Tuscan than to be native-stock words. Vulgar Latin *RATYONAT would be expected to give southern *razzuna; but, in fact, the Calabrian *ragiune* for Tuscan *ragione* displays the result of the attempt to adapt the Old Tuscan [ž], nonexistent in the south, to the local pronunciation. Hence it is more likely that, in the original of our poem, the word that corresponded to *rasona* of the Mellon text was *ragiuna*, rather than *razzuna*, which would be the regular southern reflex of the Vulgar Latin. We recommend for the execution of this song the pronunciation *ragiuna* [radžúna]. See Rohlfs, §§289, 290 for details.

Line 4. **moro** = standard Italian *muoio* 'I die'. The endings *-io* and *-eo* (VL *-yo*) are often replaced by *-o* (cf. *dormo, servo*). Another explanation may be phonetic rather than analogical, given the forms in *-oro* for *-orio*, *-iro* for *-irio* in this same poem—forms whose pronunciation is guaranteed by the rhyme with l. 1 **oro** and l. 10 **adoro**. See textual notes on l. 5 **purgatoro**.

Line 5. **Que** [ke] = modern *che*. **ne** is used as is **ci** in modern Italian, that is, here, as a redundant locative paralleling **in questo purgatoro**. **stago** = standard Italian *stò;* Rohlfs §542 cites it for Old Genoese, Old Paduan, Old Venetian, and in the modern dialect of western Venezia.

purgatoro, and l. 7 **martiro** (and possibly l. 4 **moro**) offer examples of Latin *-Vrium* > *-Vro* rather than the normal *-Vio*. Rohlfs §284 observes that most of these words are of a learned character and suggests three phases for *-orium* words: (a) *-orium* became *-oio* in native stock words, e.g., CORIUM > *cuoio* 'leather'; (b) words borrowed from Latin after change (a) had taken place lost the prevocalic *i : purgatoro;* (c) subsequent borrowings retained the *i*, and words of the -ORIUM > -*oro* type were either replaced by the new -*orio* borrowings or were remodeled—which amounts to the same thing. Such forms as *purgatoro* are now obsolete.

tranquillatate (this form from Cord): imperative of **tranquillatare*, which would be a frequentative derivative from Latin TRANQUILLARE 'to calm, to still'.

Line 6. **en ver di**: almost certainly a calque on French.

Line 7. **ja** = *già*. **martiro** is a sufficient rhyme for -*oro;* another instance of "atonic assonance" or "alliteration". See textual note on l. 5.

Line 8. **Que** [ke] = *che*.

Line 9. **Qui** [kwi] 'here'. **chome**, MS *chom:* -*e* is supplied on the model of l. 1 **come,** although -*o* could have been justified by l. 3 **Como**. The spelling with *ch*, the Italian device for spelling [k] before a front vowel, is here redundant.

chara is either a similarly redundant spelling of *cara* 'dear', or represents an attempt to use *h* as a sign of palatalization (as in Portuguese and often in Provencal), hence = *chiara* [kyára] 'bright, clear' —a reading that is supported by Cord *clara*, which represents a dialect in which *l*, preceded by an initial consonant, does not become [y].

Line 10. **quella** [kwella]; **qu'** [k] = *ch'*.

34. Il sera pour vous conbatu /
L'ome armé, ff. 44ᵛ–45ʳ [Morton]

CONCORDANT SOURCE

RomC 2856, ff. 156ᵛ–157ʳ, Borton (Morton?), (à 4)

COLLATION

With a single exception all the differences in pitch found in the single concordance result in infractions of the fifteenth-century rules of harmony in the three-voice context of Mell and must be either errors or emendations that were made when the fourth voice of RomC 2856 was added. At m. 9 (4) of the C, the variant is g-Sb (duplicating the pitch of the CT), rest-M instead of b'-dotted M as in Mell; in the T at m. 8 (4), g-M instead of e-M (a perfectly possible alternative); in the CT at m. 10 (2), f-M instead of g-M, and at mm. 4 (4)–5 (5) and 16 (2ff.), the following: e-M, f-M, d-Sb, d-M, (d-Sb, d-M only the first time). At m. 8 (4) of the C, RomC 2856 also gives for b-Sb a signed flat that is quite unnecessary in the version à 3 of Mell.

COMMENTS

Because the cadential approaches of mm. 4–5 and 16–17 consist of a lightly embellished fauxbourdon, it seemed more appropriate to raise the f of the CT to conform to the b′-natural of the unambiguously mixolydian melody of the C than to lower the same b′ in order to accommodate the written f of the CT.

The placement of the text offered no problems in T and CT, where the declamation is virtually syllabic throughout, but in order to maintain the same style in the C, it was unavoidable that some segments of the text be repeated as is done in the other two parts. If the distribution of syllables suggested for the refrain of the rondeau in the C is adopted for the long strophe, the name "Symonet" will be divided just before the final syllable by the rest of m. 8—and can be without doing violence to the meaning of the verse—but would then best be followed by a repetition of the beginning of the line, "Vive Symonet . . . " in m. 9.

Even though the mensural symbol given for this composition (C3) is the one found in Dij 517 for No. 20, Ockeghem's *L'aultre d'antan*, the unit of declamation is here the minim (rather than the semibreve as in the other work), and the basic mensural value the semibreve rather than the breve. Therefore, the observations made in connection with Ockeghem's rondeau concerning the proportional indication and the appropriate tempo cannot be construed as valid for this work as well. In this case the implicit proportion is probably sesquialteral, indicating that three minims are to be sung in the same time as two under the integral mensuration of imperfect tempus. Such an interpretation would produce the bright tempo obviously required by the character of the text and by the fanfare figures that are thrown into relief by the part writing.

1. Cantus:

      Il sera pour vous conbatu
      Le doubté Turcq, Maistre Symon
      —Certainement ce sera mon—
      Et de crocq de ache abatu.   4

      Son orgueil tenons a batu.
      S'il chiét en voz mains, le felon,   6

> *Il sera pour vous conbatu,*
> *Le doubté Turcq, Maistre Symon.*

En peu d'heure l'arés batu
Au plaisir Dieu. Puis dira-on,
"Vive Symonet le Breton
Que sur le Turcq s'est enbatu!"   10
> *Il sera pour vous conbatu,*
> *Le doubté Turcq, Maistre Symon;*
> *—Certainement ce sera mon—*
> *Et de crocq de ache abatu.*

I.   He will be fought for you,
            The dreaded Turk, Master Symon
            —there's no doubt about it—
            And struck down with an axe-spur.
                (or stalk of wild celery)

            We hold his pride to have been beaten.
            If he falls into your hands, the felon,
                He will be fought for you,
                The redoubted Turk, Master Symon.

            In a short time you will have beaten him
            To God's pleasure. Then they will say
            "Long live ol' Symon the Breton,
            Because he has fallen on the Turk!"
                He will be fought for you,
                The dreaded Turk, Master Symon
                —there's no doubt about it—
                And struck down with an axe-spur.

Variants

No texted concordant sources.

Versification

Rondeau quatrain in octosyllables, *abba*. This song is sung in the cantus simultaneously with poem ii, which is carried in tenor and contratenor.

Textual Notes

Line 2. **Le doubté Turcq** 'the feared Turk'; **Maistre Symon**, in apposition with l. 1 **vous**, is in direct address. Simon le Breton was a musician of the Burgundian court; casting him as a hero of the war against the Turks must have been an in joke in this circle of musicians. Pre-occupation with the Turks was normal at this difficult moment in history.

Line 3. 'There's no doubt about it.' **mon** is an affirmative particle; it reaffirms (or, in the negative, negates) the verb of a question, or the substitute verb *faire*, in the tense of the verb of the question and in the appropriate person and number. In an early fifteenth-century grammar of French, written for the English, these examples are proposed: "Et tousjours tu mettras devant le verbe cest mot *ce* et après le verbe cest mot *mon*, si come es cetz exemples: *le meistre est en la escolle?*, tu respondras, ottroiant: *ce est mon*, ou nient: *ce n'est mon* . . . Aussi *le meistre nous ensaigne bien?* tu respondras: *ce fait mon*, ou : *ce ne fait mon*.[1]

Line 4. **ache** = modF *hache* 'ax'; the hiatus with preceding **de** shows that the modern treatment of "aspirate h" was already current: no aspiration (as shown by the absence of the letter *h*), but no elision of the vowel of **de.** The spelling of **ache** without *h* may constitute the introduction of a comic ambiguity, for *ache* means 'wild celery'; but the failure to elide *de* to *d'*, as shown by the meter, suffices to identify the word, on a phonetic level, as *hache* 'axe'.

Line 5. **tenons a** 'we regard as'.

Line 6. **chiét** 'falls'.

Line 7. **arés** = modF *aurez* 'you will have'. A Picard form.

Line 8. **Dieu** 'of God'; in Old French a proper noun, or any noun designating a person, in the oblique case and immediately following a noun, has a genitive case function.

Line 10. **Que** 'because'. **s'est enbatu** 'has attacked'.

II. Tenor and Contratenor:

      L'ome armé doibt on doubter.

      On a fait partout crier

---

1. Treatise by Jean Barton, *Donait françois pur briefment entroduyr les Anglois en la droit language de Paris* . . ., ed. E. Stengel, *Zeitschrift für neufranzösische Sprache und Litteratur* 1 (1879): 32, quoted by Jean Gessler in the glossary (on pp. 102–03) to his edition of *La manière de langage qui enseigne à bien parler et écrire le français* (Brussels: Edition Universelle, and Paris: Droz, 1934). Gessler dates the *Donait françois* as "avant 1409" (p. 24 of *La manière*).

Que chescun se doibt armer
D'un haubregon de fer.   4

The man at arms is to be feared,
The cry has been raised all around
That every one must arm himself
With an iron hauberk.

VARIANT

L'homme armé doibt on redoubter—*Molinet D 22.*

VERSIFICATION

A monorhyme heptasyllabic (except for six-syllable last line) quatrain. However, for performance the basic poem has been adapted to the rondeau form, so that it fits in with poem I as follows (indentation of a line denotes simultaneous execution with the preceding line):

T CT L'ome, l'ome, l'ome armé,⎫ Il sera pour vous conbatu,
T CT L'ome armé doibt on   ⎬ Le doubté Turcq, Maistre
   doubter.   ⎭   Symon;
T On a fait partout crier   ⎫
CT   (A l'assault! et a l'assault!) ⎪
CT Que chescun se doibt armer   ⎬ —Certainement ce sera mon—
T D'un haubregon de fer.   ⎪
CT   (A l'assault! A l'assault!) ⎭
T CT L'ome, l'ome, l'ome armé,   ⎫ Et de crocq de ache abatu.
T CT L'ome armé doibt on doubter.⎭

This schema shows the temporal relations between poems I and II: the braces designate the lines of poem II that are sung simultaneously with one line of poem I. The expanded poem II is then adapted to the short strophe and the short refrain of poem I by singing the first two lines of the expanded version to each of these units. Then the long strophe of poem I is fitted to expanded poem II in the same way as shown in the above schema. Of course, the repeated long refrain is identical to the schema.

In the expanded version, the only new verbal material is the cry, outside the rhyme scheme, of "*A l'assault!*" If the interpolated cry is skipped, it can be observed how the sentence is passed back and forth between the two voices:

> T *On a fait partout crier*
> CT *Que chescun se doibt armer*
> T *D'un haubregon de fer.*

This technique, together with the scurrying *a l'assault!*, creates a wonderful atmosphere of excitement. The whole is a fitting accompaniment to poem I in praise of a great fighter, a poem that, in its strict adherence to the *forme fixe*, has a certain force and sobriety to complement the bustle and agitation of poem II.

Textual Notes

(line numbers refer to the basic quatrain):
    Line 1. **doubter** 'to fear'.
    Line 4. **haubregon** 'coat of mail'.

35. Tout a par moy, ff. 45ᵛ–46ʳ, Frye

Concordant Sources

*Roh, f. 83ʳ
BerK 78 C 28, ff. 29ᵛ–30ʳ
FloR 2356, ff. 69ᵛ–70ʳ
Niv, ff. xxviᵛ–xxviiʳ, Binchois
*Par 24315, f. 28ᵛ
Par 4379, ff. 18ᵛ–19ʳ
Cord, ff. 40ᵛ–42ʳ
Lab, ff. 11ᵛ–12ʳ, Frye
Wolf 287, ff. 4ᵛ–5ʳ
*Jar, f. 77ʳ

Collation

The majority of the variants for this composition proved to be either ostensible errors unique to one or two sources or details of melodic ornamentation that barely alter the musical substance. Consequently, reported here are only those seeming to have some bearing on the filiation of the different readings.
    Cantus: At m. 6(1), a′-dotted M, g-SM found in all sources except

Mell, where a′-M, g-Sm, f-Sm is given instead; at m. 9 (1), instead of b′-Sb, a′-M, a′-Sb, f-M as in Mell, Cord and Lab have b′-flat dotted Sb, a′-M, a′-M (disrupting the parallel motion of the upper pair of voices); at m. 26 (2), instead of the a′-Sb in Mell, a′-dotted M, g-Sm in all other sources; at m. 28 (1) the note values of Mell are inverted to f-Br, g-Sb in Cord, Niv, Par 4379, Lab, and Wolf 287; at m. 32 (5), instead of d-Sb as in Mell, d-dotted M, b-Sm in BerK 78 C 28, Cord, FloR 2356, Lab, and Wolf 287; and at m. 34 (6 ff.), d-M, a′-M, b′-dotted M (a more consonant reading than that of Mell) in Cord, Niv, Par 4379, FloR 2356, Lab, and Wolf 287.

Tenor: At m. 10 (2), Cord, Par 4379, Lab, and Wolf 287 have d-Br without the rest of Mell; at m. 16 (1–3), BerK 78 C 28 and FloR 2356 give d-M, c-M, a-M (a perfectly possible alternate reading); at m. 34 (3, 4), the dotted figure of Mell is reduced to even MM in BerK 78 C 28 and FloR 2356.

Contratenor: At m. 2 (1), Cord, Lab, and Wolf 287 have D-dotted Sb, E-M (a slight change); at m. 12 (1), instead of C-M as in Mell, D-M (producing a dissonant suspension with the T, but possible as an adaptation of fauxbourdon) in BerK 78 C 28, Niv, and Lab, whereas Par 4379 has E-M; at m. 20 (3) in all sources except Mell, the rest-M precedes E-M; at m. 28 (1), all other sources give a-Sb, d-Br instead of D-Sb, G-Sb, d-Sb as in Mell; and at m. 32 (3), all other sources have a-M instead of the c-M of Mell.

Par 4379, Lab, and Wolf 287 have no signature in any voice. FloR 2356 has a signed flat for the initial segment of the C only, whereas BerK 78 C 28 and Cord have written flats for several of the b′ pitches in the opening section of the C and a signed flat for the T. Niv has signed flats for both T and CT. The mensural sign, missing in Mell, can be supplied from Cord, Par 4379, or Wolf 287, where it is perfect tempus (○).

COMMENTS

The present composition exists in a keyboard arrangement included in the *Buxheim Organ Book*, f. 163ᵛ (No. 252), and was used in Italy in the fifteenth century to sing the lauda printed by Feo Belcari in *Laude spirituali* as No. cxix (p. 56). It was also cited by Tinctoris in his treatise *De inventione et usu musicae*.[1]

---

1. See the edition by Karl Weinmann, *Johannes Tinctoris und sein unbekannter Traktat 'De inventione et usu musicae,'* p. 34.

The two attributions to Frye seem to have greater weight statistically than one to Binchois, and certainly there is much both in the melodic writing and in the harmonic structure of the chanson to suggest English origins. However, because Binchois derived a great deal from the English style of the first half of the fifteenth century and often presents a musical profile similar to that of his insular colleagues, he cannot be excluded as a possible composer.

In the modern score the reading of Mell was emended in the CT at m. 20 (3) to place the E-M after the rest in conformity with all the remaining sources. The change appeared justified harmonically since a vertical tritone with the a′ of the C is thus avoided (the E-M is undoubtedly to be lowered to a perfect fifth below the b-flat of the T), and it has the additional advantage of maintaining the motion in parallel tenths with the C for the entire figure. The reading of the divergent sources is also preferable for the cadential approach in the C at m. 34 (6 ff.), but as the version of Mell is possible, it was retained.

Although relatively unimportant, the variants show that the reading of Mell is here even more independent than usual. It does not follow in matters of notational detail the tradition of transmission represented in varying degrees by all the concordant sources. Among the latter the northern MSS Niv, Lab, and Wolf 287 form a group to which Cord and Par 4379 can be assimilated, but the greatest degree of affinity is to be seen between Lab and Cord on the one hand, and Niv and Par 4379 on the other. BerK 78 C 28 and FloR 2356 are just a step removed and are more closely related to each other than to any of the remaining sources. They are also less distant from Mell than the northern collections.

Tout a par moy, affin qu'on ne me voye,
Si tresdolent que plus je ne porroye,
Je me tien seul comme [une ame esbaÿe],
Faisant regrés de ma dolente vye
Et de Fortune, qu'ainsy fort me guerroye.   5

Pensez quel dueil mon desplaisir m'envoye,   : Jar
Car j'ay des maulx a si tresgrant monjoie   : Roh
Que je crains fort que brief je ne m'occye.   : Jar   8
    Tout a par moy, affin qu'on ne me voye,
    Si tresdolent que plus je ne porroye,
    Je me tien seul comme une ame esbaye.

Mais non pourtant, se mourir je devoye   : Jar
A la poursuite de vous servir, ma joie,   : Cord, Niv
Et fussiez vous plus fort mon ennemye,   : Niv, Wolf
Je n'ay pooir que jamais vous oublie,   : Par
Car c'est mon sort que vostre soye.   : Roh, Par, Cord,
                                                   Wolf, Jar   13

Tout a par moy; affin qu'on ne me voye
Si tresdolent que plus je ne porroye,
Je me tien seul comme une ame esbaÿe,
Faisant regrés de ma dolente vye
Et de Fortune, qu'ainsy fort me guerroye.

All by myself, that I not be seen,
So very grieved that I could not be more so,
I keep to myself, like a stunned soul,
Bewailing my doleful life
And Fortune, that she wars so strongly against me.

Think what grief my displeasure sends me,
For I have woes in so great measure
That ere long I fear I'll kill myself.
    All by myself, that I not be seen,
    So very grieved that I could not be more so,
    I keep to myself, like a stunned soul.

But nevertheless, were I to die
While engaged in serving you, my joy,
And were you even more my enemy,
I have no power ever to forget you,
For my destiny is that I be yours.
    All by myself, that I not be seen,
    So very grieved that I could not be more so,
    I keep to myself, like a stunned soul,
    Bewailing my doleful life
    And Fortune, that she wars so strongly against me.

VARIANTS

The texted concordant sources are Roh (=Löp No. 138), Niv, Par
24315 (first line only), Par 4379 (hereafter Par), Cord, Lab, Wolf,
Jar, and, for the first line, Molinet O1, D64.

1 part—*Molinet O1, D64;* D64 omits affin; de paour qu'on me voye—*Par 24315;* affin qu'oil ne me voy—*Lab.* 2 Si desplaisant—*Cord.* 3 ung home esbay—*Mell;* Niv omits une (− 1 syll.). 5 qu'ansy—*Roh,* qui ainsy—*Cord* (in tenor qu'ainsi), qui si—*Lab.* (Mell ends here. Rest of text combined from various sources.) 7 Jar omits j'ay (− 1 syll.); assés et grant—*Cord.* 8 Que j'ay grant paour—*Roh,* Tant que ne craing—*Cord;* brief je ne m'octie—*Niv,* brief je ne me occye—*Cord,* briefvement m'occye—*Lab,* briefment je m'occye—*Wolf,* je ne m'en ochie—*Par.* 9 Et non—*Wolf;* Mais non obstant—*Cord;* en devoye—*Roh Niv Wolf,* j'en debvoye—*Cord;* Car j'ay perdu a sique tant chier avoye—*Lab.* 10 En la—*Wolf Jar;* poursieute—*Par;* sevir—*Wolf;* Dont ne m'atens pour nesune que voye—*Lab.* 11 Jamais de rien me trouver resjouÿe—*Lab.* 12 pouoir—*Cord,* Je pas paour—*Niv,* Je n'ay pas paour—*Roh,* Pas je n'ay peur—*Jar,* N'ayez paour ja—*Wolf;* qu'a jamaiz—*Wolf,* qui jamais—*Cord;* Mais languir jusque tant que desvye—*Lab.* 13 Car c'est force que tousjours vostre soye—*Niv;* Mon deul tenant sans avoir bien ne joye—*Lab.*

Cord adds these lines, probably to be sung to the first musical section:

> De temps jadis joieuse me tenoye
> Et doulcement je me entretenoye
> Mais maintenant a moy seule j'ennuye
> Tout a par moy.

VERSIFICATION

Decasyllabic rondeau cinquain, *a a b b a.* Epic caesura, as is shown by the uncounted -*e* after the fourth syllable in ll. 5 and 10. The short and long refrains are autonomous.

TEXTUAL NOTES

In general it has been our policy, when supplementing an incomplete Mell text, to choose a good version from a source that presents the whole poem. In the present instance, however, since no one version provides fully satisfactory readings, we have made a collage of "best lines" instead of reproducing integrally the "best manuscript."

Line 3. The Mell variant does not rhyme.

Line 5. **qu'** introduces a clause dependent on **faisant regrés**. **Fortune** is the subject of **guerroye**. Cord and Lab *qui* interpreted it as a relative clause.

Line 8. **occye** [osiɔ] 'kill'. The Cord and Roh versions of the first
hemistich (l. 8a) seem to be independent reconstructions from memory.
The second hemistich (8b) divides into two principal groups of
readings, one with **brief**, the other with *brief(ve)ment*. There is, in
addition, a reading (Par) without an adverb of this meaning ('soon'),
whose relationship to the tradition we here attempt to determine. The
ending with **m'occye** is common to both groups, a fact that casts
doubt on the authenticity of Par *m'en ochie*. We reconstruct the tradition
of the second hemistich as follows (skipping *que*, which is common to
all versions).

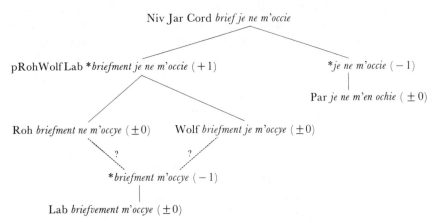

The above stemma describes the history of one line and does not tell
us a great deal about the stemma of the concerned MSS. It implies
only the following: that in the second hemistich of line 8, **que brief
je ne m'occye** (six syllables), Niv, Jar, and Cord retained the old
reading; that an intermediary, pRohWolfLab, gained a syllable by
brief > (replaced by) *briefment*; and that another intermediary lost a
syllable by omitting *brief*. There were two independent corrections of
the hypermetric version: Roh omitted *je*, Wolf omitted *ne*. A copy of
one of these versions rendered the line hypometric by omitting either
Roh's *ne* or Wolf's *je*. Lab, receiving this version, restored the lost
syllable by *briefment* > *briefvement*. Meanwhile, the intermediary that

Explanation of symbols: A reading preceded by an asterisk (*) is hypothetical, unattested. +1
means that the line has one syllable too many, −1 that it is short by one syllable, ±0 that the
line has been corrected from −1 by adding a syllable or from +1 by dropping a syllable. The
small letter p is to be read *proto*; pAB is a common ancestor of A and B. The dotted lines accompanied by question marks represent possible lines of direct descent.

had omitted *brief* (right side of the stemma) was emended by Par's addition of *en*. Clearly this scribe had no knowledge or intuition of an adverb meaning 'soon.'

The principal implication for the manuscript stemma is that there is a subgroup containing Roh, Wolf, and Lab, and excluding the others. No special relationship is proved to exist among the others, which reproduce the original version, nor is Par, which reproduces and emends a unique error, shown to be in any special relationship with any other MS by the evidence of this line.

Line 9. The first hemistich developed as follows, in our reconstruction.

Niv Par Roh Jar *Mais non pourtant*

Cord *Mais non obstant*   Wolf *Et non pourtant*

These are, then, individual changes that do not affect the manuscript stemma.

In the second hemistich all MSS agree on **se mourir ... devoye**. The eighth syllable of the line is distributed as follows:

Niv Wolf Roh	*en*
Cord	*j'en*
Par Jar	*je*

We shall suspend discussion of this stemma until we arrive at l. 12, where the significance of cross-family agreements will become clear.

From this point on, Lab's text is quite unrelated to that of the other MSS.

Line 10. As we shall see, **A la poursuite** involves a cross-family agreement that validates **A** as against **En** (Cord Niv Roh Par: Wolf Jar).

Line 12. **pooir** (= modern *pouvoir*, which was apparently remodeled on *mouvoir*) 'to be able'; here the infinitive is used as a noun. Like the modern word, it is pronounced in two syllables: [pu-oyr] up to the middle of the thirteenth century, [pu-wer] thereafter, until early modern French. The variant *paour* 'fear' proposed by Niv, Wolf, Roh, and Jar (*peur*) was pronounced in two syllables [pa-ur] in Old French and became monosyllabic [pur, pör] between the fourteenth and sixteenth centuries. Apparently the monosyllabic form existed side by side with the dissyllabic as dialectal differences during the Middle French period.[2] Thus the substitution of *paour* for *pooir* was probably metrically correct for the redactor responsible for it, but was one syllable short for subsequent (even immediately subsequent) copyists, who perceived the necessity of adding a syllable.

We reconstruct the history of the first hemistich (12a) as follows:

Par Cord *Je n'ay pooir* | *pouoir* > * *Je n'ay paour* | *peur*; for subsequent copyists the hemistich is short one syllable, that is, for those who pronounce *paour* | *peur* in one syllable. The hypometric verse is corrected in three different ways by three copyists: Roh adds *pas*, Niv agrees with Roh (but has somehow lost *n'ay*), Jar preposes *pas*, and Wolf adds *ja*. We thus begin to have the basis for constructing a stemma.

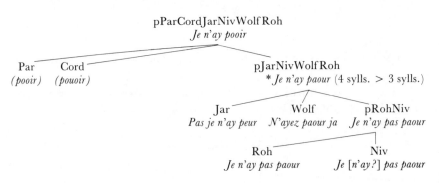

If on the basis of this hypothesis we reexamine the second hemistich of l. 9, we see that Par agrees with Jar on *je*; this cross-family agreement tends to support *je* as against Cord *j'en* (unique) and Niv Roh Wolf *en*, all, presumably, from the same source. So we can now subdivide pJarNivWolfRoh as follows.

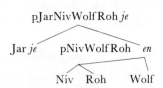

2. Mildred K. Pope, *From Latin to Modern French* (Manchester: Manchester University Press, 1952), p. 110, §242. Hans Rheinfelder, *Altfranzösische Grammatik*, pt. 1, 2d rev. enlarged ed. (Munich: Hueber, 1953) pp. 47–48, §§126, 128. Wilhelm Meyer-Lübke, *Historische Grammatik der französischen Sprache* (Heidelberg: Winter, 1934), p. 14, §138, p. 116, §143. Eduard Schwan and Dietrich Behrens, *Grammaire de l'ancien français*, trans. Oscar Bloch, 4th ed., based on 12th German ed. (Leipzig: Reisland, 1932), p. 150.

In l. 10 the agreement of Par and Cord with Niv and Roh legitimizes **A la** as against WolfJar *En*. We have evidence that WolfJar ≠ NivRoh (AB ≠ CD = 'A and B share a reading against C and D') in the right branch of the first stemma: Niv and Roh have *A la*, Wolf and Jar have *En la*. So either the divergence in l. 10a between *A* and *En* is spontaneous (or coincidental), or the three-way split of l. 9 *je : j'en : en* must be so regarded. We have also observed that Niv and Roh are close low down on the stemma by reason of their agreement on the addition of *pas* in l. 12. The agreement of Par with Cord is significant as authenticating **A la**, at least until evidence is found of a pParCord excluding the others.

We may now return to our discussion of l. 12 *pooir | pouoir*, which we find contextually superior to *paour | peur*; the idea of powerlessness is repeated in l. 13 **c'est mon sort**. Furthermore, *Je n'ay pas paour que jamais vous oublie* seems like a reassurance strangely out of place in a song of complaint rather than one promising fidelity.

36. S'il est ainsi, ff. 46ᵛ–48ʳ, Caron

CONCORDANT SOURCES

MC 871, ff. 148ʳ (p. 373), 153ᵛ (p. 384)
Pix, ff. 179ᵛ–181ʳ

COLLATION

The reading of Pix departs significantly from that found in Mell at only three places. At m. 3 (3) the C has e-M (instead of d-M as in Mell) and the T c-M (again instead of d); at m. 9 (3 ff.) of the C is written d-M, d-Sb, c-M, d-dotted M, c-Sm (differing from Mell only in the introduction of the dissonant suspension); and at mm. 44–45 there is a variant affecting all three voices: in the C at m. 44 (2), e-Br with corona and omission of the following d-Sb, m. 45 (3); in the T at m. 45 (2 ff.), c-Sb, b-M, a-M; in the CT at m. 45 (2), a-Sb, D-Sb (the three parts consequently fit together rhythmically even though T and CT are dissonant with the C on the third quarter-note of m. 45). Finally, the CT adds to the sonority of m. 29 the e a fifth above the A found in Mell.

In MC 871 the only differences with Mell are probably scribal errors despite the fact that the two sections of the bergerette are now separated physically in the MS as if they were two distinct compositions. At mm. 20 (4) and 21 (1, 2), the notes are written as MM instead of the

SSm required by the context; at 35 (5), c-M is written as Sb and the preceding rest is also Sb instead of M; and at m. 41 (5), d-Sb is erroneously written as Br.

COMMENTS

Although all three readings are closely related, Mell is nonetheless more like MC 871 than Pix for this particular composition.

The poetic-musical form of Caron's chanson is unmistakably that of the bergerette, but the verse has no long strophe in the sources now known. It is possible that the missing element has not been preserved with the rest of the poem. Nonetheless, because the transition from the end of the clos to the beginning of the refrain makes perfect sense and is syntactically correct, it is likely that the poem was actually conceived in its present form.

At the beginning of the second section of the composition Caron has introduced a proportional change of the kind to be observed in the bergerettes of Busnois (see Nos. 12 and 14 of the present collection). But although the notes are sung twice as fast under the diminished mensuration, the primary unit of declamation is shifted from the M to the Sb and hence remains essentially the same.

The melodic tritone in the T at mm. 20–21 was allowed to stand without a suggested accidental because the forbidden interval is enclosed within a line that moves through the octave from c to C without giving real prominence to either of the pitches by which the tritone is formed.

> S'il est ainsi que plus je ne vous voye,
> Et que mon oeul en desespoir s'envoye,
> Que feray je, ma damme, quel confort
> Ara mon cuer quant desja *Desconfort*
> Ou Lac de Dueil en pleurs noyer l'envoye?   5
>
> Helas, je souloye obtenir
> Par vostre amoureux maintenir
> Ce que par grace maintenir
> Me faisoit en joyeux soulas.   9
>
> Mais plus ne puis contretenir
> S'Espoir n'y veult le maintenir

Qui ne me faille maintenir
En tristresse disant: "Helas,   13
 S'il est ainsi que plus je ne vous voye,
 Et que mon oeul en desespoir s'envoye,
 Que feray je, ma damme, quel confort
 Ara mon cuer quant desja Desconfort
 Ou Lac de Dueil en pleurs noyer l'envoye?"

If so it be that I may no longer see you,
And that my eye in despair withdraws,
What will I do, my lady, what comfort
Will my heart have, when already Unease
Sends it to the Lake of Woe to drown in tears?

Alas, I once obtained
By your loving steadfastness
That which, by your grace, enabled me
To remain in joyful solace.

But I can hold out no longer
If Hope choose not a stout defense
That may not fail to sustain me,
While in sadness I say, "Alas,
 If so it be that I may no longer see you,
 And that my eye in despair withdraws,
 What will I do, my lady, what comfort
 Will my heart have, when already Unease
 Sends it to the Lake of Woe to drown in tears?"

Variants

Pix is the only concordant source. Its text is so corrupt as hardly to
be worth reproducing; however it does supply l. 4 *desconfort*, omitted
by Mell.

Versification

Technically a defective bergerette because it lacks the long strophe
that usually follows the *clos*. However, the happy union of the clos,
with its *Hélas*, to the repetition of the refrain makes it plausible that

the poet intended it so. The refrain in *aabba* is decasyllabic. In l. 3 -*e* counts as fourth syllable at the caesura; in this instance it is probably not atonic [ə], but more likely stressed [ö], so that this line is not evidence of lyric caesura. The ouvert and clos, each *cccd*, are in octosyllables.

TEXTUAL NOTES

Line 1. **voye**, subjunctive of a hypothetical condition. **S'il est ainsi que** is equivalent to a simple *if*—much like the *If it is the case that*, beloved of many in the American scientific community.

Lines 2, 5. Unless the repeated use of **envoye** at the rhyme is to be considered as homologous rhyme, it may be that the poet took the reflexive meaning as lexically different: 'retire, leave, depart'.[1] The function of **en desespoir** in this sentence is ambiguous; it is either an adverbial expression 'in despair' or it is a complement of goal to a verb of motion: 'to despair, into despair'. Our translation is based on the first assumption.

Line 4. **ara** (= modF *aura*) 'will have' is a Picard form.

Line 6. **souloye** 'used to'.

Lines 7–8. The first **maintenir** is syntactically a noun, modified by an adjective. The second **maintenir** is a true infinitive, in a causative construction with l. 9 **faisoit**. Therefore they are "different" words, that is, not in homologous rhyme. **Ce que** is the subject of **faisoit**, equivalent to modern French *ce qui*.[2]

Line 11. **le maintenir** is a verbal noun, with definite article. **le** cannot be the direct object of an infinitive *maintenir*, since in the French of this period the construction aux. verb (**veult**) + dir. obj. pronoun (**le**) + infinitive did not yet exist; in Old French, such a pronoun object would have been governed by the auxiliary verb, somewhat as follows: *ne l'y veult maintenir*.

Line 12. The antecedent of **Qui** is l. 11 **Espoir**. As in l. 8, **maintenir** is a real infinitive, here dependent on **faille**. This may be considered a case of homologous rhyme. There is a possibility that the poet, rather than attempting to avoid homologous rhyme, was instead

---

1. Godefroy, *Dictionnaire*, s.v. *envier, envoier, anvoer*, "Réfl., se mettre en voie"; Tobler and Lommatzsch, "*Refl. sich auf den Weg machen, sich in Bewegung setzen.*"

2. Lucien Foulet, *Petite syntaxe de l'ancien français*, 3d ed. (Paris: Champion, 1930), pp. 176, 178, §§247, 249.

deliberately setting himself the goal of using one word as often as possible, making a virtue of what had been traditionally forbidden.

37. O Fortune, trop tu es dure, ff. 48ᵛ–49ʳ [Busnois]

CONCORDANT SOURCES

Flo 176, ff. 15ᵛ–17ʳ, Busnois
Pix, ff. 126ᵛ–127ʳ, Busnoys
Sev 5.I.43, ff. 31ᵛ–32ʳ (Sev 1)
Sev 5.I.43, ff. 78ᵛ–79ʳ (Sev 2)

COLLATION

Leaving aside minor differences of melodic ornamentation in the C and miscellaneous errors, the following variants appear to be significant with respect to the relationships among the sources. In the T at m. 4 (3), Flo 176 has a dissonant F-Sb (definitely an error) and is joined at m. 5 (1) by Pix with D-Br, G-Sb, thus reversing the rhythmic values of Mell (a perfectly acceptable alternative); and at m. 15 (4 ff.), a′-Sb, g-dotted Sb, f-Sm, e-Sm, f-Sb, f-Sb (producing parallel fifths with the C) is found in Flo 176, Pix, and Sev 1 (ff. 31ᵛ–32ʳ). In the CT the same three sources give a rest-Sb in place of B-Sb as in Mell at m. 5 (1), a blackened Sb as D (instead of E) at m. 6 (2), and a blackened Sb as F (instead of E) at m. 17 (2). At m. 10 (1), Flo 176 and Sev 2 (ff. 78ᵛ–79ʳ) have G′-Sb instead of C-Sb as in Mell.

There is no signed E-flat for the CT of Flo 176, Pix, or Sev 2, and the written flat for e at m. 20 (2) of the T is found only in Mell.

The composition in Flo 229, ff. 124ᵛ–125ʳ, has nothing in common with Busnois's rondeau except the textual incipit.

COMMENTS

The readings given by Flo 176, Pix, and Sev 1 obviously follow the same tradition of transmission and are intimately related to one another. However, Sev 2 is considerably closer to Mell despite some minor differences of melodic ornamentation. The latter two apparently represent a distinct but not entirely homogeneous tradition in view of the link between Flo 176 and Sev 2 at m. 10 (1) of the CT.

Evidently the reference to Dame Fortune had no effect on the treatment of accidentals in this composition. The transposition involves

only the ordinary displacement of the Dorian final from D to G with
the addition of a b-flat signature and an occasional e-flat for either
harmonic or melodic reasons.

> O Fortune, trop tu es dure
> De moy faire si grant injure
> Que de [m'oster] mon esperance.
> [. . .] J'avoye a toy fait alïance,
> Mais a present je te fourjure.   5

> O Fortune, thou art too harsh
> In doing me such great injury
> As to take from me my hope.
> I had made alliance with thee,
> But now I do foreswear thee.

Variants

Texted sources are Flo (attribution and first line only), Pix, Sev
1 (first line only) and Sev 2.

1 Pix Sev 1 Flo omit O ($-$1 syll.); tu es trop—*Sev 2*; 2 injurie—*Pix*.
3 de moustrer—*Mell*, de m'oster—*Sev 2*, demostrē—*Pix*. 4 que j'avoye
Mell ($+$1 syll.); aliesse—*Pix*. 5 mais afuste iete fornire—*Pix*.

Versification

Octosyllabic cinquain, *aabba*; the structure of the music is that of
a rondeau. The concordant sources do not go beyond l. 5.

Textual Notes

Line 2. **injure** 'injury', rather than modern sense of 'insult'.
Line 3. **m'oster** (adopted from Sev) makes more obvious sense
than Mell (apparently supported by Pix) *moustrer:* 'to take away my
hope' rather than 'to reveal to me my hope'.
Line 4. Mell *Que* . . . makes a hypermetric verse. In the MS the last
syllable, *ce*, of the preceding word is written with a considerable space
before it, whence it derived a certain autonomy, as the scribe perceived
it; so he wrote *ce q̄* = *ce que*.

38. Enfermé suis je en la tour, ff. 49ᵛ–51ʳ

CONCORDANT SOURCES

Glog, No. 194

COLLATION

The variants offered by Glog are minimal. Aside from minor differences of notational and ornamental detail the only noteworthy divergence is at m. 11 (3) of the triplum, where a'-M is found instead of e-M as in Mell. However, the music of the concordant MS carries neither signed flats nor accidentals.

COMMENTS

This composition bears a marked resemblance at the beginning to *Au povre par necessité* (No. 39), one that is all the more striking because of the unusual key signature of two flats coupled with the scale structures of the Dorian mode twice transposed, features that are common to both pieces. This similarity, added to the imitative duo between C and T, both of which carry the text, points clearly to the influence—if not to the pen—of Busnois.

The formal structure of the poem is uncommon for a rondeau cinquain. The short strophe counts only two lines instead of the usual three, and the division of both music and verse thus comes after the second line of the refrain instead of after the third as in virtually every other example. Because the caesuras in the short and long strophes do not always coincide with those of the refrain, a few minor adjustments in the placement of the syllables suggested for the latter will prove necessary when the former are sung.

The contratenor fragment entered at the foot of f. 50ᵛ does not belong to *Enfermé suis* but rather to No. 54, *Ma dame de nom / Sur la rive de la mer*. The scribe may have been confused by the similarity between "Ma dame de nom" and "Dame blance comme la fleur," slight though it may be.

> Enfermé suis *je* en la tour
> De Bel Accueil par Bien Amer;
> Dame blance come la flour
> Je sers de cuer et de penser
> Au bon command de mon signeur.   5

C'est mon confort, mon seul retour,
Je treuve doulceur sans amer.   7
  Enfermé suis *je en la tour*
  De Bel Accueil par Bien Amer.

Se g'y prens deduit nuyt et jour,
Certes, nul ne m'en doibt blasmer.
Avoir ne puis milleur sejour
Par deça ne par dela mer;
J'y treuve bien paix et amour.   12
  Enfermé suis *je en la tour*
  De Bel Accueil par Bien Amer;
  Dame Blance come la flour
  Je sers de cuer et de penser
  An bon command de mon signeur.

I am locked up in the tower
Of Fair Welcome by Well-loving.
Lady, white as the flower,
I serve with heart and mind
At the good command of my lord.

This is my comfort, my only refuge,
I find sweetness without bitterness.
  I am locked up in the tower
  Of Fair Welcome by Well-loving.

If there I take my pleasure night and day,
Certainly, no one should blame me for it.
I can have no better dwelling place
On this side or that of the sea;
Here I find peace and love.
  I am locked up in the tower
  Of Fair Welcome by Well-loving.
  Lady, white as the flower,
  I serve with heart and mind
  At the good command of my lord.

VARIANTS

No concordant sources. 1 Mell omits je. 12 Je y—*Mell.*

Versification

Octosyllabic rondeau cinquain, *ababa*. Since the rhyme changes in the second line, the short strophe, like the short refrain, is only two lines long. The result is that the whole poem, not counting repetitions of the refrain, is twelve lines long; the usual rondeau cinquain has thirteen.

The repeated refrains are autonomous.

Textual Notes

This is one of the few poems in our collection expressive of the lover's complete satisfaction with his lot.

Line 1 has only seven syllables in the MS. Possible emendations are **suis je** (the one we have adopted), *me suis*, and *Enfermée*. (*Enfermé je suis* is syntactically too aberrant to warrant serious consideration.) *Enfermée* would involve a female narrator who refers to herself flatteringly as *Dame, blance come la flour*, and whose *signeur* would be the man she loved. It would be highly unusual in the courtly tradition to which this poem belongs to speak of *service* (l. 4 *je sers de cuer . . .*) with a female subject and a male object.

me suis would put the verb into the reflexive voice; *par Bien Amer* could then no longer be considered the agent of a passive verb; we would lose the allegorical figure of that expression and would, without capital letters, interpret *par bien amer* as 'by loving well'. We reject *me suis* only because the loss of this allegorical figure, *Bien Amer*, in a poem that is established at the outset as allegorical entails a loss of parallelism enhanced by alliteration (i.e., two allegorical figures, each B.A.); the rest of this poem will not be differently interpreted if we choose *Enfermé me suis* or *Enfermé suis je*.

Enfermé suis je is subject to criticism on the ground that it allows a hiatus between *-e* and a following vowel. But *suis-je* is not prosodically equivalent to *tige*. *Je* in Old French is an emphatic personal pronoun, often used where modern French would have *moi*. In Old French it appears as *gié, jou, je*, and so on. Capable of appearing in a strongly accented position, it could well have been pronounced like *Jeu* [žö]. In the song No. 36, we have l. 3 *Que feray je, ma damme . . .* , in which *je* appears in the very strong precaesural position of fourth syllable of a decasyllabic verse. It, too, must have been pronounced [žö], from an older [žu]. Therefore l. 1 of this song would not, if we adopt *suis je*, be an example of nonelided feminine *e*. The objection against it, then, is slighter than that against *me suis*; in addition to the reasons given above, the addition of *je* is a lesser alteration of the text, whereas *me* changes both the structure and the interpretation.

Line 3. **blance**: the spelling shows a Picard influence; pronounced either with [-kə], or, as in Francian, with [-šə].

Line 5. **signeur**, in spite of its spelling, is probably pronounced *signour* [siñur] for, to judge from the rhyme, the poet probably did not distinguish between *eu* [ö] and *ou* [u] in stressed position.[1]

Line 7. **treuve** exhibits the strong vowel *eu* (see p. 107). **amer** 'bitterness', a rich rhyme with l. 2 **amer**; in antithesis to **doulceur**.

Line 10. **milleur**: see textual note on l. 5. The graph *eu* has been chosen to resolve the abbreviation of Mell *mill^r* in conformity with what appears to be the scribe's practice in this poem: where the *poet* seems to have written in a dialect that does not distinguish between *eu* [ö] and *ou* [u] in stressed position, the *scribe* adopts (or keeps) the graph *ou* even in those words that would appear with *eu* in his own dialect (except for l. 5 **signeur**), as long as such words appear in the rhyming position; but where such words are not in rhyme, he adopts the spelling that reflects his own pronunciation, *eu*. Thus, though *millour* would be a better representation of the poet's pronunciation, *milleur* corresponds better to our scribe's practice, as in ll. 7, 12 **treuve**, and l. 7 **doulceur**. Our advice to the singer is to pronounce *eu* as *ou* [u] in this song to conform to the poet's pronunciation.

39. Au povre par necessité, ff. 51ᵛ–52ʳ [Busnois]

CONCORDANT SOURCES

Glog, No. 10 (Regina regnancium)
Pix, ff. 171ᵛ–172ʳ, Busnoys
Sev 5.I.43, ff. 79ᵛ–80ʳ

---

1. The failure of free, tonic [u] to become [ö] is characteristic of the northern and northeastern regions, that is, Picardy, Wallonie, Lorraine, and Burgundy, according to Pope, *From Latin to Modern French*, p. 106, §230 (i); p. 491, NE. §ii; and p. 495, E. §xviii. The *i* of **signeur** indicates a northern dialect (Picard or Lorraine); it represents the evolution of pretonic [e] before a palatalized nasal or liquid in the northern region (Pope, p. 489, N. §xviii). For discussion of the Mell scribe's spelling practice, see textual note on l. 10.

COLLATION

A comparison of Mell with Pix and Sev 5.I.43 revealed no variants of substance but did serve to identify two minor errors in the notation of the manuscript. At m. 24 (1) of the T the blackening seen here is quite unnecessary, and at m. 3 (1) of the CT the concordant sources (including Glog) give E-Sb, C-dotted M, D-Sm instead of E-Sb (later effaced), C-dotted Sb, D-M as in Mell.

The reading of Glog is only slightly more independent. In the C at m. 1 (2, 3), it gives c-dotted Sb, d-M instead of the repeated c's of Mell; at m. 6 (2 ff.), one reads e-M, f-Sb, e-Sb, a'-Sb (thus averting the cadence on g); and in the T at m. 20 (2) there is C-Br without the rest of Mell. Other differences involve only minor details of melodic ornamentation.

COMMENTS

The scribal tradition for the present work is remarkably uniform, and the similarities extend to graphical details of the notation such as blackening and the use of ligatures, especially in Mell, Pix, and Sev 5.I.43.

The reading of Mell in m. 3 of the CT is probably a scribal error that made the rhythmic values of C and D (2, 3) twice as long as they should have been. The slip must have been discovered shortly after the copying was done, for the mistake was emended by effacing the E, m. 3 (1). However, it seemed more desirable in the transcription to restore what was presumably the original notation as it is given by the concordant sources.

Au povre par necessité
Qui de touttes pars *est* cyté
De venir a ses darains jours,
Veulliés donner *aucun* secours
En *sa* misere adversité.   5

To the poor man in his need
Who is summoned from all sides
To hasten to his last days,
Deign to give some help
In his wretched adversity.

VARIANTS

Pix is the only texted concordant source.

2 Mell omits est (−1 syll.). 4 alcuni (Mell omits, −2 sylls.). 5 Mell omits sa (−1 syll.).

VERSIFICATION

One strophe of a rondeau cinquain, *a a b b a*, whose form is apparent from the music. Octosyllabic, three of its lines are hypometric but can be completed from Pix.

TEXTUAL NOTES

Line 1. **necessité** 'distress, poverty'.

Line 2. **cyté** 'summoned'.

Line 4. **aucun** 'some'.

Line 5. **misere** 'wretched'. Not recorded elsewhere as an adjective until the sixteenth century.[1]

adversité [aversite]—silent *d*.

40. Mort ou mercy, ff. 52ᵛ–54ʳ, Caron

CONCORDANT SOURCES

Flo 229, ff. 76ᵛ–77ʳ
Pix, ff. 187ᵛ–188ʳ, Caron
Tr 89, ff. 421ᵛ–422ʳ

COLLATION

The reading of Pix has no appreciable musical variants with respect to that of Mell and very few of a purely notational order. The only noteworthy discrepancy comes at m. 25 (2ff.) of the T, where the rhythmic pattern opening the second section has been changed to Sb, dotted Sb, M, Sb. The same sequence has been adopted for the C as well in Flo 229 and Tr 89, m. 26 (1 ff.), whereas in the CT those two MSS give yet another pattern, D-dotted Sb, D-M, and so forth, in m. 25 (1 ff.). The remaining differences in Flo 229 and Tr 89 consist principally in details of melodic ornamentation that do not alter essentially either melodic profiles or vertical structures. At m. 5 (4–6)

---

1. Wartburg, *Französisches Etymologisches Wörterbuch*, s.v.; Huguet, *Dictionnaire de la langue française*, s.v.

of the C, for example, both have a more conventional figure for the lower third, f-M, f-M, e-M; at m. 10 (5ff.), Tr 89 gives b′-Sb, a′-dotted M, g-Sm, g-Sb, and in the same passage at m. 10 (7 ff.), Flo 229 has a′-Sb, g-Sb, eliminating in either case some of the dotted figures of Mell; at m. 22 (3) Tr 89 has a rest-Sb instead of b′-Sb as in Mell; both MSS then avoid the dotted pattern of Mell and the subsequent syncopation with a′-Sb, g-Sb, f-Sb in mm. 22 (4)–23 (3); and at m. 28 (4ff.), both sources again eliminate the dotted pattern of Mell with f-M, d-M, d-Sb.

In T and CT the divergences are fewer, especially in Tr 89. Both MSS have d-dotted Sb at m. 36 (8) of the T, and at m. 21 (1) Tr 89 has rest-M instead of the dot for b in Mell, whereas at m. 21 (2), Flo 229 has a-M instead of G-M as in Mell. The few remaining differences are restricted to one or the other of the two concordant MSS, including a pair of errors in the CT of Tr 89 at m. 10 (5), where E-M is given instead of D-M, and m. 14 (1), where B-Sb is written instead of A-Sb. Worthy of mention in Flo 229 is the passage at mm. 4 (2)–5 (2) of the CT, which reads G-Sb, F-Br, rest-Sb, and at the conclusion of the same voice, m. 38 (1), G′-L without the rest and the figure in MM found elsewhere.

COMMENTS

The reading of Pix is so like that of Mell in virtually every detail, including the attribution to Caron, that they could have been copied from the same exemplar. In substance that of Flo 229 is not far removed despite the differences of melodic detail that apparently reflect a conscious trend toward rhythmic and melodic simplification. The Trent MS stands about midway between the two scribal traditions for this work, sharing some elements of both, but it is decidedly closer to the version given by Mell and Pix than is Flo 229.

The inconsistency of the scribe of Mell in writing out the text for only the T in the second section of the chanson has been followed in the accompanying transcription. This was done in this case because of the length of the passage involved and because of the contrapuntal and imitative character of the writing. It would be possible to place the verse under the T in the initial section as well. Certainly there are no greater obstacles there to a convincing distribution of syllables for the T than in the C with its autonomously melodic and melismatic character.

Caron's chanson was used to sing the lauda printed by Belcari, *Laudi spirituale*, as No. ccv (p. 91), an indication that it was well known in the Tuscan region.

> Mort ou mercy vous requiers si,
> Ma seulle dame;
> Car je suis si de deuil transi
> Que, sur mon ame,
> Il n'a plus triste en ce [royame].   5
> Mais j'en mercy
> Amours, qui veult qu'il soit ainsi,
> Et vous [aussi],
> Que portés l'amoureuse flamme
> Dont suis ocy.   10

> Death or mercy I ask of you, insistently,
> My only lady,
> For I am so pierced by grief
> That, upon my soul,
> There is no one sadder in the realm.
> But for this I thank
> Cupid, who wants it to be so,
> And also you,
> Since you carry the flame of love
> By which I am slain.

VARIANTS

The Pix version, exceptionally corrupt, contributes nothing to the establishment of the text.

5 royaume—*Mell*, royalme—*Pix*. 8 ainsy—*Mell*.

VERSIFICATION

Refrain alone of a rondeau cinquain layé; eight- and four-syllable lines in alternation with this rhyme scheme (the superior letters representing the four-syllable lines): $a^b a^b b^a a^a b^a$. For other rondeaux of unequal verse lengths, see Nos. 16, 41, and 48.

TEXTUAL NOTES

Line 1. **si** 'so, so much, so insistently'.

Line 5. Since Mell *royaume* does not rhyme, we have substituted **royame**, which, by the way, is etymologically more regular (cf. textual note on No. 17, l. 13).

Line 7. **Amours**, when used as proper name, most often has final -*s*, a vestige of the Old French masculine nominative singular ending, which serves to distinguish this word from the feminine abstract noun, *amour* (masculine in modern French).

Line 8. **vous**, second direct object of l. 6 **j'en mercy**. Mell *ainsy* cannot be correct, since it enters into homologous rhyme with l. 7 **ainsi**; **aussi** makes a rich rhyme with l. 10 **ocy**, and it makes better sense.

Line 9. **que** 'for, since'. The reading **que** is supported by Pix, for what that may be worth, although in this context *qui* is as plausible as *que*.

41. Paracheve ton entreprise, ff. 54ᵛ–55ʳ [Morton]

CONCORDANT SOURCES

RomC 2856, ff. 92ᵛ–93ʳ (La perontina), Morton
*Jar, ff. 67ᵛ–68ʳ
*Arn, f. lixʳ

COLLATION

The variant readings found in RomC 2856 do not alter generally the musical substance of the composition but impinge only upon matters of melodic ornamentation. For example, in the C at m. 6(5 f.) the concordant source gives f'-Sb, e'-dotted M, eliminating the d' and c' of Mell (and producing a somewhat less consonant result); at m. 8(2), the a'-M of Mell is replaced by a rest; and at m. 20(2), the c'-Sb of Mell is simply not present. In the T at m. 20(1) the other MS has a'-M, g-Sm, f-Sm, e-Sb altered (changing the music very little), and at m. 30(2) it gives e-M instead of d-M (the result being more consonant harmonically but without the exact imitation of the C found in Mell). In the CT at m. 5(3) is written G-Sb, rest-M, a-Sb without the dot of Mell (a minor alteration); at m. 16(1, 2), D-dotted Sb, F-Sb, F-M (the change of pitch coinciding with the C instead of the T as in Mell); at m. 24(1 ff.), b-M, G-Sb, F-M (eliminating the melodic flourish found in Mell); at m. 25(2), b-M, G-Sb, c-Sb (a purely rhythmic change); and at mm. 26(4)–28(1), E-dotted M, D-Sm, F-M, G-M, a-Sb, E-Sb, F-Sb (a slight difference despite the number of notes involved).

Comments

The chansonnier of the Biblioteca Casanatense apparently follows basically the same tradition of transmission as that represented in Mell despite the variants noted. Like those recorded for the previous composition in Flo 229, the divergences cited here seem to reveal a conscious simplification of melodic and rhythmic figures and are probably due primarily to the chronological gap separating the copying of the two collections and to the changes in taste that occurred in the intervening period.

Although the verse set by Morton alludes to Dame Fortune, that symbol of inconstancy, there is no hint that accidental inflections were intended anywhere except in the conventional manner for cadential figures.

Like Ockeghem's *L'aultre d'antan* (No. 20) and *Or me veult* (No. 49), the present chanson provides an example of a vocal composition included in at least one fifteenth-century collection with no more than the kind of short title usually associated with compositions of an entirely instrumental conception (see the Comments to both compositions). Moreover, because the musical phrases are often divided by articulating rests, the melodic character of the piece resembles that of a number of such works in the *Odhecaton*, which provides no text for them.[1]

Despite a style of melodic writing characterized by traits of an instrumental nature, the placement of the syllables of verse for vocal performance was not markedly more difficult than for many of the compositions published here. However, the repetition of verbal segments seemed appropriate more frequently than in most other songs because of the fragmentation of the melodic phrases. The recurring rests that interrupt the C line also make advisable a slight adjustment in the editorial syllable placement for the second line of the long strophe; it would be better divided after *tout* than after *a*.

---

1. See Helen Hewitt and Isabel Pope, eds., *Odhecaton*, the discussion on pp. 74 ff., and Nos. 44 and 80.

Paracheve ton [entreprise]
Que tu as contre moy enprise,
    Fortune adverse,   3
Et tout a ung coup me reverse,
Que mieulx morir que vivre prise,
    Tant [m'es diverse].   6

Puisque tu es de mal aprise,
Ne laisse point de moy ta prise,
    Tost me renverse.   9
        Paracheve ton entreprise
        Que tu as contre moy enprise,
          Fortune adverse.

A toy resister je n'advise;
Choulle moy du tout a ta guise,
    Vers moy converse.   12
Espand ton venin, et le verse
Sur moy; ja n'en seras reprise,
    Dame perverse.
        Paracheve ton entreprise   15
        Que tu as contre moy enprise,
          Fortune adverse,
        Et tout a un coup me reverse,
        Que mieulx morir que vivre prise,
          Tant m'es diverse.

Have done with thine enterprise
Which thou hast taken up against me,
    Contrary Fortune,
And in one go turn me around,
For I prize dying more than living
    So inconstant art thou to me.

Since thou excellest in evil
Do not release thy hold on me—
    Overturn me soon.
        Have done with thine enterprise

Which thou hast taken up against me,
Contrary Fortune.

To resist thee I have no intention,
Batter me about at thy pleasure,
    O devious one.
Spread thy poison, and pour it
On me; thou wilt never be reproached for it,
    Perverse lady.
        Have done with thine enterprise
        Which thou hast taken up against me,
            Contrary Fortune,
        And in one go turn me around,
        For I prize dying more than living
            So inconstant art thou to me.

Variants

Jar, No. 67; Fabri, *Grand et vrai art de pleine rhétorique*, ed. Héron, t. II, p. 65 (Rouen: Lestringant, 1890).

1 enprise—*Mell* (-1 syll.), entreprinse—*Jar*, entreprise—*Fab*. 2 dessus nous—*Jar*. 4 Et tout en ung coup me traverse—*Jar*, De ton dard a coup me traverse—*Fab*. 5 Car—*Jar Fab*. 6 m'est adverse—*Mell*, m'es diverse—*Jar (Fab)*. (End of Mell. The rest supplied from Fab.)

Since from l. 7 on the Jar version differs considerably from Fab, we present as a whole the remainder of Jar:

Du hault embas a la renverse
Tu ne seras par moy reprise
    Dame perverse
        paracheve ton &c.

Si je n'ay dueil assez advise
En me donnant telle devise
    Qui me renverse
A toy resister je n'avise
Comble moy du tout a ta guise
    A la reverse
        paracheve ton &c.

As will be shown in the section on versification, the Jar version has been printed erroneously in such a way as to put the last three lines in the place of the short strophe, and then to put the short strophe and the first three lines of the long strophe together, in that order, as if they constituted the long strophe. For the reconstituted version, see the section on versification. We record the variants of Jar as they correspond to Fab, in what must have been their original order.

7–9 Se je n'ay dueil assez advise / En me donnant telle devise / Qui me renverse. 10 n'avise. 11 Comble moy. 12 A la reverse. 13–14 Du hault embas a la renverse / Tu ne seras par moy reprise.

Versification

Rondeau quatrain layé. The strophe has the following structure, to which Fab adheres systematically: $a a^b b a^b$. Jar maintains the metric pattern, 884884, but its conversion of the rhyme scheme into unexpected patterns suggests that, from l. 7 on, half strophes have been shuffled, possibly due to printers' errors. We restore the immediate model of Jar, before the accidental rearrangement, as follows:

> Se je n'ay dueil assez, advise
> En me donnant telle devise
>   Qui me renverse:
>   Paracheve ton entreprinse
>   Que tu as dessus nous emprise
>   Fortune adverse.

> A toy resister je n'avise;   10
> Comble moy du tout a ta guise
>   A la reverse,
> Du hault em bas a la renverse;
> Tu ne seras par moy reprise,
>   Dame perverse.   15
>   Paracheve ton entreprinse
>   Que tu as dessus nous emprise
>   Fortune adverse,
>   Et tout en ung cop me traverse,
>   Car mieulx mourir que vivre prise,
>   Tant m'es diverse.

If I have not grief enough, be so clever
As to give me a motto
   That will overturn me:
      Have done with thine enterprise
      Which thou hast taken up against me,
         Contrary Fortune.

To resist thee I have no intention;
Heap me with everything at thy pleasure,
   Head over heels,
From top to bottom, backwards and forwards;
I'll not reproach thee for it,
   Perverse lady.
      Have done with thine enterprise
      Which thou hast taken up against me,
         Contrary Fortune,
      And with one blow run me through,
      For I prize dying more than living
         So inconstant art thou to me.

In Textual Notes below, as in Variants, when reference is made to line numbers in Jar, it is in terms of this restored order of verses.

TEXTUAL NOTES

Line 3. **adverse** [aversə].

Line 4. The Fab reading, *Et de ton dard me traverse* 'and pierce me with thy dart', is probably best; it makes the most sense in the context of l. 5, although *me traverse* is supported by Jar.

Line 5. **prise** 'I prize, I esteem'.

Line 7. 'Since you are skilled in doing harm'; Jar *advise* (*d* silent) 'Be so clever as to ... '

Line 8. Note how the restoration of verse order in Jar gives a special sense to ll. 8–9, which refer to the short refrain that follows, ll. 1′–3′, as a *devise* 'motto'. Thus the short refrain in Jar is integrated, whereas in Fab it is not.

Line 10. **je n'advise** (*d* silent) 'I have no intention'.

Line 11. **Choulle moy** 'Mistreat me'; literally it refers to the game of bowls; so it might be more vividly and accurately translated as 'knock me around'. Littré cites *chouler* still in use in Normandy,

meaning 'pousser, remuer, choquer'. **du tout** 'entirely'; but Jar
Comble moy du tout 'hit me with everything'.

Line 13. Jar 'From top to bottom, backwards and forwards'.

Line 14. **reprise** 'reproached'.

42. A vous sans aultre, ff. 55ᵛ–56ʳ [Busnois]

CONCORDANT SOURCES

Dij 517, ff. xviiiᵛ–xixʳ, Busnoys
*Jar, f. 68ʳ
*Arn, f. lixʳ

COLLATION

The reading of Dij 517 is practically identical in every detail to that
given by Mell except that the mensuration shifts in all three parts on
the third quarter-note of m. 18 to imperfect diminished tempus (₵).
However, the text is written out for the T only in Mell.

COMMENTS

Since accidentals are applied in accordance with the rules given by
Tinctoris, the melodic tritone in the C at m. 11 is not to be avoided.
If the b′, m. 11(1), is lowered it forms a diminished fifth with the e of
the CT, and if the f, m. 11(4), is raised, it sounds a diminished fifth
with the c′ of the T. The interval *ad evitandum* was consequently allowed,
melodically, both in the C and in the T, where it is heard in imitation
in mm. 11–12. It is less objectionable for being enclosed within a longer
line that uses neither b′ nor f as melodic pivots or goals, and there is a
faint possibility that the irregularity is an intentional reflection of the
corresponding line of the refrain, "A ce me contraint."

In view of the consistently imitative relationship between C and T,
it is no surprise that the scribe of Mell wrote out the text for both parts.
Since the CT is also included in the imitative structure, it too could
easily be prepared for singing. Because the first line of the long strophe
has its caesura after the fourth syllable instead of after the fifth, as in
the refrain and the short strophe, it would best be divided in performance after *dire* in both C and T with the necessary adjustments
made in the placement of the syllables. Similarly, the final line of the
long strophe is broken most naturally after *honneur*, and if that is done,
some adjustments in the suggested text placement will be required.

Like Busnois's *Bel Acueil* (No. 1) and le Rouge's *Se je fayz dueil* (No. 31), this rondeau is unusual in having its three voices written in the same range. Particularly striking here is the frequent crossing of C and T, and even the CT sometimes rises above the other two voices as in mm. 4, 7–8, 14–15, and so on.

The proportional acceleration of the tempo called for in the Dijon MS seems not only unnecessary in the context in which it occurs but also undesirable musically.

A vous sans aultre me viens rendre,
Il m'est force qu'ainsy le face;
A ce me contraint vostre face
Qui tant est belle, doulce et tendre.   4

Veuilliés vo pitié condescendre
Envers moy qui de prime face   6
      A vous sans aultre *me viens rendre,*
      Il m'est force qu'ainsy le face.

Le vous dire n'ose entreprendre,
Jamais en moi n'eust tant d'audace;
N'au moins pretendant estre en grace
En tant qu'honneur se [peult] estendre,   10
      A vous sans aultre me viens rendre,
      Il m'est force qu'ainsy le face;
      A ce me contraint vostre face
      Qui tant est belle, doulce et tendre.

To you and no other I come in surrender;
So must I do perforce.
To this your face constrains me,
[Your face] so gentle, fair, and tender.

Pray vouchsafe your pity
To me, who, at first sight,
      Come to you and no other in surrender;
      So must I do perforce.

I dare not tell you what I feel
Never could I be so bold

Except to ask the boon of being in your favor—
As far as honor will allow.
>   To you and no other I come in surrender;
>   So must I do perforce.
>   To this your face constrains me,
>   [Your face] so gentle, fair, and tender.

Variants

Dij, Jar.
3 grace—*Dij.* 5 en pitie—*Jar.* 6 (Mell ends here; remainder from
Dij.) 8 n'euz—*Jar.* 9 Ne au moins—*Dij,*[1] Neantmoins—*Jar*; d'estre—
Jar. 10 pout—*Dij,* peult—*Jar.*

Versification

Rondeau quatrain in octosyllables, *a b b a.* Acrostic: A IAQVELINE.
Line 9 is hypermetric unless *e* of *Ne* is read as elided; we have rendered
it as **N'.**

Textual Notes

Line 1. **me viens rendre** = modF *Je viens me rendre.*
Line 3. Dij *grace* is in homologous rhyme with l. 9 and is also less
apt contextually than **face**, which is supported by Jar.
Line 5. **vo** is a Picard singular, a back-formation from the plural
vos or *voz.* Jar *en* is an "emendation", either because its redactor did
not recognize *vo* or because he was removing dialectal traits.
Lines 1'–2'. The short refrain is integrated with the short strophe.
Line 7. **Le vous** was still the normal order; the modern pronoun
order, *vous le,* was beginning to make its appearance about this time
and became firmly established in the sixteenth century.
Line 8. **Jamais . . . n'eust** 'Never . . . would there be'; Jar *n'euz*
'did I have'.
Line 9. **N'** (MS *Ne*) is a coordinating conjunction introducing a
clause with a negative—even if only faintly negative—meaning. Hence
N'au moins means 'Except'. This is not *néanmoins* (Jar's *neantmoins,*
the *Trois Chansonniers* reading of Dij, *néanmoins*), since this trissyllabic
word would render the verse hypermetric. However, the meaning of
néanmoins, 'nevertheless', would fit well: '[although I dare not declare

---

1. *Trois Chansonniers français,* No. 18, p. 34 reads l. 9 of Dij as *Neanmoins,* l. 10 as *peut,* but careful
examination of microfilm confirms our readings.

my love openly to you], Nevertheless, aspiring to be in your favor, I come to surrender to you, etc.'

Line 10. 'to the degree that honor can extend'; humbly, the lover asks no more recognition, no more "grace" than honor (that is, his own low station and the reputation of the lady) will allow. Dij *pout* is spelled like an Old French preterite of *pouoir*; but perhaps it is (as *Trois Chansonniers* interpreted it) just a miswriting or bad copy of *peut*. The preterite tense is hard to justify here, so we have replaced this form with Jar **peult**.

Lines 1″–4″. The long refrain is integrated with the long strophe.

43. Triste qui sperò morendo, ff. 56ᵛ–57ʳ, Vincenet

COMMENTS

Vincenet's setting of this Italian poem, like the composition on a Spanish text that follows, appears to be unique to the chansonnier. Also unique, it would seem, is the musicopoetic structure of this work. The initial section of the piece is brought to rest on an inconclusive half cadence at m. 14 whereas the full close is reserved until the end in a manner often employed for the rondeau. However, the poem is not in that form. It consists of two four-line strophes with the rhyme scheme *abba/cdcd*, and the scribe has written it out in a continuous fashion, the first strophe with the first $13\frac{1}{2}$ measures of music (27 breves) and the second with the remaining $9\frac{1}{2}$ measures (19 breves). But if the verse is distributed in the manner thus described, two difficulties become immediately apparent. First, there are but two clearly articulated musical phrases in the second section instead of the four possible in the longer opening segment. Second, the declamation for the final strophe becomes suddenly precipitous and syllabic in contrast with the leisurely melismatic style of the preceding portion. As a result, it seemed preferable to repeat the final section of the composition for the second strophe as is suggested by the placement of the text in the modern score.

It is tempting to see this piece as a setting for a French rondeau cinquain with musical phrases ending in mm. 7, 10, 14, 18, and 23, to which a strophic Italian poem was later adapted. Such an assumption would perhaps justify to some extent the editorial latitude taken, but it must be candidly avowed that there is no explicit indication in the MS to justify the formal solution proposed in the transcription.

Notwithstanding the possibility that the music was not originally composed for the verse with which it is now associated, it is interesting to note the inconclusive termination of the melodic phrase sung to *non more* and the sparkling melisma with the word *ardendo*, either of which might be construed as a textual illustration.

> Triste qui sperò morendo
> Finire ogni dolore.
> Triste qui jamay non more,
> Va de foco in foco ardendo.   4
>
> Triste qui tene sperança
> A lo suo tempo servuto.
> Triste chi mai nulla avança
> Sinon pena per aiuto.   8

Sad [is he] who hoped, by dying,
To end all pain.
Sad he who never dies
[But] goes from fire to fire, burning.

Sad he who dared hope,
His time of service ended;
Sad he who steps not forth
Save with Pain as companion.

Versification

Shortened *barzelletta* (or *ballata*) in *ottonari piani*, that is, eight-syllable lines with stressed seventh syllable. Final vowel + initial vowel = one syllable, with the exception of l. 2, in which *-re o-* = two syllables. Musical structure is X Y Y, as follows: X (*ripresa*, ll. 1–4), Y (*prima mutazione*, ll. 5–6), Y (*seconda mutazione*, ll. 7–8). In a conventional ballata this would be followed by a *volta*, a four-line strophe sung to X. The music, however, has a final cadence at the end of the mutazione; the cadence at the end of the ripresa is not a final one, so the poem must be complete in its present form. Rhyme scheme: *a b b a c d c d*.

Textual Notes

In lines 1, 3, and 5, **qui** = standard Italian *chi*, a spelling which does occur in l. 7; all are to be pronounced [ki]. Double consonants are not spelled double (except for l. 7 **nulla**): l. 3 **jamay** = giammai, l. 5 **tene** = tenne, and l. 6 **A lo** = Allo. In the absence of incorrect doubling, or, even better, of an etymologically geminate consonant in rhyme with a single consonant, it is not possible to know whether the dialect of the poem has double consonants. **Foco**, **more** correspond to modern *fuoco*, *muore*; but note that the latter, presumably with open *o*, rhymes with **dolore**. This rhyme suggests that close and open *o* may have coalesced in this dialect; but that such rhymes were possible even in Tuscan is shown by Dante's *Purgatorio*, Canto 3, ll. 134, 136, 138: amọre : mọre : fọre.

Another, conceivable interpretation of l. 8 results from taking **pena** as a verb, the line then being translated as follows: 'Without his own striving as [sole] assistance'; i.e., the only help he will get will be from his effort. To the degree (small!) that this interpretation differs from the preceding one, it seems less concordant with the tenor of the poem. It should not end in a stiff-upper-lip counsel; it is pure plaint.

44. La pena sin ser sabida, ff. 57ᵛ–59ʳ, Vincenet

COMMENTS

As was observed in connection with the previous composition, neither the Spanish *canción* nor the strophic Italian song attributed to Vincenet appears to be found in any other source.

The mensuration intended for the initial section of this piece is almost certainly perfect tempus (○). It becomes imperfect with the setting provided for the *mudanza* and is further altered by a sesquialteral proportion for the final melisma.

The proper interpretation for the blackened brevis standing above the void one just before the repetition sign in C and CT I was not immediately clear. All six written pitches are perhaps to be sung simultaneously at the first ending to fill in and enrich the vertical sonorities. Yet it seemed more likely that the blackened notes were provided to make a smoother transition to the melisma that terminates the repetition of the section, as the coloration common to both would presumably indicate. Nonetheless, it should be remarked that an equally effective junction would be achieved by moving from m. 27 directly to the beginning of the proportional passage of mm. 30 ff.

> La pena sin ser sabida
> Es incurable dolor;

Mas quien es de mi servida
Ben sabe que por su amor
Soy triste to[d]a mi vida.   5

Et finge de non saber
La causa de mi tristura   7

Por que mas a su plazer
Me pene su fermosura.   9

La gente non entendida
Non sabe mi disfavor,
Mas quien es de mi servida
Ben sabe que por su amor
Soy triste toda mi vida.   14

Pain suffered in secret
Is incurable woe;
But she whom I serve
Knows well that for her love
My whole life is spent in grief.

And she pretends not to know
The cause of my sadness,

So that more to her pleasure
Her beauty will pain me.

The heedless and unfeeling
Cannot know my sorrow,
But she whom I serve
Knows well that for her love
My whole life is spent in grief.

VERSIFICATION

A *canción* in octosyllables (counted Spanish style), alternating *llanos* and *agudos*. *Tema* and *vuelta* are *quintillas* in *ababa*; the last three lines of the *vuelta* are identical to the last three lines of the *tema*. The *mudanza* is in *cdcd*. The musical fit is as follows: X: *tema*; Y_1Y_2:

mudanza; X: *vuelta*. See pp. 93–95, for explanation of the Spanish terms.

TEXTUAL NOTES

Line 3. **Mas** = modern Spanish *pero* 'but', until the seventeenth century; in medieval Spanish *pero* = 'nevertheless'.

Line 4. **Ben** = *bien* 'well'; possibly an Italianism.

Line 5. **to[d]a** = MS *tota*; we have restored the more authentically Spanish spelling, which is attested in l. 14. The reading *tota* may be due to the scribe's familiarity with Italian, as possibly in l. 4 **Ben**.

Line 6. **Et** [e] = modern Spanish *y* 'and'. In Spanish of the fifteenth century, *i* (*y*) and *e* (*et*) were practically interchangeable, although *i* had been specialized for use before vowels. By the seventeenth century, *y* had replaced *e* in standard Spanish. **finge** [fínže] 'feigns'. **non** = modern Spanish *no*. See also ll. 10 and 11.

Line 7. **causa** [káuza].

Line 8. **plazer** [pladzér].

Line 9. **fermosura** = modern Spanish *hermosura* 'beauty'. In the fifteenth century the phonetic change from [f] to [h] by way of a bilabial voiceless spirant [φ] was still in progress. Whether the spelling in this poem is due to dialectal factors or to orthographic lag is not determinable.

Line 10. **gente** [žénte].

45. So ys emprentid, ff. 61ᵛ–63ʳ, Walterus Fry

CONCORDANT SOURCES

BerK 78 C 28, ff. 2ᵛ–4ʳ (capital P only text given)
Esc IV.a.24, ff. 31ᵛ–33ʳ (Pour une suis deconforté)
Flo 176, ff. 60ᵛ–62ʳ (Pour une suis) Bedingan (Bellingan?)
MC 871, ff. 8ᵛ–9ʳ (pp. 262–63)
Ash 191, f. 196ᵛ (incomplete C only)
Pix, ff. 55ᵛ–57ʳ (Pour une suis deconforté)
Tr 90, ff. 283ᵛ–84ʳ (Sancta Maria)
Tr 90, ff. 308ᵛ–09ʳ
Lab, ff. 51ʳ–52ʳ (incomplete)

COLLATION

The fragment of the C preserved in Ash 191 is in black notation and comprises only the first seven measures. In contrast Lab has the T and

CT parts complete for the entire work, but f. 50ᵛ, upon which the initial section of the C was written (mm. 1–21), is missing. The second copy of the chanson in Tr 90 (ff. 308ᵛ–09ʳ) was checked but not collated in detail, since it appeared not to differ significantly from the first.

Ornamental and notational details deemed relatively unimportant have not been included in the variants recorded here. Nevertheless, enough minor differences have been included to give an idea of the degrees of affinity and independence of the various readings. Moreover, discrepancies are relatively few in C and T. In the C at m. 3(2), BerK 78 C 28, Flo 176, and Pix give f-M (eliminating the SSm of Mell); at m. 10 (1 ff.), Berk 78 C 28 has f-Sb, e-Sb (undoubtedly altered), creating a sharp clash with the CT, whereas Flo 176 has a possible e-M at m. 10(2) (instead of f-M as in Mell); at m. 22(1), there is d-Sb (without the dotted figure of Mell) in MC 871, Tr 90, and Lab; at m. 26(2, 3), Lab gives c-M, a-Sb (reversing the values of Mell, as it does even more frequently in the CT); and at m. 31(3 ff.), c'-dotted M, b'-Sm, g-M is given by BerK 78 C 28 and Flo 176, shifting slightly the rhythmic pattern found in Mell.

Only BerK 78 C 28 and Lab have variants for the T: the latter has c-M, a-Sb at m. 26(2, 3), reversing the values of Mell, and c-M at m. 32(3), forming a fourth with the CT below (instead of b-M as in Mell); the former has a rest replacing the b-Sb at m. 13(3) and two apparent errors, a missing c-Sb at m. 14(3) and e-Sb (instead of e-M) at m. 45(4).

In the CT the divergences are fairly frequent but not always particularly significant: at m. 4(1, 2), BerK 78 C 28 has c-Sb, a-Sb (altered), a slight change; at m. 6(4, 5), all sources except Mell have d-M, c-Sb; at m. 7(2), Lab has G-Sb (instead of a-Sb), probably an error; at m. 11(1), BerK 78 C 28 gives F-Sb, forming a tritone with the T (instead of G-Sb as in Mell); at m. 15(2), Lab has G-M (as possible as the F-M of Mell); at m. 18(2 ff.), Lab has an extensive variant: a-M (instead of the rest-M of Mell), d-M, b-M, c-M, b-M, d-M, c-M, a-M, F-M; at m. 27(2, 3), Lab has c-Sb, b-M (again reversing the note values of Mell); at m. 33(2), Lab has c-M (possible, but not so good as the b-M of Mell); at m. 37(2, 3), G-Sb, b-M (reversing the values of Mell) is found in BerK 78 C 28, MC 871, and Lab; at m. 40(4, 5), Lab has a-Sb, G-M (reversing yet again the values of Mell); at m. 42(1–4), MC 871 gives c-Sb, a-Sb, F-M, G-M (changing slightly the rhythmic pattern of Mell); and at m. 44(4), a dissonant E-M is found in MC 871 (instead of D-M as in Mell).

COMMENTS

The reading of Mell is most closely related to those of Esc IV.a.24 and Tr 90. Essentially similar, but somewhat more independent are MC 871 and BerK 78 C 28. Both Flo 176 and Pix can be linked to the latter by one or two shared divergences but on the whole have a greater affinity with Mell. The scribal tradition represented in Lab is evidently distinctive, but it would seem to have left at least a trace in the versions of BerK 78 C 28 and Flo 176.

Since the version of the present MS at m. 6 (4, 5) of the CT is without support in any of the concordant sources and produces parallel fifths with the C as well, it was deemed justifiable to emend the transcription in accordance with the more correct alternate reading.

The attribution to Bedingham (or Bellingham) in Flo 176 is somewhat suspect because the following composition in that MS, *Grant tempo* (see No. 47), carries the same name. In any case the careful, precise ascription of Mell is not to be ignored lightly, especially if the editor's hypothesis is correct with respect to the role played by Tinctoris in purveying the musical repertory of the Burgundian court to the kingdom of Naples and in compiling the Mellon Chansonnier.

The cadential formulas of mm. 5–6 and 40–42 pose problems in the use of accidentals because of the diminished and augmented intervals resulting from the conventional changes. Unless one assumes an English predilection for such sonorities in cadential passages, it may be preferable to eliminate the sharps in both instances and to use instead b-flat at mm. 5 (5) and 41 (4) of the C.

The mensural sign, missing in Mell, can be supplied from Flo 176, MC 871, or Pix, where perfect tempus (○) is explicitly indicated.

> So ys emprentid in my remembrance
> Your wommanhede, iour yowght, *your gentilnesse,*
> Iour g[o]odly port, your frely continance,
> Your prysid byaulte w*ith* iour *kyndenesse*
>
> —That [. . .] lord[e] [*that*] alle wot tak y to witnesse!—
> That, [wak] y, slep[e] y, or wa*t* thing y do,
> In wele, in wo, [in] joye or[e] he[v]enesse,
> M[y]n hert ys w*ith* yow, go [. . .] wey th*at* ye go.

This poem, unique to Mell, has been edited by Robert J. Menner.[1]

VERSIFICATION

Ballade in decasyllables, $a[b]a[b]bcbc$. The endings of X_1 and X_2 are written on the third stave of folio 61^v, but the scribe neglected to write the words that underlie these endings; hence four syllables of l. 2 and three syllables of l. 4 are missing. To complete these lines, we have chosen *gentilnesse* (rather than the more frequent *gentilesse*) and *kyndenesse* to conform to the rich rhyme of *witnesse* and *hevenesse* of the second stanza. The rhyme scheme of the first stanza, *abab*, conforms to that of the other English poems of this collection, in which rhyme *b* introduces the second stanza (No. 47, *abab bcc*, No. 55, *abab bcbc*).

TEXTUAL NOTES

In these decasyllabic lines the final, unstressed -*e* is not pronounced. The last syllable of every line is stressed. We have transcribed initial *i* or *I* / *J* as *i* when it is pronounced like [y]: *iour* in ll. 2, 3, and 4; but as *j* in l. 7 *joye*. The vowel *i* (*y*) is pronounced in its continental value, as in *my* [mi], *prysid* [prí : zid] 'prized, esteemed', *kyndenesse* [ki : ndənés], *y* [i :] 'I'. *Frely* is pronounced [fre : li]; that is, *e* has the value of French *é* somewhat drawn out. *Ow* and *ou* are pronounced [u:] as in modern English *you*. We have transcribed *y* and *þ* as *th* where appropriate. As in the continental scribal tradition, a raised *r* = *ur* (e.g., *yor* = *your*), and we have resolved this abbreviation accordingly.

The syntax is periodic; the sentence ends in the last line, and it could not possibly end before the first hemistich of the last line. Lines 1–4 contain the first clause: 'So deeply impressed in my memory are your qualities [seven are enumerated]'; l. 5 contains a declaration of good faith: 'I take to witness that Lord that knows all!'; ll. 6–8 set forth the result clause: 'That, whether I am waking or sleeping or whatever I do, in happiness, in woe, in joy or despondency'—now,

---

1. "Three Fragmentary English Ballades in the Mellon Chansonnier," *Modern Language Quarterly* 6 (1945): 381–87. The present edition differs in a number of details from Menner's. Since a thoroughgoing discussion of each of my independent judgments would take an amount of space inappropriate to the purposes of this edition, I shall confine my remarks to an elucidation of the Middle English text and to the justification of readings that depart from the Mell text. This will be the policy with respect to the other two English poems of this collection, Nos. 47 and 55, the latter of which has been published in an anthology of Rossell Hope Robbins (see note 1 to No. 55). The comparison of my version of these three poems with those of previous editors will be treated in a projected article. I wish to acknowledge my debt to the many valuable suggestions of the previous editors.

finally, the result clause—'My heart ıs with you' and this addendum: 'wherever you may go'.

This interpretation is somewhat different from Menner's: "One would expect a *that* after *lorde*, as well as before—'the Lord that knows all', and it would be tempting to transpose *þat* and *lorde* if it were not for the fact that the first *that* probably follows *so* of l. 1: 'so is imprinted in my memory your womanhood, . . . that I take to witness the Lord (that) knows all that whether I walk or sleep, . . .'"[2]

Line 1. The scribe tends, in the three English poems, to "see" French words; thus an original *So ys* was copied as *Soys* in all three voices (the asterisk marks a hypothetical form in the model from which the scribe was copying).

Line 3. How *goodly* was copied as *grodly* is hard to imagine. A resemblance of some English *o* to what the scribe recognizes as *r* is required. There is no ambiguity whatsoever as to the *r* that our scribe intends to write. **port** 'carriage, bearing'. **frely** 'lovely'; the semantic development is 'free', 'noble', 'graceful' in the same semantic field as Old French *gent, gentil, franc*. **continance** 'demeanor, manner'.

Line 5. **y** = 'I'.

Line 6. ***wak** 'wake' → *walk* (→ = 'was copied as'); in English handwriting an *a* often had a high rising stroke to its left, causing our scribe to see it as *al*, as here, or as *el*, as in No. 55, l. 4 *deathe* (MS *de alve*). *****slepe y** → *slepoy*; i.e., *e* → *o*. One frequently used English *e* has a closed, nearly circular form, with a counterclockwise ductus and a loop in the upper part: *ꞅ*.[3] Such an *e* would almost certainly be taken for an *o* by anyone unfamiliar with this particular form. *****wat thing** → *wathing*; the reduction of a repeated letter or sequence of letters to a single letter or sequence is a frequent scribal error, still practiced both in handwriting and in typing; it is called *haplology* by philologists.

Line 7. *****Wo in** → *Wom*; the scribe apparently perceived the three minims of **in* as *m*, and attached it to the preceding word. *****ore** → *ort*; i.e., *e* → *t*, possibly an *e* made in two strokes, like the second *e* of *helde* in Parkes, 21 (ii) l. 9 (*ꞇ*). *****heuenesse** → *henenesse*; this reading gives us a clear notion of our scribe's innocence of English.

Line 8. *****Myn** → *mijn*. Our scribe invariably makes a *y* in two separate strokes, the first nearly vertical, the second slanting back

2. Ibid., p. 383.

3. M. B. Parkes, *English Cursive Book Hands 1250–1500* (Oxford: Clarendon Press, 1969), plate 21 (ii), l. 9 *helde*, the first *e*.

under it, touching the bottom of the first stroke and descending below the base line. In English manuscripts this kind of *y* is often executed without lifting the pen from the paper; the pen then records the movement from the bottom of the first stroke to the top of the second, making a sort of bowl formed by the first stroke and the transitional movement (𝒴). The effect is that of a dotless *ij* sequence, and our scribe copied it as *ij*.[4] ***go** → *gogo;* the repetition of an element is called *dittology* by philologists; it is an error that often occurs in attempts at painstaking copying.

46. Gentil madona (Fortune elas), ff. 63ᵛ–65ʳ [Bedingham]

CONCORDANT SOURCES

Berk 78 C 28, ff. 18ᵛ–19ʳ (capital *F* only text given)
Esc IV.a.24, ff. 117ᵛ–118r
MC 871, f. 114ᵛ (p. 370) (Fortuna las)
Sched, ff. 48ᵛ–49ʳ (Fortune), Jo. Bodigham
Pix, ff. 89ᵛ–90ʳ
Par 4379, ff. 21ᵛ–22ʳ
Cord, ff. 3ᵛ–5ʳ
Pav 362, ff. 26ᵛ–27ʳ

COLLATION

Insignificant details of melodic ornamentation and isolated errors are not included in the variants reported here. Moreover, divergences worthy of note are not numerous in either of the upper pair of voices. In the C at m. 2 (4), Pix has g-M instead of f-M as in Mell; and in m. 30 (1 ff.), Berk 78 C 28, Cord, and Pix give g-Sb, a′-M, whereas Sched, after those two pitches shared with the three concordances listed, continues with c′-Sb, b′-Sm, a′-SM. In the T at m. 10 (4), BerK 78 C 28 and Sched have a-M (a possible alternative since the dissonance is correctly handled) instead of G-M as in Mell; at m. 24 (2 ff.), Sched gives c-M, d-M, e-M, f-M (running in parallel sixths with the C), and the last pitch is used also in Esc IV.a.24, Pix, and MC 871 (giving a more euphonious counterpoint than the e-M of Mell and related sources); and at m. 31 (3), BerK 78 C 28, Pav 362, and Cord have a dissonant e-M instead of the d-M of the remaining sources.

4. See Parkes, plate 21 (iii), l. 5 *hym*.

In contrast with the relative consistency of the C and T found in all the sources, the various readings of the CT give some rather extensive and independent variants. In m. 1 (1, 2), Esc IV.a.24 and Pix begin with F-Sb, c-Sb, MC 871 with F-Sb, a-Sb instead of c-Br as in Mell; at m. 2 (3) all other sources give F-M instead of the dissonant G-M of Mell; at m. 2 (4 ff.), Esc IV.a.24, Pix, and MC 871 have f-M, e-Sb (creating parallel octaves with the C), whereas Cord gives G-M, a-Sb, c-M, f-Sb, e-M, d-M (resulting again in parallel octaves with the C at the end of the passage); at m. 4 (2, 3), Esc IV.a.24 and Pix have e-M, c-Sb (moving in parallel thirds with the T); at m. 6 (1, 2), C and F are given as blackened BBr by BerK 78 C 28, Cord, Pav 326, and Sched; at mm. 8 (1)–10 (1) in Esc IV.a.24 and Pix one reads G-Sb (with no preceding rest), a-M, F-Sb, G-M, F-Sb, b-flat M, c-Sb, a-M; at mm. 12 (4)–13 (4) MC 871 has rest-M (instead of c-M as in Mell), d-M, e-Sb, c-Sb, b-M (creating yet again parallel octaves with the C); at m. 17 (1, 2), g-Sb, c-M (reversing the values of Mell) is given by BerK 78 C 28, Cord, Pav 362, and Sched, whereas Pix and MC 871 have f-Sb, d-M (either alternative is possible); at m. 20 (1) a dissonant c-M is given by BerK 78 C 28 and Par 4379 instead of d-M as elsewhere; at m. 20 (2, 3) the blackening seen in Mell seems to have no significance and is not found in concordant sources; and at m. 22 (3 ff.), Cord has c-M, a-dotted M, b-Sm, G-Sb.

Curiously, at m. 15 of T and CT, BerK 78 C 28 and Pav 362 change the mensuration to imperfect tempus (C), whereas in Cord the original perfect mensuration is iterated in the T. MC 871 provides a written flat for the b′ of the C at m. 17 (3), but the alteration does not appear necessary or desirable.

COMMENTS

The composition found in Prague, Strahov Monastery, MS D.G. IV.47,[1] f. 250ʳ (p. 498) begins in the same manner as the one published here but quickly diverges to total independence; however, one can assume a deliberate quotation. A keyboard intabulation of the song occurs in the *Buxheim Organ Book*, f. 66ᵛ (No. 124, Fortune), and a tenor–cantus firmus mass based upon it was copied into Tr 91 beginning at f. 247ᵛ. The popularity of the work in Italy is further attested

---

1. Concerning that codex, see Dragan Plamenac, "Browsing through a Little-known Manuscript."

by its adoption for the singing of two different laude, those published in Belcari's *Laude Spirituali* as Nos. lxiv (p. 34) and cxlv (pp. 65–66).

Nino Pirrotta, in his discussion of this composition,[2] suggests that the poetic form was derived from the *ballata* and apparently assumes that the musical setting attributed to Bedingham was prepared directly for the Italian verse found with it in the majority of the sources. As will be seen below, the editors have opted for a different reconstruction of the poem than that proposed by Pirrotta. But regardless of the solution adopted in that respect, an attempt to match the words with the music in a singable manner will quickly demonstrate that the difficulties involved are even more substantial than can be adequately explained by the errors and distortions of non-Italian scribes, and that the musical form has nothing in common with that of the poetry. Because such a situation is so rare in fifteenth-century secular music, it appears likely that the Italian text is actually a contrafact and that the original poem now subsists only in the fragmentary incipit, "Fortune elas," preserved in this MS and a few others. One can nevertheless surmise that it was a ballade, as witnessed by the form of the music, because the English musicians continued to cultivate the genre long after it had gone out of style on the Continent. The verse may have been French, but had that been the case, it would probably have survived in at least some of the sources. It is more likely that it was English despite the slight—and understandable—Frenchification of the Mellon scribe, a circumstance that would account for its virtual disappearance from the collections of the period.

The tradition of transmission for this work is characterized by an exceptional number of independent readings and some complex interrelationships. The version of Mell is most closely related to that of Par 4379. In essentially the same tradition but a step or two removed are BerK 78 C 28 and Pav 362, whose readings have a number of salient features in common. A separate tradition, based on the extensive and important variants in the CT, is represented by Esc IV.a.24 and Pix, which are, similarly, almost identical to each other. Mostly independent, but having some affinities with both preceding pairs of MSS are Cord, MC 871, and the rather unreliable Sched.

In m. 2 (3) of the CT the unanimous agreement of the concordant sources against Mell and the unjustifiable dissonance produced by the

2. "Ricercare e variazioni su 'O rosa bella,'" pp. 68–69.

latter's reading prompted an emendation in the transcription. In the T at m. 24 (4), by contrast, even though the pitch given by three of the sources worked more consonantly than that found in Mell, the notation of the present MS was retained because it is confirmed by some of the concordances and is not incorrect according to the contrapuntal usage of the period.

The cadential formulas of mm. 5, 13, 20, 29, and 35 pose an intriguing problem in the application of accidentals. In each case the naturally (or artificially) raised leading tone sounds a vertical tritone with the CT, but if the corresponding note of the CT is raised to obviate the tritone, it forms a diminished fifth with the previous note against which it is first introduced. Moreover, at the end of the two principal sections the melodic progression of the CT is from F to b-flat; consequently, to raise the latter would also create an unveiled melodic tritone. The only other alternative, lowering the leading tone, seemed even more unlikely than the momentary precadential clash, and so the conventional cadential alteration was allowed to stand in spite of the irregular vertical harmonies produced.

> Gentil madona, de*h* non mi habandonare,
> O precïosa gemma,
> O fior de margarita;   3
>   Tu sei aquella che [. . .] tien*e* la mia vita
> In amorosa fiama;
> De*h* non mi far' penare.   6
>
> Aymè, deb'io in questo ardore stare,
> La mya vita in dolor si guay finire,
> Perchè ansi crudel sey enver de my?
> Tu sey ben che mirando el tuo bel viso
> Tu me festi de ty innamorare.   11

>   Sweet lady, pray, do not abandon me,
> O precious jewel,
> O flower of marguerite.
>   Thou art she who ever holds my life
> In flame of love—
> Pray, do not make me suffer.
>
> Alas! I must remain in this ardor
> And finish my life so woefully in dole

Because thou art so cruel to me.
Thou knowest that, as I gazed on thy fair face,
Thou mad'st me become thy slave.

VARIANTS

The following manuscripts have texts for this poem: Esc, Pix, Par
Cord Pav. Mell, Pix, Par stop after l. 5; the rest is reconstructed from
the remaining manuscripts.

1 no—*Pav*; me—*Cord Pav*; m'abandonare—*Esc*, m'abandonnaire—
Par. 2 Pav omits O; pretiosa—*Esc Pix Par*. 3 fiore—*Esc*, flour—*Par*;
fior gentille—*Pav*; 4 se—*Pix*, soy—*Par*, sie—*Cord*; colea—*Esc*, collei—
Pix (*Par*), quela—*Cord*; qui—*Pav*; Par Cord omit sempre; che sempre
mantien—*Mell*, tien sempre—*Esc Pix*, tien—*Par*, tene—*Cord*, teny—
Pav; Esc Pix Par omit la. 5 Esc Pav omit in; amoroxa—*Esc*; in
namorosa—*Pix*; Esc Pix omit fiama; In tua guardia—*Cord*. 6 a ma
non—*Esc*; me—*Esc Pix*; fare—*Mell*, far—*Esc Par Cord Pav*, lasar—
Pix; morire—*Cord Pav*. Mell, Pix, Par end here. Lines 7–11 are shown
below *in extenso* for Esc, Cord, Pav respectively; these versions display
not only orthographic and lexical variants, but also differing order of
lines.

Esc
Aime debo sempre star in questo ardore
de ti io son servente del viso angelico
Stentar mi fay vita con doloxi guay

    Cord
    ———

    La mya vita in dolorosi guay finiere
    Per che ansi crudela soy en verso de my
    Tu scey ben che mirando el toy viso
    Tu my feste enamorare

        Pav
        Y me debio semper in questo ardore stare
        la mia vita in dolorosy guay
        Perque sey en sy crude en ver de my
        Tu sey ben che mirando el tuo bello viso
        Tu me festi dety inno mourare

Versification

This is one stanza of a canzone (see *Formes Fixes*, pp. 96–97) consisting of two piedi *A b c*, *C b a* and a sirima *A C C C A*, in eleven- and seven-syllable lines. The piedi offer two independent patterns: line lengths *Xxx Xxx*, palindromic rhyme *abccba*. Rhyme *b* is of the approximate type known to Italian metricians as *assonanza atona* or *allitterazione* (cf. No. 33), in which the concordance is between the last consonants and following atonic vowels of the rhyming lines: thus, rhyme *b* is -V́mma (V́ means any accented vowel). The *c* rhyme is a real rhyme (in -*ita*) in ll. 3 and 4 but consists of mere assonances (called *assonanza tonica* or simply *assonanza* in Italian treatises) in ll. 8–10; that is, the only part which these endings have in common is the stressed vowel *i*. We even have a *verso tronco* in rhyme with *versi piani*, if our analysis is correct. If we had taken l. 9 *my* as *me*, to conform to the dialect of Mell, Par, and Cord (see textual notes on l. 1), l. 9 would rhyme with nothing. The choice is between rejecting the possibility of approximate rhymes, with the consequent scheme *A D E F A*, and admitting the assonances described above, and with them *A C C C A*. It seems clear that the latter solution is to be preferred, especially since it repeats the palindrome effect initiated in the piedi. The use of the same rhymes in the sirima that appear in the piedi—except for the *verso chiave* and the lines that rhyme with it—is unusual for the canzone, it must be admitted.

Some adjustments have had to be made to establish a text derived from a corrupt tradition. Line 1 is one syllable too long, even assuming *mi ha-* to be one syllable. It is possible that the original poem lacked the *deh*, which, however, is supported by all concordant sources. *Deh* in the prototype to all the known MSS (the prototype is not necessarily the original poem) may have been an anticipation of the *deh* of l. 6. In l. 4 we have dropped *sempre*, which is omitted by two other sources, and the syllable *man-*, which is not supported by any concordant source. It then becomes necessary to adopt the third person singular ending -*e* provided by Cord and Pav. *Tiene* (or possibly *tenne*; see textual note on l. 4) is preferable to *mantien* because the line as we have established it has the normal rhythmic pattern 3–6–10 (see Metrics, pp. 83–84); *mantien* would shift the dominant stress to the seventh position, a most abnormal pattern. In l. 6 we have suppressed the -*e* of Mell's *fare*, which is unique to Mell.

The sirima is in a state of confusion in the three sources that preserve it. In l. 7 the rhythmic pattern is 2–4–8–10. In l. 9 there is a hiatus between *Perchè* and *ansì*; *sey enver* is run together. In l. 11, *ty* has a dominant stress (in sixth position) and is in hiatus with the following word.

Nino Pirrotta (see p. 377) has suggested a reconstruction of what he calls the *prima stanza*, presumably of a ballata, corresponding roughly to the part we have identified as the piedi of a canzone stanza:

> Gentil madona, / de non m'abbandonare.
> Hame, deb'[i]o / sempre in questo ardore stare?
>
> O pretiosa gemma, / o fior de margarita,
> tu sei colei che tien sempre mia vita
> in amorosa fiamma; / de non me far penare.

It is obvious that his analysis of the poem is radically different from ours.

In the MSS the piedi and the sirima have been taken as two stanzas, each sung to the same music, as given in vol. 1, pp. 160–63. If no MS preserves an attempt to fit the canzone as theoretically it should have been fitted to the music (piede I to X_1, piede II to X_2, sirima to Y), it is because of the difficulty of fitting the five lines of the sirima to the four well-marked musical phrases of Y. Apparently, at the beginning of this manuscript tradition, a heedless Italian scribe, confronted by an English ballade and profiting from the XXY structure common to the ballade and to many canzoni, chose to replace the English words with those of a canzone of appropriate structure whose piedi fit rather well into the first part of the ballade. Although there are awkwardnesses in fitting the five lines of the sirima to the second part of the music, it can be done, and perhaps the version given here represents best the conception of the first person to attempt to marry the present canzone to the ballade music he had before him.

According to this reconstruction of the events leading to the extant versions, the difficulty of fitting in the five lines led to a totally different notion of the structure of the song; the wide differences among the three versions of the sirima, compared with the rather fair agreement among the versions of the piedi, testify to the difficulty caused by the sirima.

Gen- til ma- do - na, non mi ha- ban- do- na - re, O
Tu sei a- quel- la — che tie- ne la mia vi - ta In

pre- ci- o- sa gem- ma, O fior de mar- ga- ri - - -
a- mo- ro- sa fia- ma; Deh, non mi far pe- na - -

1. ta; - - -

2. - - -

- - - re. Ay- me deb' i- o in ques- to ar- do-

re sta - re, La mya vi - - ta in do- lor si guay fi- ni-

re Per- chè an- si cru- del — sey — en- ver —

— de — my? Tu sey ben che mi- ran-

— do el tuo bel — vi- - so — Tu — me —

fes- ti de ty — in- na- mo- ra - - - re.

TEXTUAL NOTES

Line 1. mi is the standard Italian form of the unstressed first person singular object pronoun. The stressed form of the same pronoun, found most often as the object of a preposition, is *mè*. In most northern dialects outside of Tuscany, these forms are reversed: *me* is the unstressed form, *mì* the stressed form, as in Spanish.[3]

Mell, with unstressed *mi* in ll. 1 and 6, seems to follow the Tuscan rule. But examination of the variants reveals the following situation:

	Stressed	*Unstressed*
Mell		l. 1 mi, l. 6 mi
Par		l. 1 mi, l. 6 my
Pix		l. 1 m', l. 6 me
Esc		l. 1 m', l. 6 me
Cord	l. 9 my	l. 1 me, l. 6 my, l. 11 my
Pav	l. 9 my	l. 1 me, l. 6 my, l. 11 me

The two MSS that elide the vowel before another vowel have unstressed *me* before a consonant (Pix, Esc, ll. 1, 6). The only MSS that present an example of the stressed pronoun (Cord, Pav, l. 9) show *my*, which, because it seems to fit through assonance into a rhyme pattern (see Versification), probably belongs to the original poem and therefore does not necessarily reveal the dialect of the copyists of Cord and Pav. In the unstressed pronoun they vacillate between *me* and *mi* (*my*), but they do not have the same pattern of vacillation (cf. l. 11), in spite of an evident close stemmatic relationship. The vowel of the unstressed pronoun probably fluctuated nondistinctively between [i] and [e], perhaps without reaching either of those extremes.

Line 2. precïosa is pronounced like modern Italian *preziosa*. **gemma**: We stated in Versification that *gemma* is in atonic assonance with **fiama** (l. 5). There is also the rather remote possibility that French influence had introduced a pronunciation like **giamma* [džámma] to poetic language; the French word *gemme* at this period was pronounced [žãmə]; it rhymes with *femme* and is sometimes spelled *jame* or *jamme*. Cf. l. 9 *ansi* (var. *en sy*).

Line 3. margarita 'daisy'.

---

3. Gerhard Rohlfs, *Historische Grammatik der italienischen Sprache*, §454.

Line 4. **aquella** is unique to Mell; Cord, with its *quela* (*quella* in the tenor) is nearest to it of the concordant sources. This form, with an initial *a*, is not mentioned by Rohlfs or by Bertoni.[4] **tiene**, Mell *mantien* (see discussion of this word in the Versification section). The Cord and Pav variants (*tene*, *teny*) suggest *tenne* because the representation of geminate consonants, especially nasals, by a single letter (cf. *madona*, *fiama*) is characteristic of this period. Since the tradition is divided between the present (Mell, Esc, Pix, Par) and the *passato remoto* (Cord, Pav, if their readings do indeed represent *tenne*), and since both tenses make sense in this context, we opt for the tense exhibited by Mell.

Line 5. **fiama** = *fiamma*.

Line 7. Pav *debio* = *debb'io*, Esc *debo* = *debbo*. Since *io* bears the accent in the fourth position, the Pav reading is preferable. Esc (Pav) *sempre* can only be fitted into the line with undesirable prosodic and musical consequences; hence we drop it.

Line 9. **ansi** 'thus', **enver de** 'towards' are obvious gallicisms; they correspond to Old French *ensi* (modF *ainsi*) and to *envers*.

Line 10. **sey** 'knowest' is another gallicism; it corresponds to Italian *tu sai*, and we recommend that it be so pronounced. French influence is apparent in the spelling of the Cord variant *scey*, for at this period in French the forms of the verb *savoir* were more often than not spelled with a redundant, "etymological" *c: tu sçais* or *tu sces*, and so on.

mirando...viso by the standards of the modern literary languages would be a dangling participial phrase since it clearly does not modify the subject, *tu*, of the clause on which it is dependent, but in the Middle Ages and Renaissance such a participial construction could well modify a complement of the main clause other than the subject. Here it is the *me* of l. 10 that **mirando...** modifies.

Line 11. **festi**, second person singular, and *feste*, second person plural, correspond to standard Italian *facesti* and *faceste* (the *passato remoto* of *fare* 'make, do'). They are formed on the analogy of verbs like *dare* 'to give', whose *passato remoto* is *desti* in the second person singular. The analogy is as follows: dare : desti :: fare : festi.[5] Gerhard Rohlfs explains *desti*, in its turn, as modeled on *credei*, *credesti*, first and second person singular of the *passato remoto* of *credere*, 'to believe'.[6]

4. *Italia dialettale* (Milan: Hoepli, 1916).

5. W. Meyer-Lübke, *Grammaire des langues romanes*, French translation by Auguste and Georges Doutrepont (New York: Stechert, reprint 1923).

6. *Historische Grammatik*, 2: 378.

47. Myn hertis lust, ff. 65ᵛ–67ʳ [Bedingham]

CONCORDANT SOURCES

Esc IV.a.24, ff. 33ᵛ–35ʳ (Grant tamps ayen desiree)

Flo 176, ff. 62ᵛ–64ʳ (Gran temps), Bellingan

FloR 2356, ff. 29ᵛ–30ʳ (Grant temps)

Pix, ff. 57ᵛ–59ʳ (Grant temps aien et desiree)

Tr 90, ff. 462ᵛ–463ʳ (Beata es / Grant temps ayen desiree), Bedingham

COLLATION

Significant variants are few and minor for the most part. There is nothing of note to report in Esc IV.a.24, and in Flo 176 only one discrepancy, D-M at m. 13 (3) of the CT, a pitch (approached and left by leap) that works so dissonantly in the part writing that it must be a scribal mistake. In the C at m. 11 (4), instead of a'-Sb (as in Mell), FloR 2356, Pix, and Tr 90 give a sharply dissonant g-Sb that must surely also be a copyist's slip; at m. 15 (1, 2), by contrast, Pix and Tr 90 have g-M, e-Sb, simply reversing the notational values of Mell in parallel motion to the CT; whereas at m. 29 (2), FloR 2356 and Pix give c'-M, producing a more consonant vertical sonority than the b'-M of Mell.

The mensuration sign, absent in Mell, can be supplied from Flo 176, FloR 2356, and Pix, where it is perfect tempus (○). The b' of the C at m. 12 (2) is provided in Pix with a written flat supporting the editorial suggestion.

COMMENTS

Although the readings for this work are very similar in all six sources, there are three distinctive variants that allow the delineation of two subgroups. One consists of Mell and the two MSS to which it is most nearly related, Esc IV.a.24 and Flo 176. The other includes FloR 2356, Pix, and Tr 90, which can be linked by the divergences they shared.

The poem found with this composition in Mell is obviously the original, the French verse found in other sources a contrafact. Thus the music is undoubtedly English, as the attribution to Bedingham in two of the MSS would also show. Manfred Bukofzer, in his essay on the chansonnier,[1] gave the chanson to Frye on the basis of language

---

1. "An Unknown Chansonnier of the Fifteenth Century," pp. 24–25.

and style, presumably because he did not then know the concordant sources. Sylvia Kenney apparently accepted that suggestion somewhat uncritically and included the work in her complete edition of Frye's music,[2] but there is no compelling evidence for an attribution to Frye in preference to Bedingham either in the sources or in the compositional style.

> Myn hertis lust, sterre of my confort
> Whi[c]h is the guide unt[o] my parfaite liffe,
> Cher[a]ti, that welle of plesance and dis[p]ort,
> Whom that y [s]er[v]e w[ith] herte atenti[ff]e,
>
> And si[t]h[e] for you is my care and s[t]ri[f]e,   5
> Off wommanhede s[o] ha[v]e upp[o]n me routh[e]
> [S]i[t]h[e] y, [pr]ay y[o]u, mene veray and trou[t]h[e].
>
> My heart's joy, star of my well-being,
> Which are the guide unto my perfect life,
> Tenderness, that well of pleasure and delight,
> Whom I serve with attentive heart,
>
> And, since for you is my care and striving,
> So have upon me the mercy of womanhood,
> Since I, if you please, mean sincerity and faithfulness.

This poem, like Nos. 45 and 55, is unique to Mell, although the music occurs in five other manuscripts. For a general discussion of our policy in dealing with these English poems, see footnote 1 to No. 45.

VERSIFICATION

A septain, possibly the first stanza of a ballade. The septain is a favorite stanza of Middle English poetry. The rhyme scheme, *ababbcc*, is known as rhyme royal. This poem is metrically irregular: 9–10–11–9–9–10–9. Line 3 can be corrected from 11 to 10 syllables by reading *cherti*, or *chereti*, which are better attested than this doubtful *cherati* or *cherocti*, not found in NED (see Textual Notes). Line 4 may be increased

---

2. See "Contrafacta in the Works of Walter Frye," *JAMS* 8 (1955): 185–86, 199; also *Walter Frye Collected Works* (American Institute of Musicology, 1960), No. 4.

to 10 syllables by pronouncing the *-e* of *serve*; l. 5 may get an extra syllable from the *-e* of *sithe*, and l. 7 could get its full complement by the dissyllabic pronunciation of *mene*. This leaves only the hypometric l. 1 to explain. F. N. Robinson has observed that Chaucer "not infrequently omitted the unaccented syllable at the beginning of a line. The headless, or nine-syllable, lines . . . are by no means objectionable when the initial stress falls upon any important word."[3] Though tempting, this explanation is not very applicable to l. 1. The stress seems clearly to fall upon the second word, *hértis*, and the general iambic pattern of the poem would best be served by adding a syllable after *lust*, perhaps *that*. As a matter of pure feeling, however, these lines are not really improved by such additions of syllables. The "headless line" seems applicable to l. 4, which sounds better with monosyllabic *serve:* "Whóm that y sérve with hérte atentíffe." The poem would be in iambic pentameter, except that l. 5 seems to have no more than four strong stresses.

As Menner has observed, "Two of the English ballades, 4 and 82, attributed to Charles d'Orléans are in this stanza."[4] Among his French ballades, Charles d'Orléans has two ballades in septains, with the same rhyme scheme as *Myn hertis lust: Je n'ay plus soif, tairie est la fontaine* (cxx), and *Pourquoi m'as tu vendu, Jennesse* (ccxxi).[5] In *Secular Lyrics of the XIVth and XVth Centuries*, edited by Rossell Hope Robbins,[6] there are more than a dozen one-stanza, seven-line poems with this rhyme scheme.

Textual Notes[7]

Line 1. **lust** 'joy'; **sterre** 'star'.
Line 3. **cherati**: Menner translates this word as 'love' and interprets the line as follows: "Love, that spring of delight and discord."[8]

---

3. F. N. Robinson, *The Works of Geoffrey Chaucer*, 2d ed. (Boston: Houghton Mifflin, 1961), p. xxxvi.

4. Menner, "Three Fragmentary English Ballades," p. 381, where acknowledgment is given to Robert Steele, *The English Poems of Charles of Orleans*, E.E.T.S., vol. 215 (1941), pp. 11, 102.

5. *Charles d'Orléans: Poésies*, ed. Pierre Champion, pp. 182–84.

6. Second edition (Oxford: Clarendon Press, 1955, reprinted 1968).

7. We gratefully acknowledge the inspired suggestions of William East, Lecturer in Old and Middle English, University College, Cork, Ireland, for some of the readings we have adopted here, especially the most ingenious recognition of *pray* concealed in the Mellon scribe's *yca*.

8. P. 384.

There is no evidence from NED, however, that *charity* < Fr. *charité* (a learned borrowing from Lat. *caritas*) ever referred to romantic or carnal love. There is another Middle English word, *cherte* (or *chierte*, *cheerte*, *cherete*, or *chierte*, the last syllable also recorded as *-tee* or *-tie*), that is a direct borrowing from French *cherté*, *chierté* 'dearness' in both senses of *dear*, 'loved' and 'costly'. The Old French word is an analogical formation of *chier* + suffix *-té* rather than a direct inheritance from Lat. CARITATE. The English word is recorded in the same two meanings, described in NED as follows: "1. Dearness, tenderness, fondness, affection, esp. in phr. *to have* (or *hold*) *in chertee*. . . . 2. Dearness in price; dearth." As was true of *charity*, we find that no example of *cherte* given in NED relates clearly to sexual love.

Therefore we doubt that our *cherati* (whether it represents *charity* or *cheretie*) could be considered as a source of discord as well as of delight, since the word seems to refer only to the positive aspects of love, to *agápē* rather than to *érōs*. Hence we emend *discort* to *disport* 'joy, diversion, recreation' (< OF *deport* [deverbative from *deporter* < Lat. DEPORTARE], replaced, through prefix substitution, by *desport*). We suggest this translation of the line: "Tenderness, that well of pleasure and delight." In support of this interpretation, we may add that NED notes that the two words, and therefore the concepts *charity* and *cherte*, "were not always kept distinct; hence the forms *cherete*, *cheritie*." We have already noted that the model for our scribe's *cherocti* may well have been *chereti*, in two or three syllables. Since we have observed throughout the poem that our scribe had trouble recognizing *e* in the English original, it is no surprise that he has apparently misread it here.

and, MS *an*, *d* apparently omitted by haplology before following initial *d-*.

Line 4. **herte**: here we adopt Menner's suggestion. One could, of course, have supplied a two-syllable word, on the assumption of a monosyllabic **serve**; for example, *corage*.

Line 5. **sithe**; this is clearly *sicht* in the MS, and Menner has so read it, in the meaning of 'sighing'. Since *sicht* leaves the line one syllable short, Menner suggests that *alle* be added after *for you is*. Syntactically the line as read by Menner is hard to integrate into the poem. Our alternative is to correct *sicht* to *sithe* by the resemblance of *c* to *t* and of final *t* to *e*, thus providing this clause with a subordinating conjunction ('since') making the clause dependent upon the next line, whose nucleus is an imperative verb.

strife "effort, striving".

Line 6. Menner translates as follows: "So have pity upon me by your womanhood." He sees a similar use of *of(f)* in a poem, attributed to Charles d'Orléans, containing this line: "But an ye helpe wolde of youre woma*n*hede."

Line 7. This line is essentially a paleographical problem. We attack it on the assumption that not only was English unfamiliar to our scribe, but also that the handwriting was a typical late medieval English book hand, apt to cause our Continental scribe no small amount of trouble.

The false identifications we suppose to underlie the scribe's readings are as follows (the starred form we suppose to have existed in the English manuscript that the scribe of Mellon was attempting to copy; → = *was copied as*):

*sithe → ficht'; i.e., long *s → f, *t → c, *e → t' (t with a curved extension to its cross-bar).

*pray → yca; i.e., *p → y;[9] *r → c: the chances are that this *r* was of the variety that follows round letters ([2], as in [ɔ2], [o2], [p2], and so on);[10] and *y was omitted by haplology before a following initial *y*.

*you → ycu; i.e., *o → c of the rounder variety, not like the rather angular *c* of *care* in l. 5.

We interpret the line as follows: "Since I, if you please [*pray you* is the respectful second person plural equivalent of *prithee*] mean sincerity and faithfulness."

48. Ou lit de pleurs, ff. 67ᵛ–69ʳ

Concordant Sources

*Roh, f. 67ʳ⁻ᵛ

*Par 1719, f. 10ʳ

Comments

Since the two concordant collections contain only poetry, Mell is currently the unique source for the musical setting published here.

The composition is of more than ordinary interest because it may have been written directly in four parts—neither CT is marked *si*

---

9. See Parkes, *English Cursive Book Hands*, plate 19 (ii), l. 3 *spotte* for a *p* that could be mistaken for a *y* (ꝑ).

10. Ibid., plate 19 (ii), l. 2 *forth*, l. 3 *for*, l. 14 *pryue*.

placet—and also because of some unusual usage in the part writing. With the final of the work on C and a single flat as the signature in only three of the voices, the mode would normally be assumed to be mixolydian once transposed, but e (and a) are so frequently lowered that the scale structures are more consistently those of the Dorian mode. Striking, within that context, is the unavoidable juxtaposition of carefully written e-flats and a-flats with equally specific b-naturals; examples may be seen in mm. 8–9, 10–11, 15, 17–18, 19–20, and an analogous combination involving a written f-sharp in mm. 30–31. Besides, there is a vertical tritone between C and CT I in the cadential figures of m. 10 that is approached in a manner that suggests it was intended. It is possible that these harmonic complications are related to the meaning of the final three lines of the refrain.

If the syllabic text placement of the refrain is retained for the short strophe, the word *plourant* will be divided by the rest of m. 3, but since the pause is short and successful adjustment would be difficult, it can perhaps be allowed to stand as a fitting illustration of a *sob*. However, in the fifth line of the long strophe it would undoubtedly be more desirable to avoid breaking the word *demeure*, and a workable alternative for the placement of the syllables can readily be found.

On the top staff of f. 69ʳ, still faintly visible, is G-Br, seemingly with a dot, which have been effaced, presumably because the copyist had erred in writing it. In any case the three parts mesh correctly only with the omission of the obliterated note.

Ou lit de pleurs paré de plaintz,
Tresagrevé, de doleurs plains,
    Souspire et plains;
Et n'est aulcun qui me sequeure,   4
Ne meschief qu'en ce monde queure
    Qu'a moy n'acqueure;
L'un le couvert, l'aultre [...] l'esplains.   7

Gemir en plourant soirs et mains,
Rompre cheveux, tordre mes mains
    [Est] tout le mains
Des angoisses que j'assaveure   11
   Ou lit de pleurs paré de plaintz.
   Tresagrevé, de doleurs plains,

Souspire et plains,
Et n'est aulcun qui me sequeure.

Toulx plaisirs sont en moy estains;
Durement navré, fort attains,
    Paly et tains
De desplaisir plus noir que meure,   15
Fortune veult qu'ainsy demeure
    Et vive et meure
De ma medicine loingtains.   18
      Ou lit de pleurs paré de plaintz.
      Tresagrevé, de doleurs plains,
         Souspire et plains;
      Et n'est aulcun qui me sequeure
      Ne meschief qu'en ce monde queure
         Qu'a moy n'acqueure;
      L'un le couvert, l'aultre l'esplains.

In the bed of tears, adorned with plaints,
Heavy laden, full of pains,
    I sigh and lament,
And there is no one to help me,
Nor is there any mishap which in this world occurs
    That does not fall to me,
The one hidden, the other for all to see.

To groan while weeping, even and morn,
To tear my hair, wring my hands,
    That is the very least
Of the torments which I taste,
    In the bed of tears, adorned with plaints;
    Heavy laden, full of pains,
        I sigh and lament,
    And there is no one to help me.

All pleasures are in me extinguished;
Cruelly wounded, gravely hurt,
    Pale and discolored,
From displeasure blacker than mulberry,

So Fortune wants me to remain
And live and die,
Far from my medicine,

In the bed of tears, adorned with plaints,
Heavy laden, full of pains,
I sigh and lament,
And there is no one to help me,
Nor is there any mishap which in this world occurs
That does not fall to me,
The one hidden, the other for all to see.

VARIANTS

Par 1719, Roh.

1 Au—*Par*; parés—*Par*. 3 Soupirs—*Par*. 4 seqeurt—*Par*. 7 l'aultre
fait—*Mell* (+1 syll.). 8 Regretz en—*Par*. 9 teurtre—*Par*, teurdre—
Roh; les mains—*Par*. 10 Et—*Mell*; C'est tout—*Par*. 11 angouessez que
j'affaire—*Par* (added in another, less formal hand: Jay anstrheure).
(Mell ends here. Remainder from Roh, variants from Par.) 12 a moy
(*par* struck out, replaced by *a*, in the original hand). 13 naffré; estains.
14 (Par omits this line.) 15 Par desplaisir. 18 louentains.

VERSIFICATION

Rondeau cinquain layé in octosyllables and tetrasyllables, $a\,a^a\,b\,b^b\,a$,
in which each insert rhymes with the preceding line. The short strophe
goes as far as the first *b*-rhyme, that is, it consists of four lines, $a\,a^a\,b$.
The repeated refrains are ambiguously integrated (see Textual Notes).

TEXTUAL NOTES

Love is presented as a sickness through the vocabulary of physical
infirmity.

Line 1. **Ou** = *en* + *le*. **plaintz** 'plaints'.

Line 2. **plains** 'full', with the **-s** of the nominative singular, still
usable when the rhyme requires it. Similarly, although in l. 12 **estains**
is in the plural, l. 13 **attains** and l. 14 **tains** are in the singular.

Line 4. **N'est aulcun** 'there is no one'; **sequeure** 'helps'—present
subjunctive of *secourir*.

Line 5. **meschief** 'misfortune'; **queure** 'occurs'.

Line 6. **acqueure** 'happens'.

Line 8. **soirs et mains** 'in the evening and in the morning'.

Line 10. **Est**, emendation from Roh of Mell *Et*. The subject is the succession of infinitive phrases in ll. 8 and 9. **tout le mains** 'the very least'.

Line 12. **estains**—see note on l. 2.

Line 13. **navré** 'wounded'.

Lines 15–16. The paradox **Paly et tains** . . . **plus noir que meure** 'Pale and discolored . . . blacker than a mulberry' is probably deliberate. For pronunciation of **meure**, see p. 101.

The refrains can be read as integrated or autonomous. The sentence which begins l. 8, **Gemir en plourant** . . . , can be considered ended with l. 11 (in which case ll. 1'–4' constitute a new sentence) or as ending with l. 1', so that ll. 2'–4' constitute a new sentence. Similarly l. 18 may be taken either as ending the sentence beginning l. 16 **Fortune veult** or as leading into l. 1", ll. 2"–7" forming a new sentence. There is also the possibility of shortening the refrain to its first line, or even to the words **Ou lit de pleurs**.

49. **Or me veult bien Esperance mentir, ff. 69ᵛ–71ʳ**

CONCORDANT SOURCES

Mun 3232a, f. 65ʳ (No. 126) (Portugaler) (à 2)

Mun 3232a, f. 77ʳ (No. 149) (Portugaler) (à 2)

Mun 3232a, ff. 92ᵛ–93ʳ (No. 192) (Ave tota casta virgo / Portugaler)

Stra 222.C.22, f. 108ʳ (No. 191), G. Dufay

COLLATION

Not only do the first two versions of Mun 3232a lack the CT for the work, they are also without the entire second section, and the T is incomplete even for the fragment given. Notwithstanding these significant differences in the externals of transmission, a comparison of the extant portions with Mell uncovered only a single variant: at m. 11 (2, 3) of the C, the reading of f. 65ʳ has c-Sb, d-M, producing a markedly less consonant harmonic effect than the b-Sb, c-M of Mell.

Because the Strasbourg MS burned in 1870, no collation was possible. Therefore, the only complete concordance for the song (as a vocal work) is the third version of Mun 3232a (No. 192). The following variants may be noted. In the C at m. 38 there is d-Sb (as in Mell) rest-Sb, rest-Sb. In the T at m. 15 (1), D is Sb instead of M, and there is no rest; at m. 36 (1 ff.) d-Br, b-M, a-M; and an entire line omitted in the copying of Mell (probably because it began with the same figure as the previous one) left the present collection without mm. 38–47 of that part. In the CT at m. 10 (2)–11 (1) are written G-Br, d-M (without the rest of Mell); at m. 20 (1 ff.), D-M, F-M, E-M, C-Sb (a possible alternative); at m. 37 (1 ff.) rest-M, a-M, G-Br (without the D-Sb of Mell); at m. 40 (1), d-Sb, but without the rest of Mell at the beginning of m. 41; and at m. 52 (2), c-M, a more consonant pitch than the b-flat M of Mell.

The written flats of Mell are generally not given in Mun 3232a, f. 92^v–93^r. Not present, for example, are those given for b at mm. 5 (1) and 21 (2) of the C (given however by one or both of the versions à 2), or for the e at mm. 32 (2) and 45 (2), or for e in the T at mm. 25 (1), 35 (2), and 58 (2).

COMMENTS

An organ intabulation of this chanson was included in the *Buxheim Organ Book*, f. 21 (No. 43). In addition, as Margaret Bent will demonstrate in a study now in preparation, the T of the first section is found in the Alcetur Bible and as a cantus firmus or a square in a number of sacred English compositions from the fifteenth and sixteenth centuries.[1] Consequently she contends, with very good reason, that the attribution to Dufay in the Strasbourg MS was in error and that the composition is English. This would perhaps explain its inclusion in the Mellon Chansonnier despite its rather archaic character. Based on a French ballade, a poetic form almost never set by Continental composers after the middle of the fifteenth century, it exemplifies a number of stylistic traits more generally associated with the secular music of the fourteenth century. In Stras 222.C.22 and in Mun 3232a, f. 77^r it was even written in black notation.

The only complete version of Mun 3232a resembles the reading of Mell in C and T, but the CT has a number of variants although most of them do not affect the substance of the music. Furthermore, the scribe of the Munich MS frequently combined relatively short notes repeating the same pitch into a single symbol of longer value.

1. Concerning squares, see Hugh Baillie, *Acta Musicologica* 32 (1960): 178–93.

The missing segment of the T in Mell was supplied in the transcription from Mun 3232a. The mensuration sign, also wanting, should undoubtedly be for perfect tempus (○).

> Or me veult bien Esperance mentir
> A ceste foys et faire abusement
> De sa promesse quant me jura tenir
> Mon cuer en joye et *doulx* esbatement,   4
>
> Certefïant de voloir maintenir
> *En*vers moy ce dont m'avoit fait serment
> Et que de moy non feroit partement
> Tant que je fusse en ce point prisonnier.
> Mais je voy bien que c'est parjurement,
> Car maintenant me veult du tout lessier.   10
>
> Now would Hope deceive me
> At this time, and abuse
> The promise made when she swore she'd keep
> My heart in joy and pleasure,
>
> Certifying that she intended to honor
> The solemn oath she swore to me,
> And that she would never depart from me
> As long as I would be, to that degree, a prisoner.
> But I see clearly that it was perjury,
> For now she intends to leave me quite alone.

Versification

Decasyllabic ballade dixaine, *abab abbcbc*, with epic caesura (l. 3). We have added *doulx* to hypometric line 4. Line 6 being short one syllable, we have substituted *Envers* for *Vers*, which has the effect of placing *ce* under precaesural stress—perfectly acceptable in Old and Middle French.

Textual Notes

The poem combines legal phraseology (**abusement, jura, certefiant, serment, parjurement**) and allegory (the personification of Hope) to produce what was evidently considered a delightfully humorous effect, in full harmony with the courtly tone.

Lines 5–7. **Certefiant de voloir … et que … non feroit parte-ment** is a syllepsis (see p. 111).

Line 7. **partement** 'departure, separation'.

Line 9. **parjurement** 'perjury'.

Line 10. **du tout** 'entirely'.

50. Donnés l'assault, ff. 71ᵛ–73ʳ, Dufay

CONCORDANT SOURCES

Tr 87, ff. 119ᵛ–120ʳ, Dufay (à 3)
Tr 93, ff. 364ᵛ–365ʳ

COLLATION

The differences between the reading of Mell and that of the two Trent MSS consist primarily in the errors to be discerned in the latter two sources. For example, in Tr 93 the entire first line of the C (mm. 1–16) is copied a third too low; at m. 21 of the T the ligature is not blackened, and at m. 34 (1) c-Sb is written instead of c-M with the rest of the following measure omitted to compensate. In CT I the following errors and variants are to be observed: the opening notes are g-Br, g-Br (eliminating the rest-Br of Mell and providing one Br too many); at m. 6 (1) is written a′-M, b′-Sb, a′-M (again providing an excessive number of rhythmic units); in m. 12 the rest-Sb has been omitted; in m. 13 (2) the G-M has been omitted; in m. 14 (3, 4), G-Sb and F-Sb have been omitted; at m. 25 (1 ff.) is given c-Br, b-Sb (identical to the T) a-Br, c-Br; at m. 35 (2) a dissonant F-Sb replaces the consonant G-Sb of Mell; at m. 37 (2, 3) is given c-M, b-M (a third too low); and at m. 38 (5) is found a dissonant a-Sb instead of g-Sb as in Mell. In CT II at m. 12 (3), g is Br (a minor change) and at m. 38, the rest is Sb and the final three notes are not blackened. In Tr 87 the divergences are much fewer: at m. 27 (1) of the C, c′-Sb carries a dot (erroneously); at m. 6 (2) of CT I is written b′-Sm, g-Sm; and at m. 35 (2) the same error as in Tr 87.

The majority of the accidentals written in Mell do not occur in the two remaining sources. In Tr 97 only those of m. 18 (3) in the T and m. 25 (1) of CT I are given. In Tr 93 they are wanting in the C at

m. 21 (1, 4), in the T at mm. 14 (3) and 18 (3), and in CT ɪ at mm. 11 (1) and 22 (1), but at m. 18 (2) is written a sharp for f not given in Mellon.

COMMENTS

Although the number of variants is considerable, particularly in Tr 87, most of them are apparently due to the carelessness of the Trent scribes. It is therefore possible to assume that the exemplar used by the latter was in the same tradition of transmission as that of the present MS. Curiously, the reading of Mell is more closely related to that of Tr 87 despite the fact that it lacks the second CT, whereas Tr 93, even though copied à 4 like Mell, diverges from it more frequently and more significantly. However, the only link between the versions of the two Trent MSS is the solitary common variant at m. 35 (2) of the CT.

Like *Ou lit de pleurs* (No. 48), Dufay's rondeau à 4 has a final on c and a signature of one flat in the three lower parts, but again in this instance both e-flat and a-flat occur so consistently in the part writing that the modal character of the piece is much more clearly Dorian than mixolydian. Because so many of the accidentals are specifically indicated in the MS, editorial suggestions were needed for the most part only at cadential points. Nevertheless, one of them raises a sticky problem. In m. 20, CT ɪ has a written e-flat whereas the C touches e-natural as it moves from g to a written f-sharp, a melodic progression that makes it virtually impossible to lower the e. As a result an augmented prime between the two parts becomes practically unavoidable, and since it falls at a point in the mensural unit where dissonance is admissible, it has been permitted to stand.

> Donnés l'assault a la fortresse
> De ma gratïeuse maistresse,
> Hault dieu d'amours, je vous supplie;
> Boutés hors m'adverse partie
> Qui languir me fait en destresse. 5
>
> C'est [. . .] Anuy qui, par sa rudesse,
> De moy grever point ne se cesse
> Envers ma dame gente et lye. 8

Donnés *l'assault a la fortresse*
De ma gratïeuse maistresse,
Hault dieu d'amours, je vous supplie.

Faictes venir tost en l'adresse
Au secours, par vostre noblesse,
Pitié, Mercy et Courtoysie;
La belle soit par vous saisye,
Car le tarder trop si me blesse.   13
Donnés l'assault *a la fortresse*
De ma gratïeuse maistresse,
Hault dieu d'amours, je vous supplie;
Boutés hors m'adverse partie
Qui languir me fait en destresse.

Launch the attack on the fortress
Of my gracious mistress,
High god of love, I beg of you;
Expell my adversary
Who makes me languish in distress.

It is Ennui who by his crudeness
Injures me unceasingly
In the sight of my lady kind and gay.
Launch the attack on the fortress
Of my gracious mistress,
High god of love, I beg of you.

Summon at once, with all dispatch,
To my assistance, by your noble authority,
Pity, Mercy, and Courtesy;
May the beauty be captured by you,
For waiting causes me grievous pain.
Launch the attack on the fortress
Of my gracious mistress,
High god of love, I beg of you;
Expell my adversary
Who makes me languish in distress.

Versification

Octosyllabic rondeau cinquain, *aabba*. Autonomous refrain.

Textual Notes

Military language and imagery: the God of Love is entreated by the lover to rout the occupier (*Anuy*) from the fortress of his mistress.

Line 2. **De** may be interpreted either as the preposition of possession ('my mistress's fortress') or as the preposition of apposition ('the fortress which is my mistress').

Line 4. **m'adverse partie** [maversə partiə] 'my adversary', who is identified in l. 6 as **Anuy**.

Line 6. MS *danuy*; **anuy** = *ennui* means something between 'boredom' and 'annoyance'. In this poem it is the personification of boredom, which threatens to put the lover in a bad light in the eyes of his beloved. The meaning 'boredom' is attested as early as the thirteenth century.

Line 8. **lye** [liə] 'happy', Picard feminine form (see p. 113).

Line 9. **en l'adresse** 'directly, promptly'.

Line 12. **la belle** is likened to the fortress itself, which is to be "seized" by Love.

Line 13. **le tarder** is a substantified infinitive with definite article: 'waiting, postponing'. **si** is an emphatic particle, modified by the intensive **trop**, which can, but does not necessarily, mean 'too (much)', as it does in modern French. **trop** probably modifies **blesse** rather than **tarder** (although a substantified infinitive is capable of modification by an adverb) for two reasons: one would expect the adverb to precede the infinitive (*le trop tarder*), and the caesura after **tarder** clearly cuts the line into two syntactic constructions.

51. Par le regart, ff. 73ᵛ–74ʳ, Dufay

Concordant Sources

BerK 78 C 28, ff. 13ᵛ–14ʳ
Cop 17, No. 9 (CT only)
Esc IV.a.24, ff. 40ᵛ–41ʳ
MC 871, f. 10ᵛ (p. 266)
Pix, ff. 39ᵛ–40ʳ

Par 4379, f. 21ʳ (T and CT only, cf. Sev 5.I.43)

Pav 362, ff. 47ᵛ–48ʳ

Por 714, ff. 61ᵛ–62ʳ, Dufay

Sev 5.I.43, f. 48ᵛ (C only, cf. Par 4379)

Tr 93, f. 318ᵛ (Resone, vince)

Lab, ff. 67ᵛ–68ʳ

Wolf 287, ff. 36ᵛ–37ʳ

*Jar, f. lxxviiʳ

*Arn, f. lxvᵛ

COLLATION

The Porto MS, probably dating from about the 1440s, is written in black notation, but the reading for this work compared with that found in the later sources in void notation shows largely trivial variants, as will be readily seen if the present edition is set beside the one prepared from the earlier source by Heinrich Besseler for the collected works of Dufay.[1] Still at m. 8 (4, 5) of the T Por 714 gives d-Sb, c-M, perhaps a better reading harmonically than in Mell but found in none of the later collections, and at m. 21 (4 ff.) of the CT, the passage agrees with the concordant MSS rather than with Mell. Because of its fragmentary nature, Cop 17 was simply omitted from the comparison of the sources. The divergences among the remaining musical collections were limited for the most part to relatively unimportant melodic details, particularly in the C, that do not essentially alter the musical substance of the composition. The variants noted include a few errors and possible alternative readings but the majority are noteworthy only to the extent that they bear upon the relationships among the sources.

In the C at m. 5 (5), g-Sb (without the e-M of Mell) is given by Lab, Pav 362, and Sev 5.I.43; at m. 9 (6), a-M, rest-M (instead of a-Sb) is found in Esc IV.a.24, MC 871, Pix, Sev 5.I.43, Lab, and Wolf 287; at m. 14 (5), a dissonant f-M (instead of g-M) is written in BerK 78 C 28, Pix, Pav 362, and Sev 5.I.43; at m. 15 (3), e-M (possible but not as good as the d-M of Mell) in Lab and Wolf 287; at m. 19 (1), a'-M, rest-M (instead of a'-Sb) is given by BerK 78 C 28, Esc IV.a.24, Pix, Pav 362, Lab, and Wolf 287; at m. 21 (2, 3), f-M, e-M is found in Lab and Wolf 287, and at m. 21 (2–5), f-M, c-M, a'-M, g-M in BerK

---

1. Guillelmi Dufay, *Opera Omnia* (Corpus Mensurabilis Musicae, 1), vol. 6, *Cantiones* (Rome: American Institute of Musicology, 1964), No. 73.

78 C 28, MC 871, Pix, Pav 362, and Sev 5.I.43 (eliminating the dotted figures in Mell); and at m. 22 (3, 4), b'-M, g-M is written in Lab and Wolf 287 (with a similar result).

In the T, the most homogeneous part among the sources, at m. 6 (2) Wolf 287 has rest-M (instead of G-M) in conformity with the C; at m. 11 the D-Br is imperfected with rest-Sb in Pix, Pav 362, Lab, and Wolf 287; and at m. 13 (5), BerK 78 C 28 has b-M (instead of c-M), a possible alternative. In the CT at m. 3 (1), Lab has G-Sb (possible but not so good harmonically as the a-Sb found elsewhere); at m. 5 (3 ff.), Lab gives d-dotted Sb, b-Sm, Wolf has d-M, d-dotted Sb, b-Sm (undoubtedly a scribal error in either case), whereas at m. 5 (2–4), MC 871 and Par 4379 give a correct alternative, d-Sb, c-dotted M, b-Sm; at m. 7 (7), Pix, Lab, and Wolf 287 have a-M, rest-M, a-M (the last note being sharply dissonant), while MC 871, Pav 362, and Par 4379 give a-M, rest-M (a very slight change); at m. 21 (4 ff.), in Tr. 93 one reads c-M, a-Sb, G-Sb, d-Sb, c-M, whereas all other concordances have c-M, a-Sb, G-Sb, F-M, c-blackened Sb, b-Sm (but BerK 78 C 28 lacks the F-M).

Sev.5.I.43 has a written flat for the b of the C at m. 16 (3).

COMMENTS

Organ intabulations of this composition are found in the *Buxheim Organ Book*, ff. 11ᵛ and 12ʳ (Nos. 30 and 31).

When compared with the two northern sources, Lab and Wolf 287, whose readings are the furthest removed from Mell, that of the latter gives the impression of a conscious revision, albeit one restricted primarily to trivial melodic details. The only exception is the final passage of the CT. The degree of affinity to Mell for the versions of the remaining MSS can be gauged by the extent to which they assimilate what might be regarded as the emendations of an unusually independent reading in Mell. Closest, despite the contrafact text, is Tr 93, followed by Esc IV.a.24, BerK 78 C 28, MC 871, and Sev 5.I.43 / Par 4379. The latter two collections apparently follow essentially the same scribal tradition, judging from the number of divergences they share. To a lesser extent the same would seem to be the case for Pix and Pav 362, both of which are considerably closer to the reading of Mell than Lab and Wolf 362.

At m. 11 of the T, the transcription has been emended in accordance with four of the sources in order to give a uniform relationship among the parts for the primary internal cadence. The part writing at m. 21 (4 ff.) of the CT is more interesting in some respects in the reading of the other sources, but the passage is contrapuntally correct in Mell, and there seemed to be no justification for changing it.

Par le regart de voz beaulx yeulx
Et de vo maintieng bel et gent
A vous, [belle], viens humblement
Moy presenter, vostre amoureux.   4

De vostre amour sui desireux
Et mon voloir tout s'i consent   6
    Par le regart de voz beaulx yeulx
    Et de vo maintieng bel et gent.

Or vous plaise, cuer gratïeux,
Moy retenir ore ad present
Pour vostre ami entierement,
Et je seray vostre en tous lieux   10
    Par le regart de voz beaulx yeux
    Et de vo maintieng bel et gent.
    A vous, belle, viens humblement
    Moy presenter, vostre amoureux.

By the glance of your beautiful eyes
And (the sight) of your fair and noble demeanor,
To you, beauty, I come humbly
To present myself, your suitor.

Of your love I am desirous,
And my will assents thereto entirely,
    By the glance of your beautiful eyes
    And the sight of your fair and noble demeanor.

Now may it please you, gracious heart,
To accept me at this present moment
As your friend, wholly,
And I will be yours in all places,
    By the glance of your beautiful eyes

And the sight of your fair and noble demeanor.
To you, beauty, I come humbly
To present myself, your suitor.

VARIANTS

The texted concordant sources are Jar, Lab, Sev, and Wolf, and (for the first line) Molinet D85 Par le regard de vos beaux yeux.

2 Lab omits Et; Jar omits de; vostre—*Jar*; tresbel—*Lab*. 3 A vous me viens—*Mell* (−1 syll.); A vous servir tres humblement—*Jar*. 4 Me presente—*Jar*. (End of Mell. Remainder from Sev.) 6 tout mon vouloir—*Wolf*, mon vouloir tant—*Lab*. 8 Me retenir ores ad present—*Jar* (+1 syll.), Moy tenir or a present—*Lab* (−1 syll.), Donc moy retenir a present—*Wolf*. 10 Et je le seray—*Lab Wolf*.

VERSIFICATION

Octosyllabic rondeau quatrain, *abba*, with integrated refrains.

TEXTUAL NOTES

Line 1. **Par**, preposition of agent or instrumentality: 'by means of, by the power of'.

Lines 1–2. In the first line taken by itself, the **regart** is obviously an active property of the eyes; so one is inclined to translate it as 'glance', taking this noun as semantically in direct nominalization of *regarder* 'to look'. The next line, however, adds **Et de vo maintieng**; obviously this expression is more object than subject of the deverbative noun *regart*; it is the poet who looks, the beloved who is seen. Does this mean that we must now revise our first interpretation of **le regard de voz…yeulx**?—that the poet is smitten by the beautiful eyes that he sees? Or is this a conceit (the rhetorical figure, syllepsis) in which the noun, in the construction *le* (noun) *de* X *et de* Y, changes in meaning with each complement that is appended to it? The ambiguity was probably deliberate, and **regart** means 'glance' in construction with **yeulx** but 'sight' in construction with **maintieng**. The Jar reading of l. 2 (omission of *de* and substitution of *vostre* for *vo* to compensate for the lost syllable) might express one redactor's feeling of the impropriety of this device, as well as a normalizing effort to remove the dialectal (Picard) **vo**. (For a discussion of syllepsis, see p. 111.)

Line 3. Besides being hypometric, the original Mell reading, *me viens*, is awkward in that it does not represent a reflexive verb (*se venir), nor does it represent *viens* + dependent infinitive, as *me viens presenter*, a construction that would be perfectly acceptable in Old and Middle (and even early modern) French; but *me viens . . . Moy presenter*, as Mell has it, is redundant in a way not typical of Old French. **A vous . . . Moy presenter** is an acceptable construction and **moy** is supported by all sources (except Jar, which has *me presente* in a finite verb form). In Old French the pronoun object of an infinitive was regularly disjunctive (e.g., *moi* instead of *me*). Jar *me retenir* in l. 8 shows the beginning of the modern usage, conjunctive pronoun as object of an infinitive.

Jar *A vous servir* introduces an infinitive in l. 3 that depends on *Me presente* in l. 4.

Line 7. **plaise**, impersonal verb: 'may it please'.

Line 8. **retenir** 'keep, accept'; Lab *tenir* 'regard'.

Line 10. **vostre** 'yours'. Lab Wolf *le seray* 'will be it [your devoted friend]'. The two readings are equally fitting. From a purely philological point of view, the Lab Wolf reading may be better because the agreement of Sev and Jar, which show in this poem a rather close relationship (see ll. 6, 8, 10), does not constitute by itself a strong argument in favor of a reading; whereas Lab and Wolf show, in this poem, certain divergences (ll. 2, 3, 4) that would indicate a relative independence and lend more weight to their agreement. The evidence on filiation is so slim, however, as to fall within the margin of possible error and coincidence.

52. **Hora cridar "Oymè," ff. 74ᵛ–75ʳ**

Concordant Sources

BerK 78 C 28, ff. 44ᵛ–45ʳ (capital *D* only text given)
Esc IV.a.24, ff. 88ᵛ–89ʳ
Cord, ff. ivᵛ–1ʳ
Pav 362, ff. 25ᵛ–26ʳ

Collation

In this instance the divergences in readings among the concordant sources give no information about the interrelationships of scribal traditions except as a function of their affinity with that of Mell. All significant variants, whether due to apparent errors or the creative initiative of fifteenth-century scribes and musicians, are restricted to a single MS.

Closest to the tradition represented by Mell is the version of Esc IV.a.24, which shares with it not only the substance of the work but also many of its notational details. The same is true (to a somewhat lesser extent) of the reading of BerK 78 C 28. But at mm. 8–9 the C has c-Sb (instead of c-Br), and four rests-Sb, while the CT reads as in Mell but with a dot of perfection after C-Sb, m. 9 (1), resulting in one Sb less than in the T. The difficulty is easily mended in the CT by the alteration (doubling) of the second Sb after the dot, but there is no legitimate way to quickly bring the C into the proper vertical alignment with the other voices. Similarly, in the T at m. 2 (5), there is one e-M too many.

Cord and Pav 362 show a few additional points of substantive divergence but without meaningful agreement between them. At m. 13 (2) of the C, Cord replaces g-Sb with a rest, at m. 19 (1, 2) is written e-Sb, f-Sb (a minor change), and in the CT at mm. 6 (2)–7 (3) d-Br, E-Sb (a possible though less interesting alternative). Pav 362 alters the first phrase after the corona with F-M (instead of G-M) in the T at m. 9 (5) and, similarly, f-M (instead of g-M) at m. 10 (5) of the C, a good alternate reading. Otherwise there is a slight modification of the melodic ornamentation of m. 22 in the C with d-Sm (for e-Sm), m. 22 (2), and c-Sm (for d-Sm), m. 22 (4), and a substantial change in the CT at mm. 5 (2)–7 (2): rest-M, c-Sb, a-M, G-M, E-M, D-Br, C-Sb, displacing the short phrase of m. 6 (2 ff.) as if by a scribal omission subsequently followed by an emendation. The result is less happy than in the other sources.

The mensural symbol, absent in Mell, can be supplied from Esc IV.a.24 or Cord, where it is perfect tempus (○). At m. 10 (1) of the CT a sharp is given for b by Esc IV.a.24 to avoid the lowering of the note since it would be inappropriate to do so for either harmonic or modal reasons. (This creates a diminished fifth and mixes transposed Dorian with pure mixolydian.) But Pav 362 gives a flat at the same point (undoubtedly a slip).

COMMENTS

Despite the corona—and the corresponding division of the composition—at the end of the initial phrase, the poetry does not lend itself to any of the established fixed forms. It is instead entirely strophic. One could conceivably employ the initial line as a refrain in performance, repeating it after each strophe. Because the stressed syllables and the caesura change for any given line from one stanza to the next, some minor adjustments will have to be made in the distribution of the syllables for the second and the third in order to maintain natural patterns of accentuation and to avoid an inappropriate division of the final line by the rests in the musical phrase.

Considering the strophic structure of the secular Italian verse associated with this piece, it is not surprising that the music was also adopted for the singing of a lauda, No. lx of those published by Belcari (*Laude spirituali*, p. 32).

Hora cridar "Oymè" posso bene io
Et consumar in pianti li ochi mei
Poi che vider [più] lei
Non posso—aymè, meschino!—come solea.   4

O lingua maladicta, iniqua e rea,
Que stat'è casone de tanto male;
[Tu] m'ay conducto a tale
Que vivere m'è venuto en displacere.   8

Se yo non credess*e* più pod*ere*
[M*a*y più vedere] el myo caro *tesoro*
[Con] un' capistro d'oro
Al collo, in alto finiria la vita.   12

Now may I well cry out, "O woe is me!"
And waste my eyes in weeping
Since her no longer
May I see—O woe, poor wretch!—as once I used.

O cursèd tongue, wicked and loathsome,
Which has been the cause of so much pain;
Thou hast led me to such a pass
That living, for me, is no longer pleasing.

If I believed myself unable
Ever to see again my dear treasure,

With a golden cord
Around my neck, on high I would finish my life.

VARIANTS

Mell and Esc have only first quatrain; lines 5–12 from Cord, with help from Pav.

2 me picay dely panury ogy mey—*Pav*; l'ochi mei—*Esc*. 3 veder— *Esc Cord*, vedere—*Pav*; puy lei—*Mell*, costuy—*Cord*, coste—*Pav*. 4 oyme meschin chome solea—*Esc*, come soleva oyme come soleva— *Cord*, non posso comme sollya—*Pav* (+1 syll.). 5 Pav omits O; vinca erea—*Pav*. 6 state sey casonne—*Pav* (+1 syll.). 7 Te—*Cord*, Tu—*Pav*. 8 Che en vero me—*Pav*; a despiacere—*Pav*. 9 credesso—*Cord*; E yo non credeuio podere—*Pav*. 10 Come soleua—*Cord*, Mey piu vedere— *Pav*; tresoro—*Pav*. 11 Cū uno—*Cord*, D'une—*Pav*; capestro—*Pav*. 12 el collo mio vocereyua et ly finireyua la vita mia—*Pav*.

Due to the tight binding, the end of ll. 9 and 10 could not be read in Cord. These endings have been restored by reference to Pav and by conjecture.

VERSIFICATION

An oda, consisting of four quatrains of mixed lengths (11, 11, 7, 12), with a concatenated rhyme linking the strophes together; the first line and the last line rhyme with nothing: *ABbC CDdE EFfG* ($X = 11$ sylls., $x = 7$ sylls., $X = 12$ sylls.). There is in the traditional Italian theory of metrics a strong feeling that the twelve-syllable line is almost morally impossible; the *endecasillabo*, the most noble meter (see p. 82), is also the longest practicable line, and therefore the *dodecasillabo* receives no serious attention in the critical literature. Nevertheless, examination of the fourth line of each strophe of the present poem reveals at least a certain metrical ambiguity. Line 4 could be shortened by replacing Mell's *meschino* with Esc *meschin*; l. 8 may be shortened by the conjectural amputation of the final vowel of *vivere*, whereas l. 12 needs no material alteration, since one may choose to see in the sequence *collo, in* either a hiatus or a syneresis (p. 83).

The problem, then, is in the establishment of ll. 4 and 8—whether or not to shorten to *meschin* and *viver*. The sequence *meschin—come* is harsh, un-Italian, in that a tonic syllable, closed by a consonant, is immediately followed by a tonic syllable beginning with a consonant.

Unless one pronounces *meschin* with the velar nasal [ŋ] the transition
is difficult. In l. 8 the sequence *víver m'è*, because of its alternation of
strong and weak stress, is perhaps easier to live with, but still a shade
awkward. Tilting the balance still more in favor of the dodecasyllable
is the apparent patterning of 11, 11, 7, 12 for each strophe, in which the
12 is, if we respect the Mell text, inescapable for ll. 4 and 8, and
preferable in l. 12, considering the pause that one would expect after
the enjambment from l. 11, not to mention the syntactic pause occasioned by the end of the *se*-clause.

Finally, there is the question of the placement of the text with
respect to the music. The division of the musical phrase into three
segments (quarter notes followed by an eighth rest in mm. 18 and 21)
in each case affects the word that should, to produce an eleven-syllable
line, be shortened in a way that would be awkward, unpleasant, and
untrue to the text, solely in order to obey the dictates of a theory that
apparently did not take this poem into account.

The hendecasyllables have the dominant accent (pp. 83–84) on the
sixth position, with two exceptions. Line 6 has dominant accent on
the fifth position, an anomalous type. One might suppose an original
version, *Che stato è cason' de tanto male*, with hiatus in *stato è*. Pav would
not be hypermetric if *casonne* were relieved of its final syllable; *sey*, of
course, makes as good sense as *è*. In l. 10 the dominant stress is on the
fourth position.

Textual Notes

Line 1. **bene io**: pronounce *ben' io*.
Line 2. **Et** is a frequent medieval spelling for modern Italian *e*.
li ochi mei = modern Italian *gli occhi miei*, and must have been at
least similarly pronounced.
Line 3. **vider** = modern Italian *veder(e)*. The medieval spelling
vacillated; see l. 10. **più** for Mell *puy*; apparently the scribe perceived
p followed by three minims as *pui* and then chose to exercise the option
of *y* for *i*.
Line 4. **-so ay-** forms one syllable. Mell Esc *solea* as against Cord
soleva and Pav *sollya* (all three medieval variations on the first person
singular of the imperfect indicative ending [Rohlfs §2.333]) is assured
by the rhyme, l. 5 **rea**.
Line 5. **maladicta**, certainly pronounced *maladetta*: Latin influence
on spelling. **-ta, i-** forms one syllable, as does **-qua e**.

Line 6. **Que** = modern Italian *che* [ke]. Medieval spelling for the sound [k] varied among *c*, *k*, *ch*, and *qu*; *qu* was especially favored for words that had *qu* in Latin. Thus the graphy *qu* could indicate [k] in some words, [kw] in others. **casone** = modern Italian *cagione* 'cause' < Latin OCCĀSIŌNEM. For the development of the Tuscan form, see Rohlfs §286. In §287 he cites an Old Paduan *cason* among other words with *s* from -*sĭ*-, a feature shared with Old Lombard.

Line 7. **ay** = modern Italian *hai*; one syllable. **conducto** pronounced, as in modern Italian, *condutto*. **-to a**, one syllable.

Line 8. **Que** = modern Italian *che* [ke], and is so pronounced. **-to en** is one syllable. **displacere** = modern Italian *dispiacere* 'displeasure'. The spelling with *pl* could be a Latin orthographic influence, or it could represent a dialectal spelling. Since this form comes from the Cordiform manuscript, it could well represent a different dialect from that manifested in Mell (cf. l. 2 **pianti**). Rohlfs §186 mentions the retention of original *pl*- in the Abruzzi. Note the variant, Pav *dispiacere*.

Line 9. **se yo** = *se io*, three syllables. **credesse**: Cord *credesso*, which looks as if it had an analogical -*o* ending for the first person singular, is not recorded in Rohlfs §560, where he deals with the imperfect subjunctive. The modern ending would be -*essi*, but we have chosen to emend with -*esse* because the misreading of *o* for *e* is more plausible than for *i*, and is supported by the long period of vacillation between -*esse* and -*essi* in the first person (Rohlfs §597). The endings represented by Pav *credeuio* (apparently imperfect indicative) and in l. 12 *vocereyua* and *finireyua* (conditional?) are not in Rohlfs with exactly these spellings, but bear some resemblance to conditionals formed by infinitive plus—not HABĒBAM—but HABUĪ (Rohlfs §597). He records such forms as *sarav* (= *sarei*) and *andarav* from Milan, *pruaravi*, *vularavi*, *favelaravi* from Istria, and literary Venetian *me piaseravi*. The Pav forms, then, look like a succession or blend of several imperfect endings: -*ia*, -*eva*, and the analogical -*o* ending, which Rohlfs says (§550) is lacking in the language of Dante, Petrarch, and Boccaccio but is already present in that of Jacopone, Saint Catherine, and in the *Fioretti* and is triumphant in the modern Italian endings -*avo*, -*evo*, -*ivo*.

Line 11. **capistro** = modern Italian *capestro* 'halter; girdle of the Franciscans' < Latin CAPISTRUM 'halter, muzzle; conjugal tie'.

Line 12. **in alto** 'on high; in style'; pun on the "elevation" of a hanged man.

53. Puis que je vis le regart, ff. 75ᵛ–76ʳ

CONCORDANT SOURCES

Esc IV.a.24, ff. 38ᵛ–39ʳ
Flo 176, ff. 57ᵛ–58ʳ
FloR 2356, ff. 51ᵛ–52ʳ
MC 871, f. 137ᵛ (p. 406)
Sched, ff. 41ᵛ–42ʳ; 45ᵛ–46ʳ
Pix, ff. 70ᵛ–71ʳ
Sev 5.I.43, ff. 50ᵛ–51ʳ
*Jar, f. xcivʳ

COLLATION

Both copies of this composition in Sched have a common CT, which differs entirely from the other sources, and appreciable variants in the T as well, presumably occasioned by or connected with the redaction of the alternate CT. Consequently, only the C was included in the collation of details. The remaining MSS offer few significant divergences of substance with regard to Mell, but all show a tendency to divide the longer values of the present reading into shorter repeated pitches and to eliminate or alter the melodic ornamentation at mm. 6, 12, and, in particular, 22. Leaving aside details of that order and presumed scribal errors, the following variants were judged noteworthy as an indication of the relationships among the MSS.

In the C at m. 9 (3), a′-M is given by FloR 2356 and Pix instead of the b′-M of Mell (an acceptable alternative); at m. 10 (4), Flo 176 and Sched give c′-M (without filling in the third); at m. 14 (4–6), Sev 5.I.43 has a′-Sb, g-M, whereas Sched, at m. 14 (3 ff.) has a related reading, c′-Sb, a′-Sb, g-M, a′-Sb. In the T, Sev 5.I.43 has a lengthy but not strikingly different variant at mm. 20 (1)–22 (4): rest-Sb (instead of c-Sb), c-Sb, a-Sb, G-Sb, G-Sb, c-M, e-M (instead of c-Sb as in Mell). In the CT at m. 4 (1), F-Sb is given instead of the F-M, a-M of Mell in all other sources having the same part; at m. 10 (3), d-M (a more consonant pitch than the e-M of Mell) is found in FloR 2356, Pix, and Sev 5.I.43; at m. 20 (2), instead of c-M as in Mell, d-M is given by FloR 2356 and Pix (forming an unacceptable fourth with the T); and in m. 26 (1) the rest-M follows a-SB in FloR 2356 and Pix (instead of e-Sb as in Mell). In addition, Sev 5.I.43 varies from all other readings in a number of details: at m. 5 it gives rest-Sb, c-Sb, rest-Sb; the notes of m. 7 are omitted and the blackened L of m. 8 is c (as in the T) instead of e; at m. 12 (2) c-M is given instead of d-M (a good reading); at m. 13 (3) f is M instead of Sb and the following two pitches are omitted; and at m. 30 (3) is written g-M, g-Sb, f-M (a minor change).

Comments

The notational detail in Mell is unlike that of any other source even though the musical substance is essentially the same in a number of concordances. The two MSS with which this reading has the greatest affinity are obviously Esc IV.a.24 and MC 871. Flo 176 also has few meaningful variants, and the readings of FloR 2356 and Pix—both of which apparently follow very much the same scribal tradition—are not far removed. Sev 5.I.43 is distinguished by the lengthy variant in the T and a series of small details in the CT. The version of Sched differs much more markedly by its separate CT and the independence of its T.

That this chanson was well known in Florence is shown not only by its recurrence in the musical sources originating there but also by its use as a musical setting for the lauda published by Belcari as No. li (*Laude spirituali*, p. 30).

> Puis que je vis le regart gratïeux
> Et la beaulté de ma dame et maistresse,
> Resjouÿ suis et [recoeuvre] lÿesse,
> Réconforté [. . . .] de tous les [. . . . . .] maulx que
>   j'eux.   4
>
> En esperant que d'elle me soit mieulx
> Tout mon vivant pour servir sa jonesse,   6
>   *Puis que je vis le regart gratïeux*
>   *Et la beaulté de ma dame et maistresse,*
>
> Tenir je vueil le sentier amoureux
> Et le chemin d'amour droit a l'adresse
> Par quoy je puisse a ma belle princesse
> Briefment conter les biens que j'ay receux   10
>   *Puis que je vis le regart gratïeux*
>   *Et la beaulté de ma dame et maistresse.*

Resjouÿ suis et recoeuvre lÿesse,
Réconforté de tous les maux que j'eux.

Ever since I saw the gracious glance
And the beauty of my lady and mistress,
I am gladdened and recover my happiness,
Relieved of all the ills that I have suffered.

Hoping that I will be ever more in her favor
As long as I live, to serve her youth(ful beauty),
　　　Ever since I saw the gracious glance
　　　And the beauty of my lady and mistress,

I want to keep to the amorous path
And the road leading to love by the shortest route
Whereby I may to my beautiful princess
Soon tell the good things which have come to me
　　　Since I saw the gracious glance
　　　And the beauty of my lady and mistress.
　　　I am gladdened and recover my happiness,
　　　Relieved of all the ills that I have suffered.

VARIANTS

The texted concordant sources are FloR, Pix, Sev, and Jar.

3 réconforté—*Mell FloR*, recouvre—*Esc Pix*, recoeuvre—*Sev*, ressours de—*Jar*. 4 Réconforté suis—*Mell*; les griefs maulx—*Mell*, le mal—*Esc Sev Jar*; Pix FloR omit que j'eux (−2 sylls.). (Mell, FloR, and Pix end here. The remainder reconstructed from Sev, Esc, and Jar.) 5 me fust—*Jar*. 6 vivant serviray—*Sev*. 8 droit et l'adresse—*Sev*; Et le chemin que fine amour m'adresse—*Jar*. 9 je puis a la—*Esc*, compter a ma—*Jar*. 10 Puisse briefment les biens que j'ay receux—*Jar*, briefment conter les biens que j'ay decheux—*Esc*.

VERSIFICATION

Decasyllabic rondeau quatrain, eye-rhyme *a b b a*, ear-rhyme perhaps *a b b c* (see p. 100). In l. 4, Mell adds two syllables as if absent mindedly falling into an alexandrine, whereas FloR and Pix similarly, by losing two syllables, fall into an octosyllable. Sev and Esc maintain the decasyllable. Both the long and the short refrain are integrated, the latter uniquely (for this collection) to both the preceding and the following strophes. Our punctuation shows how the refrains have been worked into the syntactic structures of their contexts.

TEXTUAL NOTES

Line 1. **Puis que** = modern French *depuis que* 'since'. In **gratieux**, *t* = [s].

Line 3. Mell *réconforté* is unlikely, since it is followed by the same word in l. 4; hence we replace it by the Sev reading, **recoeuvre**.

Line 4. **j'eux** 'I have had'.

Line 5. *estre bien de* = 'be in the good graces of'.

Line 8. **droit a l'adresse** 'promptly; by the shortest route'.

Line 10. **Briefment** [bryeman] (2 syllables) 'soon'; **conter** 'tell, enumerate' (cf. the original meaning of *tell* in English).

54. Ma dame de nom /
Sur la rive de la mer, ff. 76ᵛ–77ʳ (also f. 50ᵛ)

CONCORDANT SOURCES

Esc IV.a.24, ff. 119ᵛ–120ʳ
BerK 78 C 28, ff. 23ᵛ–24ʳ

COLLATION

The sharp for g in m. 2 (4) of the C is found only in Mell. Otherwise the C and T are virtually the same in all three sources. The CT of Esc IV.a.24 differs from the reading of Mell only in two small details of melodic ornamentation, whereas that of BerK 78 C 28 gives two divergent pitches toward the end: C-M, D-M at m. 13 (5, 6), distinctly less euphonious than the D-M, B-M of Mell.

COMMENTS

The differences among the three MSS for this chanson are so slight that a common tradition of transmission can readily be assumed. The T is obviously based on at least one and perhaps two popular tunes, which are shared at times by the CT; the texts are sung by both lower voices. Elements of the songs cited in the second section of this piece were included in two fifteenth-century farces (*Badin qui se loue* and *Le Bateleur*). They were also quoted by Molinet and in popular poems, and provided the substance (in a somewhat modified version) for the T of another bitextual chanson included in the repertory of Dij 517.[1]

The third strophe of text in the C, *Dame de Pité ...*, presents a practical problem of performance: it is not immediately clear to which section of the music those lines of verse should be sung. Because this strophe has the same number of lines and syllables as the first, it could conceivably be adapted to the initial section, but it seems more likely that it was sung to the concluding section like the second strophe, with which it shares not only verse structure but also rhyme scheme. If this assumption is correct, there are three different ways in which the piece could be performed: (1) the entire chanson could be sung twice through—with repeats as indicated—the second time with the third strophe of text sung by the C in the second section in place of the second strophe; (2) the second section of the piece, mm. 4–14, could be sung a second time to present the additional verse; or (3) since mm. 4–7 function as a second ending for the repeat of the initial section and close with a clearly marked cadence, only the concluding phrases of the composition, mm. 8–14, need be repeated to accommodate the third strophe of the poetry.

1. Ma dame de nom
   Se ne me donnés
   De mercy le don.
   Je seray tennés.   4

   Car en verité
   Je vous ayme tant
   Qu'en suis rasoté
   Deriere et devant.   8

   Dame, de pité,
   Robin va plorant;
   Il a trop dansé
   Le pas de Brabant.   12

1. *Puis qu'autrement | Marchez la dureau* (ff. clxvi[v]–clxvii[r], No. 140); see Maria Rika Maniates, "Mannerist Composition in Franco-Flemish Polyphony," pp. 20 ff., and cf., by the same author, "Combinative Chansons in the Dijon Chansonnier," pp. 240, 261, and 258, No. 20.

II. Sur la rive de la mer
     L'aultre jour jouer m'aloye,
     La femme d'un marounier
     J'encontray en mi ma voye.   4

III. Il y a ung clerc en ceste cité,
     Il n'est pas venu pour messe chanter.   2

IV. *Hola! durié,*
     [Marchiés] la, duriau!
     Ho, la dure!   3

     My lady in name,
     If you don't give me
     The gift of mercy,
     I'll be "tanned."
     For in truth
     I love you so much
     That I am besotted
     Before and behind.

     Lady, for pity,
     Robin goes weeping
     He has danced too long
     The Brabant brawl.

     On the shore of the sea
     The other day I went to play;
     The wife of a sailor
     I did meet upon the way.

     There is a cleric in this city—
     He didn't come to sing a mass.

     Hey there, hardy,
     Step out there, toughy,
     Ho, the hard one!

Variants

Material in italics comes from Esc. 2 Marcy, marcié— *Mell.*

Versification

Song I, in the cantus, consists of three pentasyllabic quatrains, *abab cdcd cdcd*, since -és [es] does not rhyme with -é [e]. Song II, in T and CT, is sung simultaneously with the first quatrain of Song I; it is a heptasyllabic quatrain, *efef*. Song III consists of two decasyllables, *ce*. There is more verbal material, IV, consisting of interjections and nonsense syllables, to fill out the musical form.

Textual Notes

I, line 4. **tennés** 'tormented'; an extension of the meaning, 'tanned'.
Line 6. **rasoté** [rasote] (with voiceless [s]).
Line 12. **Le pas de Brabant** is the branle, a dance called the *brawl* in English, involving rocking back and forth from heel to toe.
II, line 3. **marounier** 'sailor'.
IV. Comic variations on *dur(e)* 'hard'.

55. "Alas, alas, alas" is my chief song, ff. 77ᵛ–79ʳ [Frye]

Concordant Source

Sched, ff. 80ᵛ–82ʳ (O sacrum convivium), Frey

Collation

As usual, Sched proves to be a carelessly written MS, and the majority of the variants seem to reflect errors of copying. In the C at mm. 33 (3)–34 (2), for example, the pitches are all written a step higher than in Mell; at m. 14 (1) there is a superfluous e-M; and at m. 47 (2), c-M is given (instead of b-M), theoretically an acceptable solution but with a more dissonant result. In the T at m. 31 (2), E-Sb is given (instead of F-Sb as in Mell), producing forbidden vertical intervals, and in m. 38 the rest-Sb is missing. However, the greatest number of divergences occur in the CT: in m. 4 C-Sb replaces the rest-Sb of Mell; at m. 8 (3), G′-Sb is given (instead of A-Sb), an evident error; at m. 12 (2), D-M is written, a better reading than the E-M of Mell; at m. 19 (2)–21 (3) is found D-M, F-Sb, E-M, C-M, E-M, F-M, C-M, D-M, A-Sb, G′-dotted Sb, A-Sm, B-Sm, C-Sm; at mm. 28 (1) and 29 the dot and the rest-M have been omitted; at m. 39 (1), D-Sb is given (instead of C-Sb as in Mell), obviously an error; at m. 49 (1–3) is written C-M, E-M, F-M, C-M, D-M, G′-M; and at m. 50 (4), B-Sb (instead of A-Sb), definitely a mistake.

Interestingly, Sched gives appropriately a written flat for b′ in the C at m. 31 (1), but another before C in the T at m. 32 (1) does not seem needed or even usable except to prevent raising that pitch.

COMMENTS

Errors aside, there are not a great many variants of substance between the two MSS. At m. 12 (2) of the CT the reading of Sched appeared superior enough to justify an emendation in the transcription. Similarly, at mm. 19 (2)–20 (1) an obvious error exists in the CT of Mell, resulting in parallel octaves with the C. But because the two sections "rhyme" musically, that is, terminate with identical material, it will be readily seen that the scribe has simply written those few notes a third too low. In the modern score they have been returned to their proper level.

"Alas, alas, alas" is my chief song,
ffor peyne and wo none other can y syng.
Instede of rest, a-sobbe y tale [a]mong,
ffor [m]yn one[se] and dea[th]e along siching.

The gro[u]nd[e] of wo I fele [is] departing,
The more long the more b[.]yting the peyn.
With the trew turtil all cha[u]nge fors[w]er[yn]g,
"Welchome my deth certeyne," [y] entune and pleyne.   8

"Alas, alas, alas" is my chief song,
For pain and woe none other can I sing.
Instead of rest, I talk, sobbing, ever and again,
All the while sighing for my distress and for my death.

The reason for the woe I feel is separation,
The longer [it lasts], the more biting the pain.
With the faithful turtle dove all change forswearing,
"Welcome, my certain death!" I intone and lament.

Variants

Unique to Mellon, this song has been edited by Robert Menner and Rossell Hope Robbins.[1] We wish to acknowledge our debt to the many valuable suggestions of the two previous editors.

Versification

An eight-line stanza in a rhyme scheme, *ababbcbc*, characteristic of the ballade. The fit of the music is that of the ballade. The rhythm is iambic pentameter; that is, the lines are decasyllabic with alternating weak–strong stress. Line 6 is of ten syllables only if one counts one of the occurrences of *more* as two syllables; the rhythmic pattern would require that it be the first *more*. Line 10 is of eleven syllables unless the word *y* (which is hypothetical in any case) is run together with the following initial vowel.

Textual Notes

Line 2. **ffor** 'because of'. **wo.** In the MS it is quite clearly *roo*; but an original *w*, with the right-half lobe closed (**ꞷ**), may well have looked like *ro*.[2] This spelling is repeated unambiguously in l. 7.

Line 3. **a-sobbe** 'sobbing'. **among** 'from time to time, continually' (MS *el mong*). The scribe has taken (as Menner points out) a typically English *a*, with a closed loop low on the left and a high riser on the right (**ꭺ**), for *el*, which he has then written in his own manner.[3]

Line 4. **ffor** means 'because of' when it governs **onese**, and it means 'for (goal of desire)' when it governs **deathe**; a syllepsis. **myn** (MS *nyn*). The scribe probably miscounted his minims because he was unfamiliar with the shape of *y* in English handwriting. This letter was troublesome for him more than once (cf. No. 45, l. 8, in which probably original *myn* was copied as *mijn*). **onese** (MS *onert*) 'distress, un-ease' (cf. the sense of *Desconfort* in No. 36, l. 4). Menner and Robbins see our scribe's *nyn onert* as a miscopying of *myne hert; however, *myne*,

1. Menner, "Three Fragmentary English Ballades," Rossell Hope Robbins, ed., *Secular Lyrics of the Fourteenth and Fifteenth Centuries*. The present poem appears as No. 157, "Parting is Death," p. 150, with notes pp. 275–76.

We have consulted Manfred F. Bukofzer, "An Unknown Chansonnier of the Fifteenth Century," *MQ* 28 (January 1942): 14–49, which Menner has satisfactorily taken into account.

2. For this kind of *w*, see Parkes, *English Cursive Book Hands 1250–1500*, plate 20 (ii), l. 3, *newe*, l. 7, *wordes*.

3. Ibid., plate 21 (iii), l. 1: the *a*'s of *anon*, *aftyr*, *batayle*.

even at this late epoch, is less probable as a singular than *myn*. We keep the *o*, preserve the scribe's spacing, regard his *r* as a misread *s, and his *t* as a misread *e. *On-* as a variant of *un-* is characterized by NED as "frequent ME., early modE, and dial. variant. . . ."[4]

deathe (MS *de alve*). Menner and Robbins see the MS reading as representing Middle English *thee alwey*. In our reading, we have supposed in the English model a tall *a* (see its description in textual note on l. 3) followed by thorn (*þ*) and *e*. The tall *a* may be perceived by a continental scribe as *al* as plausibly as it was *el* (as Mell l. 3 *el mong*), and a thorn such as appears in Parkes, plate 21 (iii), passim, but especially line 3 *off þis lande*, bears a marked resemblance to *v* because of the shortness of its descender (*ᵽ*).

along 'all the while'. Cf. Chaucer, *Romaunt of the Rose* ll. 1,328–29:

> And in that garden gan I goo,
> Pleyyng along full meryly.[5]

siching 'sighing' can serve both as verbal noun and as present participle; by this late period, the present participle in *-ing* has, certainly in southern texts, completely replaced the participle in *-ind* or *-and*.

Line 5. **grounde of** (MS *gronndoof*) 'reason for': original *u has been miscopied as *n*, *e as *o*, and the separation that was probably in the original has been ignored—or if the original text was also underlaid to music, it would have been next to impossible for the continental scribe to redistribute the syllables into words. **fele** 'am aware, experience, perceive, understand'.

is (a wavy line in the MS). Bukofzer suggests that the wavy line is an abbreviation of *is*, whereas Menner prefers to interpret it as a dash and translates l. 5 as follows: "The reason for the woe I feel— parting." We have chosen to follow Bukofzer's suggestion and insert *is* to facilitate the syntax, but we by no means insist on it. Our understanding of the line is much like Menner's: "Separation is the reason for the grief I feel." Robbins takes Mell *Ifele* as *Is al*, that is, *f* as original *s*, *ele* as *al*.

---

4. James A. H. Murray, ed., *A New English Dictionary* (Oxford: Clarendon Press, 1884–1928).

5. Robinson, ed., *The Works of Geoffrey Chaucer*. These lines are cited by H. Kurath and S. M. Kuhn, *Middle English Dictionary* (Ann Arbor: University of Michigan Press, 1953), s.v. *along*; they cite line numbers 1,329–30 and quote a slightly different version.

Line 6. **byting** (MS *bryting*): more trouble with English *y*; this time its left half had an elaboration that our scribe took for a round *r* (ꙗ). Menner and Robbins agree in emending to **byting**.

Line 7. **turtil** 'turtle dove'; mentioned in the bestiaries as a model of fidelity. **forsweryng** (MS *for sv̄egug*). Like Menner, we interpret the mark above *v* as an abbreviation of *er*, although it does not have the usual form, which is like an apostrophe. What our scribe has taken to be *ve* may well be a type of **w* much favored in English manuscripts of this period, the left half like a *v*, the right half a double lobe, that is, a tall rather than a wide lobe with a deep indentation like that of a 3 (ꝝ).[6] *g* for **y* is another example of trouble with *y*, this time of a transparent sort; *u* for **n* is banal. Thus we suppose **forsūyng* → *for sv̄egug*. Menner's emended text has *forsvereyng*, Robbins', *forsvering*.

Line 8. **certeyne y entune** (MS *certeynement vne*). We have seen in the *m* of the MS a misreading of **y*. This is perhaps farfetched, and we cannot insist upon it; but an *m* with a tail, that is, whose last minim is tailed like a *j*, could have been suggested to the scribe by the troublesome *y* whose effects we have already observed. This resemblance would have been accentuated by the scribe's propensity to "see" French words in the English text.

56. Nos amys, vous vous abusés, ff. 79ᵛ–80ʳ, A. Basin

Concordant Sources

BerK 78 C 28, ff. 36ᵛ–37ʳ
Esc IV.a.24, ff. 124ᵛ–125ʳ
Lab, ff. 71ᵛ–72ʳ
*Jar, f. 62ᵛ
*Arn, f. lviʳ

Collation

The reading of Mell differs from that of the concordant sources mostly in matters of melodic detail, but in this respect, as with *Puis que je vis le regart* (No. 53), it stands apart from the surprisingly unified tradition of transmission represented by the remaining three musical MSS. Specifically, the dotted figure with two FFu at mm. 5 (1 ff.),

6. See Parkes, plate 19 (ii), l. 6 *wesel*.

6 (1 ff.), and 8 (1 ff.) of the C is written in all other sources as one M and two SSm; at m. 7 (1), the d-Br of Mell is given elsewhere as d-Sb, rest-Sb; and at m. 8 (1) of the CT there is no rest in the other MSS, but d-Br instead. The few additional discrepancies are restricted to a single source. Only two are substantial enough to warrant mention and both are found in BerK 78 C 28: in the C at m. 10 (7, 8) is found a'-M, b'-dotted M (a step lower than in Mell), and in the CT at m. 6 (3, 4) is written a-M, G-Sb (also a step lower), producing in both cases sharp dissonances with the other voices.

In the Laborde Chansonnier a b-flat signature is given for both T and CT, and written flats not found in Mell are provided in Esc IV.a.24 for b' in the C at mm. 5 (7) and 8 (1), and in BerK 78 C 28 for b in the T at m. 5 (4).

COMMENTS

A keyboard arrangement of this chanson was included in the *Buxheim Organ Book*, f. 160ᵛ (No. 245), and the beginning of the C, with the verse of the refrain, was woven into a quodlibet included in Glog, No. 117.[1]

The text placement suggested for the refrain can be used without alteration for the short strophe, but in the long strophe it would be better to divide the initial line after *aultrez*, and the second line after *léal*. This can be done in either case with only minor adjustments in the distribution of the syllables.

> Nos amys, vo*us* vous abusés
> D'attendre l'amoureuse grace;
> Aultre que vous a prins la place;
> Vostre franchois en vain usés.   4
>
> Vous n'estez point dez plus rusés
> Pour prendre tel beste a la chace.   6
>   Noz amys, *vous vous abusés*
>   *D'attendre l'amoureuse grace.*
>
> Envers aultrez vous excusés,
> J'ay plus léal qui me pourchace;

---

1. See the edition by Heribert Ringmann, *Das Glogauer Liederbuch*, T, m. 20.

Pour ce querés qui pour vous face.
C'est a ung mot: plus n'y [musés],   10
    Nos amys, *vous vous abusés*
    D'attendre l'amoureuse grace;
    Aultre que vous a prins la place;
    Vostre franchois en vain usés.

Our friends, you do deceive yourselves
By waiting for the boon of love;
Another than you has seized the place—
You exercise your French in vain.

You do not have the guile
To take such game a-hunting.
    Our friends, you do deceive yourselves
    By waiting for the boon of love.

Get you hence to others—
A truer man has won my heart;
So seek some one who will do for you.
A word to the wise: Brood no more on it,
    Our friends, you do deceive yourselves
    By waiting for the boon of love;
    Another than you has seized the place—
    You exercise your French in vain.

Variants

Esc, Lab, Jar, Molinet D169 Nostre amy, vous vous abusés. FloR 2356, Nos. 5 and 28 (No. 5 = No. 28) has a similar poem with the same rhyme as our poem:

Cousine trop vous abusés
Se plus que scuser ne me fate [*sic*; probably *face* in the MS]
Qui portés l'amour a besac[e]
Dont vous amis est refuseis.[2]

2. This poem has been published by Dragan Plamenac, "The 'Second' Chansonnier of the Biblioteca Riccardiana," *AM* 2 (1954): 172.

1 Nous—*Esc*; vo vous—*Mell*, vous—*Esc Lab* (−1 syll.). 4 avés usés—*Esc*; C'est a ung mot: plus n'y musez—*Jar*. 5 pas—*Esc Jar*. 6 telle beste a chase—*Esc*, telle beste a la chasse—*Lab* (+1 syll.). (Esc ends here.) 8 prochasse—*Lab*. 9 Pour tant—*Lab*; qui mieulx vous face—*Jar*. 10 Jar omits a (−1 syll.); musés—*Lab Jar*, pensés— *Mell*.

VERSIFICATION

Octosyllabic rondeau quatrain, *abba*. Although the short refrain must be regarded as autonomous, the long one may *à la rigueur* be interpreted as integrated, as we have shown through our punctuation.

TEXTUAL NOTES

This poem, as it appears in Mell, has the orthographic peculiarity that *z* is an apparently free variant of *s* in word-final position, even when preceded by "mute e" [ə] in a final syllable: cf. l. 5 **estez** [e:tə], l. 7 **aultrez** [awtrə], whereas -*s* is used consistently in second person plural verb endings.

Lines 1–4. A scornful lady tells her suitors not to waste their time; some one else has "seized the place"—a military term.

Line 3. **prins** [pri], as in modern French.

Line 4. **franchois**, a picardism in which *ch* [š] corresponds to Francian *ç* [s]. Jar substitutes for this line what is l. 10 in the other versions, thereby giving to *C'est . . . musés* the status of a refrain in the manner of the ballade.

Line 6. **tel**: in the feminine, both *tel* and *telle* are equally appropriate in this epoch. Lab apparently used *telle*, thus giving rise to a hypermetric line; Esc *a chase* may well represent an attempt to correct a hypermetric line from the same redaction.

Line 7. **vous excusés** [vuz eküzes] is in the imperative. *S'escuser* means 'to withdraw (from a situation)'; the line means 'withdraw from the competition for my favor and turn your efforts toward others'.

Line 9. **pourchace** 'obtains, wins'.

Line 10. **C'est à ung mot** 'a word to the wise'. **musés**, supported by all but Mell, is probably correct since the *a*-rhyme is rich in all the other lines in which it occurs. Mell *pensés* is an example of synonym substitution.

57. **Virgo Dei throno digna, ff. 80ᵛ–81ʳ, Jo. Tinctoris**

CONCORDANT SOURCES

Glog, No. 259
Flo 229, ff. 19ᵛ–20ʳ, Jo. Tintoris
SG 463, No. 14, Tinctoris
PetA, ff. 49ᵛ–50ʳ, Tinctoris

COLLATION

Only the C is included in the extant part books of SG 463 (Tschudi's
Liederbuch), but it is entirely possible that Tinctoris's devotional motet
was copied directly into SG 463 from the Petrucci print; the notational
detail is practically identical in the two sources. There are no significant
variants in any of the sources despite some minor differences of
ornamental detail at cadential passages. However, Glog has no signed
flat for the C and, along with Flo 229, no E-flat in the signature of
the CT.

COMMENTS

Sev 5.I.43 is erroneously given as a source for this work by Heinrich
Hüschen.[1] (See Comments for No. 19.) It should perhaps be noted
that the manuscript tradition for this composition is remarkably
homogeneous.

> Virgo Dei throno digna,
> Spes unica musicorum,
> Devote plebi cantorum,
> Esto clemens et benigna.

> O Virgin, worthy of God's throne,
>   (or: O Virgin of God, worthy of the throne)
> Only hope of musicians,
> To the devoted throng of singers
> Be merciful and kind.

VARIANTS

Flo reproduces first line only.
Line 1. trono.

1. "Tinctoris," col. 421.

VERSIFICATION

Octosyllabic quatrain with accented penult, *abba*. Lines 1, 2, and 4 have a regular trochaic beat (accentual, not quantitative): ´˘´˘´˘, but l. 3 has a stress pattern totally unlike the others: ˘´˘´˘˘´˘. The only discernible quantitative pattern has the first two syllables long, the fifth syllable long, and the last two syllables long short: $- - \times \times - \times - \cup$.

TEXTUAL NOTES

It is likely that this song forms one of a pair with No. 19, which, dedicated to Beatrice of Aragon, was originally intended to open the chansonnier. *Virgo Dei* is in its right place as the concluding act of devotion and supplication to the highborn Virgin. As was also true for the dedicatory poem, this poem is ambiguous about the personage to whom it is addressed.

Line 1. A comma after **Virgo** renders the following translation: 'O Virgin, worthy of God's throne . . .'; without the comma it can mean: 'O Virgin of God, worthy of the throne. . . .' Perhaps the first translation is appropriate to the Virgin Mary, the second to Lady Beatrice, in which event the ambiguity could well be deliberate.

Line 3. **Devote**, medieval spelling of *devotae*.

BIBLIOGRAPHY

Anglès, Higinio. *La música en la Corte de los Reyes Católicos: I, Polifonía Religiosa.* Monumentos de la Música Española, 1. Madrid: Consejo Superior de Investigaciones Científicas, Instituto Diego Velásquez, 1941.

Atlas, Allan W. "Rome, Biblioteca Apostolica Vaticana, Cappella Giulia XIII.27, and the Dissemination of the Franco-Netherlandish Chanson in Italy, c.1460–c.1530." Ph.D. dissertation, New York University, 1971.

Auda, Antoine. *La musique et les musiciens de l'ancien pays de Liège.* Brussels: Librairie Saint-Georges, 1930.

Bancel, E. M., ed. *Cent quarante-cinq rondeaux d'amour publiés d'après un manuscrit autographe de la fin du XVe siècle.* Paris: Chez Lemerre, chez Rouquette, 1875 (Imprimé à Lyon, Louis Perrin).

Barone, Nicola. "Le cedole di tesoreria dell'Archivio di Stato di Napoli, dall'anno 1460 al 1504." *Archivio Storico per le Province Napoletane* (publicato a cura della Società di Storia Patria) 9 (1884): 5–34; 205–48; 387–429; 601–37. 10 (1885): 5–47.

Becherini, Bianca. "Alcuni canti dell' 'Odhecaton' e del codice fiorentino 2794." *Bulletin de l'Institut Historique Belge de Rome* 22 (1942–43): 327–50.

———. "Autori minori nel codice fiorentino Magl.XIX, 176." *Revue Belge de Musicologie* 4 (1950): 19–31.

———. *Catalogo dei Manoscritti Musicali della Biblioteca Nazionale di Firenze.* Kassel, West Germany: Bärenreiter Verlag, 1959.

Belcari, Feo (ed altri). *Laude spirituali.* Florence: Molini e Cecchi, 1863.

Berkovits, Ilona. *Illuminated Manuscripts from the Library of Matthias Corvinus.* Budapest: Corvina Press, 1964.

Bertoni, Giulio. *Italia dialettale.* Milan: Hoepli, 1916.

Berzeviczy, Albert de. *Béatrice d'Aragon, reine de Hongrie* (1457–1508). Bibliothèque Hongroise 4. Paris: Champion, 1912.

———, ed. *Aragonai Beatrix: Acta vitam Beatricia reginae Hungariae illustrantia. Monumenta Hungariae Historica*, Diplomataria, vol. 39 (Budapest, 1914).

Besseler, Heinrich. *Bourdon und Fauxbourdon.* Leipzig: Breitkopf & Härtel, 1950.

Borren, Charles Van den. *Guillaume Dufay.* Brussels: Marcel Hayez, 1925.

———. *Le manuscrit musical M.222 C.22 de la Bibliothèque de Strasbourg (XVe siècle) brûlé en 1870, et reconstitué d'après une copie partielle d'Edmond de Coussemaker.* Antwerp: Imprimerie E. Secelle, 1924. (Extrait des *Annales* de l'Académie royale d'Archéologie de Belgique, 1923).

———. Review of Johannes du Saar, *Het leven en de composities van Jacobus*

Barbireau, Revue belge de musicologie 1 (1946–47): 136.

———. "Tinctoris." *Biographie nationale de Belgique.* Vol. 25, cols. 288–316. (Brussels, 1930–32).

Boyde, Patrick. *Dante's Style in His Lyric Poetry.* Cambridge, England: Cambridge University Press, 1971.

Bragard, Anne Marie. "Un manuscrit florentin du quattrocento: le Magl. XIX, 59 (B.R.229)." *Revue de Musicologie* 52 (1966): 56–72.

Brandolini, Raffaelo. "De musica et poetica." *Essais de diphtérographie musicale.* Edited by Juste Adrien de la Fage. 2 vols. Paris: O. Legouix, 1864. Reprint. Amsterdam, 1964.

Bridgman, Nanie. "Christian Egenolff, Imprimeur de musique." *AM* 3 (1955): 77–177.

———. "Un manuscrit italien du début du XVIe siècle à la Bibliothèque Nationale." *AM* 1 (1953): 177–267.

Brooks, Catherine. "Antoine Busnois, Chanson Composer." *JAMS* 6 (1953): 111–35.

Brown, Howard Mayer. "The *Chanson rustique*: Popular Elements in the 15th- and 16th-Century Chanson." *JAMS* 12 (1959): 16–27.

———. "Instruments and Voices in the Fifteenth-Century Chanson." *Current Thought in Musicology.* Austin: University of Texas Press, 1976.

———. *Music in the French Secular Theater.* Cambridge, Mass.: Harvard University Press, 1963.

———. *Theatrical Chansons of the Fifteenth and Early Sixteenth Centuries.* Cambridge, Mass.: Harvard University Press, 1963.

———. "The Transformation of the Chanson at the End of the Fifteenth Century." *Kongressbericht, Ljubliana, 1967,* pp. 78–94. International Musicological Society, Report of the Tenth Congress, Ljubliana, 1967. Kassel, West Germany: Bärenreiter Verlag, 1970.

———. "Wolfenbütteler Handschriften." *MGG* 14 (1968): 810–11.

———, ed. *A Florentine Chansonnier from the Time of Lorenzo the Magnificent.* Florence, Biblioteca Nazionale Centrale, MS Magliabecchiana XIX, 59 (Banco Rari 229). Chicago: University of Chicago Press, in progress.

Brunet, Jacques-Charles. *Manuel du libraire et de l'amateur de livres.* 6 vols. Paris: Firmin Didot, 1860–65.

Bukofzer, Manfred F. "The Mellon Chansonnier." *The Yale University Library Gazette* 15, no. 2 (October 1940): 25–28.

———. "An Unknown Chansonnier of the 15th Century." *MQ* 28 (1942): 14–49.

Burbure, Léon de. "Etude sur un manuscrit du XVIe siècle contenant des chants à quatre et à trois voix." Académie Royale des sciences, des lettres et des beaux-arts de Belgique. *Mémoires couronnés et autres mémoires* 33, no. 6 (1882): 1–44.

Bush, Helen E. "The Laborde Chansonnier." *Papers of the American Musicological Society*. Annual Meeting, 1940, Cleveland Ohio. Edited by Gustave Reese, pp. 56–79. Richmond, Va.: William Byrd Press, 1946.

Cappelli, Adriano. *Dizionario di abbreviature latine ed italiane* . . . 6th ed. Milan: Hoepli, 1961.

Cartellieri, Otto. *The Court of Burgundy*. New York: A. A. Knopf, 1929.

Charles d'Orléans: Poésies. Edited by Pierre Champion. 2 vols. Paris: Champion, 1923.

Chastel, André. *Art et humanisme à Florence au temps de Laurent le Magnifique*. Paris: Presses Universitaires de France, 1961.

Commynes, Philippe de. *Mémoires*. Nouvelle édition, revue sur les Manuscrits de la Bibliothèque Royale, . . . par Mlle Dupont. 3 vols. Paris: J. Renouard, 1840–47.

Coussemaker, Charles Edmond Henri de. *Scriptorum de musica medii aevi novam seriem a Gerbertina alteram collegit nuncque primum editit*. 4 vols. Paris: Durand et Pedone-Lauriel, 1864–76. Reprint. Hildesheim, 1963.

Csapodi, Csaba, and Csapodi-Gárdonyi, Klára. *Bibliotheca Corviniana, Die Bibliothek des Königs Matthias Corvinus von Ungarn*. Budapest: Corvina Verlag (mit der Unterstützung der UNESCO), 1969.

D'Accone, Frank. "Heinrich Isaac in Florence: New and Unpublished Documents." *MQ* 49 (1963): 464–83.

————. "The Singers of San Giovanni in Florence during the Fifteenth Century." *JAMS* 14 (1961): 307–58.

D'Ancona, Paolo. *La Miniatura fiorentina* (secoli XI–XVI). 2 vols. Florence: Olschki, 1923.

Dauzat, Albert; Dubois, Jean; and Mitterand, Henry. *Nouveau dictionnaire étymologique et historique*. Paris: Larousse, 1964.

Davis, Bertran E. "Vincenet." *MGG* 13 (1966): 1652–53.

Deschamps, Eustache. "L'art de dictier" [dated 1392]. In his *Oeuvres complètes*, vol. 7, edited by Gaston Raynaud. Paris: Didot, 1891 (Société des Anciens Textes François).

Devillers, Léopold. *Chartes du Chapitre de Sainte Waudru de Mons*. 3 vols. Brussels: P. Imbreghts, 1899–1908.

Dèzes, Karl. "Der Mensuralcodex des Benediktinerklosters Sancti Emmerami zu Regensburg." *ZfMw* 10 (1927): 65–105.

Le Dictionnaire de l'Académie Françoise. Paris: Smits, l'an VII de la République (1798).

Disertori, Benvenuto. "Il manoscritto 1947–4 di Trento e la canzone 'i'ay prins amours.'" *Rivista Musicale Italiana* 48 (1946): 1–29.

Doorslaer, Georges van. "La chapelle musicale de Philippe le Beau." *Revue belge d'archéologie et d'histoire de l'art* 4 (1934): 21–57, 139–65.

Droz, Eugénie, and Thibault, Geneviève. *Trois chansonniers français du XV*e *siècle*. Documents Artistiques du XVe siècle, 4. Paris: Imprimé par F. Paillart, Abbeville, 1927.

Du Cange, Charles du Fresne, Domin(us). *Glossarium mediae et infimae latinitatis.* Paris: Didot, 1940.

Elwert, W. Theodor. *Italienische Metrik.* Munich: Hueber, 1968.

Encyclopédie de la musique. Edited by François Michel. 3 vols. Paris: Fasquelle, 1958.

Ernout, Alfred, and Meillet, Antoine. *Dictionnaire étymologique de la langue latine.* 4th ed. Paris: Klincksieck, 1959.

Fabri, Pierre (Le Fèvre). *Le grand et vrai art de pleine rhétorique de Pierre Fabri.* 3 vols. Paris, 1539. Edited by A. Héron. Reprint. Rouen: E. Cagniard, 1889–90.

Federzoni, Giovanni. *Dei versi e dei metri italiani.* 3rd ed. Bologna: Zanichelli, n.d.

Finscher, Ludwig. *Loyset Compère (c. 1450–1518) Life and Works.* Musicological Studies and Documents, 12. American Institute of Musicology, 1964.
———. "Martini," *MGG* 8 (1960): 1724–26.

Foppens, Jean François. *Compendium chronologicum episcoporum Brugensium.* Bruges: Typis J. Beernaerts, 1731.

Foulet, Lucien. *Petite syntaxe de l'ancien français.* 3rd ed. Paris: Champion, 1930.

Fournier, Edouard, ed. *Le théâtre français avant la Renaissance (1450–1550): mystères, moralités et farces.* Paris: Laplace, Sanchez [1872].

Fox, Charles Warren. "Barbireau and Barbinguant: A Review." *JAMS* 13 (1960): 79–101.

Françon, Marcel. *Poèmes de Transition (XVe–XVIe siècles), Rondeaux du Ms. 402 de Lille.* Cambridge, Mass.: Harvard University Press, and Paris: E. Droz, 1938.

Fuller, Sarah. "Additional Notes on the Fifteenth-Century Chansonnier Bologna Q 16." *MD* 23 (1969): 81–103.

Gaffurius, Franchinus. *Practica musicae utriusque cantus.* Brescia: Angelo Britannico, 1508.

Geering, Arnold. *Die Vokalmusik in der Schweiz zur Zeit der Reformation.* Schweizerisches Jahrbuch für Musikwissenschaft, vol. 6 (1933).

Gérold, Théodore. *Le manuscrit de Bayeux, texte et musique d'un recueil de chansons du XVe siècle.* Texte complémentaire pour le doctorat ès lettres. Strasbourg: L'Université de Strasbourg, 1921.

Gessler, Jean, ed. *La manière de langage qui enseigne à bien parler et écrire le français.* Brussels: Edition Universelle, and Paris: Droz, 1934.

Glahn, Henrik. "Ein Kopenhagener Fragment aus dem 15. Jahrhundert." In *Natalicia Musicologica Knud Jeppesen.* Edited by Bjørn Hjelmborg and Søren Sørensen. Hafniae: Wilhelm Hansen, 1962.
———. "Et fransk musikhåndskrift fra begyndelsen af det 16. århundrede."

Fund og Forskning 5–6 (1958–59) : 90–109.

Godefroy, Frédéric. *Dictionnaire de l'ancienne langue française et de tous ses dialectes, du IXe au XVe siècle*, 10 vols. Paris: Vieweg (Bouillon), 1881–1902.

————. *Lexique de l'ancien français*. Paris: Welter, 1901.

Gombosi, Otto. "Vita musicale alla Corte di Re Mattia." *Corvina* (Società Ungherese-Italiana Mattia Corvino) 17–18 (1929) : 110–30.

Grandsaignes d'Hauterive, R[obert]. *Dictionnaire d'ancien français*. Paris: Larousse, 1947.

Greimas, A[lgirdas] J[ulien]. *Dictionnaire de l'ancien français*. Paris: Larousse, 1969.

Guiraud, Pierre. *Le jargon de Villon ou le gai savoir de la coquille*. Paris: Gallimard, 1968.

Guicciardini, Francesco, *The History of Florence (Storia fiorentina)*, Translation, Introduction, and Notes by Mario Domandi. New York: Harper & Row, 1970.

Guiffrey, Jean. "Préface." *Catalogue de Vente, Galerie Charpentier*, 15 March 1935.

Haar, James, ed. *Chanson and Madrigal 1480–1530*. Cambridge, Mass.: Harvard University Press, 1964.

Haberkamp, Gertraut. *Die weltliche Vokalmusik in Spanien um 1500, der "Cancionero musical de Colombina" von Sevilla und ausserspanische Handschriften*. Münchner Veröffentlichungen zur Musikgeschichte, 12. Tutzing: Hans Schneider, 1968.

Haberl, Franz X. "Die römische 'schola cantorum' und die päpstlichen Kapellsänger bis zur Mitte des 16. Jahrhunderts." *Vierteljahresschrift für Musikwissenschaft* 3 (1887) : 189–296.

————. "Wilhelm duFay." *Vierteljahresschrift für Musikwissenschaft* 1 (1885) : 456.

Hamm, Charles. "Manuscript Structure in the Dufay Era." *Acta Musicologica* 34 (1962) : 166–84.

Hanen, Martha K. "The Chansonnier El Escorial, MS IV.a.24." Ph.D. dissertation, University of Chicago, 1973.

Haraszti, Emile. "Les musiciens de Mathias Corvin et de Béatrice d'Aragon." In *La musique instrumentale de la Renaissance*, edited by Jean Jacquot, pp. 35–59. Paris: Centre National de la Recherche Scientifique, 1955.

Hersey, George L. *Alfonso II and the Artistic Renewal of Naples 1485–1495*. New Haven: Yale University Press, 1969.

Hévésy, André de. *La bibliothèque du roi Matthias Corvin*. Paris: Société Française de Reproductions de Manuscrits à Peinture, 1923.

Hewitt, Helen, and Pope, Isabel, eds. *Harmonice Musices Odhecaton A*. Cambridge, Mass.: The Mediaeval Academy of America, 1942.

Houdoy, Jules. *Histoire artistique de la cathédrale de Cambrai, ancienne église métropolitaine Notre-Dame*. Lille, 1880. Reprint. Geneva: Minkoff, 1972.

Hucke, Helmut. "Neapel." *MGG* 9 (1961): 1313.

Hughes, Dom Anselm. *Medieval Polyphony in the Bodleian Library*. Oxford: Bodleian Library, 1951.

Huguet, Edmond. *Dictionnaire de la langue française du XVIe siècle*. Paris: Champion, 1925–67.

Huizinga, Johan. *The Waning of the Middle Ages*. New York: Longmans, Green, 1949.

Huon le Roi de Cambrai. *Li abecés par ekivoche*. Edited by Artur Långfors. Paris: Champion, 1913.

Hüschen, Heinrich. "Tinctoris." *MGG* 13 (1966): 418–25.

Inventaire sommaire des Archives Départementales, Nord. Vol. 8. Lille, 1895.

Jeanroy, Alfred. *Les origines de la poésie lyrique en France*. 3d ed. Paris: Champion, 1925.

Jeppesen, Knud. *Counterpoint*. Translated by Glen Haydon. New York: Prentice-Hall, 1939.

————. *La Frottola*. Vol. 2. Acta Jutlandica, 41: 1. Copenhagen: Wilhelm Hansen, 1969.

————. *Der Kopenhagener Chansonnier*. Copenhagen: Levin & Munksgaard, and Leipzig: Breitkopf & Härtel, 1927. Reprint 1965.

————. "The Manuscript Florence, Biblioteca Nazionale Centrale, Banco Rari 230: An Attempt at a Diplomatic Reconstruction." In *Aspects of Medieval and Renaissance Music*. Edited by Jan La Rue. New York: W. W. Norton, 1966.

Kellman, Herbert. "Josquin and the Courts of Netherlands and France: The Evidence of the Sources." *Josquin des Prez*, Proceedings of the International Josquin Festival-Conference, pp. 181–216. London: Oxford University Press, 1976.

Kenney, Sylvia. *Walter Frye and the Contenance Angloise*. New Haven: Yale University Press, 1964.

Kottick, Edward L. "The Chansonnier Cordiforme." *JAMS* 20 (1967): 10–27.

————. *The Unica in the Chansonnier Cordiforme*. Corpus Mensurabilis Musicae, 42. American Institute of Musicology, 1967.

Kurath, Hans, and Kuhn, Sherman M. *Middle English Dictionary*. Ann Arbor: University of Michigan Press, 1953.

Larsen, Keith. "A Reconsideration of the Pixérécourt Chansonnier." Unpublished seminar paper: Harvard University, 20 December 1965.

[Lignerolles]. *Catalogue des livres rares et précieux, manuscrits et imprimés, composant la bibliothèque de feu M. le comte de Lignerolles*. 4 vols. Paris: Charles Porquet, 1894–95.

Lille, Bibliotheque Municipale. *Manuscrits de la Bibliothèque de Lille: Catalogue général des manuscrits des bibliothèques publiques de France.* Edited by Henri Rigaux. Départements, vol. 26. Paris: Plon, Nourrit, 1897.

Linden, Herman Vander. *Itinéraires de Charles, Duc de Bourgogne, Marguerite d'York et Marie de Bourgogne (1467–1477).* Bruxelles: M. Lamartin, 1936.

Lindenburg, Cornelis. "Regis." *MGG* 11 (1963): 134–36.

Littré, Emile. *Dictionnaire de la langue française.* Paris: Hachette, 1885.

Llorens, José M. "El Códice Casanatense 2.856 identificado como el Cancionero de Isabella d'Este (Ferrara), esposa de Francesco Gonzaga (Mantua)." *Anuario Musical* 20 (1965): 161–78 [published 1967].

————. *Le Opere Musicali della Cappella Giulia.* Manoscritti ed Edizioni fino al '700 (Studi e Testi 265), vol. 1. Rome: Città del Vaticano, Biblioteca Apostolica Vaticana, 1971.

Lockwood, Lewis. "Music at Ferrara in the Period of Ercole I d'Este." *Studi Musicali* 1 (1972): 101–31.

Löpelmann, Martin. *Die Liederhandschrift des Cardinals de Rohan.* Publikationen der Gesellschaft für romanische Literatur, 44. Göttingen, 1923.

Lowinsky, Edward E. "A Treatise on Text Underlay by a German Disciple of Francesco de Salinas." In *Festschrift Heinrich Besseler,* pp. 231–51. Leipzig: Deutscher Verlag für Musik, 1961.

Maier, Julius Joseph. *Die musikalischen Handschriften der königlichen Hof- und Staatsbibliothek in München,* Erster Theil. Munich: Palm'schen Hofbuchhandlung, 1879.

Maniates, Maria Rika. "Combinative Chansons in the Dijon Chansonnier." *JAMS* 23 (1970): 228–81.

————. "Mannerist Composition in Franco-Flemish Polyphony." *MQ* 52 (1966): 17–36.

Marggraf, Wolfgang. "Bergerette." *MGG* 15 (1973) (suppl.): 684–85.

Marinis, Tammaro de. *La Biblioteca Napolitana dei Re d'Aragona.* 4 vols. Milan: Ulrico Hoepli, 1947–52.

Marix, Jeanne. *Histoire de la musique et des musiciens de la cour de Bourgogne sous le règne de Philippe le Bon (1420–1467).* Strasbourg: Heitz, 1939. Reprint. Geneva: Minkoff, 1972.

Marx, Roger, "Une salle de billard et une galerie modernes." *Art et Décoration* 12 (July–December 1902): 1–13.

Meier, Bernhard. "Die Handschrift Porto 714 als Quelle zur Tonartenlehre des 15. Jahrhunderts." *MD* 7 (1953): 175–97.

Menner, Robert J. "Three Fragmentary English Ballades in the Mellon Chansonnier." *Modern Language Quarterly* 6 (1945): 381–87.

Meyer-Lübke, Wilhelm. *Grammaire des langues romanes.* French translation by Auguste and Georges Doutrepont. Paris: Welter, 1890–1906. Reprint. New York: Stechert, 1923.

————. *Historische Grammatik der französischen Sprache.* Heidelberg: Winter, 1934.

————. *Romanisches etymologisches Wörterbuch*. 3d ed. Heidelberg: Winter, 1935.

Miller, Clement, ed. *Franchinus Gaffurius, Practica Musicae*. Translation and transcription. Musicological Studies and Documents, 20. American Institute of Musicology, 1968.

Molinet, Jean. *Les faicts et dictz de Jean Molinet*. Edited by Noël Dupire. Paris: Société des Anciens Textes Français, 1937.

Molle, F. van. *Identification d'un portrait de Gilles Joye attribué à Memlinc*. Brussels: Centre National de Recherches "Primitifs Flamands," 1960.

Montaiglon, Anatole de, and Rothschild, James de. *Recueil de poésies françoises des XIVᵉ et XVᵉ siècles* . . . Paris: Paul Daffis, 1876.

Morelot, Stéphen. "Notice sur un manuscrit de musique ancienne," *Mémoires de la Commission des Antiquités de la Côte d'Or* 4 (1856) : 133–60.

Morenas, Henri Jougla de. *Grand Armorial de France*. Paris: Les Editions Héraldiques (Presses J. Arbelot), 1934–52.

Murray, J[ames] A[ugustus] H[enry], ed. *A New English Dictionary*. Oxford: Clarendon Press, 1884–1928.

Ornithoparchus, Andreas. *Musice active micrologus*. Leipzig: Valentin Schumann, 1517.

Paris. *Bibliothèque Nationale: Manuscrits latins et français ajoutés aux fonds des nouvelles acquisitions pendant les années 1875–1891, Partie I*. Edited by Léopold Delisle. Paris: Champion, 1891.

————. *Bibliothèque Nationale: Catalogue général des manuscrits français: Anciens petits fonds français. 2: nos. 22885-25696 du fonds français par C. Couderc et Ch. de la Roncière*. Edited by Henri Omont. Paris: Ernest Leroux, 1902.

————. *Bibliothèque Nationale: Catalogue général des manuscrits français: Nouvelles acquisitions françaises*. I–III, Edited by Henri Omont. Vol. 3: nos. 6501-10000. Paris: Ernest Leroux, 1902.

Paris, Gaston, ed. *Chansons du XVᵉ siècle*. Paris: Firmin Didot, 1875.

Parkes, M. B. *English Cursive Book Hands 1250–1500*. Oxford: Clarendon Press, 1969.

Pease, Edward J. *Music from the Pixérécourt MS*. Ann Arbor, 1960.

————. "Pixerecourt." *MGG* 10 (1962) : 1316–17.

————. "A Report on Codex Q 16 of the Civico Museo Bibliografico Musicale . . . Bologna." *MD* 20 (1966) : 57–94.

Perkins, Leeman L. "Mode and Structure in the Masses of Josquin." *JAMS* 26 (1973) : 189–239.

Pernicone, Vincenzo. "*Storia e svolgimento della metrica*." In *Tecnica e teoria letteraria*. Edited by M[ario] Fubini. 2d ed. Milan: Marzorati, 1952.

Picker, Martin. "The Chanson Albums of Marguerite of Austria: MSS 228 and 11239 of the Bibliothèque Royale de Belgique, Brussels." *AM* 6 (1958–63) : 145–285.

————. *The Chanson Albums of Marguerite of Austria*. Berkeley and Los Angeles:

University of California Press, 1965.

———. Review of *Dijon, Bibliothèque Publique Manuscrit 517*, Edited by Dragan Plamenac. *JAMS* 26 (1973): 337–40.

Picot, Emile, and Nyrop, Christophe. *Nouveau recueil de farces françaises des XVe et XVIe siècles, publié d'après un volume unique appartenant à la Bibliothèque Royale de Copenhague.* Paris: Damascène Morgand et Charles Fatout, 1880.

Pirenne, Henri. *Histoire de Belgique.* 7 vols. Vol. 2, *Du commencement du XIVe siècle à la mort de Charles le Téméraire* (1903). Brussels: H. Lamertin, 1900–32.

Pirro, André. Review of Charles Van den Borren, *Guillaume Dufay. La Revue Musicale* 7, no. 8 (June 1926): 323.

Pirrotta, Nino. "Ricercare e variazioni su 'O rosa bella.'" *Studi Musicali* 1 (1972): 59–77.

———. "Two Anglo-Italian Pieces in the Manuscript Porto 714," *Speculum Musicae Artis: Festgabe für Heinrich Husmann zum 60. Geburtstag.* Edited by Heinz Becker and Reinhard Gerlach, pp. 252–61. Munich: Wilhelm Fink Verlag, 1970.

Plamenac, Dragan. "Browsing through a Little-known Manuscript." *JAMS* 13 (1960): 102–09.

———, ed. *Dijon, Bibliothèque Publique Manuscrit 517.* Introduction by Dragan Plamenac. Publications of Mediæval Musical Manuscripts, 12. Brooklyn: The Institute of Mediæval Music, n.d.

———, ed. *Facsimile Reproduction of the Manuscripts Sevilla 5-I-43 and Paris N.A. Fr. 4379.* Pt. 1. Publications of Mediaeval Musical Manuscripts, 8. Brooklyn: The Institute of Mediaeval Music, 1962.

———. "Ockeghem." *MGG* 9 (1961): 1825–38.

———. "A Reconstruction of the French Chansonnier in the Biblioteca Colombina, Seville." *MQ* 37 (1951): 501–42; 38 (1952): 81–117; 245–77.

———. "The 'Second' Chansonnier of the Biblioteca Riccardiana (codex 2356)." *AM* 2 (1954): 105–87.

———. "A Postscript to the 'Second' Chansonnier of the Biblioteca Riccardiana." *AM* 4 (1956): 261–65.

Pontieri, Ernesto. *Per la Storia del Regno di Ferrante I d'Aragona Re di Napoli, Studi e ricerche.* Edizioni Scientifiche Italiane. Naples: "La buona stampa," 1969.

Pope, Isabel (with the collaboration of Masakata Kanazawa). "The Musical Manuscript Montecassino N871." *Anuario Musical* 19 (1964): 123–53.

———. *The Musical Manuscript Montecassino 871.* A Critical Edition (in progress).

———. "La musique espagnole à la cour de Naples dans la seconde moitié du XVe siècle." In *Musique et poésie au XVIe siècle*, pp. 35–58. Paris: Centre National de la Recherche Scientifique, 1954.

Pope, M[ildred] K[atharine]. *From Latin to Modern French.* Manchester:

Manchester University Press, 1952.

Rabelais, François, *Oeuvres complètes*. Edited by Jacques Boulenger. Paris: Gallimard, 1959.

Randel, Don M. "Emerging Triadic Tonality in the Fifteenth Century." *MQ* 57 (1971): 73–86.

Raynaud, Gaston. *Rondeaux et autres poésies du XVᵉ siècle*. Paris: Didot, 1889.

Reese, Gustave. *Music in the Renaissance*. New York: W. W. Norton, 1959.

Rehm, Wolfgang. "Mellon-Chansonnier." *MGG* 9 (1961): 18–19.

Reidemeister, Peter. *Die Chanson-Handschrift 78 C 28 des Berliner Kupferstich-kabinetts: Studien zur Form der Chanson im 15. Jahrhundert*. Berliner Musikwis-senschaftliche Arbeiten, vol. 4. Munich: Musikverlag Emil Katzbichler, 1973.

La Renaissance de l'art français et des industries de luxe. "Le carnet d'un curieux," no. 8 (August 1921), pp. 444–45. "Exposition Prud'hon," no. 2 (May 1922), pp. 333–35.

Répertoire International des Sources Musicales. Recueils Imprimés XVIᵉ–XVIIᵉ siècles, 1. Munich: G. Henle Verlag, 1960.

Restori, Antonio. "Un codice musicale Pavesi." *Zeitschrift für romanische Philologie* 18 (1894): 381–401.

Rheinfelder, Hans. *Altfranzösische Grammatik*. Pt. 1. 2d rev. enlarged ed. Munich: Hueber, 1953.

Rietstap, Johannes Baptista. *Armorial Général*, 2 vols. *Armorial Général Illustré*, 3 vols. Gouda: G. B. Van Goor Zonen, 1884–87.

——. *Armoiries des familles contenues dans l' "Armorial général,"* 5 vols. Paris: Institut héraldique universel. La Haye: M. Nijhoff, 1903–21.

Rifkin, Joshua. "Scribal Concordances for Some Renaissance Manuscripts in Florentine Libraries." *JAMS* 26 (1973): 305–26.

Ringmann, Heribert. "Das Glogauer Liederbuch (um 1480) mus. ms. 40098 Berlin (Staatsbibliothek)." *ZfMw* 15 (1932): 49–60.

——, ed. *Das Glogauer Liederbuch*. Das Erbe Deutscher Musik, Erste Reihe, vols. 4 and 8. Kassel, West Germany: Bärenreiter Verlag, 1936, 1937.

Robbins, Rossell Hope, ed. *Secular Lyrics of the XIVth and XVth Centuries*. 2d ed. Oxford: Clarendon Press, 1968.

Robinson, F[red] N[orris], ed. *The Works of Geoffrey Chaucer*. 2d ed. Boston: Houghton Mifflin, 1961.

Rohlfs, Gerhard. *Historische Grammatik der italienischen Sprache*. 3 vols. Bern: Francke, 1949.

Rosenberg, Herbert, ed. *Das Schedel'sche Liederbuch*. Deutsche Liedsätze des fünfzehnten Jahrhunderts für Singstimmen und Melodieinstrumente, vol. 3. Kassel, West Germany: Bärenreiter Verlag, 1933.

Rossi, Vittorio. *Il Quattrocento*. 5th ed. Milan: Vallardi, 1953.

Salmi, Mario. *Italian Miniatures*. New York: Abrams, 1954.

Sartori, Claudio. *Bibliografia delle Opere Musicali stampate da Ottaviano Petrucci.* Biblioteca di Bibliografia Italiana, 18. Florence: Leo S. Olschki, 1948.

Schrevel, A. C. *Histoire du séminaire de Bruges.* Vol. 1. Bruges: L. de Plancke, 1895.

Schwan, Edward, and Behrens, Dietrich. *Grammaire de l'ancien français.* Translated by Oscar Bloch. 4th ed., based on 12th German ed. Leipzig: Reisland, 1932.

Seay, Albert, ed. *Johannes Tinctoris, the Art of Counterpoint [Liber de arte Contrapuncti].* Musicological Studies and Documents, 5. American Institute of Musicology, 1961.

————. *Johannes Tinctoris. Concerning the Nature and Propriety of Tones.* 2 vols. Colorado College Music Press Translations, 2. Colorado Springs: Colorado College Music Press, 1967.

Smijers, Albert, ed. *Werken van Josquin des Prés.* Amsterdam: G. Alsbach, and Leipzig: Kistner & Siegel, 1926—.

Sotheby and Company, Catalogue. 7 March 1939 (Lot 358 A).

Southern, Eileen. *The Buxheim Organ Book.* Musicological Studies, 6. Brooklyn: The Institute of Mediaeval Music, 1963.

————. "El Escorial, Monastery Library, Ms IV.a.24." *MD* 23 (1969): 41–79.

————. "Foreign Music in German Manuscripts of the Fifteenth Century." *JAMS* 21 (1968): 258–85.

Spreti, Vittorio. *Enciclopedia Storico nobiliare Italiano.* Milano: Archetipografia, 1929—.

Staehelin, Martin. "Zum Egenolff-Diskantband der Bibliothèque Nationale in Paris: Ein Beitrag zur musikalischen Quellenkunde der 1. Hälfte des 16. Jahrhunderts." *AfMw* 23 (1966): 93–109.

————. "Quellenkundliche Beiträge zum Werk von Johannes Ghiselin-Verbonnet." *AfMw* 24 (1967): 120–32.

Stevens, John. *Music and Poetry in the Early Tudor Court.* London: Methuen, 1961.

————. *Music at the Court of Henry VIII.* Musica Britannica, 18. London: Stainer & Bell (Published for the Royal Musical Association), 1962.

Stevenson, Robert. *Spanish Music in the Age of Columbus.* The Hague: Martinus Nijhoff, 1960.

Straeten, Edmond Vander. *La musique aux Pays-Bas avant le XIXe siècle.* 8 vols. Brussels: C. Muquardt, 1867–88. Facsimile reprint. Dover: New York, 1969.

Strunk, Oliver. *Source Readings in Music History.* New York: Norton, 1950.

Tatlock, John S., and Kennedy, Arthur G. *A Concordance to the Complete Works of Geoffrey Chaucer and the Romaunt of the Rose.* Washington: Carnegie Institute of Washington, 1927.

Thibault, Geneviève. "Busnois." *MGG* 2 (1952): 515–20.

———. "Caron." *MGG* 2 (1952): 859–62.

———. "Chanson II (1420–1520)." *MGG* 2 (1952): 1046–54.

Thompson, John. *The Founding of English Metre*. New York: Columbia University Press, 1961.

Thomson, James, *An Introduction to Philippe (?) Caron*. Brooklyn: The Institute of Mediaeval Music, 1964.

Tinctoris, Johannes. *De arte contrapuncti*.

———. *De inventione et usu musicae*.

———. *De natura ac proprietate tonorum*.

———. *Diffinitorium musices*.

———. *Expositio manus*.

———. *Proportionale musices*.

Tobler, A[dolf], and Lommatzsch, E[rhard]. *Altfranzösisches Wörterbuch*. Berlin: Weidmann, 1925—.

Trent (Trente, Museo del castello del Buon Consiglio). *Codices Musicales Tridentini*. Rome: Bibliopola, 1969 (87); 1970 (88); 1969 (89); 1970 (90), (91), (92), (93).

Trienter Codices. Edited by Guido Adler, Oswald Keller, et al. *Denkmäler der Tonkunst in Oesterreich*. Jahrgänge 7 (vol. 14), 11/1 (vol. 22), 19/1 (vol. 38), 27/1 (vol. 53), 31/1 (vol. 61), and 40 (vol. 76).

Turrini, Giuseppe. *Il Patrimonio Musicale della Biblioteca Capitolare di Verona*. Verona, 1952.

Vérard, Antoine, ed. *Le Jardin de plaisance et fleur de rethoricque nouvellement imprimé a Paris*. 2 vols. Edition in facsimile. Paris: Firmin Didot, 1910, and Paris: Champion, 1926.

Viollet le Duc, Emmanuel Louis Nicolas, ed. *Ancien théâtre françois*. 10 vols. Paris: Chez P. Jannet, 1854–56.

Wagner, Carolus, ed. *Epistolae Petri de Warda*. Posonii et Cassoviae, 1776.

Wallner, Bertha, ed. *Das Buxheimer Orgelbuch*. Documenta musicologica, Zweite Reihe: Handschriften-Faksimiles Heft 1. Kassel, West Germany: Bärenreiter Verlag, 1955.

———. *Das Buxheimer Orgelbuch*. Das Erbe Deutscher Musik, Vol. 37–39. Kassel, West Germany: Bärenreiter Verlag, 1958–59.

Wartburg, Walter von. *Französisches Etymologisches Wörterbuch*. Bonn: Klopp, 1928.

Weinmann, Karl. *Johannes Tinctoris und sein unbekannter Traktat 'De inventione et usu musicae.'* Regensburg, West Germany: F. Pustet, 1917. Reprint. Tutzing, 1961.

Wilkins, Nigel. *One Hundred Ballades, Rondeaux and Virelais from the Late Middle Ages*. Cambridge, England: Cambridge University Press, 1969.

Wilphlingseder, Ambrosius. *Erotemata musices practicae, continentia praecipuas eius artis praeceptiones, in gratiam & usum studiosae iuventutis* ... Nuremberg: Christophorus Heussler, 1563.

Wolff, Arthur S. "The Chansonnier Biblioteca Casanatense 2856: Its History, Purpose, and Music." 2 vols. Ph.D. dissertation, North Texas State University (Denton), 1970.

Wright, Craig. "Dufay at Cambrai: Discoveries and Revisions." *JAMS* 28 (1975): 175–229.

Zerffi, G. G. "Hungary under King Matthias Hunyady, surnamed 'Corvinus.'" *Transactions of the Royal Historical Society*. New Series, vol. 1 (Session 1882–83): 260–72. London: Longmans, Green.

INDEX